ITALIAN FASCIST ACTIVITIES IN THE UNITED STATES

GAETANO SALVEMINI

ITALIAN FASCIST ACTIVITIES IN THE UNITED STATES

by

GAETANO SALVEMINI

edited with introduction

by

PHILIP V. CANNISTRARO

1977

CENTER FOR MIGRATION STUDIES

NEW YORK

Italian Fascist Activities
in the United States

First Edition

Center for Migration Studies
209 Flagg Place
Staten Island, New York 10304

ISBN 0-913256-23-4
Library of Congress Catalog Card Number: 76-44920
Printed in the United States of America

CONTENTS

Introduction

Gaetano Salvemini was a man of strong opinions and passionate temperament. His friends and associates often felt the sting of his incisive criticism as sharply as did his opponents, and while some who knew him accused him of being a rigid moralist with no sense of reality, others saw in him an uncompromising crusader for freedom relentlessly bent on exposing both truth and falsehood with impartial severity. Cautious reserve and understatement were not his métier, for the power of his keen and agile mind was a function of his deeply felt instincts as a man. When he accused or condemned — which he did frequently — it was always with a great sensitivity for his own personal and political responsibility. It would be difficult to find a man who set such high standards for his own life as did Salvemini, and perhaps because of this he was frequently disappointed in those on whom he relied. "As for myself," he wrote his old friend Ernesto Rossi in 1944, "you cannot know how old and tired I feel. Above all it has been the defection of men...that has disheartened me."[1]

1. Salvemini to Rossi, December 4, 1944, in Gaetano Salvemini, *Lettere dall'America*, ed. Alberto Merola (Bari, 1969), p. 46.

The years that Salvemini spent in the United States as a political exile from Mussolini's Fascist dictatorship were among the most trying and disappointing in his life. He came to America with great hopes that he would find here the means and the support necessary to continue the struggle for freedom that he had begun in Europe. The American republic, with its traditions of liberty and constitutional democracy, beckoned him to its shores not with the promise of personal safety, but with the hope that its great power and resources could be marshaled in defense of the world's steadily shrinking freedoms. He respected and admired many features of American life, and after almost twenty years he was as much at home in the United States as he was in the land of his birth. He was grateful for the freedom he found here to speak and write about Fascism as he pleased, but he was profoundly disillusioned that so few Americans listened or understood. He viewed America's entrance into the war as the last chance for the survival of democracy, but he feared that the American people were unaware of the true issues at stake. Yet, in spite of his frustration, Salvemini was not prone to recrimination for its own sake, so that it must have been with a deeply felt sense of tragedy that in 1943 he and Giorgio La Piana wrote the following indictment:[2]

> We still remember with heartache our sense of dismay when we witnessed the wave of enthusiasm for Fascism and Mussolini that swept this country and flourished especially among the high political, religious, and social classes of America. We still recall how in those days we who tried to open the eyes of the American public as to the real nature and aims of Fascism were looked upon as disgruntled crackpots or, at best, as unrealistic searchers after Utopia.
>
> And we have good reason to believe that even now, more than three years after the outbreak of the present war, there are still considerable sections of American public opinion in which traces of the old myth concerning Fascism still blur the vision of the future.

If Salvemini recalled America's encounter with Fascism as a tragic mistake, he did so in the conviction that even in 1943 it was still not too late to learn from the past — even though he drew little comfort from the knowledge that he had worked and sacrificed as much as anyone to prevent that tragedy.

Salvemini had certainly not been a stranger either to political battle or to its disappointments. When he first visited the United States in 1927 as an anti-Fascist exile, Salvemini was more than fifty years old — he was born in Molfetta, Italy, on September 8, 1873 — and had already achieved international reputation as a scholar, teacher, writer, and political activist.[3] As one of Italy's leading historians he had demonstrated his belief that political history was a reflection of the struggles and aspirations of social classes. In such original and inspiring works as his *Magnati e popolani a Firenze dal 1280 al 1295* (Florence, 1899), *La rivoluzione francese* (Milan, 1905), and *Il pensiero religioso, politico, sociale di Giuseppe Mazzini* (Messina, 1905), Salvemini revealed with precision and eloquence his lifelong conviction that the life of the mind and the life of concrete action cannot be separated. "If the historian," he advised, "should not be a scholar indifferent to the moral and the political problems of his time, but a politician and a moralist who, with the discipline of his knowledge, must seek in the past the origins of the society in which he lives and works — so too the teacher of history must, even more than the historian, guard against pure, cold, and isolated erudition. In modern society he has the duty, with the help of history, to teach his students to exercise their future political functions and fulfill their social obligations conscientiously."[4]

Although he never abandoned his academic studies, Salvemini threw himself into the political life of the Italian "Liberal State" at the turn of the century and remained politically active until his death in 1957. While teaching at the University of Messina and later at the University of Florence, he became an ardent advocate of socialist reform, an indefatigable opponent of parliamentary corruption, and an uncompromising champion of what he believed was Italy's most burning political and social question — the Italian South.[5] Eventually disenchanted with the Socialist party's indifference to the problems of southern Italy, Salvemini broke with the party in 1911 and established his weekly newspaper *Unità*, in which he continued to fight his battles almost alone. During the divisive period of Italian neutrality in 1914-15, Salvemini argued for Italy's intervention in World War I, hoping that an Entente victory would result in a new, peaceful international system.

Although Salvemini had been an interventionist, he had little in common with those contemporaries who wanted Italy in the war in order to gain territorial advantages from the peace settlement that would follow. In fact,

Gaetano Salvemini (Bari, 1959); Ernesto Ragionieri, "Gaetano Salvemini storico e politico," *Belfagor*, 5 (September, 1950); Enzo Tagliacozzo, *Gaetano Salvemini nel cinquantennio liberale* (Florence, 1959); and Gaspare De Caro, *Gaetano Salvemini* (Turin, 1970).

4. Salvemini, "Pasquale Villari," *Nuova Rivista Storica*, 2, 2 (1918): 120, cited in Walter Maturi, *Interpretazioni del risorgimento: Lezioni di storia della storiografia*, 2nd ed. (Turin, 1962), p. 449.

5. In 1910 Salvemini wrote his famous attack against Prime Minister Giovanni Giolitti's corruptive influence on Italian politics, "Il Ministro della mala vita," and only began to revise his earlier views on Giolitti years later when he wrote his equally famous introduction to A. William Salomone's masterful study, *Italian Democracy in the Making. The Political Scene in the Giolittian Era, 1900-1914* (Philadelphia, 1945). See also the second, revised edition of Salomone's work entitled *Italy in the Giolittian Era: Italian Democracy in the Making, 1900-1914* (Philadelphia, 1960).

much to the disgust of the Italian Nationalists, in 1919 Salvemini advocated a peaceful agreement that would give Yugoslavia the Dalmatian coast so coveted by the Nationalists, and his support for Woodrow Wilson's principles earned him their lasting enmity. Between 1919 and 1921, during which Salvemini held a seat in the Italian parliament, he steadfastly opposed the expansionist foreign policy of the Nationalists, who were becoming increasingly allied to Benito Mussolini's Fascist party.

By the time Mussolini came to power in October of 1922, Salvemini had already been branded as a dangerous enemy of Fascism. The period from the March on Rome (1922) to his escape from Italy (1925) were years of tragic and momentous events for Italy, years which witnessed Mussolini's brutal consolidation of power and the destruction of the country's remaining civil liberties under the Fascist dictatorship. As Mussolini sought to silence the growing opposition to his regime, the first signs of systematic resistance began to take shape. Following the traumatic crisis provoked by the Fascist murder of Socialist deputy Giacomo Matteotti in 1924, Salvemini — who had meanwhile rejoined the Socialist Party — organized a group of colleagues and students at the University of Florence into the *Circolo di Cultura*, which quickly became the center of the Florentine resistance. In December 1924 the offices of the *Circolo* were raided and destroyed by local Fascist squads, and the following month Salvemini, together with Piero Calamandrei, Carlo and Nello Rosselli, and Ernesto Rossi, published one of the first underground anti-Fascist newspapers, *Non Mollare* [Don't give in!], dedicated to absolute intransigence against Fascism. As Salvemini emerged as one of the chief leaders of the resistance, the Fascist reaction mounted. Several times the halls in which he and his colleagues taught were invaded by squads of Black Shirts and he was under constant police surveillance. Finally, in June 1925 Salvemini was arrested and tried for his complicity with *Non Mollare*, only to be released provisionally after six weeks in prison. Early in August, after shaking off his police guards and traveling north to Aosta with the help of friends, he slipped across the French border and made his way to Paris, where he began an exile that was to last twenty years.[6]

Salvemini did not intend his exile to be permanent. Initially he thought that he could best serve the cause of liberty by returning to Itlay and acting

---

6. On the anti-Fascist activities of Salvemini in Italy see his *Memorie di un fuoruscito*, 3rd ed. (Milan, 1965), pp. 5-28; Salvadori, *Gaetano Salvemini*, pp. 26-34; Tagliacozzo, "La Vita," in *Gaetano Salvemini*, pp. 245-253; De Caro, *Gaetano Salvemini*, pp. 330-343; and Charles F. Delzell, *Mussolini's Enemies: The Italian Anti-Fascist Resistance* (Princeton, 1961), pp. 30-32, 49-50. On *Non Mollare* see the reproduction and essays edited by Salvemini, Calamandrei, and Rossi, *Non Mollare* (Florence, 1955); Adriano Dal Pont, Alfonso Leonetti, and Massimo Massara, *Giornali fuori legge: la stampa clandestina antifascista, 1922-1943* (Rome, 1964), pp. 85-92; and Frank Rosengarten, *The Italian Anti-Fascist Press, 1919-1945* (Cleveland, 1968), pp. 64-67

as an intellectual and moral symbol of resistance, but the growing violence and brutality of the Fascist dictatorship ultimately convinced him that it would be foolish to play into Mussolini's hands. He therefore rejected the overtures made by the Fascist government, gave up his only source of income, and on November 5, 1925, wrote an eloquent and defiant letter of resignation to the president of the University of Florence: "The Fascist dictatorship has by now completely suppressed those conditions for liberty in our country without which the teaching of history in universities — as I conceive it — loses all dignity, because it must cease to be an instrument of free civil education and must reduce itself to the servile adulation of the dominating party, or else to the level of mere exercises of erudition alien to the moral conscience of the teacher and the students."[7] Having definitely cut all bridges back to Italy with this declaration, Salvemini made a choice to dedicate his energies to the destruction of the regime that had made him and so many others outcasts. In September 1926 Mussolini 'retaliated against Salvemini and twelve other *fuorusciti* by depriving them of their citizenship and their property in Italy.

After a brief stay in Paris, where he saw Ernesto Rossi, Salvemini went to London, and while the British capital remained his base of operations until his permanent move to the United States, he spent the next ten years in frequent travel between London, Paris, and America, all the time writing, speaking, debating, and organizing. Unlike some of the early anti-Fascists, Salvemini harbored no illusions about an easy or quick victory over Mussolini's regime, and the ideas he evolved about the anti-Fascist struggle remained the more or less permanent guidelines for all his subsequent action and thought. Rejecting any hope that Fascism would fall as a result of a move by the king, the army, or the industrialists in Italy, Salvemini established two conditions under which he anticipated the end of the regime: widespread discontent and antipathy among the Italian people, and a profound national crisis that would provoke them into open opposition. Because the regime had been consolidated so firmly after the Matteotti murder, the crisis would probably have to be of an international character, and Salvemini was convinced that Fascist foreign policy would be the ruin of Mussolini.

The conclusions derived from this analysis, expressed cogently in articles and pamphlets published in Paris during the 1920's, determined the nature and purpose of Salvemini's work as an anti-Fascist political exile. "He who writes these lines is convinced," Salvemini exorted, "that the Fascist dictatorship cannot be destroyed by moral force alone, that a revolutionary

7. *Memorie di un fuoruscito*, p. 32.

crisis in Italy is inevitable if we are to overcome the real situation, and that those who refuse to assume every responsibility in the preparation of that crisis must withdraw into private life and remove themselves as dead weights from the anti-Fascist ranks. . . What action can we emigrés contribute to the struggle against Fascism? The answer to this question can be given in a few words: 'We must do that which our brothers in Italy, suffocated and paralyzed, cannot do.' Above all we can make known to the countries that shelter us the real conditions inside Italy."[8] Hence, first and foremost Salvemini's mission was to develop an active and unrelenting propaganda campaign designed to inform world opinion about the true nature of Fascism, to expose the brutal, corrupt, and suppressive nature of the dictatorship, and to shatter the false image built on lies that Mussolini's propaganda agents were spreading throughout Europe and America. Salvemini discovered quickly that for a variety of reasons the outside world had not only accepted, but had applauded, Mussolini's seizure of power in Italy and that in many cases the dictator had become the object of admiration and hero worship among uninformed foreigners.[9] The determination to devote all the powers of his mind and his energy to combating Fascist propaganda was no idle or romantic gesture, for Salvemini knew that the pressures of public opinion, especially in democracies, could exercise a real and practical influence on diplomatic and economic relations between Italy and the world's powers — an influence that could prove the ultimate undoing of Mussolini and his government.

During his years in London and Paris Salvemini wrote and lectured prodigiously on Fascism and Italian conditions, contributing articles and letters to the British and French press, speaking at rallies, universities, and public meetings, and often debating Fascist spokesmen directly in open and heated exchanges.[10] But no matter how polemical or emotional his outbursts sometimes were, Salvemini never ceased to be the historian he had been in Italy. Among his most important and influential publications during this period was the masterful volume, *The Fascist Dictatorship in Italy*, first published in the United States in 1927 and then revised and published the following year in England.[11] Although this work was motivated by his

8. "L'opera degli emigrati," in *Libertà* (Paris), July 3, 17, August 14, 1927, now published in *Opere di Gaetano Salvemini, Scritti sul fascismo*, ed. Nino Valeri and Alberto Merola, II (Milan, 1966), pp. 290-302.

9. On Mussolini's prestige and popularity abroad see Renzo De Felice, *Mussolini il duce* (Turin, 1974), pp. 534-596, and A. Berselli, *L'opinione pubblica inglese e l'avvento del fascismo* (Milan, 1971); John P. Diggins, *Mussolini and Fascism: The View from America* (Princeton, 1972); P. Milza, *L'Italie fasciste devant l'opinion francaise, 1920-1940* (Paris, 1967).

10. *Memorie di un fuoruscito*, pp. 42-58. Many of Salvemini's articles and other publications during this period are in *Scritti sul fascismo*, II.

11. *The Fascist Dictatorship in Italy* (New York, 1927) and the revised British edition, *The Fascist Dictatorship in Italy* (London, 1928). This work also appeared in a French edition, *La*

passionate hatred for Fascism, it was a model of historical research and accuracy — especially considering the limited source materials at his disposal — and it established a pattern of method and approach that guided his subsequent work in exile. In 1932, after an attentive study of Mussolini's foreign policies, Salvemini published *Mussolini Diplomate*, a scorching and powerful analysis of Fascist diplomacy from 1922 to 1931 that revealed Mussolini to be a mere shadow of the great statesman his propaganda purported him to be and a bitter exposè of the "mutilated victory" thesis upon which the Duce defended his policies.[12] Four years later appeared Salvemini's *Under the Axe of Fascism*, a penetrating study that destroyed the Fascist glorification of Mussolini's most important domestic program, the corporate state.[13]

Each of these studies incorporated a vast amount of information and data never before available to the English-speaking public, for Salvemini believed that the bare facts alone would be sufficient to belie Fascist propaganda.[14] His books were marked by a scrupulous attention to facts, and he painstakingly reconstructed the details, dates, and circumstances of events. Salvemini was constantly in search of information upon which to base his writing, and while he himself combed the British Museum, the Bibliothèque nationale in Paris, and other libraries, he also relied upon friends in France and even inside Italy to supply him with newspaper clippings, articles, and books.[15] The major source material for Salvemini's work was the press, whose limitations he himself acknowledged.[16] Importantly, the novelty of his work lay not only in the information it supplied, but primarily in the fact that he based so much of his findings and conclusions on official Fascist sources, particularly his statistical data.[17] This approach had the dual impact of demonstrating the falsity of Fascist claims and preventing the charge that he had used "prejudiced" sources — and in the process laying Fascist sources themselves open to question. The lively and direct style in which Salvemini couched his thoughts and presented his cold, uncompromising facts enabled

Terreur Fasciste 1922-1926 (Paris, 1930), and a Spanish version, *El Terror Fascista 1922-1926* (Barcelona, 1931). It has now been republished in *Scritti sul fascismo*, I, ed. Roberto Vivarelli (Milan, 1961).

12. *Mussolini Diplomate* (Paris, 1932). This work was republished in an Italian edition as *Mussolini diplomatico* (Rome, 1945), and again in 1952 in an enlarged, corrected version.

13. *Under the Axe of Fascism* (London, 1936), also published in the United States in the same year.

14. Vivarelli, *Scritti sul fascismo*, p. ix.

15. Ibid., pp. ix-x; see also *Memorie di un fuoruscito*, pp. 105-106; Salvadori, *Gaetano Salvemini*, p. 224.

16. Ernesto Sestan, "Lo storico," in *Gaetano Salvemini*, pp. 33-34; Salvadori, *Gaetano Salvemini*, pp. 218, 231; De Caro, *Gaetano Salvemini*, pp. 363-366.

17. Salvadori, *Gaetano Salvemini*, p. 225. See also *Under the Axe of Fascism* (London, 1936), pp. 12-13.

him to present the public at once with scientific methodology and powerful polemic, and the effectiveness of his anti-Fascist contributions in this sense is testified to by the close attention and frustrating alarm with which the Fascist government followed his publications.[18]

Salvemini remained a constant follower of Mazzini's dictum to combine "thought and action." As a result, he was an active participant and central figure in the political movements of the exiled anti-Fascists. When the leftist parties — excluding the Communists — joined together in 1927 to form the *Concentrazione Antifascista*, Salvemini adhered to it and supported its activities. The *Concentrazione* announced its intention to organize the exiles, to maintain contact with anti-Fascists inside Italy, to stimulate resistance through the clandestine press, and to aid the victims of Fascism. Although the group quickly adopted a republican stance in the face of the Italian king's growing complicity with Fascism, Salvemini soon found himself in opposition to its program and withdrew from the *Concentrazione*.[19] Early in 1929 Salvemini joined with the Rosselli brothers, Ferruccio Parri, Riccardo Bauer, and others in forming the supraparty coalition known as *Giustizia e Libertà*, dedicated to bold anti-Fascist resistance and the establishment of a democratic republic in Italy based on democratic-socialist principles. Salvemini, who drafted its early platform, hoped to forge the organization into a new democratic alternative to both Fascism and Communism based in part on Mazzinian principles of personal and political liberty. He rejected the Communist program because he believed that it was not in tune with the social realities of Italian life; instead, he posited an "inseparable trinity" of liberty, republic, and social justice for Italy as the long-range goal of the anti-Fascist struggle. But while the immediate goal — the destruction of Fascism — remained urgently clear, Salvemini was unwilling to tie himself or the movement to a rigidly predetermined program for Italy's future: the one, inalterable point for him was his insistence that the Italian people should determine their own destiny.[20]

Salvemini first turned his thoughts toward the United States shortly before the formation of the *Concentrazione Antifascista* and while he was busily

18. Numerous reports on Salvemini's publications by Fascist agents abroad and by the Ministry of Popular Culture reveal the deep concern that his work caused in Italian government circles. See Archivio Centrale dello Stato, Rome, *Ministero della Cultura Popolare*, busta 155, fascicolo 17, "Salvemini, Gaetano."

19. On the Concentrazione Antifascista see Delzell, *Mussolini's Enemies*, pp. 56-60, 75-80, and passim; and Aldo Garosci, *Storia dei fuorusciti* (Bari, 1953), pp. 26-54. Salvemini's role in the group has been studied by Gaetano Arfe, "Salvemini nelle Concentrazione antifascista," *Il Ponte*, 13 (1957), 1168-1171.

20. *Memorie di un fuoruscito*, pp. 115-135. See also Delzell, *Mussolini's Enemies*, pp. 60-67, passim; Garosci, *Storia dei fuorusciti*, pp. 55-70, 121-164.

engaged in his propaganda activities in London. In the spring of 1926 Francesco S. Nitti, the former Italian prime minister and now himself an anti-Fascist exile, suggested that Salvemini contact an American business agent who was seeking prominent political figures for lecture tours in America.[21] By October Salvemini had agreed to go on a long circuit of speaking engagements in the United States and Canada, fully confident that he would find fertile ground for his work — and immediately Italian authorities tried unsuccessfully to persuade the Department of State to deny him a visa.[22] Although he had not previously considered the possibility, the offer to tour America raised Salvemini's hopes of widening the dimensions of the anti-Fascist struggle. In the United States he believed he could collect a substantial amount of money for the cause while at the same time spreading his anti-Fascist message among the millions of Americans who admired and respected Mussolini. Through the intervention of Walter Lippman, who heard of his plight through Bernard Berenson, Salvemini was able to procure a visa for his now invalid passport, and he left London in December.[23]

Upon his arrival in New York on January 5, Salvemini was greeted by representatives of the Foreign Policy Association and immediately became the center of attention and polemic. The day after his arrival he appeared before the board of directors of the association, whose members questioned him sharply about Fascism and his own motives and quickly discovered that Salvemini was an extremely able public speaker in a somewhat halting but nonetheless effective English.[24] That same evening Lippman presided over a meeting of important journalists, businessmen and educators at a New York club, during which Salvemini's position was attacked by Bank of Morgan official Thomas Lamont. The two men entered into a heated debate concerning American loans to Italy, which Lamont argued were evidence of the faith Americans had in the renewed prosperity and order achieved by Italy under Mussolini. Salvemini vehemently attacked Lamont's thesis and felt that he had emerged fully vindicated from his first round of debates in America.[25] Years later he recalled with something akin to horror the hectic months that followed, as his agent shuttled him from New York to

---

21. See Nitti to Salvemini, May 15, 1926, in the Gaetano Salvemini Archives, Rome, and De Caro, *Gaetano Salvemini*, p. 357.

22. Henry P. Fletcher to William R. Castle, July 27, 1926, Box 13, *Fletcher Papers*, Library of Congress.

23. *Memorie di un fuoruscito*, p. 59.

24. Ibid., p. 60. Salvemini gave all but two of his talks in English, the exceptions being lectures in Buffalo and in New York. See "Una lettera di Salvemini," originally in *La Libertà*, August 14, 1927, now in *Scritti sul fascismo*, II, p. 303.

25. On the debate with Lamont see *Memorie di un fuoruscito*, pp. 61-62; Tagliacozzo, "La vita," p. 257; Salvemini, "G. B. Shaw e il fascismo," originally published in a series of articles in England in 1927, now in *Scritti sul fascismo*, II, p. 322, note.

Columbus, Ohio, then to Portland, Maine, to Boston, and from there to Montreal and back to New York. Traveling by train at night and speaking several times each day, Salvemini added impromptu talks of his own arranged by local anti-Fascists to his official schedule of lectures. The last important episode of his tour took place in New York in April, when he appeared once again before the Foreign Policy Association for a public debate. On this occasion Salvemini faced Bruno Rosselli, a Fascist propaganda agent who had been active among Italian-Americans for years, and who taught at Vassar College. Both speakers gave presentations on the "economic, political, and moral" condition of Italy under Fascism, Salvemini making a desperate effort to expose the false assertions of Fascist propaganda and Rosselli defending Mussolini as the savior of an Italy torn by violence and anarchy.[26] Following the formal lectures, the discussion was opened to questions from the audience, and Salvemini first encountered one of the most important Fascist agents in the United States, Count Ignazio Thaon di Revel. Revel launched a bitter tirade against Salvemini, accusing him of distorting the truth about Fascism and of having been a leader of the "anti-patriotic" forces that cheated Italy of her victory in the First World War. Here, too, Salvemini felt that he had gotten the best of his opponent, while revealing the repressive and brutal nature of the dictatorship and the lack of justice that Italy suffered under Mussolini.[27]

The United States made a profound and lasting impression on Salvemini. He expressed a measured awe at the physical expanse and power of the country,[28] and one has the impression that the experienced partisan fighter sensed a disarming and dangerous naiveté about the American people. After his six-month experience, he came away convinced that there were great opportunities to gather support and aid for anti-Fascism in America, just as there was an equally pressing need to counteract the powerful effect of Mussolini's propaganda there. On the immediate level Salvemini was deeply alarmed by the evident esteem for Mussolini which he found among American businessmen and political figures, to say nothing of the important financial credits that had been extended to the Fascist government by the Bank of Morgan.[29] On the other hand, many liberal Americans and

---

26. The text of the debate was published by the Foreign Policy Association in English and by the anarchist *Il Martello* in Italian, and is now in *Scritti sul fascismo*, II, pp. 248-270.

27. Ibid. See also *Memorie di un fuoruscito*, pp. 64-66.

28. Enzo Tagliacozzo, "L'opera di Gaetano Salvemini negli Stati Uniti d'America," *Rassegna Storica Toscana*, 10, 1 (January-June, 1974), 23.

29. "L'opera degli emigrati," p. 295. On the Bank of Morgan loans see Gian Giacomo Migone, "La stabilizzazione della lira: la finanza americana e Mussolini," *Revista di Storia Contemporanea*, II (1973), pp. 145-185, an "Aspetti internazionali della stabilizzazione della lira: il Piano Leffingwell," in *Problemi di storia nei rapporti tra Italia e Stati Uniti* (Turin, 1971), pp. 43-93. American business and political reaction to Mussolini is described in Diggins, *Mussolini and Fascism*, pp. 144-169, and pp. 262-276.

intellectuals who agreed with his ideas had given Salvemini their moral and financial support and the chance to express his views through their publications and organizations. Anti-Fascist journals such as *New Republic*, *Survey*, and *Century Magazine* published articles by Salvemini during his stay in the United States,[30] and he had been warmly received by the small but determined Italian-American anti-Fascist movement.

Perhaps the most important result of the tour was the fact that Salvemini had "discovered" the Italian-Americans. It would be a number of years before he began to devote systematic attention to them, but certainly the potential importance of the millions of Italians in the United States did not escape him. In the months that followed his first visit to America, Salvemini clearly anticipated that the majority of Italian-Americans could be converted into a powerful anti-Fascist pressure group that could turn American public opinion against Mussolini; only time would bring him to the bitter realization that a relationship existed between Fascism and the bulk of the Italian-Americans that, while indirect and fluctuating, would be difficult if not impossible to sever with propaganda and reason.[31]

If Salvemini had already established himself as a major figure of the anti-Fascist opposition in Europe, the American tour reinforced that reputation. No exile of his political or intellectual standing had carried the anti-Fascist campaign to the United States before, and his presence on American soil so disturbed Fascists on both sides of the Atlantic that Italian consular officials sent day-to-day, detailed reports on his activities to Rome.[32] Italian-American Fasicsts like Agostino De Biasi, editor of *Il Carroccio*, and special agents of Mussolini like Thaon di Revel hurled vicious abuse at Salvemini as they witnessed the impact of his work among the previously docile ethnic communities. Most revealing in this sense was De Biasi's commentary:[33]

> We intend to speak of the responsibility that you are assuming in regard to the five or six million Italians that, living and suffering the history of their emigration, have...labored so well for their distant fatherland. This, Professor Salvemini, is a patrimony that we will not permit you to touch..

30. See for example Salvemini's article "Chi si oppone a Mussolini?," originally published in *The New Republic*, May 1927, now in *Scritti sul fascismo*, II, pp. 271-274. In the same month Salvemini published an essay entitled "Mussolini, the Pope, and the King" in *Century Magazine*, now in *Scritti sul fascismo*, II, pp. 274-285. Salvemini participated in a symposium entitled "An American Looks At Fascism" published by *Survey* in March 1927; Salvemini and Prof. William Y. Elliott wrote for the anti-Fascists while Lamont and Giuseppe Prezzolini supported the Fascist case. Salvemini also wrote articles for the anti-Fascist newspaper *The Latern* of Boston, which hosted the writings of numerous prominent Italians opposed to Mussolini.
31. "L'opera degli emigrati," pp. 295-297; Tagliacozzo, "La vita," p. 258.
32. Copies of these reports are in Salvemini's police file in the Archivio Centrale dello Stato, *Cassellario Politico Centrale*, fascicolo 4551, "Salvemini, Gaetano."
33. Agostino De Biasi, *La battaglia dell'Italia negli Stati Uniti* (New York, 1927), pp. 372-377.

You are the anti-Fascist par excellance, the most rabid exile, the expatriate
from the laws of your own nation...You, Professor Salvemini, are the
leader of the opposition...We do not deny your stature as a strong ad-
versary. We lament only that you are animated by bad faith...The day on
which you denounced the decree that deprived you of your citizenship in
order to justify your anti-Italianness, you became a drifting shipwreck:
the words of protest will strangle you. The right of an Italian deprived of
his liberty no longer speaks in you; rather, the mad, bitter hatred of a man
without a country spreads throughout the world the most abject and
parricidal courses...So why do you come to disturb our exile, our work,
and our faith? Why do you come to destroy the work that we undertake
with so much love for our families, our honor, and the glory of Italy?...
What, Salvemini, is this macabre obsession that still drives your wretched
spirit?...Does your heart not still tremble with fear at the thought of that
voice which, in the midst of one of your talks, asked why Benito Mussolini,
head of the fearsome Black Shirts, does not order an execution squad to
empty into your back and those of your colleagues the last bullets spared
the Austrian enemy?...You do not have the right, Professor Salvemini, to
poison the minds of the good emmigrants; you must not be allowed to
disturb their work of passion and pride; you must not ruin the peace that
is in their midst; Let them work, let them love Italy, leave us to make
Italy loved and exalted by foreigners.

Such angry attacks only served to convince Salvemini that his work was
valuable and effective, and that his visit to the United States had not been
without result. The fact that he aroused such hatred from the Italian-American
Fascists strengthened his determination to return again. With the self-effacing
humor that balanced his grim seriousness of purpose, he wrote to his wife in
Paris that "when I die, have them place on my tomb the three great triumphs
of my life: 'he fought the annexation of Dalmatia, he learned English at the
age of fifty, and he survived a lecture tour in America.' "[34]

Salvemini left the United States in the summer of 1927 and returned to
Paris, where he immersed himself in the organizational work of the anti-
Fascist movement that gave birth to the *Concentrazione Antifascista*. Once
the volume on *The Fascist Dictatorship in Italy* appeared in the United
States that same year, Salvemini's reputation as an expert on Fascism was
firmly established there, with the result that he received an invitation from
Alvin Johnson, director of the New School for Social Research in New York,
to present a course on Italian foreign policy.[35] At the end of 1928 Salvemini
therefore sailed a second time for the United States on a visit that was to last
more than eight months and that would result in lasting friendships and
important political associations. The New School had been created in 1921

34. Cited in Tagliacozzo, "La vita," p. 258.
35. *Memorie di un fuoruscito*, p. 107. Salvemini gave the same course at the University of
London in 1923.

as a center of learning designed to promote the social and physical sciences in a liberal atmosphere, and it frequently hosted prominent European scholars who had encountered difficulties with their repressive governments.[36] Here he met a number of well-known liberal intellectuals who taught at Columbia, Harvard, Princeton, Yale, and other universities. It was also here that one cold, wintry evening a young Italian couple came to hear Salvemini lecture and began a friendship that grew and endured until Salvemini's death. Among the earliest anti-Fascists to escape Mussolini's persecution, Roberto and Maritza Bolaffio had left their native Gorizia in 1922 and settled in New York. An engineer by profession, Roberto Bolaffio was a young man of fiery democratic zeal and idealism that matched and found instinctive sympathy with Salvemini's personality and ideas. In the years that followed he and his intelligent wife worked closely and loyally with Salvemini in the anti-Fascist struggle in America and provided him with indispensable moral and practical support.[37]

As soon as his course was over, Salvemini began a second round of public lectures and debates that he arranged himself and which took him as far as California. It was on this exhausting second journey across the American continent that he had an opportunity to study the Italian-American communities closely for the first time and to form a series of powerful and lasting impressions. Indeed, Salvemini had decided to make the tour precisely in order to learn something about the Italian-Americans and to establish contacts within their communities with the hope of setting up a serious anti-Fascist organization in America.[38] In France and Switzerland he had found strong anti-Fascist sentiment among the Italian immigrants, and in the United States, "with four million Italians who had reached a level of well-being never dreamed of in Italy," he expected to find the "moral and financial basis for a vast struggle against Fascism . . . It did not take me long to discover that I was much mistaken."[39] Salvemini marveled at — and came to respect — the ability of the Italian immigrants to adapt themselves to the greatly different conditions in American society and came away with a strong impression of their initiative and hard work, especially at a time when

36. In 1933, following the diaspora of German intellectuals and scientists from Nazi Germany, Johnson established the so-called "University in Exile" as the graduate faculty of the New School, for European scholars who fled Nazi and Fascist persecutions. Among the Italians who taught there was Max Ascoli, who later became dean of the graduate faculty and a close collaborator of Salvemini. See Laura Fermi, *Illustrious Immigrants: The Intellectual Migration from Europe, 1930-1941*, 2nd ed. (Chicago, 1971), pp. 74-75.

37. The circumstances of Salvemini's meeting with the Bolaffios was recounted to the editor in an interview with Maritza Bolaffio in Florence, June 8, 1976. See also *Memorie di un fuoruscito*, p. 109.

38. Tagliacozzo, "La vita," p. 258; Valeri and Merola, *Scritti sul fascismo*, p. xx; *Memorie di un fuoruscito*, p. 109.

39. *Memorie di un fuoruscito*, p. 109.

America was experiencing the depths of the depression.[40] Yet the very ability to survive and adapt to their new home contributed to their susceptibility to Fascist propaganda:[41]

> They were almost all tireless workers, bound to their immediate and distant families by heroic ties of sacrifice. Arriving in America illiterate, bare-foot, and with sacks on their backs, they silently bore difficulties and pain, despised by all because they were Italians. And now you could hear repeated — even by Americans — that Mussolini had made Italy into a country where there was no unemployment, where everyone had baths in their homes, and the trains ran on time, and that Italy was respected and feared in the world. Whoever said that this was not so destroyed not only their ideal fatherland, but wounded their personal dignity. Italy, the Italian government, and Mussolini represented an indivisible unity in their minds; to criticize Mussolini was to fight against Italy and to offend them personally.

Disillusioned by the widespread sympathy for Mussolini that he encountered among the Italian-Americans, Salvemini concluded that the most important and successful work he could do was in English-speaking American circles, where Fascist propaganda had also made many converts but where he felt there was a strong and genuine desire to learn the truth about Italy under Fascism. As he had done in England and France, Salvemini now determined to do battle with Fascism for the conquest of American public opinion.

Returning from California in the summer of 1929, Salvemini passed through Cambridge, Massachusetts, where he visited acquaintances at Harvard and met for the first time Giorgio La Piana, who was then professor of church history, and with whom he became a fast friend and collaborator. La Piana introduced Salvemini to some of the eminent historians at Harvard, including Arthur Schlesinger, Sr., William Langer, and Samuel E. Morison, and through this visit he later received an invitation to lecture at the university.[42] Shortly before leaving New York for his journey back to Europe, Salvemini received a note from Lauro De Bosis, secretary of the Italy-America Society, requesting a meeting. Salvemini knew the Society to be a major outlet for Fascist propaganda in America, and was therefore hesitant about seeing De Bosis, but the frankness and sincerity of the young man won over Salvemini. De Bosis explained that although he had once admired Fascism, he was now thoroughly disillusioned with the movement and wanted to do something to fight Mussolini and the regime. He asked Salvemini's opinion

40. Tagliacozzo, "L'opera di Gaetano Salvemini negli Stati Uniti d'America," p. 23.
41. Memorie di un fuoruscito, p. 110.
42. Ibid., p. 112; Tagliacozzo, "L'opera di Gaetano Salvemini negli Stati Uniti d'America," p. 24.

as to the advisability of attempting an air flight over Rome to exhort the Italians to overthrow the dictatorship. Salvemini cautioned him about the practical dangers of such an effort, but gave him moral encouragement. In October 1931 De Bosis carried out his daring mission, only to crash tragically off the coast of Corsica.[43]

In February 1930, following the creation of *Giustizia e Libertà* in Paris, Salvemini made his third trip to the United States, this time to teach at Harvard University — again on Italian foreign policy — for one semester as a visiting professor.[44] This five month period was for Salvemini the most pleasant experience to date in America, for he relished the opportunity to get back into the classroom and to be in contact once again with students and colleagues in an academic environment. His stay was by no means idle, for in addition to his teaching — which he found refreshing and satisfying — he seized every opportunity to speak to political and university groups on Fascism and to carry the anti-Fascist message to the public. It was during this activity that he met still another young man who would become a close friend and supporter, Michele Cantarella, who taught Italian literature at Smith College. But certainly the most surprising and important experience for Salvemini was his discovery of the Widener Library at Harvard. Here he found all the resources of one of the great libraries of the world open to him, and he spent many long hours each day immersed in his research and the tranquility of Cambridge, profoundly impressed by the virtues of American education. The Cambridge sojourn undoubtedly planted in Salvemini's mind the idea that he might one day move permanently to the United States.[45]

Salvemini went back to Europe in the early summer of 1930, this time not to return to America again for two years. The money he had earned at Harvard, though modest enough by American standards, was sufficient to fulfill his spartan needs until his next trip. During this last extended period in Europe, he worked tirelessly and in close collaboration with the men in *Giustizia e Libertà*, continued to write for anti-Fascist and British newspapers, and began work on *Mussolini Diplomate*. He participated directly in the formation of *Giustizia e Libertà's* political program and wrote lengthy articles for its journal, the *Quaderni*, on the problems of capital and labor under Fascism, in addition to a number of pamphlets published by the Friends of Italian Freedom in London.[46] But in spite of the immense efforts Salvemini poured into the anti-Fascist struggles in London and Paris, his thoughts returned increasingly to the United States, and in October 1932 he accepted

43. On De Bosis see below, Part II, chapter 3, note 11.
44. *Memorie di un fuoruscito*, p. 136.
45. Salvemini devoted a large section of his memoirs to the joys of the Harvard library and the advantages of American education. See *Memorie di un fuoruscito*, pp. 137-146.
46. A selection of the articles published during this period appears in *Scritti sul fascismo*, II.

an offer to teach at Yale University for one semester.[47] This experience proved to be the prelude to Salvemini's eventual transfer to the United States. After a brief period in Paris during the summer of 1933 following the semester in New Haven, Salvemini returned once again to Cambridge, where he intended to resume his research and writing, and discovered to his surprise that he had been offered a permanent position on the faculty. Ruth Draper, the fiancée of the dead hero Lauro De Bosis, donated a sum of money to establish the De Bosis chair in Italian civilization at Harvard, and expressed the desire to have Salvemini fill the position, which he held until his return to Italy in 1948.[48]

In recent years the motives for Salvemini's decision to live in America have become the subject of some scholarly debate. Gaspare De Caro has argued that for personal and political reasons Salvemini felt himself isolated from and tired of the battles he had fought in Europe, and that his anti-communism had driven a wedge between himself and his friends in *Giustizia e Libertà*, so that he now wished to withdraw into his private world of books and scholarship and relinquish all political responsibility.[49] There is some measure of truth in this thesis, but only if it is seen as the momentary transition that it actually was. Enzo Tagliacozzo, on the other hand, has consistently asserted that Salvemini wanted the stability of a permanent teaching position so that he could continue his political battles without the financial uncertainties that had plagued him ever since his exile began.[50] This argument is more convincing, but it fails to provide a full explanation of Salvemini's outlook and ideas in the crucial period from 1934 to 1935. The move to the United States was not just a transfer of his old battles to a new terrain, but involved a whole series of perceptions and judgments born out of his earlier expierence in America and as a result of his interpretation of rapidly changing world events.

No doubt Salvemini himself was initially confused and torn by the choices facing him in 1934, and his ultimate decision was not easily made. He was disillusioned, depressed, and even bitter, a state of mind caused in part by his personal circumstance: his second wife, Fernanda Luchaire, refused to follow him to America, and his stepson Jean had been recently implicated in the Stavinsky scandal that toppled the French government.[51] More important, in recent months Salvemini had witnessed the seemingly inexorable march of fascism throughout Europe as well as the steady crumbling of democratic institutions and the faltering resolve of the western powers to

---

47. *Memorie di un fuoruscito*, p. 169.
48. Ibid., p. 175.
49. De Caro, *Gaetano Salvemini*, pp. 388-391.
50. Tagliacozzo, "L'opera di Gaetano Salvemini negli Stati Uniti d'America," p. 23-26.
51. De Caro, *Gaetano Salvemini*, p. 389.

resist the belligerent dictators. In January 1933 Hitler had seized power in Germany and had destroyed the Weimar republican institutions; the political crisis within Austria threatened to end democracy there; the popular front tactic seemed to be radicalizing European democracy; and perhaps most alarming, Mussolini had embarked upon his aggression against Ethiopia. The Italo-Ethiopian war had a decisive effect on Salvemini, for the enthusiasm with which the Italian people supported the war greatly disheartened him, and he was convinced that Mussolini would triumph over the League of Nations as a result of Britain's diplomatic "collusion" with the Duce.

In an important and revealing exchange of correspondence with Alberto Tarchiani, who remained in Paris until 1940, Salvemini expressed his belief that the moral protests of President Roosevelt and other statesmen would be fruitless — "You and I both know the value of useless poses against a good rifle-shot or even a simple beating."[52] Even while admitting that the Duce might be defeated in Ethiopia and that Mussolini's failure to triumph could produce a crisis within the Fascist regime, he believed that Mussolini would be replaced by an equally corrupt coalition of Fascist and liberal leaders that would include Badoglio, Balbo, Croce, Orlando, Bonomi, and the royal family, and that would probably also draw into its circle conservative anti-Fascists such as Sforza and Albertini. "I could not," he told Tarchiani, "bring myself to participate in such a festering sore." To the argument that Mussolini's fall might result in a revolution, Salvemini replied that in the hands of the Communists the revolution would create a dictatorship as repressive and unjust as the Fascist regime. Given these equally distasteful options, Salvemini felt that he could no longer fulfill a meaningful role in Italian affairs, even as part of an internal opposition.[53] Tarchiani, who knew him well, saw in this attitude not a renunciation of responsibility, but the disgust of the moralist that Salvemini was: "My dear friend and brother," Tarchiani lectured, "after a half-century of history, politics, and daily experience, are you not yet convinced that we cannot proceed except by cleansing the festering sores? If not, we remain isolated, with our own ideas, our own noble pride, with our own fierce and comforting material and spiritual integrity, but we cannot engage in politics and we will not have an influence on the destiny of our country."[54]

Repelled as he was by the political compromises and moral corruption around him, Salvemini concluded that "I do not see what a man like me can

52. Salvemini to Tarchiani, October 29, 1935, Istituto Storico per la Resistenza in Toscana, *Fondo Giustizia e Libertà*, II, fascicolo 1, sottofascicolo 55.

53. Salvemini expressed a similar attitude toward the political situation in a letter to Mary Berenson, March 15, 1935, cited in De Caro, *Gaetano Salvemini*, pp. 389-390.

54. Tarchiani to Salvemini, November 11, 1935, Istituto Storico per la Resistenza in Toscana, *Fondo Giustizia e Libertà*, II, fascicolo 1, sottofascicolo 55.

do other than asking for American citizenship . . . I had not thought about this idea of becoming an American citizen until two months ago. But the more . . . I witness these events . . . the more I am convinced that there is nothing for me to do either inside Italy or outside. I am truly becoming in these days a 'man without a country,' in the sense that I no longer feel myself even a 'citizen of the world.' "[55] The rootlessness that gnawed at his soul seemed to have been abated during his American visits. In December 1932, during a talk arranged for him in Hoboken, New Jersey by Roberto Bolaffio, Salvemini had taken the occasion to squash the rumors then circulating that he might return to Italy under the new amnesty that Mussolini had just granted. He announced that despite the revocation of his citizenship and the attacks against him by Italian-American Fascists, "I was Italian before Mussolini deprived me of my nationality. I remained Italian after Mussolini took it away. I do not feel that I have become any more Italian now that Mussolini has given it back. The soul of a man cannot be either confiscated or restored by an royal decree. My soul belongs to me."[56] With this declaration we may perhaps date the beginning of Salvemini's conscious realization that after nearly a decade in exile the concept of citizenship had come to have little meaning for him beyond the fact that the duties and obligations of a citizen to his government remain valid only as long as that government respects and maintains the conditions necessary for liberty. Several years earlier he had written:

> In our conscience as civilized men, a society is free only when three conditions are met:
>   1) if the limitations on individual liberty, made necessary by the needs of society, are equal for all citizens;
>   2) if these limitations are based on the consent of the majority and are changed as the moral criteria of the majority are transformed;
>   3) if those who disapprove of the limitations have the obligation to respect them until they are changed, but also have the right to criticize with a view toward altering the opinion of the majority and bringing about change.
>   In a free government, the liberty of the minority is limited by the majority's right to govern; but the liberty of the majority is limited by the right to dissent and to oppose that is due to every minority and to each individual.[57]

55. Salvemini to Tarchiani, cit.
56. Salvemini's speech is in *Scritti sul fascismo*, II, pp. 485-489. In the years since his New School lectures Salvemini maintained close contact with Bolaffio, and following the birth of *Giustizia e Libertà* in Paris Salvemini entrusted Bolaffio with the task of collecting much needed financial contributions in America. Bolaffio acted as secretary for the American branch of the group, edited the monthly *Bollettino della Federazione Giustizia e Libertà del Nord America*, and worked tirelessly to arouse anti-Fascist sentiment among the Italian-Americans. See *Memorie di un fuoruscito*, pp. 119, 149, 152, and the folder entitled "Giustizia e Libertà" in the *Bolaffio Papers*, Florence.
57. "Il primo dovere: conquistare la Nuova Libertà," July 1928, now in *Scritti sul fascismo*, II,

That Salvemini found these conditions more fully developed in the United States than elsewhere explains both his determination to remain there on a permanent basis as well as his eventual decision to become an American citizen. Hence, although Salvemini never ceased to be Italian in affection and sentiment, and while he remained in many ways dedicated to the Mazzinian principle that the struggle for freedom recognized no national interests, he was equally determined to give his political allegiance to the government that came closest to his deeply felt values. Years later he explained that "in December 1940 I received American citizenship. I decided on this step after a lengthy consideration of the duties that were implicit in the oath of loyalty. Those duties I assumed freely and with complete awareness because I fully agreed with the institutions of this country which, with all their defects, are those that come closest to my political and moral ideals...An oath is for me a serious thing. It will remain valid as long as America does not renounce its democratic institutions and thereby betray its ideals."[58]

In the United States of the mid-1930s Salvemini found much to restore his faith and to renew his hope. The country was undergoing a vast experiment in economic and social policy under the New Deal and the leadership of Franklin Roosevelt, who was determined to preserve democratic institutions even in the midst of the great depression and in the face of world-wide political reaction.[59] His criticism of Roosevelt's policy during the Ethiopian War was no doubt due in part to his conviction that America possessed the strength and the resources to determine or at least influence the course of world events, and in this belief Salvemini found the greatest reason for hope. While he may have protested his impotence in the face of Mussolini's successes, Salvemini never took his attention from the Italian situation and devoted all his work in America to the resolution of its problems. Even though he could recoil in moral protest against the corruption of politics, he remained a trenchant political figure who saw that the future international order would depend greatly on decisions and policies made in the United States. His assumption of American citizenship takes on its final meaning only in this light, for as a citizen he hoped not only to awaken the United States to the dangers of Fascism, but also to influence the course of American policy toward Italy.[60] Here, as in Italy, Salvemini chose for himself the difficult role of constant critic, moral conscience, and muckraker:

pp. 392-393.
58. "La risposta di Salvemini," May 17, 1944, in L'Italia vista dall'America, ed. Enzo Tagliacozzo (Milan, 1969), pp. 550-552.
59. Tagliacozzo, "L'opera di Gaetano Salvemini negli Stati Uniti d'America," p. 23.
60. Migone, "A proposito di 'L'Italia vista dall'America' di Gaetano Salvemini," in Problemi di storia, pp. 97-98.

> As a loyal American, I have the right not only to love the Italian people
> from which I came, but also the duty to demand that toward that people,
> America is just, generous, and humane. To this work of truth and justice
> for the Italian people I have dedicated my entire life outside Italy, from the
> moment I left Italy in August 1925 until today. I did not become an Ameri-
> can citizen in 1940 in order to advocate a base Italian nationalism under
> the protection of American citizenship. This would have been an abomin-
> able disloyalty on my part. But when I assumed the duties of American
> citizenship I also acquired its rights. One of these rights is to demand
> justice for the Italian people and for all peoples.[61]

Hence, despite the tempting attractions of academic life in Cambridge, which he described as an "enchanted island," Salvemini did not remain aloof from the political battles still to be fought. Tarchiani was correct — and Salvemini must have known it even in his most depressed moments — when he wrote to his friend in Cambridge, "Do you think that your tribulations would be over if you became an American citizen? Would you really abstain from taking part in the life of your new country? If you wanted to do this, Mussolini's passport would be enough. Otherwise, think of how many things you would have to reprove the United States for, from Versailles to the slippery policies of Roosevelt...Do not delude yourself: as a citizen of two countries you will have to fight on two fronts. And think of the joy!...If there is a decent way of working for our country, do not lose the chance to do so: continue and fulfill as best you can your life's work, which has been spent above all in educating by example."[62] Salvemini's instincts and character compelled him to recognize the truth of Tarchiani's words. His previous experiences in the United States now assumed a coherent political and ideological meaning, and his decision to settle in America opened one of the most fruitful and important phases in a life already filled with achieve-ment — and the burdens of political battle.

Tarchiani's forecast was almost immediately fulfilled. As soon as Salvemini had been offered the position at Harvard, his Fascist enemies began a campaign to wreck his reputation and prevent the appointment. Italian newspsapers accused him of attempting to assassinate Mussolini by planting a bomb in St. Peter's Square, and in March the *New York Times* carried the story with an editorial, while *Il Progresso Italo-Americano* of New York openly charged Salvemini with the plot.[63] With the aid of La Piana and President James B. Conant of Harvard, Salvemini hired lawyers to press a libel suit against both the Associated Press and *Il Progresso*, and he challenged Mussolini directly to present an American court with the evidence

---

61. "La risposta di Salvemini," p. 551.
62. Tarchiani to Salvemini, cit.
63. Diggins, *Mussolini and Fascism*, pp. 141-142; Tagliacozzo, "La vita," pp. 264-265; Salvadori, *Gaetano Salvemini*, p. 37.

of his complicity and to demand his extradiction. The affair eventually came to nothing and the *New York Times* reluctantly had to admit that Salvemini was innocent of the charge,[64] but it did demonstrate clearly that the Italian-American Fascists considered Salvemini's presence in the United States dangerous to their ambitions. Salvemini had no time to brood over his or the world's misery, for he began at once a bitter and relentless campaign against the Italian-American Fascists and their agents who were poisoning the ethnic communities and were making Italian-Americans "strangers in the land that harbored them."[65] Although he pursued his many other scholarly and political activities with even greater intensity than before, the war against the Italian-American Fascists remained his major preoccupation until after Pearl Harbor.[66]

During his earlier visits to the United States Salvemini had been shocked and dismayed by the extent of Italian-American support for Fascism, and he reluctantly came to realize that there was little chance for the kind of extensive anti-Fascist movement that he had once hoped to create among them. Although sorely disappointed, he understood the sources of their enrapture and harbored no ill will against them.[67] Indeed, for reasons that were central to all his work in the United States, he was outspoken in explaining to the American people why so many Italians in their country gave Fascism such enthusiastic praise. He emphasized time and again, as he had done with regard to Italy itself, that there was a basic distinction between the Italians and Fascism, and while at times the Italian people might have appeared to be zealous admirers of Mussolini, they were not Fascists. Salvemini believed that most Italian-Americans were hard-working, law-abiding citizens who wanted above all to improve their economic status and integrate into American society, and who had little interest in politics. He also saw that the pressures of American society and the stresses of assimilation isolated the Italian-Americans, burdened them with a destructive and pervasive sense of inferiority, and as a result often filled them with a bitter resentment against the United States.[68] Moreover, he argued that many Italian-Americans were still strongly attached to their former homeland by sentimental and cultural ties,[69] so that the assimilation process had not been sufficiently advanced to make them immune to Fascist propaganda. The

---

64. *New York Times*, March 21, 1934.

65. Gaetano Salvemini, "Italian Fascist Activities in the U. S.," pamphlet (Washington, D.C., 1940), p. 6.

66. De Caro, *Gaetano Salvemini*, pp. 395-396.

67. Migone, "A proposito de 'L'Italia vista dall'America,' " p. 101.

68. Salvemini, "Italian Fascist Activities," p. 6-7; *Memorie di un fuoruscito*, p. 110

69. See Salvemini's review of Carlo Sforza's book, *The Real Italians: A Study in European Psychology* (New York, 1942), originally in *The Nation*, September 26, 1942, and now in *L'Italia vista dall'America*, pp. 59-61.

Fascists claimed that Mussolini had rebuilt and modernized Italy and had made her into a powerful, respected, prosperous, and feared nation. Fascist propaganda integrated Italian-Americans into these would-be successes and gave them a long-sought sense of pride and achievement. In an alien environment that heaped abuse and disdain upon the Italian-Americans, Fascism fulfilled a much needed psychological function for them, with the result that they identified with Fascism because it provided them with a recognizable and meaningful identity in the pluralistic society that was America.[70] In concrete terms, Salvemini estimated that half of the six million Italian-Americans were oblivious to all forms of political ideology, while only about 10 percent were anti-Fascist and 5 percent "out and out" Fascists. The remaining 35 percent were not yet Fascist but could become so in an emergency that involved Italy, and it was this latter group that most worried Salvemini.[71]

The distinction that he made between Fascism and Italian-American support for it was vital to the success of his work and was the key to understanding his anti-Fascist propaganda. Particularly after the United States entered the war, Salvemini believed that this distinction would be a crucial determinant of American attitudes — and hence American policy — toward post-war Italy. There would be no hope of giving Italy a just peace or of permitting her the right to choose her own political and social institutions if the Allies did not recognize that there was no identification between the Fascist regime and the bulk of Italy's population.[72] This argument would have little credibility if Americans could point to the powerful support for Fascism among Italians in their own country, so that in Salvemini's mind it became imperative to destroy the influence of Fascism among Italian-Americans.

Salvemini's real target, then, was not the Italian-Americans, but that "five percent" that he claimed were "out and out Fascists," and especially their leaders. The chief problem, and the thing that made the war so exasperating, was that it was difficult to separate the leadership of the Italian-American Fascists from the most distinguished heads of the Italian-American communities in general — often, in fact, they were one and the same. For reasons that were easily understood by Salvemini, many important Italian-

---

70. Diggins, *Mussolini and Fascism* pp. 78-80; and the paper by Philip V. Cannistraro, "Fascism and Italian-Americans," presented to the conference on Italian-American research in New York, May 22, 1976, sponsored by the Center for Migration Studies; and "Gli italo-americani e l'Italia: un intervista di Salvemini," *Controcorrente*, December 1945.

71. Salvemini, "Italian Fascist Activities," pp. 18-19.

72. Salvemini and La Piana, *What To Do With Italy*, esp. pp. 1-32, 57-80; Elena Aga-Rossi Sitzia, "La politica degli alleati verso l'Italia nel 1943," *Storia Contemporanea*, 3, 4 (December 1972), 847-895.

American businessmen, politicians, lawyers, journalists, clergymen, physicians, and educators gave public lip service to Mussolini and lent their prestige to Fascism in America. Some, of course, were merely opportunists who rode the wave of popular enthusiasm, while others sought the honors and prestige that Mussolini and the Italian government bestowed so lavishly upon American supporters of the regime.[73] Political leaders who based their careers on the Italian-American vote were in a particularly delicate position, for even if their own philosophies opposed Fascism they were careful not to antagonize their constituents by taking a public stand against Mussolini. It seemed natural that such leaders should attend dinners and ceremonies sponsored by Italian diplomatic or cultural agents when American leaders from the president to the mayor of New York City also received official representatives of the Fascist regime. Whatever the reason, Italian-American leaders — the so-called *prominenti* — were deeply involved in creating or sustaining the enthusiasm for Fascism within the ethnic communities. In pitting himself against Italian-American Fascism, Salvemini quickly found himself facing the open hostility of the ethnic power structure.[74]

Hence, the "two front" war that Tarchiani had warned about became even more complicated in the context of the Italian-American reaction to Fascism, for by engaging in combat against the Fascists and their agents Salvemini aroused the wrath and hostility of many *prominenti*, some of whom had important connections in high government circles and controlled the ethnic information media. As a consequence, Salvemini found himself in the position that so many other leaders of the Italian-American anti-Fascist movement had already encountered — that of being regarded by American society at large as a troublemaker motivated by personal resentment or ideological radicalism, an isolated hothead who had been outcast by his own people both at home and in America.[75] Even with all the intellectual prestige he commanded, Salvemini was a lonely voice among a scattered handful of anti-Fascists across the nation, and he must have realized that alone he could do little to awaken the United States to the dangers of Fascism. Indeed, in the 1920s there had already been a number of attempts by American writers to reveal and expose the growing menace of Fascism, but such efforts had little result at a time when Mussolini's prestige abroad was at its highest.[76] What shocked and enraged Salvemini the most was the fact

73. See the manuscript by Valenti entitled "Fascist Propaganda in the United States," p. 3, in the *Girolamo Valenti Papers*, Tamiment Library, New York University.
74. Migone, "A proposito de 'L'Italia vista dall'America,' " pp. 101-102; James E. Miller, "What To Do With the Exiles? The Evolution of an American Policy Toward Italy, 1941-43," pp. 5-6 (unpublished article).
75. Valenti, "Fascist Propaganda in the United States," p. 2.
76. Among the exposès of the 1920s, see Arthur Livingston, "Italo-American Fascism," *Survey*, 57 (March 1927), 738-740, 750; Marcus Duffield, "Mussolini's American Empire," *Harper's*, 159

that the American government itself had so consistently ignored the threat of Italian Fascism within its own borders, even after Mussolini embarked upon his expansionist foreign policy. After Hitler came to power in Germany and his followers in the United States began to openly parade Nazism through the German-American Bund, he had a momentary hope that the federal government would take action against the Fascist and Nazi movements in America, but his hope turned to outrage as he witnessed the result of government action.

In the spring of 1930 the House of Representatives instituted a congressional committee under Representative Hamilton Fish to investigate subversive activity in the United States. The committee worked for six months but concentrated its attention exclusively on the communist problem. To the dismay of anti-Fascists, Fascism was totally ignored except for one curious but revealing instance: during the House debates on the committee, one member of Congress asked whether there had been "any investigation of Fascism in the United States?" The answer, from Congressman Snell of the Rules Committee, was chilling to men like Salvemini: "I guess this covers it, if it is something wrong. I do not know what that is and guess I better not discuss it at this time [laughter]."[77]

It was only in 1933, after Hitler's seizure of power, that the Congress began to take the question of Fascism seriously, but even then Salvemini experienced much the same maddening frustration. Congressman Samuel Dickstein of New York, chairman of the House Immigration Committee, began a nine month unofficial investigation of Nazi activities and the German-American Bund, and in June 1934 he introduced a resolution that created the Special Committee on Un-American Activities to put the investigations on a permanent and organized basis.[78] Chaired by John W. McCormack but codirected with Dickstein, the Un-American Activities Committee issued a report of its findings the following year which showed that considerable time and effort had been poured into investigations of Communist and Nazi subversion and propaganda — but that again nothing had been done to examine similar activities by agents and supporters of Italian Fascism.[79] Dickstein, the son of Jewish immigrants and a Tammany Hall politician

(November 1929), 661-672; "Does Mussolini Rule Millions Here?," *Liberty Digest*, 103 (November 16, 1929), 14.

77. *Congressional Record*, LXXII, Part 9 (Washington, D.C., 1930), May 22, 1930, p. 9390.

78. Walter Goodman, *The Committee: The Extraordinary Career of the House Committee on Un-American Activities* (New York, 1968), pp. 9-10; Dorothy Waring, *American Defender* (New York, 1935), pp. 119-123.

79. Report, U.S. Congress, House of Representatives, 71st Congress, 3rd Session, Special Committee on Communist Activities in the United States, *Investigation of Communist Propaganda* (Washington, D.C., 1935).

with close ties among New York's Italian-American leaders, succeeded in making a national reputation for himself as a result of his investigations into "un-American" subversion, but it was clear that his interpretation of "un-American" was limited to the Communist and Nazi movements.[80]

The fact that the McCormack-Dickstein Committee had ignored Italian Fascist activities in its investigations of foreign propaganda did not escape the notice of anti-Fascists. Indeed, Girolamo Valenti, the editor of *La Stampa Libera* and a tenacious crusader against Italian-American Fascism, had provided Dickstein with information regarding Italian agents in the United States, but the congressman took no action. Valenti then started his own private inquiry into Fascist propaganda in order to gather additional evidence, and in September 1934 the committee finally subpoenaed him to appear. But when Valenti presented himself at the hearings, he was not called to testify.[81] At the conclusion of the committee hearings even a right-wing periodical like *The Awakener* attacked "the vast areas of un-American activity which the Committee totally missed in its half-hearted researches," including "Fascist movements, inspired or subsidized by the Italian Government."[82] At the same time, the journal also called for an investigation of the lecture activities of aliens like Salvemini. To Valenti and Salvemini the consistent refusal of the committee to examine the evidence of Italian Fascist penetration in America — or for that matter even to acknowledge the existence of such penetration — appeared to be nothing less than a deliberate conspiracy; the government's lack of response certainly demonstrated to their minds the skill with which Fascist propaganda had been spread, as well as the influence of Italian-American *prominenti* in high government circles.

Nor did the McCormack-Dickstein hearings go unobserved by the Fascist government itself. In October 1934 Ambassador Augusto Rosso sent the Italian Foreign Ministry an urgent telegram about the impact of the committee's investigations. Rosso happily reported that the Nazis had been the focus of attention and that the investigation had not come up with significant evidence, but he observed with considerable alarm that American concern over German subversion was having an adverse effect on Italian Fascist work in the United States. Hitler's seizure of power and his anti-Semitic policies had caused "profound repercussions" in America, and "although the most educated and intelligent classes have been able to distinguish between Italian Fascism and German Nazism, that distinction has not always been made by the public at large, among whom the Black

80. Goodman, *The Committee*, pp. 13-14.
81. *La Parola del Popolo*, May 24, 1941. See also Valenti's articles, "Inchiesta sulle attività fasciste," *La Stampa Libera*, January 16, 1934, and "Mussolini's Agent Fosters Fascist Propaganda in the U.S.," ibid., January 24, 1934.
82. Cited in Waring, *American Defender*, pp. 211-212.

Shirt and the Brown Shirt are easily confused." While he did not want to overexaggerate the danger, the ambassador concluded that "the suspicion against foreign political propaganda provoked by Nazi activity is being extended even to us." Given these circumstances, Rosso recommended that "Fascist propaganda action be carried out *in an indirect way*, without revealing the intervention of the Italian government, and that it avoid having the character of political propaganda."[82a] If Salvemini did not know of the Italian government's concern over American reaction to the investigations, he certainly would have agreed with Rosso that the committee had done a poor job.

With a mounting sense of frustration, Salvemini and a number of other notable anti-Fascists issued an open manifesto early in 1936 demanding that a democratic government must replace the Fascist regime in Italy and blasting the "conservative forces in Europe and the United States" for their diplomatic, financial, and moral support of Mussolini.[83]

In the two years after the McCormack-Dickstein Committee submitted its report, Hitler and Mussolini marched from one success to another in Europe while Japanese aggression in the Far East spread further, democratic governments continued to weaken and crumble, and the Nazi-Fascist campaign in the United States became more intense and outspoken. Faced with these crises, Congress revived the Un-American Activities Committee again in May 1938, this time under the chairmanship of Martin Dies, a conservative populist from Texas who was bent on a crusade against "foreign influences and ideologies."[84] Although Dies announced that his committee was "going to investigate and expose the Nazi and fascist movements in this country as thoroughly as we do the Communist movement,"[85] he understood very little about either phenomenon. "The important task, as I saw it," he later recalled, "was to convince the American people that Fascism and Communism are fundamentally alike, and that the real issue is between Americanism on the one hand, and all alienism on the other."[86] Nor did Dies really believe that Italian Fascism — as opposed to German Nazism — was very strong in the United States. During the preliminary work prior to the hearings, he asked his colleagues to suggest areas that should be investigated, and McCormack replied in terms that astounded Salvemini and Valenti. He recommended

82a. Rosso to the Ministry of Foreign Affairs, October 19, 1934, Archivio Centrale dello Stato, *Ministero della Cultura Popolare*, busta 449, fascicolo "Propaganda straniera negli Stati Uniti."

83. "E dopo Mussolini?: Manifesto degli antifascisti negli Stati Uniti," January 26, 1936, *Scritti sul fascismo*, II, pp. 575-578. The manifesto appeared first in the *New York Herald Tribune* and then in the *New York Times* and other papers.

84. Goodman, *The Committee*, pp. 16-23.

85. Ibid., p. 59.

86. Martin Dies, *Martin Dies' Story* (New York, 1963), p. 130.

that the committee should concentrate on Nazi activities, since that was the primary reason why the House established it, as well as on Communism, and added as an afterthought: "If there are any Fascist 'Italian' activities herein, they should be investigated, but I doubt if any will be found connected with Italy. Italy did engage in such activities, but discontinued such efforts around 1928 or 1929. I doubt if any will be found since that time emanating from Italy itself."[87]

The same day that McCormack made this startling assertion, Valenti sent Dies a report on Italian Fascist activities in the United States along with a request that he be allowed to present his evidence to the committee. Dies thanked Valenti for his "helpful information" and assured him that "I shall certainly depend on you and your organization to supply me with additional information and to appear before our committee."[88] This time Valenti had his chance, and on October 4, 1938, he gave several hours of revealing and specific information concerning the organization, methods, and agents of Fascist propaganda among Italian-Americans. Valenti, who had been studying Fascist activities for over a decade, produced a briefcase of documents and affidavits proving that Italian consular officials were intimidating Italian-Americans reluctant to go along with Fascist propaganda, and he told the committee:[89]

> American-Italian Black Shirt legions, 10,000 strong, are marching in America with the same resounding tread as those of the goose-stepping detachments of German-American Bund storm troops.
> Behind this Black Shirt parade there are more than 100,000 Americans of Italian descent who are willing to be seen at the public manifestations of some 200 Fascist organizations throughout the United States.
> Another 100,000 fall within the influence of the powerful organs of propaganda emanating from well-knit and centralized fascistic forces which are mind-conditioning American citizens and swerving their allegiance to Italian dictatorship under the thumping fist of Mussolini.

Valenti's testimony had been a major breakthrough in the anti-Fascist effort to bring the issue of Fascism in America to the attention of public opinion. The *Washington Times* printed blaring headlines that announced "FASCIST TERRORISM IN U.S. REVEALED," and is asked pointedly, "Will the Congressional Committee Delve Deeper into Italian Fascist Activities in the United States?"[90] The answer, in spite of later claims by Dies, was not

87. McCormack to William B. Bankhead, Speaker of the House of Representatives, July 2, 1938, ibid., pp. 246-247.
88. Dies to Valenti, June 3, 1938, *Girolamo Valenti Papers*. The organization referred to by Dies was the Italian Anti-Fascist Committee, of which Valenti was president.
89. U.S. Congress, House of Representatives, 75th Congress, 3rd sess. Special Committee on Un-American Activities Hearings, *Investigation of Un-American Propaganda Activities in the United States* (Washington, D.C., 1940), p. 1182.
90. *Washington Times*, October 4, 1938.

encouraging. In August 1939, Dies brought Fritz Kuhn, the head of the Bund, before his committee and dramatized the threat of the Nazi movement, but when Goffredo Pantaleoni testified in executive session about Fascist activities the following year, Valenti was forced to leak the testimony because the committee refused to make it public.[91] Valenti's own evidence was buried in thousands of pages of official transcripts and testimony dealing with other subjects, and the official report issued in 1939 contained only passing references to Italian Fascism. Even if the committee had accepted what Valenti told them as true, it alone would not have been sufficient basis for the kind of government action the anti-Fascists wanted. It became painfully clear to Salvemini that what was needed was proof — specific, detailed, unquestionable evidence that revealed the entire history, the full scope, and the unrelenting purpose of Italian Fascism in America, proof so powerful and irreputable that it could not be ignored or hidden away by politicans and their bureaucracy. After years of congressional hearings and investigations, Italian Fascism still remained a kind of conspiracy in open daylight.

As he watched the drama of government negligence unfold in Washington, Salvemini's despair turned to anger, and then to determination. He concluded that the initiative had to be seized by the anti-Fascist forces and ultimately devised a two-pronged attack: he would organize the rapidly swelling ranks of well-known Italian exiles into a powerful organization designed to reach the American people in a systematic, carefully executed propaganda campaign, and he would mobilize the power and prestige of his own skills as an historian to provide the country with the kind of hard evidence it lacked. This new two-front war engaged Salvemini's life more or less consistently from 1939 to 1943.

Dozens of Italian anti-Fascist leaders began to make their way to the United States in 1939 following the outbreak of war, their members increasing rapidly after the fall of France in 1940. These men, representing all shades of political philosophy, included Carlo Sforza, Alberto Tarchiani, Luigi Sturzo, Aldo Garosci, Alberto Cianca, and Randolfo Pacciardi. Upon their arrival in America they joined the earlier *fuorusciti* such as La Piana, Bolaffio, Borgese, Cantarella, Ascoli, Venturi, and Salvemini himself.[92] Out of the contact between the new arrivals and the existing resistance movement

---

91. *New York Post*, March 20, 1941; *Congressional Record*, LXXXVII, Part 3 (Washington, D.C., 1941), March 25, 1941, pp. 2567-2568. Dies later claimed that his committee had exposed the Italian Black Shirts in America along with the various Nazi groups, and that "every one of these outfits folded up under the resulting publicity." See *Martin Dies' Story*, p. 159.

92. Delzell, *Mussolini's Enemies*, pp. 198-202; the same author's "The Italian Anti-Fascist Emigration, 1922-1943," *Journal of Central European Affairs*, 12 (April 1952), 20-55; Diggins, *Mussolini and Fascism*, pp. 344-345.

Salvemini forged the Mazzini Society late in 1939.[93] He infused the group with the principles that he had brought to *Giustizia e Libertà* years earlier — opposition to Fascism, communism, monarchism, and clericalism, and dedication to the Mazzinian ideas of liberty, republic and social justice — and intended it to influence "American public opinion, and possibly even those elements that direct the foreign policy of the United States, with regard to that series of problems that can be called the 'Italian question.' "[94] Its specific aims would be to inform Americans about actual conditions in Italy, combat Fascist propaganda lies, defend American democratic institutions, and undertake a major "educational" program among the Italian-American communities.[95] The Mazzini Society hammered away repeatedly at the fundamental idea that the Fascist regime did not reflect the attitudes or have the confidence of the Italian people.

At its height the Mazzini Society counted about 1,000 permanent members, but it developed branches in dozens of states across the country and — largely because of the cultural and academic prestige of its leadership — exercised an influence out of proportion to its numbers. In 1940, following Italy's entry into World War II, Max Ascoli was elected its president and Alberto Tarchiani became its secretary. Relying on membership dues and private contributions to support its activities, the group sponsored countless meetings, rallies, and marches throughout the United States, presented radio broadcasts for domestic and foreign consumption, published articles in sympathetic newspapers and magazines, and used its contacts with prominent Americans to bring the anti-Fascist case to the attention of the Roosevelt administration in Washington. One of its major weapons was *Il Mondo*, a monthly newspaper edited by the Socialist Giuseppe Lupis, who carried on a bitter, no-holds-barred war against the Italian-American Fascists and their papers.[96]

Because of Salvemini's belief that the conduct and attitudes of Italian-Americans could influence American post-war policy toward Italy, the Mazzini Society devoted much of its energy to the Italian-Americans. In this

---

93. On the series of meetings that led to the formation of the Mazzini Society, see Renato Roggioli to Salvemini, October 1, 1939, and the unsigned memorandum, "The Mazzini Society," in Istituto Storico per la Resistenza in Toscana, Florence, *Fondo Mazzini Society*, fascicolo 1, sottofascicolo 2. For sketches of Salvemini's activities during this period see also Max Ascoli, "Gaetano Salvemini negli Stati Uniti," *La Voce Repubblicana*, December 20-21, 1967; and Norman Kogan, "Salvemini in America," *Il Mondo* (Rome), October 8, 1957, pp. 9-10.

94. Poggioli to Salvemini, cit.

95. "Relazione della prima seduta della Mazzini Society," signed by Venturi and Poggioli, n.d., *Fondo Mazzini Society*, fascicolo 1, sottofascicolo 2.

96. A membership list and numerous reports on the Society's activities are in Archivio Centrale dello Stato, Rome, *Ministero dell'Interno*, DGPS (1920-1945), Cat. G-1, fascicolo 948, "Società Mazzini." See also "The Mazzini Society," cit.

connection, the organization sought first and foremost to destroy the influence of Fascist propaganda among the ethnic communities, to arouse their interest in the fate of Italy, and to defend both the Italian-Americans and the exiles against discriminatory war-time policies of the government. In its efforts to achieve the anti-Fascist politicization of the Italian-Americans, the Mazzini Society faced a difficult task, not only because of the powerful grip of Fascist propaganda, but also because of the difficulties of maintaining a united coalition among the many different trends and currents that burdened the anti-Fascist movement in America. The first serious opposition to Fascism in the United States had arisen out of the Italian-American labor movement, but it was by no means a unified or cohesive resistance. Various radicals of communist, socialist, syndicalist, and anarchist persuasions had managed to form the Anti-Fascist Alliance of North America (AFANA) as early as 1923, supported by the New York Federation of Labor, the Amalgamated Clothing Workers of America, and the International Ladies Garment Workers Union. In 1925 Frank Ballanca of the ACWA and Girolamo Valenti launched *Il Nuovo Mondo*, a daily newspaper aimed at reconciling the divisive factions with the anti-Fascist left. But efforts to create a unified front proved unsuccessful and by 1926 the socialist-liberal elements split off from AFANA and created the Anti-Fascist Federation for the Freedom of Italy. Four years later *Il Nuovo Mondo* closed down, but although the Italian-American resistance remained fragmented, local centers of anti-Fascism continued to fight valiantly, and often successfully, under the leadership of men like Carlo Tresca, Arturo Giovannitti, Girolamo Valenti, and Armando Borghi.[97]

The burden of this mixed legacy, coupled with the instinctive enthusiasm of so many Italian-Americans for Mussolini, rendered Salvemini's work all the more difficult. To add even further to his problems, Salvemini insisted that the society combine the support of American citizens with the efforts of the Italian exiles, while Ascoli wanted to stress the purely American aspects of the movement. Ascoli's strategy, designed to emphasize the group's "prevailingly Italo-American character" and "our activity as American anti-Fascists of Italian origin," meant inevitably that the Mazzini Society "must be ready to take in even men who only recently have discovered the horrors of Fascism."[98] Salvemini believed that this policy would mean the kind of moral compromise that he was unwilling to make: after Pearl Harbor most of the Italian-American leaders abandoned their earlier support for Mussolini and protested their loyalty to America and its democratic institutions, and

97. Diggins, *Mussolini and Fascism*, pp. 111-143; Delzell, *Mussolini's Enemies*, pp. 198-200.
98. Ascoli to Mazzini Society members, July 18, 1940, cited in Michele Cantarella to Philip V. Cannistraro, November 22, 1975.

Salvemini protested that the society was seeking to co-op — and eventually to form an alliance with — the very *prominenti* that he detested.

The dangers inherent in the Mazzini Society's policy of collaboration with the *prominenti* — as well as other disputes that developed later — induced Salvemini to disengage himself from the organization he had founded: he persuaded himself that the wisest course to follow was to wage his own battle against Italian-American Fascism in the way he knew best — through historical research. The failure of the Congressional investigations to confront the existence of Fascism in the United States haunted him. Although the exposés published by *Il Mondo* and other anti-Fascist newspapers had an impact in liberal circles — some English-language papers like the *New York Post*, *PM*, and *Time Magazine* even reprinted *Il Mondo's* articles — it is clear that they could not provide the basis for government prosecution or legislation.[99] Similarly, the spate of books about Fascism that began to appear in the late 1930s were too openly ideological or sensational in nature to convince any but the partisan observer.[100] The more he thought about it, the more he was certain that a well-documented, coherent study of Italian Fascism in America was the solution.

Since 1939 Salvemini had collaborated with Giuseppe Lupis in exposing Fascist activities through the pages of *Il Mondo*, the two men working on the assumption that the backgrounds and long-forgotten statements of many *prominenti* could be used to prove their complicity with Italian Fascism. Lupis and his staff combed the New York Public Library and private collections to locate back issues of Fascist journals like *Il Carroccio* and *Il Grido della Stirpe* for this purpose and provided Salvemini with an informal research service for his articles.[101] It was about this time that Salvemini began to collect such information in a systematic manner, and it is probable that he had helped Valenti gather his material for the Dies hearings.[102] In the summer of 1940 Salvemini wrote the twenty-three page pamphlet entitled "Italian Fascist Activities in the U.S.," published in Washington by the American Council on Public Affairs after Italy's declaration of war.[103] The

99. "The Mazzini Society Influences the Italian Language Press," September 18, 1941, *Fondo Mazzini Society*, fascicolo 1, sottofascicolo 2.

100. See for example George Seldes, *Sawdust Caesar: The Untold History of Mussolini and Fascism* (New York, 1935); A. B. Magil and Henry Stevens, *The Peril of Fascism: The Crisis of American Democracy* (New York, 1938); Max Ascoli and Arthur Feiler, *Fascism for Whom?* (New York, 1938); George Britt, *Fifth Column in America* (New York, 1940); and John R. Carlson, *Under Cover* (New York, 1943).

101. See the exchange of correspondence in 1939 between Lupis and Salvemini in the Salvemini Archives, Rome.

102. Valenti told the Dies Committee that other anti-Fascist friends had helped him to collect his data. *Investigation of Un-American Propaganda Activities*, cit., p. 1186.

103. The pamphlet was published with an introduction by Prof. William Y. Elliott of Harvard,

council, which included well-known liberals such as Harry Elmer Barnes, Paul Kellog, Stephen P. Duggan, and Max Lerner, maintained close relations with Salvemini and relied upon him for information and commentary concerning Italian affairs.[104] Toward the end of the year a number of mass circulation magazines ran a series of alarming articles on foreign political subversion in the United States and honed in for the first time on Italian Fascism. The evidence would indicate that the editors either based their stories on Salvemini's pamphlet or received his active assistance in compiling their information.[105]

It is clear that during the course of 1940, while he worked on these projects, Salvemini developed the idea of writing a full-length study of Italian Fascist activities in the United States. The result was the present work. Although it is not certain whether he intended to publish the book at once,[106] Salvemini's first concern was to produce a lengthy chronicle of Fascist propaganda and subversion in America for the Dies Committee that would force Congress to confront the issue squarely and take action against the Fascists and their agents. The project, begun in earnest in 1941, consumed enormous amounts of his time and energy, and he worked on it steadily when not engaged in his many other activities. When Tarchiani pressed him to contribute essays to the Mazzini Society newspaper, *Nazioni Unite*, Salvemini explained that he could not do so because "I intend to finish the memorandum for the Dies Committee by next December. And I will do nothing else until this nightmare that has poisoned my life for a year has vanished."[107]

The nature and purpose of the painful history he intended to write determined from the outset that it would follow the same pattern he had established for his books on the Fascist regime. Here, too, he worked to achieve that peculiar balance of objective history and political indictment that characterized his anti-Fascist historiogrphy.[108] Because the burden of

"Why Tolerate Mussolini's Agents?" Large portions of this essay were reproduced under the title "Mussolini's Empire in the United States" in a book by Salvemini's secretary, Frances Keene, *Neither Liberty Nor Bread: The Meaning and Tragedy of Fascism* (New York, 1940), pp. 336-349.

104. M. B. Schnapper to Salvemini, December 23, 1940, *Fondo Mazzini Society*, fascicolo 1, sottofascicolo 2.

105. See "The War of Nerves: Hitler's Helper," *Fortune*, 22, 5 (November 1940), 85-87, 108, 110, 112; Dale Kramer, "Survey of Fascist Organizations in the United States," *Harper's*, 180 (September 1940), 380-393; "Lay Off the Italians," *Collier's* 106:5 (August 3, 1940), 54-56. The term "Fascist transmission belt" which Salvemini coined and used in his writings to describe subsidiary propaganda organizations appears several times in these and other articles.

106. Cantarella to Cannistraro, June 30, 1976.

107. Salvemini to Tarchiani, November 5, 1941, *Fondo Giustizia e Libertà*, II, fascicolo 55. In 1941 Valenti submitted reports on Fascist propaganda to the FBI and the Federal Communications Commission. See *The New York Sun*, July 12, 1941.

108. Salvemini explained these ideas about the writing of history in a series of lectures at the

proof lay with him, Salvemini's methodology relied heavily on the use of quotations, footnotes, and documentation to establish the credibility of his argument. Within this framework he also believed that it was crucial to let the Fascists and their supporters incriminate themselves, so that the bulk of his documentation came from Fascist and philo-Fascist newspapers, journals, and other publications. The predominance of Fascist materials in this study allowed him not only to establish the objectivity of his sources, but also to obtain details and information not available elsewhere. If the enemy's own published words sometimes exaggerated the importance of their activities or the zeal of their commitment, so much the better. Salvemini never shrunk from making accusations about specific individuals, whether they were notable personalities or minor characters; even in his articles for *The Nation*, the *New Republic* and similar journals he had refused to hide behind abstractions,[109] and if this work was to have the intended result it was all the more important that it provide the reader with the names and activities of all those who had acted as knowing or unconscious agents of Italian Fascism in America. But his determination to expose individuals was always tempered by his refusal to stoop to personal invective or to attack his opponents on any but the political level. Although the innumerable references to names — which sometimes appear as little more than lists — detracted from the flow of his narrative, they constituted a powerful and inescapable testimony of the extent to which Fascism had penetrated into the Italian-American communities.

Salvemini had chosen a monumental task for himself, for it required endless sifting through thousands of pages of newsprint and periodicals and the compiling of copious notes. In the process of gathering the evidence, he often relied on his devoted friends and secretaries to help locate a quotation, check a source, or find a piece of information about a specific event, and he ultimately accumulated thousands of typed pages and index cards.[110] He began writing before he had completed the last bits of research and then went back and filled in gaps and additional information later. He wrote in English, using a direct and agile style which, though not flawless, was highly effective for his purpose.[111]

Salvemini started the actual writing of the book sometime early in 1941, but although he had completed a number of drafts, the momentous events of

University of Chicago in 1938 and published as *Historian and Scientist: An Essay on the Nature of History and the Social Sciences* (Cambridge, Mass., 1939).

109. Migone, "A proposito de 'L'Italia vista dall'America,' " p. 98.

110. Cantarella to Cannistraro, June 30, 1976. See also Tagliacozzo, "L'opera di Gaetano Salvemini negli Stati Uniti d'America," p. 27; and his introduction to *L'Italian vista dall'America*, pp. xiv-xv.

111. See Roberto Vivarelli's introduction to Gaetano Salvemini, *The Origins of Fascism in Italy* (New York, 1973), p. vii.

1942-43 caused him to put it aside. The Allies landed in North Africa in November 1942 and by the following spring they had laid their plans for the invasion of Sicily. In view of the impending attack against the Italian mainland itself, Salvemini saw the urgent need for the Allies to adopt a definitive and organic policy for the Italian occupation and the post-war period. He and La Piana therefore worked feverishly to compose *What To Do With Italy*, a comprehensive critique of the forces at work in Italy and a plea for a policy based on Salvemini's ideas on the kind of government Italy required.[112] This volume appeared several weeks prior to the coup d'état that toppled Mussolini from power in July 1943, and Salvemini continued to work on his study of Italian-American Fascism on and off throughout that year. But by then the logic of events and the rapid momentum of the war had superceded the once burning need for his history of Fascism in the United States.[113]

Salvemini left a rich legacy for later generations, and surely one bequest of value is the lesson that if Fascism must be studied and understood with the reason and logic of the mind, it should also be fought with the instincts and passion of the soul. This dialectic of human reactions formed the source of his political action and the inspiration for his historical opus during three tumultuous decades. *Italian Fascist Activities in the United States* cannot be properly understood outside of this context, for although — and perhaps because — his perception was molded by moral outrage, the work remains an important and valuable contribution to historical knowledge. Today, thirty-five years after it was written, the passion that infuses it may appear excessive to modern readers and some of his judgments of men and events may be dismissed as the overreaction of a partisan motivated by the heat of political battle. But then, such judgments have been made by critics of his other writings as well, and it is safe to say that he expected them.[114]

On an immediate level, the appearance in print of an unpublished work by a figure as important as Salvemini would be justified on its own merits, if for no other reason than the fact that it documents a phase of his political and intellectual formation during a crucial period of his life. In the perspective of his evolving attitudes toward Fascism and Italy it provides a multi-level bridge between his analysis of Fascism as expressed in *The Fascist Dictator-*

---

112. Salvemini used portions of his manuscript on Fascist activities in *What To Do With Italy*, especially in regard to the attitudes of American clergymen toward Fascism. See below, Part II, chapter 4, notes 1 and 10A, and also "Italian Fascism in America," *Il Mondo*, February 15, 1941.

113. On the writing and publication of *What To Do With Italy*, see Tagliacozzo, "L'opera di Gaetano Salvemini negli Stati Uniti d'America," p. 33, and his introduction to *L'Italia vista dall'America*, p. xxv.

114. Migone, "A proposito de 'L'Italia vista dall'America,' " pp. 95-96.

ship in Italy, his political ideas for *Giustizia e Libertà* as articulated in the Mazzini Society, and his program for a new Italy free of Fascism as revealed in *What To Do With Italy*. In the context of a renewed interest in the study of ethnic minorities in the United States, this book furnishes modern historians with considerable insight and raw material for a re-evaluation of the intricate processes of political socialization and assimilation. A study of the complex reaction of Italian-Americans to Fascism not only raises many questions regarding the social and cultural adjustment of a particular immigrant group in the United States, but also comes to grips with a far more important issue — America's own encounter with Fascism. Salvemini certainly anticipated that this work would be a contribution to both problems, and modern scholarship will no doubt sustain his expectations. Salvemini worked long and hard, and sometimes suffered, in order to produce an uncompromising measure of truth about a painful and tragic moment in the life of the nation he had adopted as his own. His prupose and his inspiration are perhaps best explained by what he himself had written many years before about another Italian political exile: "This suffering was accepted by Mazzini because he had a heroic vision of the world, of history and of life; because he thought that, in toiling and enduring, he could contribute towards a great work of universal equity; and because he was convinced that his efforts were not confined to their immediate ends, but that every beat of his heart responded to a rhythm of eternal and inviolable justice."[115]

---

115. Gaetano Salvemini, *Mazzini* (London, 1956), p. 192. This is an English edition of the work Salvemini first published in 1905.

Editor's Notes

When Salvemini returned to Italy for the last time in 1948, he took with him a large collection of notes, correspondence, and research material which he had accumulated during his years in America. Following his death in 1957, the bulk of these papers passed into the keeping of his close friends Ernesto and Ada Rossi, while another part remained in the possession of his long-time friends and collaborators, Roberto and Maritza Bolaffio. The work published here for the first time exists in two slightly different versions. One copy is in the Bolaffio papers in Florence. The draft used in compiling the present edition is from the Bolaffio typescript. However, one brief section of part III, chapter one (indicated by brackets) was missing. In an effort to give the work as much continuity as possible, the editor has reconstructed this missing portion of the work along the lines that Salvemini apparently intended.

Given the condition in which this work was found, it has also been necessary to make certain decisions regarding the overall format of the book, although the editor has taken great pains to leave Salvemini's words intact and unaltered. Salvemini did not give the last draft a final structure, and he changed the organization of the chapters several times by shifting them to different parts of the book. The present arrangement conforms to his last and presumably final design. The chapter titles (again with the exception of part one, chapter one) and the titles of the three main parts of the work were his. The editor has, however, numbered the footnotes and placed them at the bottom of each page, as Salvemini had done for his other scholarly publications. In order to offer the reader the benefit of recent scholarship and previously unavailable documents, and also to provide explanations of obscure references, the editor has added footnotes of his own; these are indicated by brackets and the abbreviation "Ed. Note." Finally, since Salvemini never got to the stage of preparing a final version of the work for publication, he did not write a general introduction or a conclusion. The editor has therefore selected suitable portions of Salvemini's 1940 pamphlet on the same subject to serve both functions.

While he probably would have altered or expanded some aspects of this book had he had the opportunity, Salvemini would no doubt have approved of its publication even in its present form. In 1925, two decades after he had first published his study of Mazzini, he wrote "After so much labour by others and the passing of twenty years, I am conscious of a sense of dissatisfaction on re-reading this book of mine written in what seems another age. Not that there are errors of fact to be put right, or that I feel prompted to modify the conclusions I then reached. But there is a great deal more that I would like to add in order to make the book fully worthy of its subject."[1] The editor has been guided by these considerations in preparing this volume for publication.

The editor wishes to express his grateful thanks to the individuals and institutions that facilitated his research and made the publication of this book possible. First and most importantly, he had the privilege of a number of delightful, informative, and moving conversations with Maritza Bolaffio, who granted him free access to the papers in her husband's collection, where the present typescript was found. Signora Ada Rossi also gave the editor permission to consult the papers in her possession, and Professor Elena Aga-Rossi Sitzia of the University of Pisa furnished him with parts of one of the drafts.

The following persons also gave the editor information, the benefit of their personal knowledge of Salvemini's life and work, or material used in the introduction: Professor Michele Cantarella; Dr. Max Ascoli; Professor

1. See Salvemini's 1925 preface to the English edition of *Mazzini* (London, 1956), trans. I. M. Rawson, pp. 7-8.

John P. Diggins; Dr. Theodore P. Kovaleff; and Mrs. Laura Tucci. The directors and the staffs of the following libraries and archives all greatly assisted the editor with his research: the Istituto Storico per la Resistenza in Toscana, Florence; the Biblioteca Nazionale Centrale, Florence; the Archivio Centrale dello Stato, Rome; the Florida State University Library; the Tamiment Collection of New York University Library; and the Library of Congress. Professors Lawrence Cunningham and Ralph V. Turner of Florida State University kindly read drafts of the introduction and offered valuable comments and criticism.

Drs. Silvano M. Tomasi and Lydio F. Tomasi of the Center for Migration Studies supported and encouraged this project with their usual energy and dedication. Charles Moore and Mattie Sims typed portions of the manuscript with diligence and accuracy.

Needless to say, none of the above individuals or institutions are liable for any errors in the introduction or the editing of the present volume, the editor assumes that responsibility.

Abbreviations

The following abbreviations were used by Salvemini in the footnotes of his typescript:

AF........................Ario Flamma, ed., *Italiani di America* (New York, 1936).

Gio........................*Giovinezza*

GS........................*Il Grido della Stirpe*

IAW......................Giovanni Schiavo, ed., *Italian American Who's Who* (New York, 1935).

PIA........................*Il Progresso Italo-Americano*

Roman Numerals (i.e., XXII) ...*Il Carroccio*

The historian is strictly limited by the data furnished by his sources. He is not permitted freely to invent or combine events, their details, and the circumstances in which they took place. Only a Philistine expects the artist to give proofs of what his immagination has created, whereas any sensible man demands of the historian proofs and documents.

I, for my part, declare that my mind is carpeted with biases — religious, philosophical, scientific, social, political, national, and even personal — and that I constantly make use of my biases in my studies. I am not ashamed of this fact, because biases are not irreconcilable with scientific research.

The old historians who candidly displayed their ethical judgments were more intelligent than those modern historians and social scientists who think that they avoid ethical judgments when they "objectively" balance "data" against "data" on scales which are swayed by the influence of unconscious ethical judgments, even if they themselves do not realize this fact.

I should be deeply distressed if, from the doctrine that history and the social sciences cannot provide us either with absolute truths or with secure previsions, any of my readers were to come to the conclusion that they must be indifferent to the question of truth or error, good or evil.

Gaetano Salvemini, *Historian and Scientist*
(Cambridge, Mass., 1939), pp. 62-63, 75, 157.

Preface

Recently, one of the leading Italian dailies, *Il Corriere della Sera*, asserted that all of the ten million Italians living in foreign countires — among them, four million, one hundred fifty thousand persons in the United States — "gaze with faith upon the great imperial and Fascist Fatherland." In view of the fact that the 1930 census indicated that four million, six hundred thousand persons in the United States are American citizens or residents of Italian origin, one must conclude that Mussolini is evidently generous enough not to claim as his subjects almost half a million men and women. However, when President Roosevelt condemned Mussolini's intervention in the present war as an act of treachery, prominent personages of Italian descent made it widely known that all Italo-Americans are loyal to America and only to America.

Where does the truth lie?

This is no easy question to answer. A mass ranging between four and five million persons is not a compact bloc that may fit into a single formula. Be that as it may, while it is perhaps wise to say, it certainly would be unwise to believe, that *all* Italo-Americans cherish untainted democratic ideals.

Most citizens and residents of Italian origin and their descendants have been, by and large, completely assimilated by their American environment. They have not seldom translated their family names into English: Viciguerra, for instance is now Winwar. If there are among them people who favor Fascism, they share their personal faith with other more or less authentic sons and daughters of the American Revolution. Mayor Rossi of San Francisco is popular among Italian Fascists in his city. Mayor LaGuardia of New York is enemy number one of the Italian Fascists in his community. Both are of Italian descent. It would be absurd to exclude La Guardia of New York from, and to include Rossi of San Francisco in, Mussolini's American empire. Both are American and nothing else.

Most Italians of recent immigration have other problems on their hands than studying the constitution of either the United States, Italy or any other country. They have to earn their living. Not long ago one of these immigrants in Boston applied for citizenship. The judge asked him who was president of the United States, who was governor of the commonwealth, how many states form the union, etc. The answer was a consistent: "I don't know." "Then, you don't know anything?" "Mister Judge, do you know how many bananas there are to a bunch?" "No, I don't." "Do you know how many bananas I have to sell every day to make a living?" "No, I don't." "Well, this is my business and that is your business." Another Italian of New York, who had thirteen children in America — all American citizens by birth — had never had the time either to learn to read and write or to become an American citizen himself. Finally, when his children persuaded him to take the examination, he knew how to tell who he was, what was the name of the president of the United States and who was governor of the State of New York. But when the Judge asked him if he — the father of thirteen children — could become president of the United States, he was seized by a moment of panic and answered "Excuse, Mister Judge, I have thirteen children; I am too busy."

Even though they know little about the nation's governmental structure, hard-working, decent, law-abiding men and women are not dangerous to the democratic institutions of the United States — if they are left alone.

Those of Italian descent have not been left alone.

Although Italian immigration to this country has virtually ceased since 1924, the staffs of the Italian embassy and consulates have grown busier and busier from year to year. Their primary duty consists in organizing Fascist activities on the radio, through the newspapers, and in the schools, churches and clubs of their own districts. The more important consulates now have a "cultural agent" who controls all Fascist activities in their districts. These cultural agents receive their instructions from an office in the embassy at Washington, which has been directed by Signor Luigi Villari. It should be noted that Signor Villari, after having directed Fascist propaganda in England for several years, was transferred to America to perform similar functions.

The consuls have found among the population of Italian extraction plenty of persons who can serve their purposes. Italian emigration has always been accompanied by parasites of one sort or another — most of whom belong to those intellectual lower middle classes that are the curse of Italy; people without will or power to work, who have always lived off the poor, and who call themselves intellectuals because they have been educated above their intelligence. After Italian immigration ceased, these people would have remained in America without raw material to feed upon if they had not found a new means of livlihood in Fascist activities under the leadership of the consuls. Edmondo Rossoni, now one of the ministers of Mussolini's cabinet, was one of them before the war of 1914-18. On June 1, 1912, during a demonstration before the Garibaldi monument in New York "amidst a delirium of applause, he spat with all his might on the King's tricolor" (Il Proletario, New York weekly, June 2, 1912). Others have not had such auspicious careers. They are satisfied in this country with far humbler offices in the propaganda machine, such as radio speakers, journalists, elementary school teachers, or ward-heelers.

Thus, since the advent of Fascism in Italy citizens and residents of Italian extraction in this country have been subjected to a vast and relentless barrage of propaganda. They have been told day after day that Italy is no longer the country where they or their ancestors were once so unhappy. Italy, thanks to Mussolini's achievements, has become "rich, prosperous, respected and feared." Fascist propaganda is careful not to show any clearly defined anti-American bias. It confines itself to offering about things American no more than scanty, banal, and frequently disparaging information. Most Italian immigrants know only the hardships of America where they have been looked down upon as dagoes and wops. Fascist propaganda keeps them strangers in the country that harbors them and reserves all of its praises for Mussolini's Italy.

The results of this methodical drill came to the surface during the Ethiopian War several years ago. At that time most Italians in this country were driven into a state of nationalistic frenzy, the mainsprings and intensity of which remained mysterious to those not familiar with the Little Italies. I know of a New York restaurant employing thirty-four Italian waiters. Only one of them remained untouched by the contagion. None of the others would have been so cruel as to maltreat a dog. Yet all felt endowed with

heroic souls when they read the shrieking headlines of the Italian papers of
New York announcing that Mussolini's son and son-in-law had dropped
bombs from their planes on Ethiopian villages. "We are proving," they said,
"that we know how to hit hard."

During the Ethiopian War there was no contrast between Fascist and
American loyalties since the government of the United States allowed
supplies to go to Italy while Ethiopia was in no position to buy supplies
here. As long as there is no reason for a clash between Fascist and American
loyalties, Fascist agents see no reason for hastening an outbreak. Their
interests are best served by retarding it, provided that the seeds of Fascist
mentality develop underground. They expect that when the conflict bursts
out into the open, American democracy will have to reap what Italian
Fascism has sown.

Strangely enough, the determined and consistent Fascists, besides the
agents directly connected with the propaganda machine, may be found
mainly among the offspring of successful immigrants who could afford to
send their children to college. These young men have often felt themselves
discriminated against because they are Italian. Among those who are out of
work, discouraged, and embittered, Fascist propaganda acts like a spark in a
haymow. Playing on their inferiority complex and their reaction against real
or imaginary injustices, it stirs them to hatred of this country which they
feel is a stepmother rather than a mother to them.

PART I

FASCIST ORGANIZATIONS
1923 — 1929

1

Pre-Fascist Organizations

Half a century ago the Italian immigrant to this country came from the poorest classes of the most backward sections of Italy. He was, as a rule, a day laborer and illiterate. On landing in New York or Boston he was suspicious of all strangers, and a stranger to him was anyone who did not come from his own town. Some fellow townsman *(paesano)* who had preceded him to this country would receive him at the very harbor and take him to the district where his fellow townsmen were living.

The men coming from the same town formed mutual aid societies which granted relief and medical care in case of illness and a lump sum to families in case of death. In addition, most of these parochial organizations every year celebrated with religious ceremonies, pantagruslian banquets, and noisy fireworks, the festivity of the town's patron saint. Every time the native town needed money for a hospital, for a school, for an emergency, the club of its far away American sons was ready to step in with amazing generosity. The club reached the peak of prestige when it was in a position to build a hall where the members could hold their meetings and spend their leisure hours.

Here are the words by which the origins are described of a mutual aid society which arose in 1912 among immigrants from the Sicilian town of Marsala in Brooklyn, New York. The same would suit any other similar association.

> As soon as they arrived in America, the townsmen of Marsala, who were not used to a roving and wandering life, found themselves bewildered. They felt intensely their separation from their native land and the weariness of solitude. It was a torment that pushed them to return home, a martyrdom that gave them no peace: exile. One had no longer the sweet comfort of one's own family, one had no place of recreation where one could pass the winter evenings and the hours of enforced idleness. There was no exchange where one could be hired for his work. There were American trade unions, but who could understand the talk? One was like a Turk at a Christian sermon, as the saying goes. We were living in such a state of utter dejection when someone happily got the idea of starting a Club.[1]

The Italian immigrants were looked upon by the other workers with distaste, because they were satisfied with less pay, worked harder, and had a lower standard of living and crude habits. Moreover, they were among the most recent arrivals. The day of the pioneer had gone. Room was already becoming scarce. There was competition in labor markets between the early and late comers. In all countries the lot of the poor man is grievous. But when the poor fight each other for bread, they harm each other in the cruelest ways. There is no one more ruthless than one underdog running another underdog out, or an underdog who believes himself born in the lap of the gods. The Italian immigrants had to face terrible hardships.

In such straits they realized that they belonged to a national group different from all others. They had never felt themselves to be Italians as long as they had been living in the old country, among people who spoke their same dialect, who had their same habits, and who were laboring under their same poverty. National consciousness awoke in them when they came in touch (which often meant to blows) with groups of different national origins in America. Italy now seemed to them no longer a land from which they had been forced to leave in search of a less distressing life. Italy became in their minds a land from which they felt exiled, of whose past glories they felt proud, and for whose present fortunes or misfortunes they felt glad or miserable.[2]

---

1. PIA, July 5, 1939.
2. The "rediscovery" of national consciousness among Italian-Americans was also noted by fellow exile Massimo Salvadori, *Resistenza ed azione* (Bari, 1951), pp. 162-163. See also Humbert S. Nelli, "Italians in Urban America," in S.M. Tomasi and M.H. Engel, eds., *The Italian Experience in the United States* (New York, 1970), p. 79, and John P. Diggins, *Mussolini and Fascism: The View from America* (Princeton, 1972), pp. 78-80. [Ed. Note]

An organization, the Order of the Sons of Italy, endeavored to give a response to such national feelings. It summoned the Italians to break away from their parochial mutual aid societies and establish an all-embracing organization which would imitate the Jewish, German, Swedish, etc. associations and protect the interest and rights of the Italians in the United States.

Mr. Aquilano, to whom we owe the official history of the order, admits that "in its first period the Order had a frankly Italian patriotic nature. There was some sense of attachment to America, but that attachment confined itself to obedience to the laws of the United States. We were American in body, but not in spirit." The order had an ultra-nationalistic task. "It had to keep Italian energies outside Italy tied among themselves and to the fatherland." It was to represent "the greater Italy which was outside the natural boundaries of Italy." Each gathering had to be "a memory, a call, an exaltation" of the faraway fatherland. The order had "to make Italianism respected and triumphant" at all times and in all places.[3] This word Italianism *(Italianità)* is pregnant with many connotations. It means: 1) the national character of the Italian; 2) the moral prestige of Italy; 3) the real or alleged needs and rights of the Italian nation; and 4) the international activities of the Italian government.

Thus the first four constitutions of the order from 1905 to 1910 gave as one of its aims that of "maintaining alive in the hearts and minds the worship of the Mother country, participating in her joys and sorrows, and keeping aflame her cult, and intact the faith in her future, a future as radiant with glory as her past." America did not exist.

The first years of the order were difficult. In 1905 there were no more than nine lodges, and in June 1910 there were forty-two of which several were only on paper. But during the First World War, a wave of national enthusiasm carried the Italo-Americans away. Moreover, the order, by establishing mutual aid for its members and their families in case of illness or death, drew to itself an increasing number of members. Its membership jumped from 316 lodges at the end of 1914 to 590 lodges and 125,000 members in twenty-four states by the end of 1918.[4]

At the same time, the war put the order face to face with the duty of the Italian immigrant towards the country which sheltered him. The fifth constitution of 1915 did not confine itself to saying that "the Order had to keep aflame the cult of the Mother country and intact the faith in her future." It added that "however much the ties which bind us now and

3. Baldo Aquilano, *L'Ordine dei Figli d'Italia in America* (New York, 1925).
4. Ibid., pp. 61, 74, 99.

always to our country are dear, strong, and indissoluble," "the emigrants have also a debt of gratitude and the duty of becoming citizens of the United States, of respecting its laws, holding dear its institutions, and taking an active part in its public life." Yet the fatherland remained always Italy, and there was an evident difference in temperature between keeping aflame the cult and intact the faith and the debt of gratitude and respect which was due the country which harbored the emigrant. The order undertook to "encourage, prepare, and assist the brothers to obtain American citizenship and the franchise," but it was not clear whether the brothers were to make use of their rights in the service of the United States, or whether they were not rather to profit by the rights granted them by the American constitution to further the interest of their country of origin. The Italian language remained always the only official language of the order.

The intervention of the United States in the war brought about a more radical change. The constitution of 1917 no longer spoke of Italy as the only fatherland of the Sons of Italy. It enacted that beside the "country of origin" the Sons of Italy had an "adopted country"; "if the cult of the country of origin is worthy of admiration, that of the adopted country is a sacred duty." The brothers should not only become naturalized, but also "favor the economic and civil growth of the adopted country, live a public-spirited life, defend its existence, independence, liberty, in short consent to all the duties that weigh upon the American born citizens, in order to obtain their rights." The English language was adopted as the official language along with the Italian language.[5] At that time, America and Italy were fighting together against a common enemy, and no one encountered the slightest difficulty in reconciling the cult of the country of origin with the sacred duty to the country of adoption.

To give the final touches to the picture of the Italian organizations existing in America before the Fascist onslaught upon them, we must not overlook those which were made up, not of the vast mass of the working classes or of the lower middle classes, but of those elements which belonged, or pretended to belong to the better classes. These organizations were the Tiro a Segno Nazionale, the Dante Alighieri Society, and the Italian Chamber of Commerce of the City of New York.

"Tiro a Segno Nazionale" is being translated for the use of the gullible English speaking public into the "Italian National Rifle Shooting Society of the United States." The fact is that the Tiro a Segno Nazionale in Italy has always been a part of the military system, has always been controlled by the minister of war, and has always been aimed, not at teaching men to shoot

5. Ibid., pp. 42-49.

pigeons in time of peace, but other men in time of war. It was established in Italy in 1882, and it was imported into the United States in 1888.[6] One who was admitted to this association could consider himself a member of the Italo-American high life.

The Dante Alighieri Society was established in Italy in 1889 as a counterpart to the German and Slav nationalistic organizations which were multiplying their schools in the Italian territories then annexed to the Austrian-Hungarian Empire. The Dante Alighieri Society subsidized the Italian schools in those territories. At the beginning of the present century the society began to found its own schools even among the Italian communities scattered in the Mediterranean basin, in France, and in North and South America. The Dante Alighieri in the United States was the organization of the Italo-American intellectual or would-be intellectual classes.

The Italian-born businessmen established in 1888 the Italian Chamber of Commerce of New York.

The Tiro a Segno Nazionale has never had great importance, and the other two only began to play a conspicuous role after the coming of Fascism, that is to say, after October 1922. Before then, the ground was held by the mutual aid societies of a parochial character, and by the Sons of Italy.

There is no doubt that these organizations held back the Italian immigrant from adjusting himself to the American ways of life, in so far as they segregated him, encouraged him to keep the habits he had brought from home, and prevented him from mingling with groups of other nationalities. But his associations, while segregating him, protected him, and protection was his first need. Without such protection he would have been even more unhappy in America, and even more hostile to her way of life, and therefore, less liable to assimilation. First it is necessary to live, and only he who finds good living conditions in the country to which he immigrates becomes attached to it little by little, and in the end feels tied to it by bonds of loyalty. The living conditions in the Little Italies were appalling. But the immigrant would have been much worse off if not even the Little Italies had existed. And the association he joined was an integral part of his Little Italy.

Thus in themselves the Italian organization, both parochial and national, would have been at least for a certain time entirely beneficial if their leaders had been well-intentioned men. Too often this was not the case. Italian emigration has always been accompanied by parasites of one sort or another — most of whom belong to those intellectual lower middle classes that are the curse of Italy; people without the will or the power to work, who have always lived off the poor, and who call themselves intellectuals because they

6. *Almanacco*, p. 149.

have been educated above their intelligence.[7] The humble, illiterate Italian laborers in America were the predestined prey of these parasites. Padroni (recruiters of man power), local politicans, directors of the small mutual aid societies, liaison officers between the Italians and the outside world, too often abused without pity the good faith of the immigrants. The wealth nowadays enjoyed by not a few *prominenti* ("prominent persons") or sons of *prominenti* of Italian extraction has been the fruit of vicious rape.

The Sons of Italy were born with the promise of fighting the padroni and the *prominenti*. But from the first year, there was among them "some secretary who took hold of the funds and vanished."[8] Graft became more active as the organization grew more complex, and above the local lodges were formed the Great State Lodges, and from these the Supreme National Lodge. One of the supreme venerables of the order, Mr. Stefano Miele, said in 1926: "If we had not done illegal and immoral things in the Order, we would never have done anything in the past."[9] In fact, in May 1941, he was sentenced in New York City's Court of General Session to a probationary sentence of three years for embezzling funds entrusted to him by a working man.

The Sons of Italy had hoped to absorb and supersede the little parochial mutual aid societies. These have survived because on the whole their members can better supervise their own funds and their own immediate officers, have acquired experience, and can take care of themselves, whereas the state and national headquarters of the order are too far away.

During the world war of 1914 to 1918, the agents of the Italian government imported into this country anti-Yugoslav propaganda. This propaganda did not bring about any results among the English-speaking people, but made inroads among the Italians. These revolted to a man against President Wilson when he came to grips with the Italian representatives at the peace conference in 1919, and voted against him in the election of 1920.[10]

As a consequence of this experience, the Italian government realized the advantage it could reap from the loyalty of the Italian-born in America if they were cleverly handled. In 1920 it recognized the Order of the Sons of

---

7. This sentence also appears in Salvemini's pamphlet, "Italian Fascist Activities in the U.S.," p. 5. [Ed. Note]

8. Aquilano, p. 62.

9. Roberto Ferrari, *Days Pleasant and Unpleasant* (New York, 1926), p. 79.

10. On the Itlaian-American reaction to Wilson see Joseph O'Grady, *The Immigrants' Influence on Wilson's Peace Policies* (Lexington, 1967); John B. Duff, "The Politics of Revenge: The Ethnic Opposition to the Peace Policies of Woodrow Wilson," Ph.D. dissertation, Columbia University, 1964; and Louis L. Gerson, *The Hyphenate in Recent American Politics and Diplomacy* (Lawrence, Kans., 1964). [Ed. Note]

Italy as the official representative of the Italian emigrants,[11] and from that year on, the Italian consuls everywhere favored the spreading of the order. All the *prominenti*, padroni and nouveau riches, for whom a knighthood was the culmination of felicity, flocked to the order. The lodges increased to 1,110 in 1924 with 160,000 members. This increase of knights, lodges and members did not raise the intellectual or moral level of the organization.

In 1928 the Italian ambassador, Signor Rolandi-Ricci, toured the Italian communities "urging his fellow-countrymen to become naturalized so that they could vote and cast their ballots unitedly to foster Italian interest."[12] The problem became acute when he attacked a tariff bill which was before Congress, on the ground that the matter was of vital concern to Italy, and that by criticizing the bill in public meetings he was carrying out that open diplomacy which had been inaugurated by President Wilson.[13] As a result of his open diplomacy he left for a vacation, never to return again to America.[14]

11. Aquilano, pp. 114, 122.
12. *New York Times*, April 22, 1922.
13. Ibid., June 9, 10, 1922.
14. On Rolandi-Ricci's activities see Gian Giacomo Migone, "Il regime fascista e le comunità italo-americane: la missione di Gelasio Caetani (1922-1925)," in *Problemi di storia nei rapporti tra Italia e Stati Uniti* (Turin, 1971), p. 26. [Ed. Note]

2

The Fascist Central Council
and the Fascist League of North America

In the meantime, the Fascist movement had come to light not only in Italy, but also in America. In 1921, the first fasci[1] arose in New York and Philadelphia. In 1922, in Italy, the directorate of the Fascist party passed a resolution to the effect that the Fasci Abroad should act as "posts for the rescue of threatened Italianism."[2]

In the spring and summer of that year, the Italian Chamber of Commerce of New York and the Supreme Executive Council of the Sons of Italy organized an excursion of twenty-eight young Italians to Italy, accompanied by the secretary of the chamber, Dr. Alberto Bonaschi, and by the supreme venerable of the order, Giovanni Di Silvestro.[3]

Di Silvestro had started his political career in the United States during the first decade of the present century as a socialist of the extreme left, and as

1. Fascio (a bundle of men) is the local branch of the Fascist movement. Fasci is the plural of fascio.
2. *Enciclopedia Italiana*, XIX, p. 1032.
3. Aquilano, pp. 128-29, 148.

such he had spent several months in prison. But soon he grew wise, and became assistant supreme venerable of the Sons of Italy in 1917, and in November 1921, he reached the highest post of supreme venerable.[4]

In Rome, in June 1922, Di Silvestro reached an agreement with the nationalist leaders who, at that time, were collaborating with Mussolini but had not yet been absorbed by the Fascist party. Between Di Silvestro and the Lega Italiana per la tutela degli interessi nazionali ("Italian League for Safeguarding of National Interests"), controlled by the Nationalists, a "covenant" was drawn up to the effect that the league acknowledged the order as the only body entitled to represent the Italians in America, and in turn Di Silvestro agreed that the league should represent the order in its relations with the Italian government.[5]

When the March on Rome took place (October 28-30, 1922), and Mussolini became prime minister, Di Silvestro hastened to hail these events as the beginning of a new era of glory and happiness in Italian history. Addressing the Sons of Italy in New York on November 10, 1922, he warned them that they "should be Americans" and were to "cooperate to the greatness of America," but he also reminded them that they should not forget that they were to cooperate also "to the greatness and prestige of Italy": "the Order of the Sons of Italy must take inspiration from Fascism." The Italians of America should "feel and put into practice the new discipline and make Mussolini realize that he could expect from them vigorous brotherly cooperation." The meeting ended with a telegram of devotion to the king and to Mussolini.[6] The telegram sent to Mussolini runs as follows:

> While Fascism under your leadership lifts Italy up in the Roman way, the 300,000 members of the Order of the Sons of Italy send you their greetings and good wishes. Your rise as the ruler of the Fatherland will give back the Nation her old faith and the spiritual discipline necessary to dare and to succeed. The new Government, gathering together the youthful energies of the country for fecund and efficient work, will instantly renew confidence and prestige abroad. The Order of the Sons of Italy, knowing this, follows you with faith. G. Di Silvestro

Toward the end of November, Di Silvestro was honored at a dinner in Philadelphia, attended by one hundred guests, including the ambassador. The order "sent to the ceremony its most eminent delegates from all over the United States." "Fascism was well celebrated and reasserted its mission in America so in harmony with that of the Order of the Sons of Italy."[7] During the dinner, Di Silvestro repeated on behalf of the Sons of Italy "before the

4. Ibid., pp. 112, 128.
5. Ibid., pp. 130-131.
6. PIA, November 10, 1922.
7. XVII, p. 121.

Stars and Stripes the oath of the adopted sons," but at the same time, before the representative of the Italian embassy in Washington, "he repeated solemnly, with deep and secure sense of his responsibility...the oath of worship to Italy." He announced that "the Order of the Sons of Italy is today a 'Fascio' for the safety of Italy and America":[8]

> The Order of the Sons of Italy in America was the forerunner of the Italian Fasci. The Order today hails Him who has assumed for Himself the hard task of giving back to Italy that spiritual discipline, which is the foundation for her economic rebirth and for her prestige abroad. In this hour of difficult experiment, may all Italians assure Him of their brotherly urge to cooperate with Him.

Di Silvestro addressed a Fascist meeting in New York on December 19, 1922.[9] In January 1923, in the lodge of the Sons of Italy of Bridgeport, Connecticut, he illustrated "the last events which have made the people of Italy aware of their new duties," arousing an "indescribable enthusiasm" for the Duce.[10] In February 1923, in Stamford, he took part in a ceremony of the Sons of Italy where the official Fascist anthem "Giovinezza" was sung.[10A] When the Nationalist and the Fascist parties amalgamated in Italy into one, single National Fascist party (February 1923), the Italian League for the safeguarding of National Interests, to which Di Silvestro had associated the Order of the Sons of Italy, was disbanded[11] and the "covenant" of the preceding year was inherited by the Fascist party.

In May 1923, Di Silvestro made the following statements:[12]

> Italy is the supreme thought of our Order. We only know our faith in Italy...The faith in Italy gave us a Fatherland. The faith in Italy allowed Italy to become a great nation. The faith in Italy allowed the laboring classes to vindicate their rights. The faith in Italy had created and made gigantic our Order.

There was no longer any trace of faith in America. The supreme venerable of the Order of the Sons of Italy, having become Fascist, returned to the "ultra-nationalistic" sentiments of the years which had inspired the order before the world war of 1914-1918.

Di Silvestro remained as one of the pillars of the Fascist movement in North America until 1935, when he suddenly resigned as supreme venerable of the Sons of Italy and went out of circulation, no explanation given. Those

8. XVII, p. 123.
9. PIA, January 7, 1923.
10. Pibid., January 29, 1923.
10A. Ibid., February 2, 1923.
11. Ibid., March 8, 1923.
12. XVII, p. 643.

who were in the know whispered that he had had to decamp because he had been unable to keep the money of the order separate from his own.[12A]

In the meantime, in Italy, the Fascist party had established a secretariat general of the Fasci Abroad,[13] which entrusted the Fascio of New York with the task of acting as central Fascio of the Italian Fasci in North America.[14] The directorate of the Italian Fascio of North America made the following announcement:[15]

> Italy's Fasci in North America, with headquarters in New York, adhere to the principles of the Fasci of Italy. Their members in every word, manifestation or action must aim at the sole purpose of making the Fatherland strong and powerful from an economic and political standpoint, drawing all implied advantages from the Italian Victory in the World War, and asserting the national prestige among the strangers in the midst of whom they live. Therefore, they must carry to the highest possible level the culture and the feeling of Italianism among the masses of emigrants, making use of every means which the circumstances and the environment suggest and allow . . . One of the members of the Directorate will represent the American Fascio at the National Council in Italy, and will keep in constant touch with the Central Directorate in Italy for the coordination of work . . . The Italian Fascio of New York will have sections in all the Italian colonies in the United States. These sections will receive instructions from it in regard to their political activities, administration and discipline.

Soon the directors of the Fascio of New York were unable to cope with the "incompetence, simple-mindedness, ignorance and opportunism"[16] of many of the members and chieftains of the multiplying local fasci. Thus in the summer of 1923, the national directorate of the Fascist party in Italy dissolved the Fascio of New York in order to reorganize it on a new basis. It delegated the job of controlling the Fascist organizations all over North America to a Fascist Central Council ("Consiglio Centrale Fascista") as distinguished from the directorate of the Fascio of New York. It formed this Fascist Central

---

12A. In 1933 Di Silvestro's home was bombed by unknown assassins; his wife was killed, four of his children and several neighbors were injured. Police authorities agreed with Di Silvestro that the bombing was the work of anti-Fascists, but no one was ever arrested. Di Silvestro's sons, who were members of the Fascist party, were later given an audience by Mussolini. See Diggins, *Mussolini and Fascism*, p. 133. [Ed. Note]

13. XVII, p. 501. [The first director of the Segreteria generale dei fasci all'estero was Giuseppe Bastianini, followed by Cornelio De Marzio and then by Piero Parini. See Enzo Santarelli, *Storia del movimento e del regime fascista*, 2 vols. (Rome, 1967), I, pp. 476-483; Alan Cassels, "Fascism for Export: Italy and the United States in the Twenties," *American Historical Review*, 69 (April 1964), pp. 702-712; Santarelli, "I fasci italiani all'estero," in *Ricerche sul fascismo* (Urbino, 1971), pp. 105-132; and Giorgio Rumi, *Alle origini della politica estera fascista* (Bari, 1968), pp. 241-245. Ed. Note].

14. PIA, January 7, 1923.

15. Ibid., January 27, 1923.

16. Gio., April 8, 1923.

Council with a president and eleven councilors,[17] and appointed as president, Giovanni Di Silvestro, as vice-president, Giuseppe Previtali, and as secretary, Agostino De Biasi.[18]

In 1924, De Biasi resigned from the office of secretary and from the party,[19] and the secretaryship was taken up by Ornello Simone, who was a member of the council.[20] Another member of the central council was Francesco Paolo Macaluso.[21] Since there were eleven members of the Fascist Central Council, and so far we have enumerated no more than five (Di Silvestro, Previtali, De Biasi, Simone, Macaluso), it would remain for us to make the acquaintance of the other six. But a complete, official list, in so far as we know, was never published. *Giovinezza*[22] announced that two persons, J. J. Licari and Almerindo Portfolio, would be called to take part in the council, but we do not know whether this ever came about.

The council held its first meeting in September 1923.[23] At the beginning of October 1923 it issued the statutes to which the local fasci were to conform.[24] On October 29, 1923, the first anniversary of the March on Rome, it issued a manifesto "to the dependent fasci and the fellow-nationals in North America" in which we read:[25]

> Fascism, which, no longer as a party but as the Nation itself, controls the destinies of our nation, entrusts to the Italians who have emigrated the task of cooperating with its work of restoration. In America, more than anywhere else, we have to form an Italian block in order to compete with the nationalism of other groups...We have to be, overseas, the foremost defenders of the Fatherland's supreme interests.

At the end of 1923, the directorate of the Fascist party in Italy announced that all the fasci which, in North America, were not recognized by the central council located in New York were "to be regarded as miserable and ridiculous communist deceits."[26]

In July 1925, the Fascist Central Council was superseded by the Fascist League of North America. It seems that this change was prompted by the need of disjoining the activities of president of the Fascist Central Council from those of the supreme venerable of the Sons of Italy, which were united

17. Ibid., August 25, 1923.
18. XVIII, pp. 294, 406; XIX, p. 238.
19. XXVII, p. 19.
20. XVIII, p. 405; XXIV, p. 88.
21. XVIII, p. 405.
22. Gio., August 25, 1923.
23. Ibid., September 15, 1923.
24. Ibid., October 3, 1923.
25. PIA, October 29, 1923.
26. Ibid., January 1, 1924.

in the person of Di Silvestro. We have to say it seems because the reasons for the change were never divulged. Most of the reforms in Fascist apparatus which we shall witness in the course of our survey, took place for reasons which remained mysterious to the membership of the organization.[27]

President of the newborn league was Count Ignazio Thaon di Revel, delegate of the secretariat general of the Fascist National Party Abroad,[28] Giuseppe Previtali was vice president, and the treasurer was Count Alfonso Facchetti-Guiglia. These three persons held those offices for the entire span of life of the league, that is to say from July 1925 to December 1929.

Besides the president, vice president and treasurer, the league had five councilors in 1925: Giannetto Bottero, Giuseppe Castruccio, Enrico Citriolo, Mario Montrezza, and Domenico Trombetta.[29]

In October 1925, the American fasci held their first convention in Philadelphia. The convention decided that "all Italians and Americans of Italian origin" were eligible for membership in the League, but also "individuals well known to be filo-Fascists of every nationality" could be affiliated as "associate members," besides those "distinguished personalities" to whom would be conceded the honorary membership. The president and the central council were to be elected at the annual convention of the league. In their turn, the president and the central council were to designate for every state of the union their own delegate. He, in his turn, was to designate a committee which would assist him in the job of controlling the movement within their own state. The branches were not entitled to promote any public manifestation without first getting permission from the state delegate.[30] There were fasci also in Canada, especially in its eastern provinces, and they too, were under the jurisdiction of the League. The headquarters were in New York.

The central council, when it deemed it necessary, passed over the head of the state delegate and its commission, took the initiative to found local fasci,[31] and sent its own commissioners to check the work of the local

---

27. Salvemini was largely correct. The new Italian ambassador to the United States, Gelasio Caetani, had to deal not only with frequent disputes between local Italian-American Fascists, but also with American public and government opinion. He therefore advised Mussolini that the Sons of Italy should remain an "a-political" organization without direct connection to the fasci. Moreover, Di Silvestro's open support of Mussolini had provided cause for a serious split in the ranks of the Sons of Italy, with State Senator Salvatore Cotillo and State Representative Fiorello La Guardia leading the break against De Silvestro. See Migone, "Il regime fascista," pp. 31-33; Diggins, *Mussolini and Fascism*, pp. 89-91; and Cassels, "Fascism for Export." [Ed. Note]
    28. XXV, p. 166; Gio., May 1, 1927.
    29. Gio., November 30, 1925; XXII, pp. 276, 409.
    30. Gio., November 30, 1925.
    31. PIA, December 14, 1926.

directorates,[32] or else it presented to the local fasci the persons destined to manage it.[33] We are confronted, therefore, with a centralized system in which, conforming to the Fascist rule, authority comes from above. Even when they tell us that the president of and the central council have been elected by the convention, we must remember that it is not a question of what Mussolini called *ludi cartacci* ("paper games"), that is to say a vote by secret ballot in which the voter could choose between two or more competing candidates. The Fascist election, when the leaders deigned to summon an election, merely was an acclamation without discussion of the candidates nominated by one or more henchmen in agreement with the higher-ups, who, in actual fact, made the choice. Whoever opposed that acclamation and demanded a discussion and a regular vote, would commit an act of undiscipline and would be expelled from the party. The president and central councilors of the league of North America were *announced at*, and not *elected by*, the convention.

At the beginning of 1927, the council appointed Macaluso as its secretary in place of Citriolo,[34] took over *Giovinezza* as the official bulletin of the League, created a press bureau, and chose Toto Giurato as its head. Furthermore, it established a Court of Discipline with jurisdiction over all the sections "in order to enforce more rigid order and justice," and appointed Thaon di Revel as president; Previtali, Facchetti-Guiglia and Vincenzo Martinez as judges; Toto Giurato as chancellor; and Macaluso and Laspia as league consultants.[35] The court tried and expelled members to the right and the left,[36] when the punishments were not inflicted by the central council itself without consulting the court.[37]

In 1927 the centralization of powers in the council was more and more intensified. The state delegate and his committee were invested with the authority of appointing the directors of the local fasci[38] unless the appointment was made directly by the central council.[39] All the resolutions of the local Fasci had to be sent not only to the state delegate, but also to the secretary general of the council.[40] The council proscribed anyone who

32. Ibid., June 18, 1926.
33. Ibid., December 5, 1926.
34. Ibid., March 7, 1927.
35. Ibid., March 7, 1927; January 15, 1928; Gio., March 15, 1927.
36. Gio., March 15, 1927; PIA, July 11, August 16, 1927, February 3, 1928.
37. PIA, February 20, May 19, 28, 1927.
38. Ibid., February 3, 1927.
39. Ibid., February 17, 1927.
40. Gio., March 1, 1927.

published Fascist magazines without its authorization.[41] It appointed inspectors to supervise the sporting activities of the local fasci,[42] and special commissioners, not only for individual local fasci, but for vast territories. They had power to disband fasci which were working badly, and to reorganize them and choose their directors.[43] The Duce Fascist Alliance, created as an autonomous body in the Bronx by a certain Caldora, expelled from the league, was solemnly and repeatedly proscribed,[44] and it never had any importance.

The second convention held by the league in Hartford, Connecticut in December 1927, elected, that is to say acclaimed as president, Thaon di Revel, as vice-president, Previtali, and as secretary, Macaluso, acknowledged as legitimate Fascist papers *Giovinezza* and *Il Grido della Stirpe*, and decided that besides those, there was need of an official bulletin of the League.[45] The convention made the centralization of powers even more rigid, grouping more states under one single commissioner.[46] Up until then the choice of the directors of the local fasci had taken place according to methods which differed from place to place and from time to time, however always keeping away from elections by secret ballots. Sometimes the fascio acclaimed its directorate under the chairmanship of a representative, *fiduciario*, of the central council[47] who proposed the names of the assembly. Sometimes, always in the presence of the delegate of the central council, the assembly appointed, without secret voting, the nominating committee, which without further ado, announced the names of the directors who had evidently been previously chosen.[48] Or the representative appointed by the central council to found a fascio was adopted as its president.[49] But not even these elections were fitting perfectly into the framework of the Fascist doctrine. Therefore, the convention at Hartford abolished every form of intervention, even though illusory, of the members in the choice of their directors. The appointment from then on was to be made by the central council through its state delegates "with great benefit accruing thereby to the unity of the membership who remain immune from the degrading struggles of petty factions."[50] Therefore, in 1928 we find that the central council directly appoints the directorates of the local fasci or sends commissioners who

41. PIA, August 16, 1927.
42. PIA, March 7, 1927.
43. Ibid., March 7, June 12, September 23, November 13, 1927.
44. Ibid., February 15, March 15, June 1, August 4, 1927.
45. Ibid., December 13, 1927.
46. Gio., December 15, 1927.
47. PIA, April 20, 1924.
48. Ibid., February 25, 1926.
49. Ibid., January 29, 1927.
50. Gio., December 15, 1927.

propose the names which the assembly approves without discussion, or takes over directly the direction of a fascio after the resignation of the special commissioner.[51]

At the beginning of 1928, Martinez took his seat on the central council as representative of the Court of Discipline, and the Court of Discipline was reorganized. Thaon di Revel and Previtali left the bench, and it now consisted of Martinez, Francesco Ragno, Antonio Di Marco, Pietro Garofalo and Alberto Bonaschi, judges; F. A. Siclari, legal consultant; and Salvatore Bonanno, chancellor.

The central council of the league formed a Central Committee for Press and Propaganda with the following persons: Mario Billi, Vinzo Comito, Mario Soave De Cellis, Beniamino De Ritiz, Giovanni Favoino di Giura, Remo Fioroni, Cesare Maccari, Francesco Moschetti, Nino Perciavalle, Armando Romano.[52]

In October 1928, Angelo Flavio Guidi appeared on the scene and was appointed chief editor of the bulletin. In February of 1929, another Fascist agent came from Italy to the United States, Cammillo Canali, who immediately became the secretary general of the league in place of Macaluso.[53] *Carroccio* defined him as the "official representative of the National Fascist Party in the United States"[54] and revealed that he received a monthly salary from the Rome government.[55]

The third convention of the League, held in February 1929, transferred to the president all the powers which had formerly pertained to the council, and furthermore conferred upon him the authority to choose, "according to his prudent judgement," the secretary, treasurer, and the members of the general council who would assist him with a simply advisory vote. The president, always the same Thaon di Revel, after having been elected by acclamation, announced then and there to the convention that he was appointing Facchetti-Guiglia, Giurato and Guidi to their positions again, leaving out Macaluso, Martinez and Trombetta.[56] When Giurato left the United States there was no need to find a substitute because Guidi, as director of the bulletin, was already there ready to act as chief of the press bureau.

There is not the slightest doubt that the directors of the Fascist Central Council from 1923 to 1925 and the president of the Fascist League of North

51. PIA, June 14, July 28, August 23, 1928; January 20, 1929.
52. Ibid., January 26, May 18, 1928; Gio., February 1, 1928.
53. Ibid., February 5, 1928.
54. XXX, p. 372.
55. Ibid., p. 300.
56. PIA, February 20, 1929.

America were appointed from Rome and carried out orders from there, and that all the Fascists, both the leaders and the rank and file, regarded themselves as members of a political party which had its headquarters in Rome. De Biasi, who, as we have seen acted as secretary of the Fascist Central Council in 1923, stated in 1923 that "secret and open instructions" sent out from the secretariat of the Fasci Abroad at Rome, were in his possession, and all gave proof that "the American Fasci directly originated from the authorities of the Fatherland and depended on the leaders of the Party."[57]

In 1923, the headquarters at Rome entrusted to a Fascist who "had gained great favor in high political circles of the Fascist Party" with the task of organizing fasci in Louisiana, Alabama, Texas, Arkansas, Georgia, Florida, and North Carolina, on the condition that he always depend on New York.[58] The task of spreading the fasci in Ohio was entrusted to a commissioner.[59] Giovinezza[59A] stated that the political secretaries of each fascio had been instructed by Rome to respect the laws of the country, as if those living in America had to receive from Rome orders to respect those laws. When Fascist ceremonies were held, telegrams were sent to Mussolini "offering devoted homage and unconditional obedience,"[60] "pledging him loyalty."[61] When in Italy in May 1924, the secretary general of the Fasci Abroad started a weekly bulletin entitled Fasci Italiani all'Estero [Italian Fasci Abroad], this was announced also in the United States,[62] and therefore it addressed itself also to the Fascists of North America. In 1925, when that bulletin was replaced in Rome by a review Legionario, organo ufficiale dei Fasci all'estero [The Legionaire, Official Organ of the Fasci Abroad], the headquarters in Rome appointed a representative of the publication in New York, Carlo Vinti.[63]

In April 1927, the secretariat general of the Fasci Abroad, which until now had been an organ of the Fascist party, was superseded by Direzione Generale a bureau of Italians abroad, established as one of the branches of the Foreign Office. The Fasci Abroad were not only de facto, but also de jure put under the jurisdiction of the Foreign Office. No exception was made in the case of the Fasci of North America. A certain "Captain Terranova, Special Representative of the Government and Commissioner for the Fascist

57. XXVII, p. 180.
58. PIA, May 9, 1923.
59. Ibid., April 14, 1923.
59A. August 4, 1923.
60. Lawrence, Mass., PIA, September 10, 1923.
61. New York, PIA, March 28, 1924.
62. PIA, May 14, 1924.
63. XXII, p. 106.

movement in these States," founded Fasci.[64] In Montreal, Canada, the secretary of the fascio announced officially that he had been summoned to take the position "on the proposal of the Royal Consul, by the Special Delegate of the Secretariat General of the Fasci Abroad on a tour of inspection of North America."[65] *Giovinezza*, which had become the official organ of the League, published orders given to the Fasci Abroad by the secretariat general of the Fasci Abroad in Rome.[66] The ambassador and his attachés, the consuls, vice-consuls and consular agents paid official visits to the headquarters of the fasci,[67] they took part in and spoke at ceremonies of the fasci.[68] They promoted the foundation of new fasci.[69] They acted as mediators in the disputes between the factions into which the fasci were splitting.[70] The directors meetings of the fasci were sometimes held in the offices of the consuls or vice-consuls.[71] In 1928, the consular agent of Utica, New York, Salvatore Martino, acted as commissioner of the League in upper New York state.[72] Those Fascists who showed a lack of respect towards the representatives of the Italian government, were punished by the central council.[73]

The Fasci of North America sent their delegates to the conventions of the Fascist party in Italy.[74] High Fascist personages, coming to the United States, addressed Fascist meetings, and brought them the greetings of Mussolini and the secretariat general of the Fasci Abroad.[75] Before speaking they had to obtain leave from Mussolini and the secretariat general through the ambassador.[76] In January 1928, the central council announced that "according to the directions received from Rome" the league had succeeded in forming a united front among fasci, war veterans, Orders of the Sons of Italy, etc.[77]

64. Baltimore, Md., PIA, January 9, 12, 1927.
65. PIA, August 19, September 22, 1928.
66. Ibid., January 26, 31, 1927.
67. Baltimore, Md., PIA, May 5, 1928.
68. I.e., Chicago, PIA, November 16, 1925; New York, PIA, October 30, November 30, 1926; Baltimore, PIA, January 12, 1927; Newark, N.J., PIA, January 27, 1927; New York, PIA, October 30, 1927; Pittsburgh, PIA, November 6, 1927; Milford, Mass., PIA, December 7, 1927; Niagara Falls, N.Y., PIA, August 2, 1928; Portland, Me., PIA, September 1, 1928; Newark, N.J., PIA, September 27, 1928; New York, PIA, October 11, 1928.
69. Baltimore, PIA, January 10, 1929.
70. Pittsburgh, PIA, November 23, 1928.
71. Newark, N.J., PIA, January 3, 1927.
72. PIA, August 12, 1928.
73. Ibid., February 3, 1928.
74. Chicago, PIA, February 25, 1926; Lawrence, Mass., PIA, March 28, 1926.
75. Representative Pili, New York, PIA, April 15, 1926.
76. Luigi Freddi, vice-secretary general of the Fasci Abroad, PIA, October 27, 1926; February 17, 1927.
77. PIA, January 30, 1928.

3

Fascist Leaders in North America

The preceding chapter was laden with names, names, names. It was impossible for us to avoid this bore because in those lists are almost all the persons who will assume a permanent position of leadership in the Fascist movement. [The persons whose acquaintance we have made so far have been described by De Biasi as "about forty, not more, irresponsible good-for-nothings, in search of jobs and free support,"[1] "pompous fools and rodents who use the League to strut around in, and then peck at it,"[2] "a ragged gang of two or three noblemen who have gone to the dogs, four or five unsuccessful lawyers looking for clients they can't get their hands on, half a dozen restless bureaucrats and eight or nine beggars who, in the act of stretching out their hand, made two different gestures simultaneously: they gave the Fascist salute and they asked for charity."[3] To be sure there is, in these words, the bitterness of the would-be fuehrer who has been disappointed

1. XXVII, p. 395.
2. XXIX, p. 305.
3. XXX, p. 374.

in his ambition. But only from the disgruntled member of a gang can one learn the secrets of the gang. Another Fascist, and this time not a disgruntled one, tells us that "incompetence, simplemindedness, ignorance, and opportunism" were in the cradle of the league when it was born. Men like Martinez and Garofalo certainly did not wait until 1940 to give evidence of their prowess. De Biasi could have remarked also that among the leaders of the league there were [not] only war veterans, and among them one, Castruccio, who had the highest Italian war decoration, the gold medal, but also people who, during the world war, had been deserters. Probably he avoided this point because he, too, in 1914 was no more than forty years old, unmarried, not an American citizen, and therefore there would have been a place also for him on the Italian-Austrian fighting front. He also thought it convenient not to cross the ocean, but to save Italy in America. In short, the Fascists who were directing the movement in America were neither better nor worse than those who were living in Italy. One might say that those in America were perfectly representative of those in Italy.] Let us survey these people one by one in alphabetical order.

M. Billi. He is unknown to us unless there has been an error in giving his first name, and he is really Giovanni Billi, one of [the] editors of the Fascist daily *Progresso Italo-Americano*.[4]

S. Bonanno. War veteran. Captain in the Fascist militia.[5] Executive of the Bank of America in Harlem.[6] In 1924 one of the directors of the New York Fascio.[7] He took part in many Fascist manifestations.[8] In 1929 member of the special committee to reestablish order in the Fascio Benito Mussolini of New York.[9] In 1930 and 1931, president of the New York branch of the Italian War Veteran Federation.[10]

A. Bonaschi. Secretary of the Italian Chamber of Commerce until 1939, a strategic position of the first order for the control of businessmen who had connections with Italy. We have seen that in 1922 he accompanied Di Silvestro to Italy. In 1925, he returned to Rome "to confer with the Government."[11] Di Biasi did not slander him in 1929 when he affirmed that he was a duly enrolled member of the Fascist party.[12] In fact, in 1927, the

---

4. IAW.
5. PIA, April 17, 1924.
6. XXXI, p. 426.
7. XIX, p. 473; PIA, April 17, 1924.
8. XXXI, p. 333; XXXIII, pp. 279, 366; XXXVI, pp. 103, 504; GS, April 18, 1931; GS, March 3, April 21, November 3, 1934; GS, March 30, 1935; GS, March 30, October 24, 1936.
9. PIA, January 13, 1929.
10. XXXI, p. 426; XXXIII, p. 108.
11. XVIII, p. 406.
12. XXX, p. 351.

Court of Discipline of the league suspended him for a month from "Fascist activities" for not having walked out from a luncheon attended by "anti-Fascist agitators,"[13] and after having been punished by the Court of Discipline in 1927, he was summoned to take part in it in 1928. Very active speaker.[14] In 1927, he published an article to show that the Italians had a right to change the name of Mont Blanc to Monte Mussolini: "Let them plant there and display the flag of glorious Italy and of admonishing Fascism."[15] In 1928, he tendered his resignation from the sectretaryship of the Chamber of Commerce, "holding his position to have become untenable after the embezzling of funds of the Chamber, steadily perpetrated by one of its employees. For a long time the administrative records entrusted to that individual had not been checked."[16] In 1931, he was re-appointed secretary of the Chamber.[17] In 1934, Mussolini bestowed upon him a decoration on account of his "fascist devotion" and his "activities in culture, journalism, finance and patriotic organizations."[18] In 1935, Mayor La Guardia, having to appoint one of the five members of the New York board of education for a period of seven years, chose none other than Dr. Bonaschi. In February 1941, Mayor La Guardia explained the blunder he had made in appointing him as judge by the crack: "When I make a blunder it's a beaut." He should make the same comment about the appointment of Dr. Bonaschi to the board of education. On that occasion, Trombetta praised Bonaschi as "our dearest friend and comrade."[19] When Italy's participation in the New York World's Fair was announced, the Chamber of Commerce entrusted Dr. Bonaschi with the task of issuing a handbook to be put on sale at the fair, *Agenda of Italians Abroad*. Thanks to the above volume, the Italians living in the United States would "live again the glorious moments of the annexation of the vast territory of Ethiopia to the Empire, and the incessant work of the Duce to give power and strength to the nation." They would enjoy also the Duce's speech at Palermo, "Mussolini's memorable voyage to Germany" and "the celebration of the March on Rome."[20] When Dr. Bonaschi resigned from his secretaryship of the Chamber of Commerce, the super-Fascist *Grido della Stirpe*,[21] in announcing the event, sent "to Commendatore Bonaschi wishes of great success in his new cultural activities." One of the key men in the Fascist movement.

13. Gio., January 6, 1927.
14. XVII, p. 391; XIX, pp. 152, 357, 474; XXV, p. 490.
15. XXVI, pp. 153-154.
16. XXVIII, p. 247.
17. XXXIII, p. 107.
18. XXXVI, p. 325.
19. GS, June 18, 1935.
20. *Rivista Commerciale Italo-Americana*, March 12, 1938, p. 7.
21. December 9, 1939.

G. Bottero. War Veteran. In 1923 secretary of the Fascio of Boston, Massachusetts.[22] In 1924, one of the directors of the Fascio of New York.[23] Appointed in 1925 by the headquarters at Rome as delegate of the Italian Naval League in the United States.[24] In 1926 on the staff of the magazine *Giovinezza*.[25] Active in the Fascist movement of Boston.

G. Castruccio. War Veteran. In 1924, one of the directors of the New York Fascio.[26] In 1925, president of the Federation of the Italian War Veterans in the United States.[27] In 1926, appointed by the government at Rome as consul to Pittsburgh, Pennsylvania,[28] and moved in 1928 from the consulate of Pittsburgh to that of Chicago.[29]

E. Citriolo. Attorney-at-law. In July 1926 held the office of secretary general of the League.[30] At the beginning of 1927 still a member of the central council.[31] Special commissioner to manage the Fascio of New York, Benito Mussolini, from the fall of 1925 to the spring of 1926.[32]

V. Comito. War veteran. In April 1927, we meet him as centurion in command of one of the squads of the New York Fascio Benito Mussolini.[33] In May 1927, the central council entrusted him with the organization of a fascio in Brooklyn, district of Williamsburg.[34] Official speaker at the inauguration of the banner of the Fascio Armando Casalini of Brooklyn.[35] From then on, he appears an infinite number of times as speaker in Fascist ceremonies. In July 1927, he was one of the three directors of the New York Fascio Benito Mussolini.[36] In December 1927, he was one of the directors of the Dante Alighieri Society,[37] and represented the Fascio Rizzo of Brooklyn at the convention in Hartford.[38] In October 1928, he represented the central council of the league at a ceremony of the Fascio Umberto Nobile of Brooklyn.[39] In January 1929, he was chosen by Giurato to take part in the

22. XVII, p. 268.
23. XIX, p. 474.
24. XXI, p. 359.
25. XXIV, p. 566.
26. XIX, p. 474.
27. XXI, p. 459.
28. XXIV, p. 88.
29. PIA, July 4, 1928.
30. Ibid., July 16, 1926.
31. Ibid., February 1, March 7, 1927.
32. Ibid., November 10, 1925; May 21, 1926.
33. Ibid., April 26, 1927.
34. Ibid., May 26, 1927.
35. XXV, p. 577.
36. PIA, July 23, 1927.
37. XXVX, p. 460.
38. PIA, December 13, 1927.
39. Ibid., October 8, 1928.

special committee to reorganize the New York Fascio Benito Mussolini.[40] Towards the end of 1929, he was inspector of the Fascist League of North America.[41] In 1935, editor-in-chief of the review *Il Combattente* [The War Veteran], "official organ of the Federation of Italian War Veterans in the United States."[42] According to IAW, head of the press bureau of the above mentioned federation. In 1939, he published a book *In difesa della mia gente* [In defence of my race], (New York, Union Press Co.), aimed at stirring up anti-Semitic and nationalistic exaltation among citizens and residents of Italian origin. In 1939 and 1940, he was a member of the committe which, under the chairmanship of Consul General Vecchiotti, allotted prizes to the Italian language schools which had taken part in dramatic and musical competitions.[43] He took the place of the consul in signing the circular letter by which the committee for the Italian language announced the ceremony of April 21, 1940, where the prizes for 1940 were to be announced. During that ceremony, he was rewarded by Consul Vecchiotti with a certificate of merit for his services as radio speaker on radio station WHOM, and as one of the editors of the Fascist daily *Progresso*.[44] Left the staff of *Progresso* in November 1940, and seems to have gone to South America for a few months. Then in the spring of 1941, he reappeared in New York. One of the key men in the Fascist movement.

A. De Biasi. Newspaperman and publisher. If one were to believe him, Italy and Mussolini were indebted to him and him alone if, in the United States, the ship of Italianism not only stayed afloat, but triumphed against the waves of the subversive doctrines, that is to say, anarchist, socialist, and all those hostile to the House of Savoy:[45]

> What the Italian colony is now, — he wrote in the *Carroccio* — a colony from 1900 on up to the present day educated to be Italian, a colony ready to understand Italy, to defend her and to support her in this new continent: all this is my greatest accomplishment. Of an Italian colony of anarchists, socialists and republicans, I made a super-Italian colony. I founded *Il Carroccio*, and gathered around me the soul, the thought, the gratitude of all the Italians . . . I molded the Fascist soul of the Italians of North America and made of it a gift to Mussolini.

After he had resigned from the party in 1924, he continued to take part in Fascist ceremonies and to flaunt himself as the only authentic interpreter of the thought of Mussolini. Still in 1926, the president of the Fascist league

40. Ibid., January 13, 1929.
41. GS, January 11, 1930.
42. Ibid., June 1, 1935.
43. PLO, p. 52.
44. GS, April 13, 27, 1940; PLO, p. 151.
45. XXVII, p. 10.

praised him "for the work he had done and was doing in the service of the Fascist cause."[46] In 1928, for his bitter criticisms against the Italian and American leaders of the movement, he was expelled from the party. His magazine, mercilessly boycotted by the Fascist organizations, breathed its last sigh in 1935, and he, having lost his sounding board, fell into almost complete oblivion.[47]

M. S. De Cellis. War veteran. "Since 1921, he has taken an active part in the National Fascist Party both in Italy and in America. In 1924 he came to the United States...In 1925 he began to take part in the editing of *Giovinezza*, a magazine of Fascist propaganda."[48] In 1926 one of the directors of the Fascist Association of Italian Newspapermen in North America.[49] In July 1927, speaker at the opening of the Fascio Francesco Crispi of New York.[50] In September 1927, speaker at the Fascio D'Ambrosoli of Brooklyn, at the Fascio Aurelio Padovani of Hoboken, New Jersey, and at the Fascio Armando Casalini of Camden, New Jersey.[51] In November 1927, special commissioner to reorganize the Fascio Italia of Jersey City, New Jersey.[52] In December 1927, he represented the same Fascio Italia at the convention at Hartford. In 1933 he started the "Foreign Language Features" which supplied the press with Fascist news and photographs. Correspondent of the Milan daily *Corriere della Sera*, and of the super-Fascist *Regime Fascista* published by Roberto Farinacci.[53]

B. De Ritis. In 1923, sub-editor of the Fascist daily *Corriere d'America*.[54] In 1925 he joined the staff of the Fascist daily *Progresso*.[55] In 1927 he came back to the *Corriere d'America*.[56] From 1930 to 1934, secretary of the Italy-America Society, and editor of its publication *Italy-America Monthly*. On July 3, 1934, he gave at the Institute of Public Affairs of the University of Virginia, an address on "Aims and Policies of the Fascist Regime in Italy," which was reprinted by the *International Conciliation* of the Carnegie Endowment for International Peace[57] as a document of exceptional importance, though it was full of misstatements from the first to the last word. During the second half of 1934, he left America to go to Malta as inspector

46. XXIII, p. 677.
47. See Agostino De Biasi, *La battaglia dell'Italia negli Stati Unite* (New York, 1927). [Ed Note]
48. AF.
49. XXV, p. 171.
50. PIA, July 30, 1927.
51. Ibid., September 17, 19, 1927.
52. Ibid., November 13, 1927.
53. IAW.
54. XVII, p. 270.
55. XXI, p. 265.
56. XXV, p. 491.
57. *Documents for the Year 1935*, December 1935, n. 315.

of the Italian schools. Malta was a hot-bed of Fascist and anti-British activities, and Mr. De Ritis' mission was "most delicate and of extreme political importance."[58] In the summer of 1940, he reappeared in New York. With what new delicate mission had he been entrusted? We do know his present whereabouts. He is one of the cleverest Fascist agents.

A. Di Marco. War Veteran. In 1924, one of the directors of the Fascio of New York.[59] One of the directors of the Bank of Sicily Trust Co.[60] In December 1926, he spoke at a meeting of the New York Fascio Benito Mussolini.[61] In 1928 he went to Rome to represent the Italian War Veteran Federation in the United States at the national convention of the organization.[62] At the end of 1929, he was inspector of the Fascist League of North America.[63]

Count A. Facchetti Guiglia. "Interested in the silk industry in the United States, and therefore obliged to reside in New York, he nevertheless did not want his sons to be deprived of Italian schooling. His young daughter is doing well in a Milan school."[64] President of the committee which prepared a permanent exhibition of Italian books at Columbia University.[65] Councilor of the Italian Chamber of Commerce.[66] Vice-president of the Italian Child Welfare Committee.[67] Admirer of the super-Fascist weekly *Grido* and its publisher.[68] The admiration was mutual.[69] In 1936, [*Il Grido*][70] defined him as "permanent trustee and leader" (*fiduciario e gerarca permanente*) of the Fascist movement. In that year he was holding the office of general director of the educational clubs,[71] which had taken the place of the old fasci. Untiring speaker at Fascist ceremonies and banquets. In 1940, those of the Fascists of New York who were in the know asserted that the task of keeping the roster of the Fascists who had sworn allegiance to Mussolini was held by Count Facchetti-Guiglia and Miss Amelia Maghini. The latter, in July 1941, was one of the persons chosen by Consul General Vecchiotti to leave for Italy with the personnel of the consulate. A key man.

58. *Carroccio*, July 1934, p. 227.
59. PIA, April 17, 1924; XIX, p. 473.
60. XXV, p. 267, XXXIII, p. 199.
61. PIA, December 5, 1926.
62. XXVII, p. 574.
63. GS, January 11, 1930.
64. XVIII, p. 491.
65. XXII, p. 511.
66. XXIII, p. 167, XXV, p. 168.
67. IAW.
68. GS, November 5, 1932; October 28, 1933.
69. Ibid., March 31, 1924.
70. August 22, 1936.
71. GS, October 3, 1936.

G. Favoino di Giura. In December 1924, held the office of great commissioner of the Fascio of New York.[72] "From 1925 to 1930 he founded and directed *Il Vittoriale*, a fine Fascist magazine...Was Secretary and Delegate of the Italian Fasci Abroad for the State of New York from 1929 to 1930."[73] The delegation was given him by the headquarters of the Italian Fasci Abroad in Rome. Editor and publisher also of the magazines *Italia Madre* and *Noi*.[74] Until October 1940, one of the sub-editors of the Fascist daily *Progresso Italo Americano*.

R. Fioroni. He came to the United States in 1925; and in 1926 he became one of the executives of the Bank of Sicily Trust Co.[75] From 1926 on, a pillar of the Dante Alighieri Society.[76] In 1926, spoke at the opening of the Fascio in the Bronx,[77] in 1928 at the Fascio of Orange, New Jersey[78] and at the Fascio Umberto Nobile of Brooklyn.[79]

P. Garofalo. War veteran. In 1925, he was vice-president and in 1927 president of the New York branch of the Italian War Veterans.[80] Active propagandist in all kinds of Italian organizations.[81] Agent of LUCE, the motion picture company controlled by the Fascist government. In *Nuova Italia*, a Fasicst weekly which he edited, he boasted on December 24, 1939, that during the Ethiopian War he had found a way of sending Italy 1,232,000 copper postcards, amounting to 200 tons of copper, in spite of an embargo placed on copper exports by the United States government. General Francesco Gangemi, inspector of the Fascist Abroad, congratulated him for this achievement in a radio broadcast from Rome printed in *Il Progresso*.[81A] Later he thought up a similar scheme involving the sale of postcards to be sent to Italy bearing a heart in gold leaf.[82] On December 2, 1940, was sentenced by Judge Bondy of the United States District Court, southern district of New York, to two months imprisonment and a $2,000 fine for defrauding the government of the amusement tax on the Italian moving-picture theater, Cine Roma.[83]

72. PIA, December 24, 1924.
73. AF.
74. IAW.
75. AF.
76. XXVI, p. 460; PIA, November 2, 1926; IAW.
77. PIA, November 2, 1926.
78. Ibid., March 21, 1928.
79. Ibid., May 18, 1928.
80. XXI, p. 363; XXVII, p. 249; PIA, June 5, 1927.
81. GS, March 14, July 18, August 8, 22, 1936.
81A. June 11, 1939.
82. *Il Mondo*, January 1940.
83. *The New York Post*, December 3, 1940.

T. Giurato. "Fascist from the very first hour."[84] Co-editor of *Il Grido.*[85] He was one of the most untiring speakers in Fascist ceremonies and meetings.[86] In the spring of 1927 he went to Rome "in special mission to Mussolini," had "important conferences with the Secretary General of the Party and with the Secretary and Vice-Secretary of the Fasci Abroad," was detained "a long time by Mussolini talking about the situation of the Fasci in America," and Mussolini made him a present of his photograph with a dedication.[87] In March 1929, he left the press bureau of the league to go to Buenos Aires and found there a new daily.[88] In 1937, he was serving the Fascist government in Peru.[89]

A. F. Guidi. War Veteran. One of the most important, if not the most important, key man in the apparatus of North American Fascism. From A.F. we gather that during the Italo-Austrian War of 1915-18, he acted as "head of secret inquests" (*capo ufficio delle inchieste riservate*), i.e. he took part in espionage work. As soon as he arrived in the United States, he made a "tour of Fascist lectures" all over the country.[90] In February 1928, the central council entrusted him with the job of editing the *Bulletin of the Fascist League of North America.*[91] At the same time he was co-editor of the *Progresso*, correspondent of Italian dailies, consul of the Republic of San Marino, and commissioner of the Syndicate of Fascist Journalists of Rome for the United States (Fiduciario del Sindacato dei Giornalisti fascisti di Roma per gli S.U.).[91A] "Several times he has been appointed to accompany various Italo-American missions to Italy, which, because of his influence, were received by the Duce, the King and the Pope."[92] In the spring of 1934, he returned to settle down in Rome. In the fall of 1934 he came back again to the United States "for a short mission,"[93] and from then on he acted in Rome as head of the offices of the *Progresso Italo-Americano* and of the *Corriere d'America*, and traveled steadily between Italy and America, acting as contact man. *Carroccio* wrote to him then:[94]

His present task gives our worthy comrade the opportunity of crowning

84. XXIII, p. 363.
85. *Annuario della stampa italiana* (Rome, 1931-32), p. 655.
86. PIA, January 4, July 25, 30, September 19, 1927; February 4, June 28, August 2, October 28, 1928; March 3, 1929; XXII, p. 527, XXIII, p. 461; XXIV, p. 658; XXVI, p. 186.
87. XXV, p. 576; XXVI, p. 59; Gio., May 15, 1927.
88. PIA, March 17, 1929.
89. *Annuario della stampa italiana* (Rome, 1937-38), p. 345.
90. XXVIII, p. 454; PIA, October 25, November 2, 24, 1928; January 8, 11, 19, February 10, March 4, 1928.
91. PIA, February 20, 21, 1929.
91A. *Annuario della stampa italiana, 1931-32*, p. 656.
92. AF.
93. XXXVI, p. 614.
94. XXXVI, p. 105.

in Italy the work which he was carrying on here with intelligence and zeal among the emigrants. He knows their soul, their conditions, and the ardor with which they participate in the life of the Italian peninsula. Therefore, his daily telegrams, his comments, the articles which he sends across the ocean respond perfectly to the state of mind of his readers and to their patriotic devotion. In Rome he enjoys the same confidence of the Regime which he enjoyed in the past years in the United States as a journalist, lecturer, organizer and commissioner of the Italian Press. In the reception of the Secretaries of the Fasci Abroad held by the Duce at Palazzo Venezia on the 4th of June, he represented the Fascists of the United States, and on their behalf acted as sentinel at the Exhibition of the Revolution.

In short, all the whole machine of the Fascist propaganda in North America was maneuvred by him. During the first half of 1940 he was in New York. He left for Italy a few days before Mussolini declared war upon France and England.

John Laspia. In 1926 gave an address at the Fascist popular university of New York.[95] In 1927, one of the directors of the Italian Historical Society.

J. J. Licari, Attorney-at-law. In 1923, he was supreme venerable (the highest office) in the Independent Order of the Sons of Italy, and in this capacity in June, at the closing of the annual convention of his order, he sent an admiring telegram to Mussolini, "Duce of the destinies of Italy, true exponent of the Latin Race."[96]

F. P. Macaluso. Attorney-at-law. He was twenty-nine years old when the Italo-Austrian war broke out in 1915. Instead of going to the fighting front, he found it more healthful to be a member of the Italian Military Mission to Washington.[97] In January 1923, founded *Giovinezza* [Youth], "a monthly magazine of Fascist propaganda."[98] "*Giovinezza* and *Grido*" — stated Macaluso in the October 1925 issue of his review — "were the first organs of our faith." In 1925, vice-president, and in 1926 and 1927 president, of the New York branch of the War Veterans Federation.[99] A very active speaker.[100] In 1928 he went to Italy, and on his return he reported that the authorities in Rome were "satisfied with the work of the Fascist League."[101] In 1929, "appointed by His Excellency Piero Parini [then director of the Italians Abroad at the Rome Foreign Office] honorary consultant in Italian Law at the Italian Consulate of New York."[102] In 1940 he gave IAW the following

95. PIA, January 5, 1926.
96. Gio., June 23, 1923.
97. IAW.
98. AF.
99. XXI, p. 363; XXV, p. 490; PIA, July 15, 1926.
100. XVIII, p. 405; XIX, pp. 244, 361; XX, pp. 286, 490; XXIV, p. 84; PIA, October 28, 1929; GS, February 12, November 11, 1934; February 26, May 5, November 2, 1935.
101. PIA, July 22, 1928.
102. AF.

information: "Lawyer, publicist and film distributor. Director, Italian American Community Center of Brooklyn, N. Y., President, Esperia Film Distributing Company, distributors in the U. S. of Luce Newsreels and E.N.I.C. films of Rome, Italy." The Esperia Film Distributing Co, LUCE Newsreels, and E.N.I.C. are controlled by the Italian government. Therefore, Macaluso registered with the secretary of state as an agent of the Italian government. In 1940 Macaluso was one of the two managers of Cine-Città in New York,[103] a carrier of Fascist propaganda, of course. At the world's fair of 1939-40, one of the halls was placed at his disposal for his films, and one can imagine the use he made of this opportunity. One of the key men.

C. Maccari. In 1928 speaker at the Fascio Umberto Nobile of Brooklyn.[104]

V. Martinez. War veteran. Former employee of the Italian consulate in New York.[105] In 1925, in Italy, "he presented to the King the homage of the Federation of Italian War Veterans in the United States" and represented the New York Fascio at the conference of Fasci Abroad.[106] In 1926, chairman of the New York Fascio Benito Mussolini[107] and president of the Association of the War Maimed Men (Mutilati).[108] In 1928, one of the directors of the New York branch of the Italian War Veterans.[109] It is impossible to count the ceremonies and demonstrations at which he has spoken, and the banquets which he has devoured. On December 21, 1940, as a result of an investigation conducted by Assistant District Attorney William Murphy, he was indicted and then released on $1,000 bail under charge of extortion in his capacity as secretary of the Macaroni Employees Association, 225 Lafayette Stree, New York City. Rather than a key man, he is one of the parasites of the movement.

M. Montrezza. He is unknown to us.

F. Moschetti. Co-editor of the *Grido*. Died in 1933. One of the wildest Fascists. Director, 1927, of the Fascist Association of Italian Journalists of North America.

N. Perciavalle. Speaker in Fascist ceremonies.[110] In 1933 he was appointed chairman of the Fascist Association of Italians Abroad.[111]

A. Portfolio. A prosperous industrialist who retired from business in 1927. *Giovinezza*, when giving the notice about his probable appointment,

103. PLO, p. 157.
104. PIA, March 18, 1928.
105. XXVII, p. 314.
106. XXII, pp. 409, 528.
107. PIA, May 19, 1926.
108. Ibid., June 15, 1926.
109. XXVII, p. 249.
110. PIA, September 19, 1927; January 15, 1928.
111. GS, November 11, 1933.

described him not as a full-fledged Fascist, but as a "filo-Fascist." Was a shareholder of the Fascist magazine *Il Carroccio*.[112] In 1928, attended a dinner of the Fascist historical society in honor of the American Colonel Howard, a "fervent propagandist of the New Italy and the Fascist regime."[113] In 1933, he was one of the honorary presidents of a committee to present Mussolini with a medal commemorating the so-called Fascist Revolution.[114] In October 1934, he proclaimed that "the dawn of the 13th year of Fascism finds the Italians of America more closely cemented to the country of origin."[115] In April 1935, he was sure that "the fearless Italian Youth is walking towards...high mirages [most likely he meant ideals] under the leadership of Benito Mussolini."[116] For the anniversary of the March on Rome in October 1936, he ejaculated other nonsense of the same sort.[117] "He went to Italy several times and was received by the King, by the Duce Benito Mussolini and by the Pope."[118] Received a high decoration from the Rome government.

G. Previtali. War veteran. Teacher of pediatrics, first at Columbia University and then at New York University. Member of the Pontida (Italy) fascio.[119] In the spring of 1923, before the directorate of the party in Rome established the Fascist Central Council for North America, he was received by Mussolini as representative of the Fascio of New York, together with the American, James P. Roe, who "gave evidence before Mussolini of the fact that Italian Fasci were useful and necessary in America.[120] When he returned to New York, he became "active in all the manifestations of the Italian colony."[121] In 1923 and 1924, he was president of the Italian War Veterans.[122] Speaker in an infinite number of ceremonies in New York and outside.[123] In 1927, he accompanied Thaon di Revel in Italy in his visits to Mussolini and other Fascist leaders, and on his return to America he made a tour of Canada on behalf of the league.[124] Member of the directorate of the Dante

112. XXX, p. 371.
113. PIA, December 15, 1928.
114. GS, February 4, March 11, 1933.
115. Ibid., October 27, 1934.
116. Ibid., April 20, 1935.
117. Ibid., October 24, 1936.
118. AF.
119. Ibid.
120. XVII, p. 692; XVIII, p. 84.
121. XIX, p. 238.
122. XVII, pp. 147, 588.
123. See for instance PIA, April 27, December 24, 1924; January 29, 1925; April 2, December 3, 1926; January 4, April 22, June 25, September 22, 30, 1927; October 28, November 5, 1928; January 1, 23, 1929; XXIV, p. 567.
124. PIA, September 22, 1927.

Alighieri Society.[125] Chairman of the Italian Historical Society.[126] One of the governors of the Italian Medical Society.[127] Member of the advisory committee for the year book of the Italy-America Society,[128] and a higher-up in we do not know how many other associations. Representative (*fiduciario*) for the United States of the Italian Fascist federation for the fight against tuberculosis.[129] One of the key men in the movement.

F. Ragno. Served during the Italo-Austrian War of 1915-1918 as judge in those military tribunals[130] which left a terrible record of insensate ferocity in the memories of the Italian soldiers. In 1925 chairman of the Federation of Italian War Veterans.[131] In January 1929, commissioner to manage the Fascio Podestà-Priori in the Bronx.[132]

A. Romano. Born in Italy in 1889 and settled in New York in 1912, he did not find it convenient to return to Italy during the Italo-Austrian war 1915-1918. Co-editor of the Fascist dailies *Il Bollettino della Sera*, 1924-1931; *Opinione*, 1931-1932; *Progresso Italo-Americano* since 1932;[133] and the magazines *Giovinezza* and *Vittoriale*, 1929. In 1926, official speaker at the celebration of the March on Rome at the fascio of Montreal, Canada.[134] On May 24, 1932, at the Dante Alighieri Society of Jersey City, New Jersey he hailed "the Fatherland, reborn because of the Duce."[135] Member of the committee which, under the chairmanship of Consul General Vecchiotti, in April 1940, awarded prizes to Italian language schools.[136] Awarded with a prize for his activities in behalf of the Italian language.[137] In October 1940, signed a telegram to the *Grido della Stirpe* voicing full agreement with its political faith.[138] In 1925 he composed the words of the hymn "March on Rome," set to music by Curci.[139]

F. A. Siclari. In December 1927, he represented the Fascio Martiri Fascisti of Portchester, New York at the convention at Hartford.[140]

125. Ibid., January 16, 1926; January 19, 1927.
126. Ibid., May 22, 1927; XXV, pp. 167, 488.
127. XXV, p. 487, XXVI, p. 241; IAW.
128. XXIV, p. 567.
129. AF.
130. XXXVI, p. 235.
131. XXI, p. 363.
132. PIA, January 20, 1929.
133. AF.
134. XXIV, p. 459.
135. GS, May 28, 1932.
136. PLO, p. 52.
137. Ibid., p. 151.
138. GS, October 12, 1940.
139. XXI, p. 456.
140. PIA, December 13, 1927.

O. Simone. War veteran. In 1926, one of the directors of the Fascio Benito Mussolini of New York.[141] In 1927, was appointed by the government at Rome as vice-consul at San Francisco, California.[142] From 1928 to 1931, vice-consul at Newark, New Jersey.[143]

I. Thaon di Revel. A Piedmontese nobleman, who came to the United States in 1922 as the representative of a moving picture concern.[144] In 1923, he was one of the commissioners appointed by the central council for the New York Fascio.[145] Mussolini's daily paper *Il Popolo d'Italia*, in 1927, described him as "a Fascist shock trooper."[146] In July of that year he went to Italy with Previtali as delegate of the league at the ceremony in honor of two Fascists killed in New York.[147] He "reported to the Secretary General of the Fascist Party on the organization and development of the Fasci of North America"; he was also received by the under secretary at the Foreign Office, and was given a special audience with Mussolini. All were "vitally interested in his reports and opinions about the organization and development of the Fasci in the United States and Canada."[148] After the Fascist League of North America had to disband, in December 1929, he continued to live in New York and to take part in Fascist demonstrations until 1935, when he was appointed inspector of the Fasci Abroad by the Fascist government, and left the United States. *Grido*,[149] in giving this news, assured him that "the comrades of America remember his merits as a leader and as an Italian."

D. Trombetta. In his autobiographical sketch given by IAW we read:

> Editor and publisher. Fifty-five years old. In America since 1905. United States citizen, 1917. Catholic. Democrat. Editor *Il Grido della Stirpe*, a Fascist weekly since 1922. Former editor (with Edmondo Rossoni, now member of the Italian Cabinet) of *L'Italia Nostra*, a weekly, 1914-1916. Dress manufacturer from 1915 to 1924. Past member of Central Council of the Fascist League of North America 1925-29. Organized the first Fascist Club in New York. He has been arrested several times for his activities in the Fascist movement in the U. S.

Thus while Italy was fighting her war with Austria and Germany from 1915 to 1918 Trombetta, born in 1885 and being thirty years of age, instead of rushing to his beloved country and heroically serving it chose rather to remain in America, started a newspaper with Rossoni, and in 1917 became

---

141. Ibid., May 19, 1926.
142. XXV, p. 488.
143. PIA, October 14, 1928; XXXIII, p. 109.
144. *New York Times*, December 23, 1929.
145. Gio., December 29, 1923.
146. "Ardito Fascista," XXV, p. 573.
147. XXV, p. 639.
148. XXVI, pp. 56, 184; PIA, August 13, 1927.
149. June 15, 1935.

an American citizen, renouncing most solemnly all allegiance to every foreign potentate or government, and particularly to the King of Italy whose subject he had been. Rossoni, on June 1, 1912, during a demonstration before the Garibaldi monument in New York "amidst a delirium of applause, spat with all might on the King's tricolor."[150] Thus, one could believe that Trombetta also was a socialist syndicalist, an extremist, a believer in social revolution and a hater of the bourgeoisie and therefore did not need to go and fight in Italy a capitalist war. But this would be a mistake. Rossoni, in 1914, had already refound his national Italian soul, and his paper *Our Italy (L'Italia Nostra)*, of which Trombetta was one of the editors, was an organ of super-Italianism. But Rossoni returned heroically to Italy, and there found a way of remaining as far from the fighting front as possible. Trombetta preferred to save Italy in America and in 1917, he took his second papers. Why, with his super-Italian soul, he became an American citizen, and what meaning the oath of allegiance had for him is a mystery beyond human understanding. He, too, will act as a key man.[151]

At the beginning of their movement, the Fascists had to meet not only the open hostility of anti-Fascist groups, but also the unwillingness of many consuls who still belonged to the old Italian diplomatic tradition. They thought that the fasci in America were not needed, that they would cause not only conflicts in the Italian communities, but also diplomatic friction with the state department. The self-appointed leaders in America, however, supported by Fascist chieftains in Italy, dictated laws to ambassadors and consuls, usurped their powers, and by denouncing them as anti-Fascists, destroyed their reputation at home. The conflict came to an end only when new consuls, 100 percent Fascists, were gradually sent over to replace those whose political faith was either doubtful or lukewarm.[152]

When a consulate was fascistised, the Fascist consul worked hand in hand with the Fascist chieftains of his jurisdiction. The consulate turned into a station of the Fascist secret police. The consul refused to grant passports or visas to those who did not make a profession of Fascism. He denied

150. *Il Proletario*, New York weekly, June 2, 1912.

151. Domenico Trombetta was one of the most fanatical of the Italian-American Fascists, and his *Grido* supported all aspects of Mussolini's policies, including anti-Semitism. In 1928 as a result of a rift between the leaders of the Duce Fascist Alliance of New York and Trombetta, the latter was accused of killing a Fascist named Salvatore Arena. He published a scurrilous attack against the anti-Fascist leader Carlo Fama entitled *Pervertimento: L'antifascismo di Carlo Fama* (New York, n.d.). [Ed. Note]

152. The consuls were the chief agents of the Fascist government in the Untied States and elsewhere, and despite a sharply declining Italian immigration rate, their numbers began to increase sharply by the 1920s. Santarelli, *Storia*, I, p. 481, calculated that between 1928 and 1929 about seventy new consulates were opened by the Italian government, while 120 newly appointed Fascist career consuls were appointed in the same period. [Ed. Note]

affidavits needed to settle family affairs, or documents necessary for business transactions. He strove by all means in his power to hinder the lives and business of all anti-Fascists, especially if they were political refugees. Signor Rolandi-Ricci's open diplomacy had been too crude a method of action. The consulates carried on a more efficient secret diplomacy, while the task of carrying on open diplomacy was entrusted to the League and to journalists, school teachers, lecturers, radio commentators and other more or less conscious fellow-travelers and transmission belts of the League and the consulates. Only in rare cases did the ambassador come to the fore to protect the machine.[153]

Under the pretence of assisting the American people to fight against communism, the League and the consulates were managing to enroll as members of the fasci both citizens and residents of Italian extraction and thus to create a powerful pressure group in American political life.

---

153. By the mid-1930s the consuls in the United States were resorting to high-handed tactics in order to Fascistize Italian-American communities and sparked growing protests from government officials and the anti-Fascist press. See Diggins, *Mussolini and Fascism*, pp. 102-104, and Philip V. Cannistraro, "Fascism and Italian-Americans in Detroit, 1933-1935," *International Migration Review*, 4, 1 (Spring 1975), 30-31. See also Salvemini's pamphlet, "Italian Fascist Activities in the U.S.," p. 5. [Ed. Note]

4

The Fasci in New York City

At the end of 1922 in New York there was one single "Fascio Italiano di New York" which boasted of "being headed by *our* Prime Minister, Benito Mussolini."[1] The Black Shirts made their first public appearance in New York on the Fourth of July, 1923.[2] The first anniversary of the March on Rome (October 28, 1923) was celebrated in Carnegie Hall, with the attendance of the consul general and squads of Black Shirts.[3]

In 1925 the New York Fascio assumed the name of Benito Mussolini and had its headquarters at 220 East 14th Street.[4] At the beginning of 1927, it moved to 145 West 45th Street.[5]

In 1926, the Fascio Benito Mussolini produced an offspring, that is to say

1. PIA, November 24, 1922, italics ours.
2. XVIII, p. 87.
3. XVIII, p. 405.
4. PIA, March 12, 1925.
5. Ibid., February 12, 1927.

a ladies' auxiliary,[6] which in 1927 took the name of Queen Margherita.[7] In July the ladies' auxiliary received its banner from the wife of one of the directors of the Fasci Abroad in Rome.[8] Its "untiring" president since the middle of 1927 was Countess Olga Facchetti-Guiglia.[9] In 1928 and 1929, it had a "triumvirate for propaganda" in which Mrs. Rina Ciancaglini-Gera took part.[10]

Countess Facchetti-Guiglia, in October 1928, was received in Rome by Mussolini, by the secretary general of the party, and by the secretary of the Fasci Abroad, and when she returned to New York, she "reported on the instructions given by Mussolini."[11]

Mrs. Rina Ciancaglini-Gera. From the *Italian American Who's Who* of 1935, we learn that this lady, educated at the University of Turin, came to America in 1920. Here, in 1924, she became instructor in Italian at the Washington Irving High School, and in 1932 at Teachers College of Columbia University. In 1934, "appointed by the Board of Examiners of the City of Newark, N. J. to pass on qualifications of candidates for teachers of Italian." Contributor to *Il Carroccio*. In 1928, she was received by the Fascist section Vittoria Colonna of Providence, Rhode Island as one of the "true examples of the feminine Fascist world in America."[12] *Il Grido della Stirpe*, in 1935, credited her with "the soul of a patriot and a true Fascist."[13] In 1934, she taught Italian in the school of the Fascist Abraham Lincoln Club in the Bronx,[14] and she took part in a ceremony in celebration of the Birthday of Fascism.[15] We shall come across her again. One of the most efficient Fascist agents.

In the meantime it had become clear that one fascio alone was insufficient to cover the entire city of New York. Therefore, in 1925, new fasci began to appear in Manhattan, Brooklyn and the Bronx. We will enumerate them here in chronological order, according to the information we have found about them:

1925, January — Brooklyn: Armando Casalini, 2325 Atlantic Avenue;[16] named after a Fascist who was killed by a madman in Rome in 1924.

6. Ibid., April 26, 1926; January 16, 1927.
7. Ibid., February 1, 1927.
8. Ibid., July 27, 1927.
9. Ibid., August 18, 1928.
10. Gio., April 8, 1928; January 1, 1929.
11. PIA, October 17, November 15, 1928.
12. Ibid., December 18, 1928.
13. GS, June 15, 1935.
14. Ibid., February 2, 1934.
15. Ibid., March 31, 1934.
16. PIA, January 29, 1925.

1926, June — The Bronx: Umberto Nobile;[17] named after the well known aviator.

1926, June — The Bronx: Mario Sonzini, 606 East 187 Street;[18] named after a nationalist who was killed by Communists in Turin in September 1920. Moved to 697 East 187 Street in August 1927.[19]

1926, November — The Bronx: Filippo Corridoni, 1193 Spofford Avenue;[20] named after a Socialist of the extreme left who had been Mussolini's follower when Mussolini was also an extreme left Socialist, and Corridoni killed in battle during the world war. This fascio was promoted by the Clement Contractor Co., whose manager, Gaetano Clemente, without further ado, enrolled all his workers.

1926, November — The Bronx: Nicola Bonservizi;[21] named after a Fascist who was killed by an anarchist in Paris in 1923.

1926, December — Brooklyn,Greenpoint: Umberto Nobile, 212 Union Avenue;[22] moved to 28 Conselyea Street in September 1928.[23]

1927, January — The Bronx: Vittorio Podestà-Luigi Priori, 3550 White Plains Avenue;[24] named after two Fascists killed in Italy in 1920.

1927, March — Brooklyn, Bensonhurst: an unnamed fascio with a ladies' auxiliary.[25]

1927, March — Brooklyn, Flatbush at Nostrand Avenue: another unnamed fascio.[26]

1927, May — Brooklyn: Angelo Rizzo;[27] named after a Fascist youth killed in Sicily in 1921 during the civil war.

1927, May — Manhattan: Francesco Crispi, 429 First Avenue;[28] named after the Italian prime minister who is regarded by the Fascists as the forerunner of Mussolini, and who in fact was responsible for the military disaster of Adua in March 1896.

1927, May — Brooklyn: an unnamed fascio in the district of Williamsburg.[29]

17. Ibid., June 24, 1926.
18. Ibid., June 29, 1926.
19. Ibid., August 27, 1927.
20. Ibid., November 2, 17, 1926.
21. Ibid., November 2, 1926.
22. Ibid., December 27, 1926; January 18, 1927; April 25, 1928.
23. Ibid., September 27, 1928.
24. Ibid., February 1, 1927.
25. Ibid., March 13, 1927.
26. Ibid., March 19, 1927.
27. Ibid., May 23, 1927.
28. Ibid., June 30, 1927.
29. Ibid., May 26, 1927.

1927, September — Brooklyn, Bath Beach: D'Ambrosoli;[30] named after a Fascist who was killed in new York by unknown persons, most likely anti-Fascists, in 1927. In 1928, held its meetings at the Dyker Heights Club.[31]

1928, April — Brooklyn: Domenico Mastromuzzi, 3112 Church Avenue;[32] named after a young Fascist killed in Italy in 1921 during the civil war.

1928, May — Manhattan, Bleeker Street: Aurelio Padovani;[33] named after a Fascist leader who in Naples, in 1924, died as a result of an accident.

Almost all of these fasci had internal crises which did not show in their leaders and followers a great capacity to command and to obey.

The first fascio of New York had to be disbanded as early as February 1923, because of lack of discipline.[34] Its reorganization must have been very difficult if, at the end of 1923, the fascio was still entrusted to the care of three special commissioners.[35] In March 1924, the Secretariat of the Fasci Abroad announced that one sole fascio in New York was legal, and it was that one which depended on the Fascist Central Council.[36] In April 1924, the Fascio, Benito Mussolini, was working in a normal way with a directorate of its own.[37] But in the fall of 1925, it was once again undergoing a crisis and the central council of the league had to entrust it for nine months to the care of one of its members, Citriolo.[38] In November 1927, there was a new crisis, and Giuseppe (or Peppino) Ganci was appointed by the central council as "Special Commissioner with full powers."[39] Ganci still continued to hold this office in May 1928.[40] In January 1929, a new special commissioner, Giurato, became necessary,[41] who appointed a special committee to assist him in his work.[42] The Fascio Francesco Crispi also, in January 1928, was placed under the surveillance of a special commissioner.[43]

In the Bronx, in February 1927, the central council of the league had to announce that the only fascio which it recognized was that named after Mario Sonzini. "Every other initiative was the work of anti-Fascist agents,"[44]

30. Ibid., September 17, 1927.
31. Ibid., September 29, 1928.
32. Ibid., April 6, May 18, October 22, 1928.
33. Ibid., May 10, 18, 1928.
34. Ibid., February 9, 1923.
35. Gio., December 29, 1923.
36. PIA, March 2, 1924.
37. Ibid., April 17, 1924.
38. Ibid., November 10, 1925; May 21, 1926.
39. Ibid., November 13, 1927.
40. Ibid., May 10, 1928.
41. Ibid., June 9, 1929.
42. Ibid., January 13, 1929.
43. Ibid., January 30, 1928.
44. Ibid., February 1;5, 1927.

as if the Fascio Filippo Corridoni and the Fascio Vittorio Podestà-Luigi Priori had not been inaugurated with addresses by Thaon di Revel, Trombetta, Giurato and other full-fledged Fascists. In June 1927, the Fascio Bonservizi was baptized again as legitimate,[45] and in May 1928, the Fascio Vittorio Podestà-Luigi Priori was also welcomed back into the fold.[46] But in January 1929, it was managed by a special commissioner.[47] The Fascio Sonzini must also have been failing if, in January 1927, it was in the process of reorganization,[48] and only in June 1927, the special commissioner was able to proceed to the appointment of its directorate.[49]

In 1924, the anti-Fascists maintained that the Fascio of New York was made up of "a few titled aristocrats who met together in elegant hotels of the metropolis." In order to discredit this charge, the *Grido della Stirpe* in April 1924 arranged for the Fascist celebration of the Birthday of Rome to be held in the Thalia Theatre.[50] In 1926, if we believe what the Fascists tell us, 400 members were present at a meeting of the Fascio Benito Mussolini.[51] In May 1927, at a meeting in Brooklyn, they gathered together "more than 2,000 Fascists."[52] On October 28, 1927,[53] "more than one thousand Fascists in Black Shirts" gathered together to hear Thaon di Revel. The head of the press bureau of the league, Giurato, then announced that the Fascio Benito Mussolini "counted its members by the thousands,"[54] and in January 1929, he announced that the Fascio numbered "3,000 enrolled members."[55] But these round figures of "400," "more than one thousand," "thousands," and "3,000" raise doubts in the mind of whoever knows how easily the Fascists, Nazis and Communists invent statistics.

Anyhow, quality counts more than quantity. In the Fascist as well as in the Communist movement one must bear in mind that there are different streams of people: 1) comrades proper, i.e. duly enrolled members of the party; 2) fellow travelers, who swear that they are not actually regular members of the party, but they are always to be found at the right moment and at the strategic point where the party line must be upheld; 3) people who may be termed prisoners of war because they have become members of the party under pressure from their relatives in Italy who have asked them

45. Ibid., June 12, 1927.
46. Ibid., May 29, 1928.
47. Ibid., January 26, 1929.
48. Gio., January 31, 1927.
49. Ibid., June 12, 1927.
50. PIA, April 12, 22, 1924.
51. Gio., October 28, 1926.
52. PIA, May 23, 1927.
53. Ibid., November 7, 1927.
54. Ibid., October 27, 1927.
55. Ibid., January 9, 1929.

to join the party in order to avoid trouble over there; or people who, if they did not show sufficient Fascist zeal in this country, would have their business connections with Italy seriously disturbed, or would not get any facilities here from the Fascist controlled Italian banks, or find it advisable to procure a membership card before going to Italy for business or to see their families; 4) fronts or people who lend their names to committees, give money, sign proclamations, or even become members of the organizations without realizing that they are made use of for purposes wholly alien to their thoughts: flies that are trapped in spider webs or moths who are attracted to the light. Most of them are patriots who do not understand anything about Fascism or anti-Fascism, but think that to be a Fascist is to be a good Italian; 5) good natured people who allow themselves to be dragged along by whoever succeeds in reaching them with no competition from other quarters.

According to De Biasi, the rank and file of the Fascists in this country consisted of small groups of "good people, credulous, deluded, attracted around the swollen grosbonnets, and lured with their innocent ambitions into the shadow of the Consulates,"[56] or else a "sly and cautious element who, before going to Italy on business, thought it well to put a membership card in their pockets to exhibit as proof of their devotion to the Duce." "Fascists for pure opportunism, who requested the card in hope of getting easier terms and favors."[57] The fact that many people "succeeded in seizing the membership card just on the eve of their return to Italy" was deplored by Giurato.[58] Thaon di Revel also explained in an interview with the *New York Herald Tribune*[59] that "membership cards are in form of passports and serve as links between the Fascists of Italy and those of the United States . . . Anyone who belongs to the Fascist League of North America, finds on going to Italy that his card serves as a means of identification when presented to the National Fascist Party there." He was careful not to explain why the official passport was not a sufficient means of identification, and what would happen to the man who did not possess the Fascist card or was denounced from America to the Fascist party there as an anti-Fascist.

Under such circumstances, it would be unfair and dangerous to brand and treat as Fascists all those people whose names appear among those attending Fascist demonstrations or contributing to Fascist subscriptions or devouring Fascist dinners. Not even those who now and then become directors of some Fascist organization should be listed as active Fascists unless a more intimate connection with the Fascist party can be proven through other evidence.

56. XXX, p. 374.
57. XXIX, p. 369.
58. PIA, June 9, 1929.
59. September 5, 1926.

The Fascists founded, or boasted that they would found, schools. For example, in 1924, the Fascist Central Council announced that they had opened at the headquarters of the Fascio of New York a school of English, two schools of design, a quick theoretical-practical course of radio, and it promised to open "other courses of every kind." All courses were to be free.[60] In 1926, the Ladies' Auxiliary Queen Margherita opened courses in Italian and English.[61] Two years later, the Fascio Umberto Nobile of Brooklyn also opened a free school of Italian.[62] In 1926, the central council inaugurated a Peoples' Fascist University in New York, which gave courses of lectures on the history and philosophy of Fascism, Fascist legislation, etc.[63] The spirit which prevailed in these people's universities may be gauged by a lecture which was held in Boston's university in 1928. In this lecture, the speaker discussed a problem on which the experts in Dante studies have racked their brains for centuries: of whom was Dante thinking six centuries ago when making the prophecy that Italy would be saved by a greyhound (veltro)? The Fascist lecturer of Boston enumerated all the candidates who have been put forward to claim the glory of acting as the greyhound, but concluded that all hypotheses were groundless. Then he asked who this greyhound of Dante would possibly be? "All those present answered with him: 'Mussolini!'"[64] In 1928, the Fascio Benito Mussolini thought of promoting the rise of a dramatic and a philharmonic society.[65]

More than in teaching the Italian language or the philosophy of Fascism or in solving the riddles of Dante, the leaders of the league and the directors of the local fasci were interested in promoting sports among their flock. Every fascio tried to form among its members a squad of Black Shirts under a caposquadra ("leader").[66]

The New York Fascio Benito Mussolini in June 1926, displayed on Memorial Day a group of two hundred Black Shirts who were passed in review by the president of the league.[67] In Providence, in November 1926, Captain Angelo Martella "undertook the command of all the squads which, in a demonstration of force and discipline, marched into the hall, giving the

60. PIA, October 26, 1924.
61. Ibid., June 21, 22, 1926; March 11, 1927.
62. Ibid., April 25, September 28, 1928.
63. Ibid., March 5, 20, May 5, 8, June 1, 19, 1926.
64. Ibid., June 10, 1928.
65. Ibid., October 18, 1928.
66. See for instance the fascio of Lawrence, Mass., PIA, April 20, 1924, January 20, 1926; Fascio Italia of Jersey City, New Jersey, ibid., December 24, 1924; Fascio Ala Umberto Nobile, West New York, N. J., ibid., January 10, 1927; Fascio Nicola Bonservizi, Newark, N.J., ibid., February 11, 1927; Fascio Rino Moretti, Wierton, Pa., ibid., November 8, 1927; Fascio Vittorio Veneto, Providence, R.I., ibid., August 25, 1928.
67. PIA, June 3, 1926.

Roman salute."[68] In January 1927, in New York, "600 Fascists in Black Shirts, in perfect formation, with 50 flags" appeared in the stadium.[69] In February 1927, the press bureau of the League called together "the First and the Second Centuries" for practice in sport.[70] In March 1927, the central council appointed Giuseppe (or Peppino) Ganci inspector of the sport squads,[71] and in April 1927, "the Fascist Centuries in uniform" were present at the reception for the aviator De Pinedo, commanded by six centuries, among whom was Comito.[72] We come across squads also at one of the fasci of Brooklyn in May 1927.[73] In November 1927, the central council concentrated all the sport activities of the Fascists of greater New York in the Fascio Benito Mussolini.[74] In West New York, New Jersey, in June 1927, "more than two hundred men in uniform" under three *capisquadra*, took part in the commemoration of Memorial Day.[75] In Boston, November 1927, a group of two hundred Black Shirts paraded through the streets to the strains of the anthem "Giovinezza";[76] and in October 1928, at a celebration commemorating the March on Rome, the president of the League passed in review the Black Shirts "in military formation."[77]

These sportive activities were considered so important that at the beginning of 1928 the inspector of the Fascist squads, Ganci, was called to take part in the central council of the League.[78]

G. Ganci. War veteran. "Participated in the first movements of Fascism in Milan and had the opportunity to know Benito Mussolini personally. Returning to the United States in 1919, he was one of the first to organize the Fasci of North America, in which he was director of squads."[79] In 1923, the national directorate of the Fascist trade unions in Italy appointed him as commissioner *(fiduciario)* to organize Italian trade unions in the United States.[80] In 1926, was one of the directors of the Fascio of New York.[81] In 1927, "Special Commissioner with full powers" to reorganize the Fascio Benito Mussolini of New York.[82] Business manager of the super-Fascist

68. Ibid., November 10, 1926.
69. Gio., January 31, 1927.
70. PIA, February 19, 1927.
71. Ibid., March 7, 1927.
72. Ibid., April 26, 1927.
73. Ibid., May 26, 1927.
74. Ibid., November 27, 1927; Gio., January 1, 1928.
75. Ibid., June 2, 1927.
76. Ibid., November 2, 1927.
77. Ibid., October 27, 1928.
78. Ibid., February 2, 1928.
79. AF.
80. Gio., July 28, 1923; XVIII, p. 295.
81. PIA, May 19, 1926.
82. Ibid., November 13, 1927.

Grido.[83]

Nothing is more healthful from a physical and moral point of view than sport. But every European knows that sportive associations from one moment to the next can become armed and aggressive political organizations. *Squadre* ("squads") and *squadristi* ("members of squads") meant in Italy at the time of the civil war (1921-1922), and still mean in Fascist terminology, those armed units which carried out acts of violence against the anti-Fascists. The Fascio Benito Mussolini of New York offered free lessons in fencing,[84] and the Fascio Nicola Bonservizi of Newark, New Jersey drilled its *squadristi* in the arts of "fencing, boxing, etc."[85] The Fascist squads were units for fight and not for sport. An act of February 16, 1926, granted the same pension as that which was given to soldiers who were wounded or killed in war to Italians abroad who incurred wounds or death fighting for the "national" (Fascist) cause. No discrimination was made between Fascists who were injured in self defense or in attacking other people. This was plain incitement to violence and murder.[86]

The Fascists boasted that their aim was "to cooperate with the various American societies in the noble campaign for spreading the respect of religion, of the nation, of the family, of private property, and for gathering all social classes in the fight against atheism, internationalism, free love, Communism and class hatred."[87] "Either Communism or Fascism" was their slogan. This was also the Communists' slogan. In America, as in Italy, as in Germany or anywhere else, democratic institutions had to be crushed between the wall of Fascism and the door of Communism. The trick played first in Italy, then in Germany, and later in Spain by the Fascists to undermine the institutions of a democratic country and finally to destroy them, consisted in pretending that their political opponents were all Bolshevists and were planning leftist revolutions. Therefore, they must be done away with. Then the Fascists rushed on the stage as the saviors of society from Communist danger.[88] They must take the law into their own hands and overthrow the democratic government as incapable of keeping peace and order. To tell the truth, in America during the twenties, the Fascists did not yet dream of overthrowing democratic institutions. This phase of the movement has begun to develop

83. *Annuario della stampa italiana, 1931-1932*, p. 287.
84. PIA, October 14, 1928.
85. Ibid., February 11, 1927.
86. The emphasis on sports which Salvemini noted among the Fascists in the United States conformed to the regime's policies in Italy. See Felice Fabrizio, *Sport e fascismo: la politica sportiva del regime* (Rimini-Florence, 1976). [Ed. Note]
87. *New York Times*, December 23, 1929.
88. On the use of anti-communism in Fascist propaganda see Philip V. Cannistraro and Edward D. Wynot, Jr., "On the Dynamics of Anti-Communism as a Function of Fascist Foreign Policy, 1933-1943," *Il Politico*, 38, 4 (December 1973), 645-681. [Ed. Note]

in this country only during these last few years. During the first year of their activities the Fascists' aims were more limited in scope. They only wanted to throw a sinister light over anti-Fascists as breakers of the peace, trouble-makers and Bolshevists. To reach this second aim, all that they needed was to start riots and street fighting. This was not difficult. Unpleasant incidents became too frequent. Most Italian communities fell prey to a kind of civil war. In an article in the *Carroccio* of January 1928, De Biasi wrote: "As soon as a Fascist parade is out, there are riots, blows and wounds, and the next day there is an explosion of indignation in the American newspapers."

In 1926, on Memorial Day, a Fascist group wearing black shirts marched through the streets of New York. When they reached 113 Street there was a sudden riot and an exchange of blows and shots.[89] Two Fascists fell dead in the encounter. The investigation made by the police never succeeded in discovering the truth as to who started the fray. Some said that the Fascists were the first to attack an anti-Fascist group who jeered at them; others affirmed that the attack came from the anti-Fascists. In such affairs it is almost impossible to find out who fired the first shot.[90]

Fascist witnesses denounced as authors of the murder of two workers, [Cologero] Greco and [Donato] Carrillo, who were arrested and a certain Longhetti who was never found. The two murdered Fascists were glorified as martyrs of the Fascist cause. They were given a gorgeous funeral — graced by the presence of the ambassador — and their bodies were taken to Italy to receive further honors and to be laid to rest with the Fascist martyrs. The Fascist League and its president Thaon de Revel, assumed the task of securing the conviction of the two accused men. He even went to Italy to report the affair to the Duce and to secure funds for the purpose.

The trial took place at the Bronx county court from December 9 to 24, 1927. The Fascist witnesses involved themselves in such contradictions as to lose all credit. The star witness of the prosecution, a certain A. [lexander] Rocco, one of the founders of the Fascist league and leader of the fascio of the Bronx, immediately after the murder had given to the district attorney a detailed description of one of the murderers whom he later identified as Carrillo. But the description did not fit the accused man at all. Furthermore, it was ascertained that Rocco, before identifying Carrillo in the line up, had been given by a policeman the opportunity to take a look at the man. Another witness for the prosecution, a certain Umberto De Simone, confessed that he was a Fascist, but had feigned to be an anti-Fascist and had become a member of the anti-Fascist alliance in order to spy upon its activities and

---

89. Salvemini is mistaken in two minor details. The correct year is 1927, and the incident occured at 183 Street. [Ed. Note]

90. *New York Times*, May 31, June 1, 2, 1927. [Ed. Note]

report them to the Fascist league.

Greco and Carrillo proved satisfactorily that when the murders were committed they were in other distant parts of the city. Among the witnesses for the defense there appeared [Giacomo] Caldora who admitted that he was a Fascist, though not belonging to the official League but to the outlawed Duce Fascist Alliance. He had seen the murderers and denied that they were either Greco or Carrillo or Longhetti, all of whom he had known personally for some time. He declared also that a certain [Carlo] Vinci, former member of Fascist squads in Italy, had approached him the day after the murder, and had offered him $5,000 if he were willing to accuse the three men and to affirm that he had seen the murderers alight from the motor car of Dr. Fama, the leader of the anti-Fascist alliance. Questioned as to why he belonged to a different Fascist organization than the League, he answered that it was because he felt disgust for the criminal activities of the League and of its president, Thaon de Revel. Invited to explain what he meant by criminal activities, he mentioned the plan of throwing bombs at anti-Fascist meetings. The two accused men were pronounced not guilty by the jury.[91]

Meanwhile another incident had occurred. On September 11, 1926, an anti-Fascist open air meeting was being held at the corner of 116 Street and First Avenue. A car which was running towards the meeting, just before it arrived there, was forced to stop by the red light and the policeman who was there in control of the traffic. At this point an explosion blasted the car. The explosion shattered many windows, and of the men who were in the car, two were reduced to pieces and the third severly wounded. Their bodies were blown twenty feet away. All of them were Fascists. All those present affirmed that the explosion sounded like the blast of dynamite compressed in a steel bomb. One does not need to be a competitor of Sherlock Holmes to guess that the Fascists had intended to throw a bomb at the assembled anti-Fascists and then make a getaway in their car. This would have been their revenge for the killing of their two comrades on Memorial Day. The bomb exploded in the car because it had already been lighted when the car had to stop on its way.

But 1926 was the happy time when loans for hundreds of millions of dollars still were to be floated on the American market and it was not expedient to show Fascism in America in an unfavorable light. That was also the happy time when Mr. James S. Walker ruled New York City. As the Grido della Stirpe wrote on October 12, 1940, he was "undoubtedly the

91. The Greco-Carrillo case caused great notoriety and became a cause célèbre among anti-Fascists. Clarence Darrow led the defense and a committee headed by Arthur G. Hays, Isaac Schorr, and Arthur Levy was established to raise funds for the defendants. See Diggins, Mussolini and Fascism, pp. 129-131. [Ed. Note]

most sincere friend that the Italians have had among the politicians of America." Mussolini recognized his merit when, in June 1927, he conferred upon him a high decoration,[92] and in September 1927 he received him cordially in Rome.[93] No wonder, therefore, if in 1926 the New York police were of the opinion that probably the blast had been caused by an explosion in the gasoline tank, and the *New York Times*, September 12, 1926, took good care not to say that the men in the car were Fascists, while inventing that the meeting was being held not by anti-Fascists but by Fascists. Thus, even if one surmised that the car had been blasted not by a gasoline explosion, but by a bomb, one was left to surmise that the bomb was destined to fall among a meeting of Fascists, and therefore that the three men in the car probably were anti-Fascists.

92. PIA,   June 22, 1927.
93. Ibid., September 20, 1927.

5

Fascism and Americanism

With the establishment of Fascist organizations in the United States, a basic problem had to be solved, the same problem which had confronted the Sons of Italy from 1905 to 1922. Were the citizens and residents of Italian origin in this country to become American citizens, or were they to retain forever their Italian citizenship, or even worse, were they to become American citizens in order to take advantage of their rights as citizens to promote the policies of the Italian government in this country?

Another problem interrelated with the first arose which had never existed before. Were the fasci in America to be under the jurisdiction of the headquarters in Rome or were they to be autonomous American organizations? The former solution had the disadvantage that the Fascist League would run against American traditions and laws and it would assign to the Italian diplomatic and consular agents a task not reconcilable with good diplomatic behavior. The second solution, that of granting autonomy to the American fasci as American associations under American law, did not secure unity of action, made clashes with the headquarters at Rome possible, and gave no means of enforcing discipline.[1]

The Fascists in this country never felt any doubts about these problems. The editor of the Fascist magazine *Carroccio*, De Biasi, in the issue of January 1923, described in the following terms the task of the Italian fasci in the United States:

> The aim of Fascist foreign policy is in one word, expansion . . . To be sure Italian Foreign policy must be carried on by the government and its diplomacy: but in great part it must be the concern of *us Italians who have emigrated* [italics in the original] . . . Italian foreign policy is one of the most delicate tasks for us Italians who militate abroad . . . In Washington the effects of an Italian diplomatic action, virile, robust, frank and powerful are to be felt . . . Thus the necessity of a Fascist plan . . . We, in America, possess excellent forces of persuasion . . . Fascism will watch carefully over Italian foreign policy in Washington. When we have organized Fasci in all our communities as scouts and observatories of our fatherland, then our ambassador will find in the masses with whom he will come in contact, a more intelligent readiness to work with him. We, the vanguard on this side of the Ocean of irresitible Fascism, make this promise to our Italy.[2]

Thus, the masses of Italian extraction in this country, organized into fasci, were to act as pressure groups at the service of the Italian ambassador in his dealings with the American government.

In the summer of 1925 a member of the Italian senate, Antonio Cippico, the official speaker for Italy at the International Institute of Politics of Williamstown, uttered the following statement:

> Whoever wishes to secure Italian workmen must make provision as to prevent those immigrants from losing their nationality, so that their absence from Italy should not cause their political separation from Italy. Either colonial territories are assigned to Italy where her sons can settle under the Italian flag . . . or the Italian immigrants in foreign countries sparsely populated must remain grouped together and keep always their Italian citizenship.

1. The problems discussed in this and the preceding paragraph were crucial for the Fascist regime. While there were some enthusiasts among the Italian-American Fascists and in Rome who argued for strong and direct connections between Italy and the American fasci, Italian diplomatic officials in Washington generally favored a cautious and low-keyed propaganda strategy designed to avoid arousing the anxiety of American public opinion and adverse reaction from the government. On this question see Migone, "Il regime fascista"; Philip V. Cannistraro and Theodore P. Kovaleff, "Father Coughlin and Mussolini: Impossible Allies," *Journal of Church and State*, 8, 3 (Autumn 1971), 427-443; Diggins, *Mussolini and Fascism;* Daria Frezza Bicocchi, "Propaganda fascista e comunità italiane in USA: la Casa Italiana della Columbia Univeristy," *Studi Storici*, 11, 4 (October-December 1970), 661-697; Cassels, "Fascism for Export." There is also considerable documentation on this problem in Archivio Centrale dello Stato, *Ministero della Cultura Popolare*, buste 105, 163, 166. [Ed. Note]
2. XVII, pp. 1-7.

America, being computed among the nations sparsely populated in comparison to most European regions, was obviously one of the countries for which this measure was proposed. The claim of Cippico was denounced and sharply criticized by American newspapers, as for instance by the *New York Times*.[3] To dispel the bad effects of Cippico's indiscretion the Fascist daily *Corriere d'America* bluntly condemned the Italian senator.

> The idea of Cippico is a mistake. It would give rise to endless struggles and paralyzing rivalries. It is understood that Cippico speaks for himself. But even when he speaks for himself, a man who is a Senator of the Realm has abroad an authority and a prestige which imply delicate responsibilities. He knows well that America is the product of the transformation of European immigrants into American citizens.

Cippico rushed to protest that he excluded America from the list of the countries to which his plan could be applied. This explanation did not satisfy the *Corriere* which suggested that the senator's speeches were good for "home consumption but out of place in America." The fact was that America was precisely the country in which the Fascists were eager to keep the Italian immigrants under Fascist control. America alone has almost one-half of the ten million Italians abroad. And the Fascist thinkers in expounding Fascist policies towards the Italians abroad, have never made any exception in favor of the United States.

To avoid possible storms, the Fascist convention at Philadelphia, in October 1925, stated that the League was an "autonomous organization, which received no orders from the outside," but it "wished to be sanctioned by the Secretary General of the Fasci Abroad at Rome as the only official organization in America," and "the line of action in America was to be the same as that ordained by the Secretary General of the Fasci Abroad." The League acknowledged Mussolini as its spiritual leader. Its action was parallel to that of the Fascist party in Italy. But there existed a reciprocity of agreement and not dependence. The League was at the service of America.[4] Yet, chairman of that convention was a consul of the Fascist militia and member of the national directorate of the Fascist party who had purposely come from Italy, Alessandro Sardi.

Even after the convention at Philadelphia had proclaimed the autonomy of American Fascism from Rome, this Fascism continued to remain directly dependent on Rome. Fascist meetings voted messages to Mussolini, "renewing their oath of faith to Italy and Fascism"[5] and their "oath of intangible Fascist

3. August 3, 1925.
4. Gio., October 28, November 30, 1925.
5. Lawrence, Mass., PIA, September 25, 1925; March 28, 1926.

faith";[6] "reasserting their faith and discipline";[7] "reiterating their oath of loyalty to the Fatherland, the King and the Fascist Regime, always ready to take up arms again if necessary."[8]

Once in a while the Fascists remembered that there existed also America and they cried "Three cheers for the Duce of the Fascist Militia, for Italy and for America."[9] Or else, after proclaiming that "it was the sacred duty of all Italian forces to keep aflame their love for the far away Fatherland," they shouted "Long Live America, long live the Duce, long live Italy."[10] Sometimes they even went so far as to send messages of greeting not only to Mussolini, but also to the president of the United States.[11] Whoever was prepared to believe them was told that the Fascists in America aimed at "keeping alive among the Italians the love for Italy and absolute respect for the laws of this land."[12] Mussolini had given them orders that they should show themselves "worthy of Italy's new destiny and useful to the land which shelters them and their mother Fatherland."[13] Citriolo, secretary general of the Fascist League, maintained in 1926, that the League was but an "educational and cultural organization." The fasci were wholeheartedly to cooperate with America institutions. No violent activities were permitted to Fascist squads. These were sporting and not fighting groups.

> Our foes endeavor to prove that we are against Americanism, that we are a branch of the Fascist Secret police, that we are members of the Fascist Militia. We would regard as an honor to be members of the Militia . . But we know that in this country we cannot and must not be . . . We are only soldiers of an ideal.[14]

Macaluso maintained that there was no conflict between the Fascist doctrine and the democratic American doctrine:

> The democratic ideas embodied in the Constitution of the United States have always been exalted by the Fascist Government . . . Fascism, from both a theoretical and a practical standpoint, is a higher form of hierarchical and centralized democracy.[15]

The press bureau of the league was eager to explain that "whoever accepted the Fascist doctrine, showed himself to be also an American hostile to

6. Newark, N.J., PIA, March 14, 1926.
7. Ibid., February 3, 1927.
8. Ibid., March 19, 1929.
9. Ibid., October 30, 1926.
10. Ibid., December 9, 1926.
11. Ibid., December 13, 1927.
12. Ibid., May 9, 1923.
13. Ibid., May 30, 1926.
14. Ibid., January 12, 1926.
15. Gio., October 15, 1927.

subversive doctrines":

> What we ask of American citizens of Italian origin is to keep alive their cult for the Fatherland and to realize the wondrous renaissance which Fascism has brought to it. These tasks do not conflict with their duties of American citizenship.[16]

The Fascio of Trenton, New Jersey, in February 1924, commemorated Lincoln in a truly Fascist meeting. The speaker put into one and the same category Lincoln and Mussolini.[17] Could one be more American than that?

Thaon di Revel "did not see any contrast between being an American citizen and being a Fascist": "one who is loyal and obedient to the laws of this country can at the same time have spiritual links with the Fatherland from which he came,"[18] meaning by spiritual links that the Italian Fascists of America were "tied to the Duce and Italian Fascism by deep ideal and spiritual links which never could be dissolved."[19] He admitted that America, "because of her special conditions, had no need for Fascism *today*" (italic ours). Yet, he suggested discreetly, we must not exclude the "eventuality that some of the most typical laws of Fascism may come to be applied in America," for example the laws which had created the corporate state.[20]

The Fascist ambassador in Washington, De Martino, went so far as to assure his comrades that "the President of the United States knew that the Italo-Americans were loyal to their adopted Fatherland while keeping alive the cult of the Fatherland from which they came."[21]

The Americans were not as gullible as the Fascists believed. Only people who had taken a vow to remain stupid at all costs could fail to sense the difference which existed between the love for the adopted country and the cult of the country of origin; between the obedience to American law and the never to be dissolved links with Italy. Links cultural and spiritual which can never be dissolved will dissolve love and obedience as soon as a clash arises between love and cult, between obedience and ties with Italy.

Therefore, a cloud of suspicion steadily hovered over Fascist activities. In 1926, an American agent of Fascist propaganda, Mr. James P. Roe, endeavored to maintain that the only purpose of Fascist organizations in the United States was "to counteract unfair propaganda": "there is no mystery or secrecy about the League, its membershp, its activities, methods or purposes."[22] But

16. PIA, July 17, 1928.
17. Ibid., February 17, 1929.
18. Ibid., September 8, 1928.
19. Ibid., February 20, 1929.
20. Address at the Army and Navy Club of New York, PIA, January 15, 1927.
21. PIA, April 6, 1929.
22. Gio., February 15, 1926.

two weeks later, he had to express the opinion that the fasci in America were "so misunderstood that they did more harm than good."[23] In 1929, Macaluso complained that "the innuendos were going on" in spite of the fact that the Fascists were taking part in American celebrations and repeated constantly that the League "received no orders from the Government of Italy," "was not a military organization, had no bonds of interdependence with the Fascist Party" but merely had been recognized by the Secretariat General of the Fasci Abroad as the "sole interpreter to the United States of Fascist doctrine."[24]

The most disturbing fact to the Americans was the oath of blood which the Fascists were said to take in the act of being admitted to the party. No doubt, on receiving his membership card, the newly baked Fascist took an oath. The directors of the fasci took their oath in the presence of a commissioner of the central council.[25] But the content of this "ritual oath"[26] was not revealed. Most certainly it contained a pledge of "absolute and unconditional fealty to the Fascist League of North America."[27] The Fascist was to be loyal to the Fascist cause and to the Fascist authorities who bestowed upon him the very high honor of terming himself a Fascist soldier.[28] In September 1927, secretary of labor in the Coolidge administration, Davis, expressed the opinion that whoever had taken the Fascist oath could not be a good American citizen, and he ordered an investigation of Fascist activities in the United States, "especially in regard to the presumed oath of blood."[29] The League hurriedly sent out an official protest that there existed no oath of blood and stated that the Fascist oath ran as follows:[30]

I swear upon my honor to serve with loyalty and discipline the Fascist Idea of Society based upon Religion, Nation and Family, and to promote respect for Law, Order and Hierarchy and for the Tradition of the Race.

To love, serve, obey and exalt the United States, its Constitution and Laws.

To keep alive the worship for Italy as our Fatherland and as the eternal light of civilization and greatness.

To fight with all my strength the doctrines and thoughts aiming at subverting, corrupting and disintegrating Religion, Love of Country and Family.

To make all efforts to better my culture and myself, physically and morally, so as to deserve to be among those who can serve and guide the

23. Ibid., March 1, 1925.
24. Ibid., Ocotober 1, 1929.
25. PIA, July 9, 1926.
26. Ibid., August 18, 28, September 17, 1928.
27. Ibid., November 21, 1928.
28. Ibid., August 8, 1928.
29. Ibid., September 25, 1927.
30. Ibid., September 25, 1928. [This oath is also printed in Diggins, *Mussolini and Fascism*, p. 92. Ed. Note]

Nation in its greatest moments.

To be disciplined under the leaders of the Fascist League of North America.

This formula represented a huge lie. In the book, *Atto di Fede* [Act of faith], published by Scilla di Glauca in 1937, the Fascist oath was the authentic one:

> In the name of God and of Italy, I swear to carry out the orders of my Duce and to serve with all my strength, and if necessary with my blood, the cause of the Fascist revolution.

On January 28, 1928, Mussolini announced the laws under which the Fascists abroad should live:

> Art. I. — The Fasci abroad unite in one organization the Italians living abroad, who have chosen as the rule for their civil and private life, obedience to the Duce and to the Fascist laws. They have the purpose of gathering around the Fascist emblem the Italian colonies in foreign countries.
> The Commandments drawn up by the Duce to serve as a guide for the everyday life of the Fascists abroad are:
> a) Fascists abroad must obey the laws of the country that gives them hospitality. They must give a daily example of this obedience even to the citizens.
> b) They must not take any part in the internal politics of the country that houses them.
> c) They must not be the cause of dissensions within the colonies, but rather must bring all its components under the Fascist emblem.
> d) They must be models of public and private integrity.
> e) They must respect the official representatives of Italy abroad, obey their directions and follow their instructions.
> f) They must defend Italianism, past and present.
> g) They must assist the Italians who are in need.
> h) They must keep discipline, as I exact and obtain discipline from the Italians at home.
> Art. II — The organs of the Fasci abroad are: 1) the General Secretariat located in Rome; 2) the Fasci abroad.
> Art. III — Each Fascio must organize a section of *Avanguardists*, a section of *Balillas* and a Women's section. The Fasci abroad are under the direct dependence of the General Secretary in Rome.
> Art. IV — The secretary of a "zone" is appointed directly by the General Secretary in Rome.
> Art. V — The secretary of each Fascio is appointed directly by the General Secretary in Rome.
> Art. VI — The first duty of the Fasci is the assistance of Italians abroad. The Secretary of each Fascio must keep in touch with the official representative of the Fascist State and cooperate with him in all measures to be taken in current affairs.
> Art. VII — The Secretary of each Fascio is directly responsible for its administration and must make each year a report to the General Secretary in Rome.

Art. VIII — Blanks and cards of registration are furnished by the
Secretariat General in Rome and badges are provided by the same.

Art. IX — A Fascio may be organized only upon authorization of the
Secretary General in Rome.

ARt. X — The disciplinary punishments are: a) Reprimand; b) Suspen-
sion either for a definite or for an indefinite period; c) Expulsion. No punish-
ment may be inflicted without notifying the party and giving him a hearing
All punishments must be approved by the Secretary General and cannot
be enforced without his ratification.

Art. XI — The General Secretary can inflict punishments directly on
those guilty of: a) causing dissensions within the Fasci or within the colony;
b) counteracting the orders of the consular authorities, or damaging their
prestige before the Italians and the foreigners.[31]

The first of the eight commandments ran: "Fascists abroad must obey the
laws of the country that gives them hospitality. They must give a daily
example of this obedience even to the citizens." If anyone feared that the
Fascists abroad might cause troubles, let him be reassured. The Duce had
spoken. Yet there was a chasm between the duty to obey the laws of a
democratic country like the United States and the dotting of the country
with organizations which carried on a noisy propaganda against the
fundamental principles of all democratic constitutions and hence against the
whole legal system of the United States. The truth of the matter was that the
first commandment had only one purpose, that of fooling the enemy, as the
Fascists called the countries where the Italians were living. Fascist doctrine
teaches that emigration of Italians to other than Italian lands is an evil, since
the emigrant, coming into contact in foreign lands with a civilization
different from his native one, soon becomes denationalized. He is lost to the
mother country not only in the flesh, but also in spirit. In the event of war,
he will have to take arms against the country of his origin. This enormity
must be stopped. Italy must no longer "lavish with culpable generosity her
demografic resources, either on young nations desirous to increase their
restricted man-power or on old nations desirous to reinforce their impover-
ished strength with young blood."[32]

In discussing the budget of foreign affairs in the lower house on March 31,
1927, Signor [Dino] Grandi (at that time under secretary of Foreign Affairs),
made the following declarations:

Emigration tends to diminish the strength of our race. We must have the

31. The regulations for the fasci abroad cited by Salvemini conform in their essential points
to the statement issued by the Fascist Grand Council in Rome on July 28, 1923. See Partito
Nazionale Fascista, *Il gran consiglio nei primi dieci anni dell'era fascista* (Rome, 1933), pp.
96-97. The test of the actual regulations reproduced by Salvemini is in *Opera Omnia di Benito
Mussolini*, ed. Edoardo and Duilio Susmel, 35 vols., XXIII (Florence, 1957), pp. 89-91, "Nuovo
statuto dei fasci all'estero." [Ed. Note]

32. Offical communique published by the Italian press on April 30, 1928.

boldness to assert that the emigration of our citizens to those countries which are not under direct Italian soverignity, is a danger. Those of our citizens, especially those of the lower classes, who are forced to live among other races, are inevitably and violently (!) assimilated with them. Why must our race continue to be a sort of human reservoir at the disposal of the other countries of the world? Why must our mothers continue to furnish soldiers for other nations?

The Fascist government consents to, nay favors, the expatriation of intellectuals, traders, professionals, and technical men, provided they are of Fascist sentiments, because they are "national pawns on the foreign chess board." For the same reason it favors also the expatriation of active Fascists, "politically fresher elements, even if economically inferior, which can take the place of elements politically less secure, but economically better."[33] When there are no political reasons to allow the expatriation, emigration is made difficult, and in many cases impossible or even prosecuted as a crime.

In January 1928, in an interview granted to the *Christian Science Monitor,* Mussolini was quoted as saying: "We are glad that our people in the United States become naturalized . . . The United States is the only country in which we encourage the Italians to become citizens." The oracle spoke again in the following month, March 1928. To a correspondent of the *New York Sun,*[34] who had asked several questions in writing, Mussolini handed a written statement in which it was said:

> The tendency which you say exists in the United States to believe that Italy considers Italian-born citizens as its own citizens with duties towards their mother country, is absolutely unfounded. In the Italian view, naturalized American citizens of Italian origin are from the civil and political point of view American citizens with all inherent duties and rights. Italy does not consider them as her own citizens, but as foreign citizens, to whom, however, she feels herself bound as much as they themselves feel bound to Italy, through a community of blood, tradition, religion and culture. Surely in this spiritual tie there is nothing to offend anyone's feelings.

In the same vein, Mussolini exhorted a delegation of the Sons of Italy to be "faithful to the United States, but remember Italy."[34A]

33. Signor [Andrea] Torre's report on the budget for foreign affairs, 1928-29. [The report referred to here by Salvemini is in *Atti parlamentari, Camera, Documenti,* XXVII, n. 1837-A. Ed. Note]

34. The interview cited here by Salvemini was actually given to Carrol Binder, Rome correspondent for the *Chicago Daily News* on March 14, 1928. See "Sugli oriundi italiani naturalizzati americani," *Opera Omnia di Benito Mussolini,* XXIII, pp. 124-125. On Italian policy regarding naturalization see also Gianpiero Carocci, *La politica estera dell'Italia fascista* (Bari, 1969), pp. 27, 322. [Ed. Note]

34A. *New York Times,* September 25, 1929. [On September 24, 1929 Mussolini received four hundred members of the Sons of Italy at Villa Torlonia in Rome, when he made the statement cited by Salvemini. See "A quattro cento 'Figli d'Italia' venuti dagli Stati Uniti d'America," *Opera Omnia di Benito Mussolini,* XXIV (Florence, 1958), p. 150. Ed. Note]

Viceversa, Piero Parini, who in January 1928 had become director of the bureau for Italians abroad in the Foreign Office, in his first message to the Fascist organizations in foreign countries, said:

> You must remain profoundly Italian and must kindle the sacred fire in the hearts of those in whom that fire has died out, because of their long contact with peoples of other races.

In the following article the same Parini expounded more in detail his thoughts:

> For Italy this problem is of the utmost importance, because there are ten million Italians scattered throughout the world and if they do not organize themselves for the defense of their nationality, within a few decades they will become foreign to Italy. The means employed by the States to denationalize the Italian settlers are formidable: They range from flattery to threats. Above all they make use of economic pressure. To resist such pressure it is necessary to create the spirit of solidarity among the Italians living abroad: they must present a united front. The name of those Italians who, to preserve their nationality, have renounced economic advantages, must be put in the list of honor, as soldiers who remained faithfully at their place of combat *in the face of the enemy* [italic ours].

Parini spoke of ten million Italians abroad. Among those ten million there were more than four million Italians of the United States. These also were to oppose a united front against their being assimilated by the country of adoption. They had to remain Italians from generation to generation, always foreigners in a country which, in fact, had become their own. Mussolini's own words were:

> My order is that an Italian citizen must remain an Italian citizen, no matter in what land he lives, even to the seventh generation.[35] I consider all Italians, in whatever part of the world to which their work takes them, as impassioned and faithful collaborators in the great work of Fascism for the prestige and the power of Italy.[36]

The review *Il Legionario*, published in Rome by the Fascist party for the fasci abroad wrote:

> With strenuous effort all the nations are preparing to face new events, so that we may say that another war is being deferred only by economic difficulties. It is essential that we organize ourselves in order to face a situation every day more perilous. Fascism abroad should organize to combat the first and most imminent problem, that of denationalization of our communities abroad and their division into scattered foreign groups. The

35. Quoted by Duffield, "Mussolini's American Empire," in *Harper's Magazine*, November 1929, p. 662.
36. XXXVI, p. 302.

United States is trying by every possible means to absorb them. If Italian communities in foreign lands are not defended, we shall soon see ten million Italians lost to the mother country.[37]

In September 1928, Parini "made it a duty in all foreign countries for the Fascists to wear the emblem of the Party," and proclaimed that those Fascists abroad who sent their sons not to the Italian schools, but to the French, English, German or Spanish schools, were traitors.[38]

The same system which existed in Italy existed also in America. There was a dual hierarchy, that of the officials of the government, and that of the officials of the Fascist party. Ambassadors, consuls and consular agents, as official representatives of the Italian government, were bound by rules of diplomatic behavior. The secretaries of the fasci, although also representatives of the Fascist regime, had no diplomatic character, and were free to carry on activities forbidden to the former. The abnormal situation of the fasci in America and in all foreign countries, consisted precisely in the fact that, according to the law of the countries where the fasci were established, they were only private associations, whereas according to the Italian law they were organs of the Fascist regime. Their highest officials were all appointed by Rome, their constitutions were dictated by the head of the Italian government, and they had as their basic duty, "obedience to the Duce and to the Fascist law."

The appeal to join the fasci was made to all Italians living abroad. No difference was made between those who had retained Italian citizenship and those who become naturalized. Both classes were represented in the fasci from the very beginning. In not a few cases, the leaders and the officers themselves were Italians who had renounced their allegiance to the Italian king and to its government, and had assumed American citizenship.

The character of the fasci was emphasized by the statutory obligation to receive and carry out the orders given either through the secretariat general of Rome, or through the diplomatic representatives of Italy. This duty of obedience was stressed as the most important of all. In the report of the committee on the budget laid before the Italian parliament for the year 1929-30, it was said:

> In the same way that the Secretary General of the Fascist Party in each Italian province is the direct co-operator of the Prefect, so the Secretary of a Fascio abroad is the faithful and blind co-operator of the Ambassador and the Consul. His devotion and obedience must be even more absolute, because if it is conceivable that a limited freedom of action may be allowed

37. Quoted by Duffield, p. 664.
38. Gio., September 1, 1928.

in some cases to subordinates in Italy, abroad on the contrary, individual will must give way to the will of all, and this must be uniform even to
excess.

"The will of all" was the will of the secretary general in Rome, or of the
Italian representatives abroad.

To sum everything up, the Fascist League of North America was an
American organization, incorporated under the laws of the State of New
York. But the consul was to be "the real head of the Fascio according to the
Duce's commandment,"[39] and the officers of the League, either sent from
Rome or appointed by the consul, were to be responsible to him, who in his
turn was responsible to Rome. The president of the League, its treasurer and
its secretary were all members of the Fascist party in Italy. As such, they had
taken the Fascist oath of personal allegiance to Mussolini.

We may now begin to understand what Mussolini meant when he was
advising the Italo-American Fascists to be loyal to America, and what the
Fascists mean when they advise people of Italian origin to become "good
Americans."

Whoever believes in the doctrine of democracy, whatever his European
origin, can be a rightful member of the North American democratic
community while keeping alive in his heart a legitimate affection for the
land of his ancestors. The English remain attached to England, the Irish to
Ireland, and so on, [as with] all the other groups which make up the North
American nation. Even if Italy or Germany or France have gone totalitarian,
the citizen of democratic America is allowed to go on loving the people from
which he came. But only on the condition that he bear in mind that if, in his
oath of citizenship, he never renounced his love for the people from whom
he came, he did renounce any allegiance and fidelity "to any foreign Prince,
Potentate, State or Sovereignty." This is what the Fascist (or the Nazi)
cannot grasp. Until 1922, one was able to feel Italian and at the same time
Catholic, anti-Catholic, conservative, democratic, monarchic, hostile to
royalty, socialist, communist, anarchist and what not. After 1922, as we
said a little while ago, the Fascist party became Italy, and the term Italianism
came to mean Fascism, and any anti-Fascist was a trator to Italy, or at least
a bastard. Many innocent people swallowed this deceit hook, line and
sinker. They were patriots who were unable to disentangle one from the
other the notions of nation, state, government, and party in power. Not
only Italians, but people of all countries find it difficult to proceed to such a
discrimination, especially when they are abroad. Many Frenchmen today
feel duty bound to remain loyal to the Vichy government, or at least do not

39. XXVII, p. 395.

give vent to their grievances against it, because it is the government of France. The Fascists exploited to the full this prejudice, which led many Italians outside Italy to make one and the same thing of the Fascist government and the Italian nation, as if the Italian nation had not existed before Mussolini and would vanish when he is gone.

What, then, does the Fascist mean when he maintains that Lincoln and Mussolini are twin brothers and that Fascism and American democracy are one and the same thing? He means that the democratic constitution of the United States grants the citizen the right to scorn, undermine, and overthrow the democratic constitution of the United States. An American is entitled by the constitution to be a Fascist and to maintain that the only good Americans are those who are persuaded that America will become good only when she adopts Fascist institutions. Thus if one has to be a good American he has to become a Fascist. Mrs. Rose Marrow Previtali wrote in *Carroccio:*[40]

> Ye Gods! How we do need Fascism in America!. . . So great is my faith in our American education, that let the idea of Fascism once take hold of the youth of the country, the flame will be stronger and brighter than that which first showed the way in Italy. . . When America will have Fascism, then there will be true American Liberalism.

When the Fascist advised the Italian born guest to become an American citizen, he means that the citizen must remain loyal to the Fascist government of Italy even after he has gone through that silly procedure which, before he becomes an American citizen, forces him to answer a certain number of insignificant questions and take an insignificant oath. And when he has become an American citizen, he has to work for the importation of Fascism into America, and above all he must remain loyal to Italy, that is to say, to Fascism and his Duce, and as such he has to work in the United States.

An authority on Italian affairs, Professor Arthur Livingston of Columbia, in an article on "Italo-American Fascism" in the *Survey Graphic* of March 1927, p. 750, wrote:

> Recognizing the growth of American sentiment among Italo-Americans, Fascist propaganda favors "Americanization" of the immigrant on the theory that as a participant in the political life of the new country he will be better able to defend the interests, policies and ideals *of his real country* [italics ours]. In America, and to Americans this is represented as a step towards "international understanding" and "world peace." However, Fascists in Italy understand the mutuality in a onesided sense. While great applause is bestowed on such enterprises as the House of Italian Culture at Columbia University [Casa Italiana] and the Italy-America Society in New York, Fascists have to exercise great restraint to tolerate the Methodist

40. XXII, p. 201.

Missions in Rome and the Italian establishments of the Y.M.C.A.,[41] while a unisonous press is loud in its denunciation of America and everything that smacks of American influence. Even in America, the "pinks" take little stock in "international understanding." Their leading intellectuals make habitual and much coddled boast of their contempt for things American, and of the purely practical nature of their residence here.

By "pinks" Livingston meant "Italian transients, recently arrived immigrants, representatives of Italian firms, businessmen with interests in Italy, a few 'intellectuals' of higher grade, a few non-Italian 'lovers of Italy,' and a certain number of wealthy Italo-Americans...Accepting the Fascist dogma that Italy is Fascism and that Fascism is the Fascist regime, many of the 'pinks' consider themselves the appointed bishops of the Fascist religion in this country...These individuals constitute a nucleus of active and self-conscious Fascist propaganda in this country."

In 1933, Mario Orsini Ratto, who had acted as Italian consul in Baltimore and in Philadelphia, published a book *L'Avvenire degli Italo-Americani* [The Future of the Italo-Americans].[42] In it we read:

Thanks to the Italo-Americans, Italy has been able to lay the demands of Fascism before the United States in a much more favorable light. Obviously the Italian policy of advising the emigrants to keep Italian citizenship as long as possible has been forced to give way in North America to the necessity for Americanization. But we have gotten in exchange other advantages. And we can develop these advantages if we inject into the Italo-American masses the habit and need for returning from time to time to the Fatherland...Italo-American citizens remain in constant touch with the diplomatic and consular authorities, and the latter pay special attention to them. Italo-Americans can, in a ten-year period of serious organization, become a formidable electoral and financial force and offer unprecedented opportunities for intellectual and economic influence...The masses of emigrants have a strongly American mentality, but they are sensitive to the honors, encouragements and provisions which the Italian Government devises in their favor.

Fascist policies in the matter of Americanization have always been based on cunning and deception.

41. The YMCA was banned in 1938; the Methodist Missions, especially after the Concordat of 1929, have been in all ways hampered, notwithstanding the abject servility of their ministers.
42. Milan, Istituto Fascista di Cultura, 1933.

6

The Disbanding of the League

Nineteen twenty-nine opened with events which gave the Fascists of New York and of the United States, at large, grounds for expecting further and more sparkling triumphs.

On January 3, Italo Balbo was solemnly received in the New York City Hall. The committee which organized the ceremony had as its honorary chairmen the Italian ambassador, the governor of the State of New York, Franklin D. Roosevelt, and the mayor of New York City, James Walker. Mr. Roosevelt, most likely, had never heard anything about Italian affairs and only meant to extend American hospitality to a high Italian official personage and well known aviator. Mayor Walker knew about Italy and Fascism what he had learned in 1927 when Mussolini bestowed a high decoration upon him,[1] and when he went to Italy and was received there as if he were the emperor of the United States.[2] But the Italian ambassador knew quite well

---

1. PIA, June 22, 1927.
2. XXVI, pp. 177, 255. [Walker visited Rome in September 1927 and had a half-hour interview with Mussolini; in July 1933 he passed through Rome a second time but did not see the dictator.

that as far as the Italians in the United States were concerned, Balbo's reception was to be regarded as a Fascist demonstration, and the same holds true for those other Italian gentlemen who formed the executive committee for the reception. They were the Italian consul general: Thaon di Revel; Judge Francis X. Mancuso; Garofalo and Bonaschi.

This executive committee surrounded itself with a general committee of 180 persons who were enumerated by *Il Progresso*.[3] Since its is probable that a part of these persons gave their names for the same reasons as Governor Roosevelt, or for vague patriotic sentiments which could not be defined as Fascist, it is not the case to give all their names here. But those who represented associations on the general committee are worth being recorded, because it is probable that among these associations there may be some Fascist transmission belts which we have not yet come across in our survey.

1. Dr. Mario Abbene, Italian Medical Association, Brooklyn. 2. Luigi Barzini, chief editor of the Fascist daily, *Corriere d'America*. 3. L. Berizzi, Victor Emanuel III Foundation. 4. Velino Carradini, Fascist Longshoremen League. 5. Vito Contessa, Legion of Sons of Columbus. 6. Rocco Cortese, Federation of Apulian Associations. 7. Mario Cosenza, Italian Teachers' Association. 8. Dr. A. G. De Sanctis, Italian Medical Association of New York. 9. G. Di Silvestro, Order of Sons of Italy, National Executive Council. 10. A. Facchetti-Guiglia, Tiro a Segno Nazionale. 11. I. Falbo, Dante Alighieri Society and Fascist daily *Progresso Italo-Americano*. 12. Favoino di Giura, Fascist review *Vittoriale*. 13. F. M. Ferrari, Italian Hospital. 14. Judge J. J. Freschi, Order of Sons of Italy, New York State. 15. A. Giannini, Italian Chamber of Commerce. 16. V. Giordano, Fascist daily *Bollettino della sera*. 17. T. Giurato, press bureau of the Fascist League of North America. 18. R. Ingargiola, Independent Order of Sons of Italy, New York State. 19. A. Macaluso, Fascist review *Giovinezza*. 20. P. Margarella, Italian Child Welfare. 21. V. Martinez, War Maimed Men Association. 22. Angelo Pacelli, Italian Barbers Association. 23. Lionello Perera, Italian Red Cross. 24. Dr. A. Pisani, Italian Educational League. 25. G. Pope, Fascist daily *Progresso Italo-Americano*. 26. G. Previtali, Italian Historical Society. 27. Felice Rossetti, Italian Sports Union. 28. Dr. F. Trapani, Independent Order of Sons of Italy. National Executive Council. 29. V. Vedovi, Italian War Veteran Association.

Of the twenty-nine persons enumerated above, twenty-two are shown to be fullfledged Fascists or fellow-travelers by other sources. To these must be added Perera (no. 23), shareholder of *Carroccio*,[4] who would

See Gene Fowler, *Beau James: The Life and Times of Walker* (New York, 1949), pp. 203-204, 342. Ed. Note]
3. PIA, January 1, 1929.
4. XXX, p. 371.

never have been chosen as representative of the Italian Red Cross by the government of Mussolini, nor would he have been accepted as one of the directors of the Italcable,[5] had he not been a man of unquestionable Fascist faith; and Felice Rossetti (or Rosset) director of the two Fascist transmission belts. For only five persons (nos. 1, 5, 8, 22, 24) is definite information lacking.

A few weeks after the reception in Balbo's honor, Piero Parini, director of the bureau of Italians abroad and director general of the Italian schools abroad at the Rome Foreign Office, arrived from Italy. He was received at the New York pier by "a large group of Fascists" who gave him an "enthusiastic demonstration" with the Roman salute and cries of *alalà*. *Giovinezza*,[7] in giving this information, asserts that Parini had come to study American cultural institutions and to arrange with these institutions for the exchange of students between America and Italy. "Our enemies would want to make it appear that Parini came to America in his capacity of Secretary General of the Fasci Abroad, to give orders to the Fascist League of North America. Any such attempt is so ridiculous that it isn't worth denying." The Italian Fascists in America were dependent "solely" upon the leaders of the League, and they only obeyed orders which came down "directly" from such leaders. Their "autonomy was made necessary by the environment in which they lived, and was the best available method for gathering under one single institution, the Fascist League of North America, all Italians in America, whether citizens of Italy or of the U.S.A." But they "felt spiritually united in common ideal and faith, with the comrades of the Italian Fascist Party," and, therefore, they regarded "the directions given by Parini, who faithfully interpreted the thought of the Duce for the Italians living abroad, as a magnificient beacon whose clear light shined afar." In other words, the Fascist organizations of North America were autonomous from the Fascist party in Italy, but Mussolini gave the directions for the Italians living abroad. Parini interpreted those directions, and the leaders of the autonomous league of North America handed over those directions to its dependent organizations. Autonomy was a meaningless word. The fact was that Parini *was* director of the bureau of Italians abroad, and director general of the Italians schools abroad, and that it would have been strange indeed if, in the United States, he had limited himself to studying the educational institutions of the country, and had abstained from imparting any orders to the leaders of the Italian Fascist institutions. *Carroccio*[8] explicitly stated that Parini had come "to examine *de visu* the Fascist

5. XIX, p. 587; XXVI, p. 378.
6. IAW.
7. February 1, 1929.
8. XIX, p. 128.

organizations."

Parini made his first visit to the headquarters of the Fascist League of North America. From New York he went to Boston, accompanied by Di Silvestro. When he returned to New York "he was given an enthusiastic welcome" in a reception held in his honor at the headquarters of the Fascio Benito Mussolini of New York. In the reception participated the representatives of several other fasci of New York and neighboring cities. Thaon di Revel spoke, presenting Mrs. Terruzzi, wife of the chief of the general staff of the Fascist militia, "American by birth, Italian by sentiment," and he rehashed the formula which by now had become official, according to which "the Fasci of America will be autonomous under the jurisdiction of the leaders of the League, but will be spiritually united to the regime, which will always bestow its moral protection upon them."[9] Parini also visited the Fascio Margherita di Savoia and the orphanage of the Order of the Sons of Italy at Nutley, New Jersey where he was received to the strains of "Giovinezza."[10]

While he was in New York the honorary title of deputy sheriff of New York County was bestowed upon Thaon di Revel by his friends in Tammany. The decree of nomination was granted him at a dinner given by Generoso Pope for his "very dear friend."[11]

When Parini left, "a crowd of Italians and Italo-Americans, and the representatives of the Fasci" were at the pier to bid him good-bye.[12]

If we gather together the names of the persons who a) went to greet Parini at the pier, b) took part in the dinner given in his honor by Pope, and c) went to see him off, we have the following list with the applicable letter:

1. Barra, b; 2. L. Barzini, b, c; 3. T. Bernabei, b; 4. Billi, a; 5. Bruno, b; 6. Canali, c; 7. Comito, a; 8. G. Cosulich, c; 9. Judge Cotillo, b; 10. De Bosis, a; 11. De Cellis, a; 12. De Ritis, c; 13. Di Silvestro, a, c; 14. Facchetti-Guiglia, b; 15. Countess Facchetti-Guiglia, a, c; 16. Falbo, b, c; 17. Favoino di Giura, c; 18. F. M. Ferrari, b; 19. Judge Freschi, b, c; 20. Gallo, b; 21. Garofalo, c; 22. Gentile, b; 23, 23. Gerli, b; 24. V. Giordano, a, c; 25. Giurato, b, c; 26. A. F. Guidi, c; 27. Konta, b; 28. Macaluso, b, c; 29. Malnati, b, c; 30. Judge Mancuso, b; 31. Martinez, c; 32. Palermi, b, c; 33. G. Paterno, b, c; 34. Judge Pecora, b; 35. Previtali, b; 36. Antonio Quintieri, c; 37. Rubino, b; 38. Thaon di Revel, c; 39. Dr. Tomarkin, a; 40. Trombetta, a, c; 41. Ferruccio Vecchi; 42. Judge Vitali, c; 43. Zinito, c.

Among the persons enumerated above, De Bosis (no. 10) was already undergoing that moral crisis that was to make of him one of the heroes

9. PIA, February 8, 1929.
10. Gio., February 15, 1929.
11. PIA, January 23, 1929.
12. Ibid., February 10, 1929; Gio., February 15, 1929.

in the fight for Italian freedom; at that moment he was there as a full-fledged Fascist. Barra (no. 1) was a tenor by trade, Rubino (no. 36) was a music teacher; political opinions of musicians have no importance since they change with the changing wind, unless they are men of exceptional intellectual and moral fiber, like Arturo Toscanini. The family name Bruno (no. 5) is so common that without knowing the personal name it is impossible to determine whether it belongs to Dr. J. F. Bruno, a full-fledged Fascist[13] who in 1929 was secretary of the Association of Italian Physicians of Brooklyn.[14] Cosulich (no. 8) would not have been director of the Italian line, and he would not have received a decoration from Mussolini[15] if he had not been a loyal Fascist. The family name Gallo (no. 20) is even more common than the family name Bruno, and therefore we cannot be sure in this case whether it belongs to Fortunato Gallo, shareholder of *Carroccio*[16] who was decorated and received in audience by Mussolini in 1926.[17] For the family name Gentile we find the same difficulty. Konta (no. 27) without doubt is Commander Alexander Konta, who would not have been appointed consul general of the Republic of San Marino,[18] had he not been a loyal Fascist. Malnati (no. 29) is without doubt the director of the Biltmore Hotel, decorated twice by Mussolini, the first time in 1923,[19] and the second time in 1931.[20] Quintieri (no. 36) was decorated by *Grido della Stirpe*[20A] with the title of comrade, and this shows that he was a full-fledged Fascist. Ferruccio Vecchi (no. 41) was one of the most notorious Italian Fascists, a man capable of any crime whatsoever. Bruno Zinito (no. 43) was a shareholder of *Carroccio*[21] and one of the directors of the Italian Welfare League.[22] We do not know what Dr. Tomarkin (no. 39) was doing in that company because there is no evidence that he ever had Fascist inclination. The same question must be asked for Judge Vitali (no. 41) and for Judge Pecora (no. 34). Probably the latter attended the dinner at the home of Generoso Pope as a personal friend of Pope. In any case, these judges should have understood that their names printed in the Italian newspapers along with those of other judges who, if not full-fledged Fascists, were certainly fellow-travelers, and with the names of the leaders of the Fascist League of North America, would give the Italian public the impression that too many judges in New York were under Mussolini's thumb. A finer sense of their responsibility would have only lost them an invitation to dinner from Pope or a handshake from Parini. T. Bernabei (no. 3) is unknown to us, unless he is Erasmo Bernabei, shareholder of *Il Carroccio*.[23]

13. PIA, April 28, 1926.
14. XXX, p. 450.
15. XXXV, p. 256.
16. XXX, p. 371.
17. XXIII, p. 251.
18. XXXII, p. 243.
19. XVII, p. 389.
20. XXXIV, p. 80.
20A. August 22, 1936.
21. XXX, p. 371.
22. XXXII, p. 323.
23. XXX, p. 371.

> To sum up everything, if we exclude from the forty-three persons who
> attended the meetings in honor of Parini those for whom we have no sure
> proof to label them full-fledged Fascists or fellow-travelers, we find that
> thirty-two certainly belong to one of these two categories.

While Parini was in the United States, Mussolini, on January 28, 1929,
established a National Foundation for the Sons of the Lictor, more commonly
termed the Lictor Foundation. Its aim was "to give physical and spiritual
assistance to the sons of Italians abroad" and "to save and revive in them
Italianism." One can affirm without running the risk of being wrong, that
the new institution had been decided upon before Parini left for the United
States to bring instructions concerning the setting up of the new machine.

In the April 11, 1929 issue of *Popolo d'Italia*, Arnaldo Mussolini, the
Duce's brother, under the caption "National Defense," minced no words in
stressing the urgent need of saving the children of the Italian immigrants in
any country from being assimilated by the local population. Italy's right and
duty to look after her national defense could be expected and fulfilled only
by having those children brought up as Italian Fascists, no matter where
they happened to live:

> Ten million Italians live in foreign lands. This is another national
> community scattered in the farthest regions of the world. This is a second
> national community which has a sacred duty to accomplish; that of pre-
> serving the soul and the national character of the coming generations in
> such a way that the Fatherland should not be defrauded of so many
> precious energies and that the sons of the Italians abroad should be brought
> up to feel, to think, to love, to act and to hope as do the sons of the Italians
> at home. . . Young people are the prey sought by preference by the nations
> eager to assimilate foreigners. They are easily denationalized. The en-
> vironment often twists by violence the character, the tendencies, and the
> education of young people who have lost contact with the national soul
> and who do not have the consciousness of the bond that ties them to the
> national soul. Italians abroad have to endure a great struggle, and in certain
> countries this struggle assumes the tragic form of a combat between giants
> and pigmies. . . The guardianship of young Italians abroad is a matter of
> greater importance than any function of protection or assistance of our
> emigrants: it is a measure of national defense. . . The sons of Italians abroad
> must be trained to feel that their material absence from their country of
> origin has no importance; they must feel to be not only spiritually, but
> almost physically united to and included in the great national family.
> This is the aim of the Lictor Foundation. . . The stubborn efforts and the
> brutality by which, through various ways and means, foreigners try to
> absorb the masses of our citizens and to obliterate even by changing their
> family names, all traces of their Italian origins, ought to awaken the Italians
> to the danger to which our youth abroad is exposed and to the worth of
> safeguarding their attachment to the Fatherland. Great, endless and ever
> present is the ambush: just as great and more efficient must be the defense.

In May, a message of the secretary general of the Fascist party was still more heroic than the grandiloquent appeal of the Duce's brother. He began by remarking that "we of the older generation" have accomplished the miracle of the Fascist revolution, "an event of an ideal beauty never tarnished by human weakness." The children would have the fortune to see "in all its splendor the greatness and the power of this country of ours which we have loved and served in the heroic period of the battle."

This preamble was followed by an eloquent peroration:

> All these things must be told to the Italian children and especially to the children who live abroad, because on them all shall fall the duty of carrying still higher the flag which one day we shall entrust to their hands. They must understand that March twenty-third 1919 [date of the foundation of foundation of the first fascio in Milan by Mussolini] marked the day when the Italian Fatherland ceased to be the nursery of immigrants for the whole world and became again the mother of pioneers of all civilizations . . The children living abroad must understand that if today they can feel the incomparable pride of being Italians, this was made possible by the Fascist Revolution which gave to Italy ideal and political greatness that now marches forward through the ways of the whole world.

The secretary of the League in the United States, in issuing the above documents, added an encyclical letter of his own in which he stated that "the Lictor Foundation which has in Rome its headquarters, carries out its aims by providing institutions for the education of Italian children and children of Italian origin living abroad, through summer colonies, scholarships and all other means of assistance in order to preserve and to revive among them the memory of the country of origin." He ended with an urgent appeal addressed to all Italians in the United States for cash contributions to the great work of "national defense" inaugurated by the Lictor Foundation.[24]

Meanwhile the Lateran Agreements between Pius XI and Mussolini had made of the Catholic clergy in America, no matter what its tongue, an orchestra glorifying Mussolini. The pilgrims who went to visit Italy, returned relating marvelous stories of what they had or had not seen. Nineteen twenty-nine may be considered as the triumphal year for Fascism in the United States.

All of a sudden, the structure which had seemed so promising broke down. In its issue of November 1929, *Harper's Magazine* published an article under the title of "Mussolini's American Empire: The Fascist Invasion of the United States." The author, Mr. Marcus Duffield, stated that "il Duce had set up a political organization in the United States which resembled an unofficial government of his own to claim the allegiance of Italo-Americans

24. XXIX, p. 374, ff.

and enforce their obedience." He described the inaugural meeting of the
Fascio D'Ambrosoli in Brooklyn in the following terms:

> Dr. Giuseppe Previtali, a Columbia University professor presided in the
> absence of Count di Revel, who was on one of his periodical trips to Rome
> to report to Mussolini. When Dr. Previtali entered, the members, standing,
> gave the Fascist salute, upraised arm, palm forward, and their chant "Mus-
> solini: Eja! Eja! Alalà!" After the ruling triumvirate was installed the group
> sang "Giovinezza" and other Fascist anthems, and then dispatched this
> cablegram to Mussolini: "Inauguration with great manifestation of enthu-
> siasm new section D'Ambrosoli, Brooklyn. Beg your Excellency, founder
> of the fortune of our country, to accept our devotion and homage." The
> initiates then took the oath at the tribune, received their membership cards,
> and walked backward to their seats, saluting.

Mussolini's American empire late in 1927 had established a rudimentary
judicial system:

> The newspaper *Il Grido della Stirpe* which calls itself "organ of Fascist
> Propaganda," announced the formation of a *Corte di disciplina*, officially
> authorized by the executive committee of the League. The Court was de-
> signed after the fashion of the special military tribune in Italy, for the
> purpose of *preserving rigid discipline among the Fascists here and to mete
> out exemplary punishments.* A Captain Martinez, formerly a military
> tribunal judge in Italy, drew up its rules and has presided over its sessions.
> The various Fasci handle their own minor infractions of discipline, with
> the triumvirate sitting as a court, sometimes joined by one of the judges
> sent out from the central court. Suspension or expulsion from the Fascist
> League is the commonest form of punishment imposed by these courts;
> but for more grave offenses there are penalties of corresponding severity.
> Confiscation of property, revocation of Italian citizenship and boycott lie
> in store for him who turns anti-Fascist, for he is a traitor. The League ipso
> facto penalizes any of its members who become naturalized citizens by
> taking away their rights and privileges as members of the Fascist organiza-
> tion in Italy. This may constitute a deprivation of no mean significance, for
> without the magic membership card, Italo-Americans travelling in Italy or
> transacting business there, are likely to find their way beset by innumerable
> difficulties... When Rudolph Valentino took out first citizenship papers
> the Fascists were indignant, and threatened to boycott his films in Italy, but
> when he did, they claimed him.

Mr. Duffield found great difficulty in gathering evidence because of the
fact that the Fascist league was going "to extremes which were quite
undreamed of by most Americans."

> With a few exceptions, Italians blacklisted by the Fascists are afraid to
> speak lest they suffer reprisals. Their questioner might be a Fascist spy; their
> names may appear in print. They have learned that it is dangerous to
> criticize Mussolini in this country even in the banks where they cash their
> pay checks or in their restaurants. Only by the patient building up of con-
> fidence can they be induced to tell the stories of persecution that reveal the

methods only too suggestive of despotic terrorism with which the Fascist League is crushing Italian opponents in America.

Yet even under such difficult circumstances, Mr. Duffield gathered enough evidence to reach the following conclusions:

> The first and most powerful weapon of the Fascists here is economic. Put boldly, they know that they can silence most of their foes if they can starve them. Most Italo-American firms do part of their business in Italy, notably the banks, importers, steamship lines and a few manufacturers. Unless they are obedient to Mussolini, their business in Italy will promptly be ruined, since Il Duce has industry under his thumb. The Italian Chamber of Commerce in New York City is, and obviously had to be, pro-Fascist. These Italian firms in America are perforce subject to the orders of the Fascists. This makes possible the employment of both the boycott and the lock-out against critics of the regime . . . When their opponents cannot be reached by business pressure, the Fascists have found an equally effective and even more vicious weapon in the intimidation of relatives in Italy of anti-Fascists here.

The issue of the magazine was put into circulation during the last of the decade, October 1929. The reaction of American opinion was quick and strong. The press spoke of an investigation which the State Department was supposed to have made into the activities of the embassy, the consulates, and other Fascist authorities in American territory.[25]

The Italian ambassador, De Martino, had taken part in infinite Fascist demonstrations, ceremonies, dinners, etc., and had delivered in them an infinite number of addresses in glorification of Mussolini and the Fascist regime. "The National Government" — wrote the *Progresso Italo-Americano*[26] — had had in him an authoritative and efficient propagandist, who had not confined himself to his delicate and high office of plenipotentiary to the Government of the United States." On October 28, De Martino flatly asserted that Mussolini had never demanded fealty from Italian emigrants.[27] Then on November 26, in an address given in Philadelphia, he said:

> Let us consider in what consists this formidable Fascist Italian organization in the United States. First of all, it is not an Italian but an American organization, or if you wish, an Italo-American organization, incorporated in New York according to American laws. We have always considered it as an autonomous organization. If sometimes we had to take an interest in it, it was only to prevent excesses of zeal which could have made room for misunderstandings. This organization is formed mostly of young people, noisy and filled with enthusiasm, but having little capacity for discernment . . . They are few and they have no large following in public

25. On the impact of Duffield's article see Diggins, *Mussolini and Fascism*, p. 93 [Ed. Note]
26. December 23, 1928.
27. *New York Times*, October 28, 1929.

opinion, because of the make-up of the organization. I may well recognize that these good boys sometimes have made mistakes, carried away by too much zeal, but really, I cannot believe that any American could see in the little work done by the Fascist League of North America a menace to the institutions of this country.

An ambassador is a gentleman who lies abroad in the service of his own government. It was ridiculous to affirm that the league was an autonomous body and at the same time to admit that the embassy had taken an interest in its activities. If the League consisted of noisy young men having little capacity for discernment, why had the ambassador participated in and delivered speeches at so many of its ceremonies and demonstrations? It was dishonest to term as American an organization, the president and the treasurer of which were Italian citizens, and whose secretary, Canali, had been "sent from Rome and was paid monthly by the public treasury of the Italian State, was an agent of the Italian Foreign Office, and received and carried out orders from Minister Grandi and from the Director of the Bureau of Italians Abroad."[28] Thaon di Revel himself admitted that among the League's members "the percentage of American citizens ranged from about fifty in New York to one hundred in smaller communities."[29] Thus, about fifty percent in New York were still Italian citizens.

The campaign against the League in the American press went on. As a consequence, on December 23, 1924, Thaon di Revel announced to the leaders of the League that the League "had fully carried out the aims which it had set for itself" and proposed that it disband. The meeting naturally approved the proposal unanimously and decided that "as a symbol of the devotion of the League to the Fascist ideal, the banners and the history of each Fascio in America should be sent to the Historical Museum of Fascism in Rome."[30] A few days later, Secretary Stimson announced that the investigation on the activities of the embassy and the consulates had revealed no reprehensible activities.[31] A government which announces publicly that it has made an investigation of the activities of an ambassador, certainly pays him a peculiar compliment. But De Martino was happy to have obtained a clean bill, and the State Department was happy to be able to tell the country that the Fascist League of North America no longer existed. And the leaders of the Fascist League of North America were happy to have had no worse trouble than to disband.

What was the number of Fascists in the United States from 1923 to 1929?

28. XXX, p. 300.
29. New York Times, December 23, 1929.
30. PIA, December 23, 1929.
31. New York Times, December 28, 1929.

At the beginning of 1923 the Fascists claimed to have twenty thousand members in their organizations, to the great dismay of Judge Cotillo, who took such humbug seriously.[32] In September 1926, Thaon di Revel claimed "about seven thousand" members, grouped into forty-seven branches mostly east of the Mississippi River, eighteen of which were in New Jersey. But he judiciously added that "members do not seem to be the only index of its influence, for the League seems to be largely composed of Key men." He estimated that in this country, of the population of Italian origin "fully 70 percent were admirers of Mussolini," "another 10 percent were eager advocates of the ideas of the Duce, veritable partisans"; and there was "another 20 percent who were rather indifferent" but who "might be enlightened by a campaign of education." "In the 20 percent are included also persons of recalcitrant or of extreme ideas, who could not number more than fifty thousand in all."[33] In August 1927, Thaon di Revel announced that the League had "about one hundred branches" with fifteen thousand members, but he considered "the quality more important than the quantity."[34] In the same month, the League announced that the branches of Brooklyn "comprised in all about five thousand members, but the sympathizers and admirers of the Fascist regime numbered hundreds of thousands among the Italians of that Borough and the entire Metropolitan area."[35] In November of that same year, Thaon di Revel announced that the membership was "from twelve to fifteen thousand," and he raised his estimate of Italians in the United States who were in favor of Fascism to 90 percent: "every Italian daily is for Fascism; every merchant and industrialist of a certain importance, every professional man, intellectual, scientist or educator is in favor of Fascism."[36] A few days later the sections of the League were always "about one hundred" as they had been the preceding August, and the "enrolled members" were twenty thousand but the "holders of Fascist membership cards were twelve thousand.[37] We do not understand the difference between enrolled members and holders of the Fascist card, unless the latter were those who had taken the oath of fealty, whereas the former were merely the catechumens. In April 1928, the number of the branches were precisely ninety-four,[38] and this number remained more or less unchanged in the following months.[39]

32. PIA, March 26, 1923.
33. *New York Herald Tribune*, September 5, 1926; Gio., October 28, 1926.
34. Gio., August 15, 1927.
35. PIA, August 6, 1927.
36. Ibid., November 16, 1927.
37. Gio., December 1, 1927.
38. PIA, August 15, 1928.
39. Ibid., August 9, October 28, 30, 1928.

In December 1929 the branches numbered eighty-seven,[39A] and Thaon di Revel stated that the membership had amounted to six thousand in 1926, to between nine and ten thousand in 1927 and to about twelve thousand by the end of 1929.[40] God only knows what faith we can put in these figures. Even the three hundred thousand Sons of Italy offered in November 1922 by Di Silvestro to Mussolini were no more than one hundred fifty thousand, and they continued to be three hundred thousand in 1926, except to go back again to one hundred fifty thousand in a legal document of 1927.[41] No one ever saw those "approximately thirty thousand" war maimed veterans who, according to Martinez, in 1926 were in the process of organizing with the support of the League.[42] Statistics are instruments of class war for the Communists and instruments of nationalistic bluff for the Fascists.

Fascist penetration in the Italian communities up until the end of 1929 was not very extensive. In April 1930, De Biasi described the results of Fascist action in the following terms: "At every step where one calls himself a Fascist, another jumps up proclaiming himself an anti-Fascist, and against the pair of them arise eight who say that we are in America and the political quarrels of Italy have no place here." De Biasi questioned the right of those eight to count because they were "men of no faith, lacking in courage, reeds that bend in the wind."[43] But he admitted that they numbered eight out of ten. And this is what is important to notice.

39A. Ibid., December 23, 1929.
40. *New York Times*, December 23, 1929.
41. PIA, May 18, 1927.
42. Ibid., May 30, 1926.
43. XXXI, p. 233.

7

The Lictor Federation

The Institute of Living Law (340 Woodward Building, Washington, District of Columbia), in studying the devices by which foreign agents carry on their work in this country, has noticed that one of the commonest and handiest tricks they make use of for obscuring their own identity is to do business first under one corporate or associate name until it has been discredited in the eyes of the public, then to close shop and open up shortly thereafter under a new corporate name. The Fascists have repeatedly made use of this device with great success.

In December 1929, the central headquarters of the Fascist League of North America in New York ceased to exist. But merely a wrong method had been discarded in favor of a more suitable, or would-be more suitable, method of attack.

As soon as the disbanding of the League was announced, Trombetta, in the December 28, 1929, issue of his *Grido della Stirpe*, published an article under the title "Let Us Return to Our Origins" *(Ritorniamo alle origini):*

Those who should grieve over this happening are precisely our enemies. These gentlemen will realize now that the really annoying Fascism was not that of the "Fascist League." The latter operated as a brake. From now onwards single Fascists and single groups will act individually, will be responsible to no superior authorities. From now onwards Fascism will be able to defend itself and attack its foes with words, with the Press and, if necessary, with blows. Who can forbid us in America to express and to further our ideas by all means allowed us by the laws of the land?... Now we are free to speak more clearly, assuming our own responsibility. Sometimes, when needed, we shall be able to break a few skulls. We alone will answer for our actions before the laws of this country...His Excellency, the Ambassador, will no longer have to disturb himself for us American citizens. We are bound to the Mother Country by spiritual ties and we are here free to serve Fascism. For the defense of Fascism each one of us is ready to serve. Fascism. For the defense of Fascism each one of us is ready to give everything, even life itself. The laws of this country cannot forbid us to spread this faith of ours. If we wish, as Brisbane[1] says, we can even form the American Fascist Party, with all the rights which are granted to political parties here, though we are far from thinking that. By disbanding, the League has deprived its foes of their target. Now those gentlemen ought not to forget that in the place of one League, hundreds will arise. They will have to settle accounts with us. In all cities of America Fascism will be stronger, better equipped, less disciplined, more efficient, and if necessary, more violent...The end of the Fascist League does not mean the disbanding of our forces nor a renunciation of our ideas. The *Grido della Stirpe* is always the banner of our faith and the mouthpiece of Italian Fascism.

In the same issue of *Grido della Stirpe*, Trombetta's twin brother, Moschetti, wrote as follows:

The Fascist League has done a work of penetration in the interests of Italy. If the Order of the Sons of Italy now is favorable to the institutions of the Fatherland and admits the greatness of the Revolution which has taken place in our country and the civil improvements which it has introduced or is introducing into the Peninsula, this has been in great part the work of the Fascist League...The disbanding of the Fascist League does not mean that the Fascist movement in this country is dead. Quite the contrary...Fascists can form societies according to the laws of this country, and these societies or sections can federate and create state or national organizations...Fascism can live in this country by its own resources and on its own responsibility, in the interests of America...From this movement a new life begins. We are sure that all Fascists, wherever they may be, will be equal to the situation in the name of Italy, of Fascism, of il Duce.

In the January 4, 1930, issue of his paper, Trombetta returned to explain that "Fascism in America is Not Dying":

---

1. The well known pro-Fascist columnist of the Hearst press.

We are volunteer soldiers in an army which today, more than ever, must show its courage and remain with its flags flying in the front line . . . Fascists of America, let us consolidate our ranks, and let us shout with all our might: Long live the Duce! Long Live Fascism . . . The *Grido della Stirpe* remains unshaken at its battle post.

On January 20, 1930, the *Grido della Stirpe* issued a proclamation signed by Trombetta in which one reads:

The *Grido della Stirpe* today calls together all Fascists of America to unite under the great "Lictor Federation" . . . This stand of ours does not mean disobedience to the decision of the last meeting of the Fascist League . . . Every Fascio should carry out its clearance. After this, however, every group acquires absolute independence and no longer has anything to do with the old leaders . . . These must remain far away and leave us to work undisturbed.

A Lictor Federation already existed. When it became necessary to disband the Fascist League of North America, the Lictor Federation took its place.

In an interview with the *New York Herald Tribune*,[2] Trombetta announced that the thirty-seven of the ninety-three branches of the Fascist League had reorganized themselves and become a part of the federation; the Lictor Federation would organize "one million members": "only the external symbols of Fascism have been abandoned: flags, banners, black shirts; the names have been changed. But the purpose of the Federation is to continue the work of the dissolved Fascist League." Trombetta maintained that the Italian consuls gave no help to the organization: the branches of the federation were "completely separate from the political movement in Italy."[3] The prospective members of the federation were informed that at their head there would only be American citizens "in order to be able to fight their adversaries on equal ground."[4]

On February 23, 1930, a meeting was held at Newark, New Jersey, which entrusted the task of drawing up the constitution of the federation to a committee of seven comrades: Angelo Bianchi, Salvatore Caridi, Ercole Prezioso, Francesco Renzulli, Roberto Toberti, Eugenio Sturchio, and Domenico Trombetta.[5]

Four of these full-fledged Fascists were M.D.'s: Bianchi, Caridi, Prezioso, Sturchio. Five of the seven lived in Newark; Caridi in West New York, New Jersey and Trombetta in New York.

2. Reprinted in GS, February 15, 1930.
3. XXXI, p. 334.
4. GS, February 8, 1930.
5. Ibid., March 1, 1930.

Before revealing the commandments of the new laws, the Fascist Moses asked the opinion of several luminaries of American politics about the lawfullness and advisability of the new organization. All answered in the affirmative,[6] most likely without taking the slightest trouble to understand what it was all about. One of these oracles was Representative Dickstein, who came out with the following verdict:

> Dear Mr. Trombetta:
> I am in favor of every movement which aims at the Americanization of the foreign-born and makes them good citizens. If your organization wishes to act along the lines of your letter of March 12, I do not believe that any fair-minded American will have any objection to your activities. Very truly yours, Samuel Dickstein.

Dear Mr. Trombetta made fun of such a monument of political idiocy by displaying it under a big title: "Fascism Necessary for Italian Mind, Superior Form of Life. We need to March."[7]

In May 1930, at the convention of the federation held in New York, instead of the thirty-seven sections imagined by Trombetta, no more than twenty-three of them took part. Some called themselves sections of the Lictor Federation, others openly called themselves Fascio Alfonso Arena of Binghamton, New York,[8] Fascio Carlo Delcroix of Montclair, New Jersey,[9] Fascio Principe Umberto of West New York, New Jersey,[10] Fascio Fiamme Nere of Hoboken, New Jersey. The latter was made up of "about one hundred fifty Fascists, all tried and true Black Shirts."[11] It was rebaptized with the name of Arnaldo Mussolini in 1932[12] and in 1935 it continued to term itself as a Fascist section.[13] The directorate of the Francesco Crispi branch of Glen Cove, Long Island, New York consisted of "very good Fascists."[14] In the city of New York there were two branches and in addition an orchestra named after Giuseppe Verdi and a Bari football club.[15] One of the two sections of New York took the name of Theodore Roosevelt, doubtless to demonstrate the 100 percent Americanism of its members; Peppino Ganci was a member of its directorate;[16] Theodore Roosevelt served as a front for Mussolini. The other section was the old Queen Margherita which had lightly changed its

6. Ibid., March 1, 15, 1929; April 4, 1930.
7. Ibid., March 22, 1930.
8. Ibid., August, 2, 1930.
9. Ibid., February 8, 1930.
10. Ibid., January 11, 1930.
11. Ibid., March 29, 1930.
12. Ibid., April 10, 1932.
13. Ibid., June 19, 1935.
14. Ibid., March 26, 1932.
15. Ibid., March 5, May 24, 1930.
16. Ibid., April 1, May 31, 1930.

title to Margherita di Savoia, probably so as not to offend the republican sentiments of the gullible Americans with the word queen.

The convention created a federal council made up of seven persons: Dr. Salvatore Caridi, Professor Castellano, Dr. E. A. Manginelli, Dr. Francesco Renzulli, Dr. Eugenio Sturchio, Dr. Tomaiuolo, and Trombetta.

The federal council elected as its own president, Dr. Manginelli, who in 1928 had belonged to the Fascio Mario Sonzini of the Bronx.[17] The newborn president announced that the basic purpose of the federation was "to propagate Italian culture in all its phases, based mainly on the spirit and the principles of Fascism."[18]

The federal council appointed delegates for Connecticut, Pennsylvania, California and the city of Hoboken, New Jersey; added to their own ranks Francesco Mario Gerbini, "long-time Fascist," and entrusted the press bureau to Dr. Ugo Bontempo.[19] The latter made the following announcement:

> We have always maintained that after the triumph of Fascism in Italy, there is no longer any place for half-hearted people in the Italian communities abroad. Italians abroad must either be Fascists because Italy is Fascist, or anti-Fascist, which today is equal to anti-Italian...Fascism is part and parcel of everything in our communities. Whatever we do in the name of Italy, we do also in the name of Fascism.[20]

The federation repeated day in and day out that it "was in no contact whatsoever with Fascism in Italy" and that it was not dependent upon the bureau of Italians abroad at Rome. However, it felt "the pressing need" to assert in America "those principles, those constructive methods which had made of Italy, once headed for disaster, a country and a nation envied by all Europe, nay by all the world."[21] It was absurd to pretend that American citizens of Italian origin ceased taking part in Italian affairs: "They have already made a sacrifice when they renounced their Italian citizenship to become American."[22]

The second convention of the federation was called in February 1931.[23] Fourteen branches took part in it, including the Theodore Roosevelt and the Margherita di Savoia of New York. As members of the federal central council for 1931, the following persons were chosen: Giuseppe Alessandro, Vincenzo Ascrizzi, Salvatore Caridi, E. A. Manginelli, Raffaele Muccilli,

17. PIA, October 27, 1928.
18. GS, May 24, 31, 1930.
19. Ibid., July 5, 19, 1930.
20. Ibid., July 27, 1930.
21. Ibid., September 6, 1930; September 3, 1932.
22. Ibid., January 9, 1932.
23. Ibid., January 24, 1931.

Giuseppe Santy, and Trombetta, federal secretary.

The convention created a Permanent Great Council of the Lictor Federation, made up of Fascists of proven faith, who were to work in collaboration with the federal central council.[24]

The creating of this new organ did not augment the number nor the activity of the sections. In April 1931, Trombetta complained that "many sections were dormant": in many states, organizations were lacking entirely. This did not hinder him from announcing that "In this work of ours the Duce and all the Hierarchies of Italy are following us with admiration."[25] Neither did such admiration prevent him from asserting in January 1932 that "no Fascist propaganda exists in any form in America; there exists only information about Italy as is the case for every other country."[26]

In the third convention held in New York in April 1932, only eight branches were represented. In the hands of Trombetta the sections, instead of multiplying, vanished. New York alone was an exception to this rule, since here two new branches had sprung up in the Bronx, the Abraham Lincoln and the Iolanda of Savoy. The federal council for that year consisted of the following persons: G. Alessandro, V. Ascrizzi, Vincenzo Beltrone, S. Caridi, Gennaro Giorgi, G. Santy, and Trombetta, secretary.[27]

The federal council issued an appeal to the "dependent branches" to remind them that "the duty of Italians abroad was conforming to the thought of the leaders in Italy."[28] In May 1932, a certain Mayer, "delegate in America of the German Fascist movement" was a guest of the Theodore Roosevelt fascio, and extended the greetings of the German comrades to the Italian comrades.[29]

In that year, Peppino Ganci, manager of *Il Grido della Stirpe*, in outlining Trombetta's merits in the *Annuario della Stampa Italiana* [Yearbook of the Italian press], issued by the National Fascist Association of Italian Newspapermen for 1931-32,[30] stated that it had been due to Trombetta's "constance and fighting fiber" that the first fasci had arisen in America, and then the Fascist League of North America had been formed, "and now the organization of a Fascist movement which goes under the name of Lictor Federation or Foundation" was working.

24. Ibid., February 7, 1931.
25. Ibid., April 11, 1931.
26. Ibid., January 9, 1932.
27. Ibid., April 3, 1932.
28. Ibid., April 30, 1932.
29. Ibid., May 7, 1932.
30. (Bologna, 1932), p. 287.

The attitude of the federation towards American institutions is easily defined. In *Il Grido*,[31] Moschetti stated that the duties of a good Fascist were: "absolute respect for the country of origin and defense of Fascism in America . . . as a historical (?) and ideological movement": "the obligation to defend in America against all slanderers the good name of Italy, Fascism and the Duce"; and "maximum" (mind not absolute) respect, not for the country of adoption, but for "the representatives of American authority and law and for the American constitution."

> As far as democracy is concerned, the Federation maintains that every form of government must aim at granting prosperity to the people: Even the democratic form, when it fails in this regard, by degenerating first into demagogy and then into chaos, loses every authority, every credit and every right. Whoever accepts in the name of democracy all the errors and and the horrors of disorganization, creates a fetish which increases the dangers of national disorganization. The Lictor Federation, *composed of American citizens, or imminent or future American citizens* can even think that this degenerated state of affairs has not yet been reached in America. Therefore, although not renouncing its right to criticize, it requires of its members respect to the American constitution in its entirety.

American democracy was still given a span of life. But this was not of long duration. When Lindbergh's son was kidnapped, the *Grido* proclaimed that this fact was the consequence of the conditions created "by the much extolled American liberty and democracy";[32] it "was eloquent evidence of the debacle of democracy"; it showed "what could become of a country under the throes of anarchy and disorder";[33] " 'we need a Mussolini' is not a mere cry; the people are beginning to see the futility of democracy."[34] A proclamation of May 24, 1932, announced that "the duty of every Italian worthy of the name was to gather closely around the Duce, obey him and follow him in the path of destiny."[35]

In short, the Lictor Federation resembled the Fascist League of North America as one rotten egg resembles another. The only change was in the names of the directors. Those of the old League were all substituted by new names, except Trombetta, who, for that matter, had already been excluded from the central council of the league in 1928.

In April 1930, De Biasi, who had now become a bitter personal enemy of all the old leaders of the League, revealed that the latter had convinced Cardinal Hayes to give instructions to the rectors of Italian parishes to the

31. February 8, 1930.
32. GS, March 12, 1932.
33. Ibid., March 19, 1932.
34. Ibid., May 14, 1932.
35. Ibid., May 21, 1932.

effect that they should designate a committee of ten persons who would assume the tasks which hitherto had been held by the central council of the League.[36] The plan was never carried through, although it was proof of the inclination of Cardinal Hayes and the Catholic clergy to favor the Fascist movement among the Italians.

On the other hand, it is doubtful whether the former chiefs really remained inactive. Thaon di Revel remained in New York, and in New York remained also another key man of the movement, A. F. Guidi. In March 1934, Thaon di Revel was invited as guest of honor to a dinner where the Birthday of Fascism was celebrated, and Trombetta, who had taken the initiative for this dinner, wrote in his *Grido:*[37] "Although diplomatic exigencies have forced Fascist organizations in America to disband, the old Fascists have never ceased to consider Count Ignazio di Revel as their chief" (*gerarca*). Thus it is most likely that Thaon di Revel and Guidi continued to pull the strings behind the scenes.

The Order of the Sons of Italy, already captured in its leadership, continued along the road on which it had set out in 1922. The rivalry between Cotillo and Di Silvestro in the state of New York was eliminated in 1931, and Cotillo from that time on, competed with Di Silvestro in the display of Fascist enthusiasm. The first gathering of the Grand Lodge of the State of New York after the end of the schism, "leapt to their feet when the name of Mussolini was mentioned."[38]

The Independent Order of the Sons of Italy, in 1930, elected as its supreme venerable, Vincenzo Titolo,[39] who, in 1926, had spoken at the inauguration of the Fascio Arnaldo Mussolini of Brooklyn.[40] In 1931, the ex-supreme venerable, Ingargiola, conducted to Italy one of these pilgrimages which were aimed at bamboozling innocent people.[41]

In June 1930 an attempt was made to create a federation of all the clubs made up of Italo-Americans in the United States. This federation was given the name of Unico Clubs. Its purpose was "to work for the betterment and the social progress of the Italian element." A. De Biasi was one of the speakers at its first convention.[42] Nothing came of this initiative.

In 1931 *Il Carroccio*[43] mentioned a Federation of Sicilian Societies, which included about three hundred groups and had been started in New York by

36. XXXI, p. 233.
37. March 31, 1934.
38. PIA, October 10, 1931.
39. XXXVI, p. 418.
40. XXIV, p. 658.
41. XXXIII, p. 369, XXXIV, p. 76.
42. XXXI, p. 429.
43. XXXIII, p. 197.

Frank P. Cantinella; and of which Carmelo Amoruso, one of the sub-editors of the Fascist daily *Progresso*, was to be secretary. This federation also remained on paper.

Again in 1931 it was said that at least three hundred delegates of Italian clubs, belonging to the Democratic party in New York, had met in Atlantic City to "discuss the problems connected with the participation of the Italo-American electorate in the public life of the metropolis."[44] This mountain did not produce even the proverbial molehill.

All in all, the years 1930 to 1932 in which the Lictor Federation held the field, must be considered as a period of stagnation. The scarcity of branches in the federation shows that Trombetta did not enjoy great prestige. Neither did the Fascists make greater inroads into Italian societies than they had done in the preceding years. To cap the climax, in the second half of 1932, Trombetta scarcely escaped being electrocuted.

In Staten Island, New York, there is still the little house where Garibaldi lived in exile, earning his bread as a candlemaker. It is a holy shrine for the Italians in this country and at stated days every year patriotic societies never fail to make a pilgrimage there. Orders from Rome bade the New York Fascists to prepare a monster Garibaldi celebration for the centennial. The Order of the Sons of Italy took the initiative; thousands of circulars were sent to all Italian societies and to prominent individuals requesting their participation and contributions. The main feature of the celebration was a great parade in the streets of New York and a pilgrimage to the shrine. The Italian ambassador to Washington and various Italian consuls of nearby cities came purposely to decorate the event with their presence and were escorted by two hundred policemen, sent not so much to do honor to the exalted Italian officials, as to meet possible disturbances.

The anti-Fascist alliance of New York had urged the Italians to protest against the Fascist desecration of Garibaldi's memory. The Fascist parade at various points of its march was greeted by anti-Fascist groups shouting "Down with Mussolini" and "viva Matteotti," but the whole celebration was carried on with no incidents other than occasional fisticuffs among individual contenders.

When the ceremony in Staten Island was over, a squad of about one hundred Fascists who had served as a bodyguard of the parade and who were armed with canes, led by Mr. Trombetta, took the return train to New York at the Rosebank station. In the next car of the same train there were already a small group of some twenty anti-Fascists who had paid their own

44. XXXIII, p. 197.

homage to Garibaldi's shrine. How the riot started is not known. A shot was heard and a man fell down.

When the train stopped and the police rushed to the battlefield, it was found that the wounded man was a Fascist, Salvatore Arena, member of the Fascio Fiamme Nere of Hoboken, New Jersey,[45] and that he had been hit by a bullet in the back of the head. He died two hours later at the hospital without having regained consciousness. One of the anti-Fascists, a certain Lista, whose head was bleeding and who had been seen grappling with Arena, was arrested and charged with murder.

Arena was proclaimed a martyr of the Fascist cause and the victim of anti-Fascist criminals. As such, he was given a royal funeral in New York with the intervention of the Italian ambassador, of all Fascist authorities and crowds of Fascists and admirers of Fascism. His body was taken aboard an Italian liner, and laid in state in a special funeral chapel with a Fascist guard of honor. At Naples all the high Fascist authorities and endless cohorts of the Black Shirts paid extraordinary honors to the dead comrade. The Fascist newspaper published glowing eulogies of the martyr. The Rome *Giornale d'Italia* described the story of his death as follows:

> Salvatore Arena, an indefatigable worker, a fervent patriot, a steadfast Fascist, one of those heroes who abroad fight the battles of the Fatherland, on the Fourth of July went with the Fascist ranks to the Garibaldi com- memoration...A group of armed renegades attacked the Fascists during the ceremony. Hit in the heart, Arena fell dead. Thus he consecrated once more with his blood the glorious emblem of the Lictor and the great cause of our revolution.

Meanwhile the investigation of the New York police ascertained a few facts. Lista was grappling with Arena face to face while Arena was killed by a bullet in the back of his head. It was evident that Lista could not have been the murderer. Witnesses affirmed that the man who did the shooting was Trombetta, the Fascist leader. It was stated that Trombetta carried the revolver. The reconstruction of crime by the police investigators showed that Trombetta, who stood behind the grappling pair, aimed at Lista, but in the confusion or because of the brusque motion of the train missed his aim and kiled Arena. Lista was then released; Trombetta was arrested, sent to prison without bail and, when the grand jury sustained the indictment, was held for trial.

The discoveries went still further. The police of Montreal, Canada, reading in the newspapers the name of Salvatore Arena, remembered that a man of this name had been one of a gang of twelve bandits who in 1924 had made a

45. GS, January 3, 1931.

bold attempt to steal $150,000 from the Hoselaga bank while the sum was being transferred in an armored truck. One of the messengers was killed and another wounded. One of the bandits was also killed. Four others were arrested, found guilty and hanged in the prison of Montreal. Arena escaped and took refuge in the United States. The Montreal police had his photograph and his fingerprints. These were sent to the police of New York. The Montreal newspapers *La Presse* and the *Daily Star* published, a few days later, a communication of the police inspector Armand Brodeur, that the New York police had definitely identified the bandit of 1924 as the dead Fascist hero.

The news appeared also in the American papers. The *World Telegram*, after telling the story, advised the Italian ambassador to be more careful before paying such honor to a Fascist as he had to Arena. The Fascist Italian daily of New York, *Il Progresso Italo-Americano*, on July 7, had published a short biography of the dead hero and stated that Arena had come to America in 1922, that he had served in the Italian army with the class of 1896. These dates corresponded exactly with those of the police record concerning Arena the gangster. When the identification of the hero as the gangster became public, the *Progresso*, with the typical Fascist ease in denying today what was said yesterday and vice versa, revised Arena's biography and affirmed that the hero had come to America only late in 1924 and that he belonged to the class of 1899. The Fascist press of New York even went so far as to circulate a spurious communication attributed to the New York police, stating that there was nothing in common between the two Arenas. This communication was denied by the police and it was stated again that the fingerprints left no doubt whatever that the gangster and the martyr were the same person.

The initiative for Trombetta's defense was taken by the Sons of Italy. Trombetta was not only a member of the order, but one of its dignitaries, great delegate of the Brooklyn lodge Perseverance.

At the trial which closed on October 29, 1932, a significant incident came to light. A certain Francesco Cerbini, by bribery and by threats, had tried to persuade the two main witnesses of the prosecution to take back their statements at the trial. The witnesses had feigned willingness to negotiate and had notified the police. Hence, when at the arranged meeting Cerbini repeated his proposition, the police who had listened in hiding, arrested him.

The whole affair turned out to be an imbroglio within the Fascist family. The man who was murdered was a Fascist, the man who was indicted was a Fascist, and the two star witnesses of the prosecution who affirmed that Trombetta was the man who did the shooting were Caldora and La Motta, both members of the Fascist Alliance Il Duce and both disreputable people. Trombetta was acquitted by the jury for lack of evidence.

Trombetta although acquitted had become unfit, for the moment at least, to appear publicly as leader of a respectable movement. The remedy for the evil was right at hand: closing up shop and opening up shortly thereafter under a new name.

PART II

FASCIST TRANSMISSION BELTS

1

The Sons of Italy

The Fascist League of North America and the local fasci which were under its jurisdiction, had the ambition to act as the moving wheels of a vast system embracing all Italian organizations existing in the United States and Canada. The Fascist convention of Philadelphia, in November 1925, entrusted a Central Bureau for Propaganda with the task of "setting up Fascist infiltration into political organizations and mutual aid societies so as to create friendly ties and spiritual agreement."[1] In January 1928, the League announced that it had been able to gather "into a single bundle" the fasci, the Orders of the Sons of Italy, the Tiro a Segno Nazionale, the Dante Alighieri Society, the Chamber of Commerce, the War Veterans, the Maimed War Veterans, the Blue Ribbon (Nastro Azzurro, i.e. the association of those war veterans who had been decorated for acts of bravery), the Italian Historical Society, the Italian Hospital, the daily press and the periodical magazines.[2]

1. PIA, November 30, 1925.
2. Gio., January 15, February 1, 1928; PIA, January 30, 1928.

The most coveted conquest was the Order of the Sons of Italy (OFDI). As we have already seen, their loyalty was offered to Mussolini by Di Silvestro in the telegram of November 11, 1922. The supreme venerable's Fascist zeal aroused protests from many quarters. Even a 100 percent Fascist had to admit that Di Silvestro had "outstepped his own rights" when making such an offer "on behalf of the 300,000 Sons of Italy."[3]

This quarrel intermingled with another previous quarrel between the national headquarters led by Di Silvestro and the headquarters of the state of New York led by Judge Cotillo. Cotillo, no less than Di Silvestro, claimed to be an admirer of Mussolini for life and death, but he maintained that Fascism must remain an Italian affair and not be imported into America.[4] He charged Di Silvestro with altering the Order's nonpolitical nature, "dividing the Italian family in this country" and thus "harming Italy."[5] Personal rivalries lay beneath the resounding phrases and revived the controversy when it seemed on the point of subsiding. At the bottom it all narrowed down to a quarrel as to who should administer, that is to say squander, the pension fund, which amounted to $200,000, and the educational activities fund, which amounted to $200,000, and the schism was patched up,[7] and soon nothing was left of the pension and the educational funds. For the purposes of our research, we can ignore that incident. We need only follow the general movement of the Order.

In October 1925, the supreme executive council of the order endorsed Di Silvestro's telegram of November 1922, but to allay protests, they interpreted it as "a simple message of well wishing directed to the Head of the Government of all Italy" and not as an "enlistment with a part of Italy," the Fascist party.[8] Di Silvestro himself, at the national convention held in Providence, Rhode Island, rejected the charge that he "was plotting" to make the order a Fascist organization: "there is no room for the Order in the Fascist Party"; the order respected Mussolini as the head of the government,

3. Salvatore Benanti, La secessione della Sons of Italy Grand Lodge (New York, 1926), p. 51. [On the Sons of Italy see also Ernest L. Biagi, The Purple Astor: A History of the Order of the Sons of Italy in America (New York, 1961); D. Sandino, "Il fascismo alla conquista dell'ordine figli d'Italia," La Parola del Popolo, 9, 37 (December 1958-January 1959), 247-256; and the documentation in Archivio Centrale dello Stato, Ministero della Cultura Popolare, busta 452, fascicolo "Figli d'Italia." Ed. Note]
4. PIA, March 26, 1923. [On Cotillo see the contemporary biography by Nat Joseph Ferber, A New American: The Life Story of Salvatore Cotillo (New York, 1938). Ed. Note]
5. PIA, November 11, December 17, 1923.
6. Gio., September 15, 1925; New York Times, August 30, 1926; PIA, August 7, 1925; May 29, 1929. [As a result of the dispute, the New York State branch, led by Cotillo and La Guardia, broke away and formed a separate fraternity. See Diggins, Mussolini and Fascism, p. 95. Ed. Note]
7. XXXIII, p. 279.
8. Aquilano, p. 134.

not as the leader of a party.[9] The fact was that Mussolini did not admit any difference between himself as a leader of the party and himself as head of the government. In Italy the party had become the whole, and one could not hail the whole without swallowing down the party. In America the supreme venerable of the order was also president of the Fascist Central Council. He could not leave his Fascist overcoat in the vestibule of the order. Although the order had not officially joined the Fascist party, an interlocking had come about between the supreme executive council of the Order and the Fascist Central Council. De jure the two bodies were distinct; de facto the supreme executive council of the Order had become a transmission belt of the Fascist Central Council. The very choice of the day for the inauguration of the convention in Providence, October 28, that is, the anniversary of the Fascist March on Rome, which had taken place the preceding year, revealed the intention to give the convention a Fascist color, and in fact most vociferous Fascist manifestations took place in it.

The convention endorsed the work of the supreme venerable and elected for the period November 1923 to October 1924, a supreme executive council consisting of Di Silvestro, supreme venerable, and twelve other members, all of whom remained in office until 1929.[10]

Baldo Aquilano. New York City. Born in Italy in 1885 and naturalized not before 1921, he could have returned to Italy to fight in the war against Austria, 1915-1918. He preferred to keep his Italian patriotism intact in America for better times. In March 1923, the rumor went around that the Fascist government proposed to summon the Italians settled abroad to cast abroad their ballots in national elections. If such a plan had been carried out, the governments of all those countries who had received Italian emigrants, would have forced them either to renounce the privilege of electing deputies to Rome or to go back home. Likely as a result of diplomatic protest, Mussolini announced that "the Italian Government had decided not to grant the franchise to the emigrants."[11] But Aquilano, director of the press and public relations bureau of the OFDI in New York claimed for the order the credit for making a similar proposal before anyone else had thought of it.[12] In 1925, he was one of the directors of the Dante Alighieri Society, a Fascist outfit.[13] "In 1927, he founded the Italian Tourist Institute to create

9. Ibid., pp. 134, 137-38.
10. PIA, April 7, 1929.
11. The original idea of giving the vote to immigrants had been suggested by the Fascist deputy Antonio Casertano and had been initially supported by Mussolini. But the dictator changed his mind almost immediately as a result of the fears of American reaction expressed to him by Gelasio Caetani. See Migone, "Il regime fascista," pp. 38-40. [Ed. Note]
12. PIA, March 7, 19, 1923.
13. XXI, p. 263.

and develop an ever expanding tourist current between Italy and America, specializing in the organization of groups of students, female teachers and professors."[14] These trips to Italy by students and teachers were one of the favorite devices of Fascist propaganda. Aquilano could not have built up such a business had he not been palatable to the Fascist authorities. In 1932, he hailed the "superb vision of Mussolini's Italy."[15] In 1933, he became representative in America of the "Italian Tourist and Propaganda Institute."[16] In 1933, he hailed the superiority of the Fascist over the American press: "here, too, Fascism means wisdom and political education."[17] In 1935, he described the United States of America as "a conglomeration of diverse and multiple interests, all motivated by a common urge, always the same, the selfish and fierce purpose to exploit events to one's own profit"; in America "a mixture of peoples and races had found an Eldorado for their beastly passions"; this was the reason why America "did not feel and never could feel any real friendship towards our country."[18] His office in New York was at 225 Lafayette Street, a beehive of Fascist activities.[19]

Count Umberto Billi. New York City. In 1937, contributed the following gem to the book, *Atto di Fede: Per il Duce d'Italia* [Act of faith: for Italy's Duce] (edited by Scilla di Glauco, New York, Economic Printing Service):

> If I fight far from the Fatherland, I know that I am fighting with the sacred song of the Fatherland in my heart and with the manly face of the Duce fixed in my eyes.

His wife, Countess Nadina Billi Pappano, contributed to the *Atto di Fede* the following nonsense:

> In this glorious hour of our Italy,, the NEW MAN really enlightens the peoples and the world. With Mussolini, the prediction of Dante is coming true. We see in Him the man "who moves everything, penetrates and shines in the Universe." The doctrine expounded by our great Duce has upset the world. Like a new Messiah, He intends to remove the world in order to carry it on to the heights of humanity and peace. I feel sure that his powerful voice will triumph over adverse powers.

Billi's office as registrar (Supremo Archivista) of OFDI gave him wide opportunities to furnish the Italian consuls with precious information about names and addresses of citizens and residents of Italian origin in this country. He returned to Italy a short time before 1940.

---

14. AF.
15. GS, November 5, 1932.
16. Ibid., April 29, 1933.
17. Ibid., December 23, 1933.
18. Ibid., September 3, 1935.
19. IAW.

Luigi Cipolla. Providence, Rhode Island. In 1924, he acted as godfather in the headquarters of OFDI of Providence at the inauguration of the banner of the newborn fascio.[20] In 1926, he took part in the ceremony for the founding of the Fascist ladies' auxiliary.[21] In 1926, he was rewarded by Mussolini with a knighthood for his services.[22]

Oreste Giglio. Williamsport, Pennsylvania. Unknown to us.

Ubaldo Guidi. Boston, Massachusetts. In Italy he was known as Butrini. He emigrated before the Italo-Austrian war of 1915-1918. With the outbreak of the war it would have been his duty as an Italian citizen to recross the ocean and go to the defense of the country he so devotedly loved. *Carroccio* defined him as "the most intelligent, most congenial, most popular propagandist of Italianism in New England."[23] As speaker in an infinite number of meetings and as radio commentator, he has always been one of the most efficient agents of Fascist propaganda in this country.[24]

L. Lanza. Unknown to us.

Giorgio A. Mazzacane. New Haven, Connecticut. In 1925 he acted as toastmaster at a dinner given by the Fascio of New Haven to celebrate the Birthday of Rome.[25] In August 1935, spoke at a meeting expressing indignation against the hostility of the local press towards Italy and Mussolini in the Italo-Ethiopian dispute.[26]

Stefano Miele. In 1925 attended the Fascist celebration of the Tiro a Segno Nationale. In 1933, he exhorted the American young people of Italian origin to "go ever forward, listening to the words of Il Duce, Mussolini: 'march and not rot.' "[27] In March 1934, he attended the celebration of the Birthday of Fascism.[28] In October 1935, during the Italo-Ethiopian War, he stated that "at this moment all Italians are following their heroic Duce, banded together in one single powerful Fascio."[29] In November of that same year, on succeeding Di Silvestro as supreme venerable of the Order, he hailed, "the Italian legions, trodding again the routes which belonged to their ancestors and will again belong to Rome."[30] From 1936 to 1941, assistant corporation

20. PIA, November 14, 1924.
21. Ibid., October 11, 1926; December 18, 1928; January 11, 1929.
22. XXIV, p. 304.
23. XIX, p. 367.
24. Guidi spoke on station WCOP in Boston three times a day during the week and once on Sunday. See Salvemini's pamphlet, "Italian Fascist Activities in the U. S.," p. 8. [Ed. Note]
25. PIA, April 29, 1925.
26. GS, August 10, 1935.
27. "Marciare e non marcire." GS, December 2, 1933.
28. GS, March 31, 1934.
29. Ibid., October 12, 1935.
30. Ibid., November 23, 1935.

counsel for the City of New York.[31] In 1940, in his capacity as great venerable of the Order, attended the annual festival of the super-Fascist and anti-Semitic *Grido della Stirpe*.[32] On April 9, 1941, was sentenced by Judge Donnellan in New York City Court of General Sessions, to a probationary sentence of three years for embezzling $1,500 entrusted to him by a working man, C. Galetta, and which he should have invested in Italian government bonds. Only Mr. Miele's admission of guilt and his privately concluded arrangement to reimburse his victim saved him from a sojourn in the penitentiary. He was the supreme venerable who, in 1926, said: "If we had not done illegal and immoral things in the Order, we would never have done anything in the past."

Salvatore Parisi. New York City. In 1924, he was overtaken by poetic inspiration and brought forth a poem on the March on Rome.[33] In 1926, "passing through Rome, he was received by the Head of the Government, Benito Mussolini. In 1928, he was decorated with a Knighthood."[34] In 1934, he took part in the celebration of the Birthday of Fascism.[35] In 1936, he took part in the same celebration "as representative of the Supreme Council of the O.F.D.I."[36] In 1937, he contributed the following verdict in the book *Atto di Fede: Per Il Duce d'Italia:* "A new Caesar has revived Italy, giving her new face, new dignity, new power. I send him my greetings of admiration and devotion."

Saverio R. Romano. Boston, Massachusetts. Knighted in 1926[37] and then promoted to the rank of Commander of the Crown of Italy.[38] In 1927, in a Fascist ceremony, he exalted Mussolini as "apostle of humanity."[39] In 1929, gave an address on "liberty exempt from disorder," maintaining that "that which flourishes in Italy is true liberty under the protection of the sovereign State."[40]

Vincenzo Serafini (Reverend). Trenton, New Jersey. We do not know whether he is one and the same Rev. Serafini who, in April of 1940 was rewarded by Consul General Vecchiotti for the services rendered by him in the diffusion of the Italian language in the school annexed to the church of the Mater Dolorosa in New York.[41] According to Fascist doctrine, the Italian

31. IAW.
32. GS, February 1940.
33. XIX, p. 473.
34. AF.
35. GS, March 3, 1934.
36. Ibid., March 28, 1936.
37. XXIII, p. 577.
38. IAW.
39. PIA, March 30, 1927.
40. Ibid., January 15, 1929.
41. *Primo Libro d'Oro*, p. 150.

language must be the carrier of Fascist thought alone.

John Spaniola. West Hoboken, New Jersey. Sometimes he is named Spanolia.[42] Member of the transmission belt Dante Alighieri Society.[43]

In conclusion, from 1924 to 1929, of the thirteen highest-ups of the OFDI, eight were either full-fledged Fascists or fellow-travelers, and three of them were among the most active Fascist agents, without counting the fact that perhaps some of those whose political opinions we know nothing about belonged also to either of the two categories.

In 1925, Di Silvestro and Parisi went to Italy, and were received by Mussolini, and two Fascist high personnages in Rome, Senator Corradini and General Guglielmotti, represented the OFDI in a grand Fascist ceremony.[44]

In the state of New York, the headquarters of the Order were, and still are, at the beehive of Fascist activities, 225 Lafayette Street. If we survey the members of the executive council in the state of New York for a year, 1925, chosen at random, we find that the highest office, great venerable, was held by Judge John C. Freschi.

J. C. Freschi. In the controversy arising from the Fascist stand taken by Di Silvestro, he was one of the leaders of the group which upheld Di Silvestro and by this group was elected great venerable for the state of New York in August 1925.[45] In October 1923, at a Fascist ceremony for the celebration of the March on Rome, he presented a film whose subject was "the education of the young Italian in America through the knowledge of the unending glories of Italy and through the work of her sons in America."[46] Again in 1923, he gave an address "of accentuated Fascist tone."[47] He participated in and spoke at many Fascist celebrations on board Italian liners.[48] He deserved the praise of *Il Carroccio*.[49] In 1927, he spoke at the ceremony for the transformation of the Fascist Italian Digest News Service into the Fascist Italian Historical Society.[50] In April 1928, he was present at the celebration of the Birthday of Rome given for the benefit of the Fascio of New York on board the *Duilio* where "groups of Fascists in Black-Shirts" received the guests.[51] In December 1923, attended the dinner in honor of Colonel Howard.

42. PIA, March 12, 1924.
43. Ibid., March 3, 1924.
44. XXV, pp. 263, 669.
45. *New York Times*, August 10, 1925.
46. XVIII, p. 405.
47. XIX, p. 474.
48. XXIX, p. 697; XX, pp. 90, 277, 286, 401; XXI, p. 416.
49. XXI, p. 670.
50. XXV, p. 488.
51. PIA, April 24, 1928.

In 1930, he was declared professor *honoris causa* by the Law School of the University of Palermo.[52] In 1933, he was a member of the committee which organized a celebration for the foundation of the Fascist weekly *Grido della Stirpe*.[53] In November 1935, he spoke at a ceremony promoted by the Fascist Italian Union of America.[54] Again in 1936, he was official speaker at the Drama-Musical Society Benito Mussolini.[55] Member of the Fascist transmission belts, Dante Alighieri Society and Italian Historical Society. On the advisory board of the Fascist outfit, Italian War Veteran Federation.[56] One of the directors of the Bank of Sicily Trust Co. of New York, an office which he would not have obtained had he not given proof of his loyalty to Fascism. Trustee of the Italy-America Society, a carrier of Fascist propaganda. "The King of Italy and His Excellency Mussolini have bestowed various decorations upon him as recompense for his fervent and sincere love for his country of origin and for his numberless activities on behalf of the Italians of America and Italy."[57] If this judge is not a duly enrolled member of the Fascist party, he is no doubt one of the most effective fellow-travelers.

Among the other ten members of the executive council, five are unknown to us (Alfa Angrisano, S. De Stefani of Rochester, Gaetano Galante, Umberto Miele, O. Provenzano). If none of these men was connected with the Fascist movement, we must remember that especially in New York, the order was under charge of being affiliated with Fascism, and therefore the Fascists needed a certain number of fronts. The other five directors were as follows:

Francesco P. Catinella. Took part in Fascist ceremonies in 1934, 1935, and 1936.[58] Trombetta defined him as "our very dear friend, a perfect Italian."[59]

Vincenzo Jannone. "Well deserving patriot" according to the super-Fascist *Carroccio*.[60] In 1935, took part in the celebration of the Birthday of Fascism.[61]

C. Pitocchi. Delegate of the Fascio of Hackensack at a Fascist ceremony in honor of the mayor of Rome.[62]

G. Rossi. Physician in Utica, New York. "Founder of the Fascio Giovanni Berta."[63] In 1928, as commissioner of the central council of the League, took

52. XXXII, p. 172.
53. GS, May 27, 1933.
54. Ibid., November 9, 1935.
55. Ibid., February 22, 1936.
56. AF.
57. Ibid.
58. GS, March 31, 1934; March 30, 1935; March 28, 1936.
59. Italian means Fascist; GS, June 15, 1935.
60. XXI, p. 674.
61. GS, March 3, 1935.
62. PIA, May 18, 1928; misprinted as Pistoccio.
63. IAW.

part in the celebration of the March on Rome at the headquarters of the OFDI in Utica.[64] In 1931, he handed over to the *Grido della Stirpe* his Fascist enthusiasm on the anniversary day of the March on Rome.[65] When he was knighted by the Fascist government, the *Grido della Stirpe*[66] defined him as "comrade [Fascist] of old standing." In 1934, he proclaimed that "Rome has made three contributions to the world: 1) the foundations of law; 2) the religion of Christ; 3) the word of Mussolini which will purify present civilization."[67] In 1936, he exalted "the Duce's healthy and straightforward guidance."[68]

G. Stramiello. In the convention of the state of New York held in Utica in 1941, he opposed the proposal to condemn Fascism.[69]

Secretary of the order in the state of New York was Luigi Campione.

L. Campione. "It is to him that we owe the sending of an expensive silk flag to the Fascio of Regalbuto, Sicily, on behalf of the women of New York who had come from Regalbuto." Knighted in 1925.[70]

The Fascist penetration did not stop with the state of New York. Let us give some dates to substantiate this fact for other states.

In 1923 and following years Eugenio V. Alessandroni was great venerable of the state of Pennsylvania. In 1927 at the headquarters of the OFDI he attended a ceremony at the Fascio of Philadelphia.[71] In 1928, he accompanied Di Silvestro to Italy to organize the pilgrimage of the OFDI in the coming year. "In 1930 he was made Commendatore by the Italian Government in acknowledgment of his fervid Italianism."[72] In 1931, he took part personally in another similar pilgrimage.[73] In 1934, he spoke at the inauguration of the flag of the Fascist club Italo Balbo.[74] In 1935, he was the official speaker at the celebration of the Birthday of Rome, promoted by Fascist associations.[75] This judge also, if not a full-fledged Fascist, is a good fellow-traveler.

Great Venerable in the state of Massachusetts from 1923 to 1925 was Luigi Fiato, "very fine Fascist,"[76] and secretary of the Italian Chamber of

64. PIA, November 6, 1928.
65. GS, October 24, 1931.
66. January 21, 1933.
67. GS, April 21, 1934.
68. Ibid., April 18, 1936.
69. *Il Mondo*, August 1941, p. 3.
70. AF.
71. XXV, p. 380.
72. AF.
73. XXXIII, p. 366.
74. GS, May 5, 1934.
75. Ibid., May 11, 1935.
76. XXVII, p. 498.

Commerce in Boston in 1928.[77] In September 1923, the OFDI combined with the fascio in common manifestations[78] and Fiato sent a telegram of homage to Mussolini.[79] In 1927, Vittorio Varriale, great financial secretary of the OFDI, founded a Fascist club in Watertown and became one of its directors: "many of the new champions of Fascism belong to the O.F.D.I."[80]

Great venerable in the state of New Jersey from 1917 to 1923 was Francesco Palleria. In 1924, he was proclaimed "Honorary Great Venerable for life for the State, with the right of participating in the meetings of the Executive Council and having a consultive vote."[81] He acted in 1927 and 1928 as commissioner of the Fascist league in his state, and was one of the most active Fascist agents.[82] In 1927, he addressed "an imposing manifestation of Fascist faith" in Paterson, New Jersey, holding the flag of the Fascio Roma for baptism.[83] In 1934, 1935, and 1936, he took part in the celebrations of the Birthday of Fascism.[84]

In 1924, when he left the office of great venerable of New Jersey, Palleria was followed in the same office by "comrade" Torquato Mancusi,[85] "worthy champion of the Fascist Revolution";[86] in 1927, secretary of the Fascio Aurelio Padovani of Hoboken,[87] and from 1933 onwards, president of the same club[88] which was none other than the old fascio. Great admirer of Trombetta.[89]

In 1924, great venerable of the OFDI in Rhode Island was Vito Famiglietti, who boasted of "educating his sons in the highest Italian [Fascist] faith," and was received in audience by Mussolini.[90] The meetings, ceremonies and receptions of the local fascio took place in the headquarters of the OFDI.[91]

Among the founders of the Fascio in Baltimore in 1927 were the great venerable of the state, De Marco, and three other persons, V. Flacomino, Rev. L. Arena and R. Del Giudice, who had held high offices in the OFDI in preceding years.[92]

77. PIA, July 31, September, 1928.
78. Gio., September 8, 1923.
79. Ibid., September 15, 1923.
80. PIA, November 23, 26, 1927.
81. Ibid., September 13, 18, 1924.
82. Gio., January 31, March 2, October 2, 1927; January 29, 31, 1928; XXV, p. 488.
83. XXV, p. 488.
84. GS, March 31, 1934; March 30, 1935; March 28, 1936.
85. Ibid., August 3, 1930.
86. Ibid., August 22, 1936.
87. Gio., January 31, 1927.
88. GS, January 28, 1933; October 24, 1936.
89. Ibid., September 3, November 5, 1932; October 26, 1935; October 24, 1936.
90. XIX, p. 242.
91. PIA, November 14, 1924; March 27, 1926; December 18, 1927.
92. Ibid., January 9, 1927; Aquilano, p. 323.

In West New York, New Jersey, one of the founders of the fascio was an authoritative member of the OFDI, Antonio Nuccio.[93]

In Cleveland, a lodge organized a lecture of A. F. Guidi "propagandist of Fascism" at which the "Venerables of many Lodges" were present.[94]

The Venerables of several lodges attended a lecture of Fascist propaganda at Akron, Ohio.[95]

A lodge of the OFDI at Garfield, New Jersey, took on the very name of Benito Mussolini.[96]

In the state of Illinois, the great venerable, George Spatuzza, spoke at the super-Fascist ceremony for the reception of Ambassador De Martino in Chicago.[97] In 1933 he received Trombetta, editor of the super-Fascist *Grido della Stirpe*, with great pomp,[98] and gave an address on the March on Rome.[99] He would not have been the legal advisor of the Italian Chamber of Commerce, an institution supported financially by the Rome government,[100] had he not been a full-fledged Fascist. In *Grido*[101] a correspondent from Chicago extolled Spatuzza who, as head of the Sons of Italy, "in his well defined Italianism, cultivates and develops Americanism."[102]

These and other facts, which could be culled by the hundreds from the contemporary press, show that the upper layers of the Sons of Italy soon were flooded with Fascist agents, but not that the lower strata consisted of wholehearted Fascists who actively agreed with the leaders. A well organized minority which gains control of the strategic positions in an organization always succeeds in speaking and acting in the name of the leaderless multitude. For the OFDI, not only must we repeat all that we have said about the membership of the party, but we must add that the OFDI was not a political organization: it was a confederation of benevolent societies. The member of a political association whose directorate had been captured by Fascist agents, could relinquish his membership if he did not like to be a tool in Fascist hands and if, outside the association, the Fascists could not bring any pressure to bear upon him and force him to swallow everything they did. Quite different was the matter in the OFDI. There if one resigned from

93. PIA, January 27, 1927.
94. Ibid., December 21, 1928.
95. Ibid., February 8, 1929.
96. Ibid., June 1, 1925.
97. Ibid., January 26, 28, 1927.
98. GS, September 23, 1933.
99. Ibid., November 25, 1933.
100. IAW.
101. May 3, 1941.
102. For the significance of the word Americanism in Fascist terminology, see above, Part I, chapter 5.

one of its lodges because he did not like Fascists in its directorate, he forteited his share in the common fund, i.e. he would not be taken care of in case of illness, nor would his family get relief if he died. He might keep his membership and oppose the directorate. But he would be expelled without further ado. Since the society was legally incorporated, he could go before the court to revindicate his own rights. But this would mean waste of time, money and worry. Very few, and only exceptionally obstinate people, could face such strains. If a group of non-Fasicst members succeeded in controlling one of the local lodges, and passed over to the opposition, the state or national headquarters were entitled to disenfranchise the lodge, to get hold of its assets (buildings and funds), and to hand them over to their own friends. The outlawed group could get redress only through a costly procedure in the courts. Thus the OFDI could be managed by its leaders as if its members were a flock of sheep. The principle of leadership from above and obedience from below was the basic assumption of Fascist philosophy and practice.

Year by year, links of good neighborliness and cordial understanding between the Order and the Fascist League became closer and more obvious. In September 1928, the national convention of the Order held at Syracuse, New York, decided to organize for the following year a pilgrimage of its members to Italy. These pilgrimages to Russia or to Italy with the purpose of indoctrinating the innocents of all countries were fashionable in those times. When the convention closed, Di Silvestro and Alessandroni rushed to Italy to make the necessary arrangements with the Italian authorities for the success of the excursion. The pilgrims were to visit the "birthplace of the Duce"[103] in the village of Predappio, "whose name resounds in the world for giving birth to the Man sent by Providence to forge the destinies of youthful Italy."[104] They were received by the Duce, by the secretary general of the Fascist party, by the minister of justice, by Rossoni, by Arnaldo Mussolini and by the director general of the Italians Abroad.[105] In short they made what the Catholic pilgrims to Rome call the visit to the seven churches. Among the concessions which they obtained for the travelers, there was one worthy of special notice. Those who were out of line with the military service, that is to say the draft dodgers and deserters from the First World War, were not to be annoyed if they took part in the pilgrimage.[106]

103. PIA, September 25, 1928.
104. Words of Di Silvestro, PIA, April 7, 1929. [On the use of Mussolini's birthplace in Fascist propaganda see Philip V. Cannistraro, *La fabbrica del consenso: Fascismo e mass media* (Rome-Bari, 1975), p. 83. See also Salvemini's pamphlet "Italian Fascists Activities in the U.S.," p. 10. Ed. Note]
105. PIA, October 6, 12, 14, 1928; Gio., January 10, 1928.
106. XIX, p. 502; XXX, p. 140.

In February 1929, the annual convention of the Fascist League sent a message to Di Silvestro expressing their "brotherly thoughts towards the Order of the Sons of Italy" and their wishes and hopes that it would display "an ever greater activity on behalf of the Fatherland." Di Silvestro answered stating that the order "for more than twenty years had kept its faith and passion for Italy's greatness," and therefore was prompted by the same thoughts as those of the League.[107]

The convention of the Order in July 1929 was held in Montreal, Canada, on the eve of the departure of the pilgrims for Italy. "The telegrams of well-wishing sent to the Convention by the Magnificent Duce, Benito Mussolini, and by Ambassador De Martino, which were read by Di Silvestro in a deeply moved voice, caused patriotic manifestations and surges of enthusiasm."[108] Di Silvestro proclaimed that "Fascism and Italy today are one and the same thing," and was reelected by unanimous vote for a third four-year term. The *Opinione*[109] described this reelection as "a supreme and unforgettable triumph for Di Silvestro and for the political lead which he had given to the Order." *Giovinezza*,[110] explained that, according to the constitutions of the order, Di Silvestro could not have been elected for the third time had he not received a unanimity of votes. This unanimity he had obtained: "The re-election has the significance of a plebiscite which cancels any uncertainty. The words 'brothers of Italy' are no longer empty and meaningless. They resound through the spaces and reach the first source from which our concept of the Fatherland springs."

The review *Vittoriale*, edited by Favoino di Giura, in the July-August issue of 1929, stated that "the Order, even without adopting as an organization the insignia of Fascism, adhered to Fascism." Trombetta was carried away by enthusiasm. In the *Grido della Stirpe*,[111] he put a headline six colums long on the first page saying: "No more ambiguity! The Order of the Sons of Italy gives a mortal blow to the non-political character which shields anti-Italy." In the August 17 issue, he praised the Order as "the only institution which was always conspicuous for its patriotism and for its unconditional support of Fascism."

In August 1929, under the guidance of Di Silvestro, eight hundred Sons of Italy left on their pilgrimage.[112] They "expressed the devotion of Italo-Americans to Italy, the Fascist regime and Premier Mussolini."[113] They were shown all

107. PIA, February 22, 1929.
108. *Opinione*, Philadelphia, July 22, 1929.
109. July 22, 1929.
110. August 1, 1929.
111. July 27, 1929.
112. *New York Times*, August 24, 1929.
113. *New York Times*, September 29, 1929.

the Potemkin villages, the purpose of which was to bamboozle pilgrims. And they came back to the United States of America repeating in unison under Di Silvestro's guidance: "We, too, in America need a Mussolini."

If from the OFDI we pass over to the Independent Order of the Sons of Italy (OIFDI). We have already seen that its supreme venerable, Jerome J. Licari, was a member of the Fascist Central Council. In June 1924, Francesco Trapani succeeded Licardi in the office of supreme venerable[114] and he kept this office for many years.

F. Trapani. In 1924 spoke at a meeting held by the veterans and the Fascists in Boston.[115] In 1926, was a member of the committee which organized the celebration of the Birthday of Rome under the auspices of the central council of the Fascist League.[116]

If from the national headquarters we pass over to the leaders of the organization in the state of New York, we find that great venerable in this state in 1924 was John W. Perilli.[117]

J. W. Perilli. In 1926, he presided at a dinner in honor of the super-Fascist priest, F. Grassi.[118] Shareholder of the super-Fascist *Carroccio* and efficient propagandist for its diffusion.[119] In April 1924, representatives of the OIFDI took part in the Fascist ceremony organized by the *Grido della Stirpe* at the Thalia Theatre.[120]

Successor to Perilli in 1926 was Rosario Ingargiola,[121] who was still great venerable in 1930.

R. Ingargiola. In 1930 in the *Carroccio*[122] protested against those who accused his order of being anti-Fascist, finding listeners, nevertheless, among "those who say that they represent the interests of the Government of Italy," that is in the embassies and in the consulates.

> If we were in Italy we would not hesitate a minute to choose our battle post. But here, so many miles away, what can we do for Fascism and for Italy?...For us, Italians in America, Italy is not and cannot be a political entity: but it is and it will always remain a spiritual entity...To consider Italy a political entity...would be undoubtedly an act of disloyalty toward America and her institutions. The juridical renunciation of Italian citizenship in order to assume American citizenship does not imply at all a re-

114. PIA, June 21, 1924.
115. XX, p. 397; PIA, September 12, 1924.
116. PIA, April 28, 1926.
117. Ibid., August 2, 1924.
118. XXIII, p. 465.
119. XXIV, p. 313.
120. PIA, April 22, 1924.
121. Ibid., October 14, 1926.
122. XXXI, pp. 346-347.

nunciation of all that store of memories, affections and traditions which tie us to the country where we were born and which no *artificial oath* [italics ours] can ever cancel from our interior world, exactly because these ideal and imponderable feelings represent the voice of the blood which does not admit nor consent to abjurations of any kind. Naturalized or not, the Italians who live in this country owe to America maximum faithfulness, absolute loyalty, unconditional respect of her laws. A fortiori, if naturalized, their duty becomes imperative and categorical obligation.

It was, in other words, the theory of Cotillo that Fascism was good for Italy, but not for America, as if people could let themselves be convinced that Fascism was good for Italy without reaching the conclusion that it would be good for America too.

At Boston, in September 1923, the fascio, the Dante Alighieri, the War Veterans, the OFDI and the OIFDI got together to send a telegram to Mussolini in which they expressed "unconditional consent and approval" in behalf of "the whole of the Italian community of Boston, united and compact for the first time."[123] In this year Mario Conti represented the OIFDI at a ceremony held by the Dante Alighieri Society.[126]

In 1923, both C. Guarini and J. Langone attended a Fascist ceremony.[127]

M. Conti. Was one of the most active Fascist agents in Boston. In July, 1941, left for Italy together with the Italian consul.

At Philadelphia, in June 1923, the Italian consul invited to attend the final exercises of the Italian school supported by the OIFDI, did not allow the occasion to pass without proclaiming that "Italy had been reborn thanks to a man, Benito Mussolini, who had known how to enjoin the admiration of all the world and to whom all we Italians must show the utmost approval and co-operation."[128]

There did not exist in Italy any organization which was analogous to that of the two Orders of the Sons of Italy in Ameirca and with which these could coordinate themselves. But the Order of the Sons of Italy kept in Rome at its own expense a permanent office. The weekly *Il Paese* of Philadelphia, June 29, 1940, gave the facsimiles of two vouchers, one for $400 and another for $300, signed by the financial secretary of the Order for the state of Pennsylvania and initialed by Judge Alessandroni. The money was to be paid to Senator Corradini, representative of the order to Rome.

123. Gio., September 8, 1923.
124. PIA, September 6, 1925.
125. Ibid., December 22, 1926.
126. Ibid., April 24, 1925.
127. XVIII, p. 499.
128. PIA, June 6, 1923.

2

Other Transmission Belts

The Dante Alighieri Society

This association had always been controlled by Nationalists who, in February 1923, combined into a single party with the Fascists. Therefore it was even easier to capture than the Orders of the Sons of Italy. To show that the New York chapter was under Fascist control we need only give the names of the people who formed its directorates from 1924 to 1929.[1]

1. Gaetano Ajello.[2] Unknown to us.

2. Mrs. Giulia Grilli Angelone.[3] The wife of an attachè at the Rome embassy to Washington.[4] It is unlikely that she quarreled with her Fascist husband about Mussolini or Fascism.

1. On the Dante Alighieri Society and Fascist propaganda see Cannistraro, *La fabbrica del consenso*, pp. 28, 121-123. [Ed. Note]
2. XIX, p. 248; PIA, August 7, 1924.
3. PIA, December 23, 1928.
4. IAW.

3. Baldo Aquilano.[5]

4. Luigi Berizzi.[6] One of the shareholders of the super-Fascist *Carroccio*.[7] President of the Victor Emanuel III Foundation of War Maimed Men,[8] an institution subsidized by the Fascist government. One of the directors of Italcable, this too an office which could be trusted only to a loyal Fascist.

5. L. Bertelli.[9]

6. Dino Bigongiari.[10] Member of the Fascio of New York.[11] In 1923, vice-president of the New York Association of War Veterans.[12] In 1935, one of the promoters of the Fascist Italian Union of America.[13]

7. Miss Vera Billi.[14] We do not know whether she belongs to the Billi family.

8. Mrs. Rosalina Boeuf.[15] Fascist; in February of 1931 she represented the Margherita di Savoia club at the second congress of the Lictor Federation.[16]

9. F. Boglione.[17] Employee of the Banco di Napoli Trust Co.,[18] and therefore a Fascist.

10. Giovanni Caggiano.[19] In 1923 he spoke at a banquet of the Dante Alighieri Society in honor of Eleonora Duse, during which the ladies were presented with bonbon dishes decorated with the Fascist emblem of the Lictor Fascio: "thus the meeting of the Dante Alighieri Society had a Fascist seal."[20]

11. Vincenzo Caiano.[21] Unknown to us.

12. Antonio Campagna.[22] Wealthy contractor. Shareholder in the *Carroccio*.[23] In December 1928 attended the Fascist dinner in honor of Colonel Howard. Donated to the Fascist party in Italy 300,000 lire to be devoted to

5. PIA, January 16, 1926; January 15, 1927.
6. Ibid., December 23, 1928.
7. XXX, p. 371.
8. XXVII, p. 183.
9. PIA, October 23, 1928.
10. Ibid., December 23, 1928.
11. Gio., August 11, 1923.
12. XVII, p. 147.
13. GS, August 31, 1935.
14. XIX, p. 248; PIA, August 7, 1924.
15. PIA, January 15, 1927.
16. GS, February 7, 1931.
17. PIA, December 23,, 1928.
18. XXXI, p. 322.
19. XIX, p. 248; PIA, August 7, 1924.
20. XVIII, p. 500.
21. PIA, January 16, 1926; January 15, 1927; December 21, 1927.
22. Ibid., December 23, 1928.
23. XXX, p. 371.

educational and welfare activities. In 1939 made a count.[24]

13. Guiscardo Cinquini.[25] "Very ardent Fascist."[26]

14. Filippo Cipri Romano.[27] In 1933 secretary of a committee which intended to offer to the Duce a medal in commemoration of the tenth anniversary of the March on Rome.[28] "Fascist of the old guard."[29]

15. Vinzo Comito.[30]

16. Mario Cosenza.[31] President of the New York Italian teacher's association which in December 1922 presented a parchment to Mussolini, "regenerator of Italy." Mussolini answered praising "the precious work performed by Italian teachers in foreign lands."[32] Mussolini had come to power on October 30. Thus no more than forty-seven days had sufficed him to regenerate Italy. Cosenza was an admirer of the super-Fascist *Carroccio*,[33] "vibrant asserter of nationalism" and delegate in the United States of the Italian Inter-Universitarian Institute of Rome,[34] a Fascist institution, of course. Was decorated by Mussolini in 1925.[35]

17. Baroness Elvira Curci,[36] see following name.

18. Baron Gennaro Mario Curci.[37] In 1925 attended the celebration of the Birthday of Rome organized by the *Grido della Stirpe* where a hymn, "The March on Rome" set to music by him, was played.[38] His name was misprinted as Barone Cocco among the names of the Fascists who spoke at the inauguration of a fascio in the Bronx in November 1926.[39] In 1928, took part in a Fascist reception at the Ladies Auxiliary Margherita di Savoia.[40]

19. Natalia Danesi Murray.[41] Unknown to us.

20. Mario Soave de Cellis.[42]

24. XXX, p. 64.
25. PIA, January 15, 1927.
26. XXIV, p. 306.
27. PIA, January 16, 1926.
28. GS, January 14, 1935.
29. Ibid., November 11, 1934.
30. PIA, December 21, 1927.
31. Ibid., December 23, 1928.
32. XVII, p. 383.
33. XVIII, p. 96.
34. XXXV, p. 68.
35. XXI, p. 359.
36. PIA, January 16, 1926; January 15, 1927.
37. Ibid., January 16, 1926; January 15, 1927; December 21, 1927; December 23, 1928.
38. XXI, p. 456.
39. PIA, November 26, 1926.
40. Ibid., December 25, 1928.
41. Ibid., December 23, 1928.
42. Ibid., December 23, 1928.

21. Margherita de Vecchi.[43] Unknown to us.

22. Lucille de Vescovi Whitman.[44] Unknown to us.

23. Countess Olga Facchetti-Guiglia.[45]

24. Italo Carlo Falbo.[46] Chief editor of the Fascist daily *Progresso Italo-Americano*. In 1923 he made a speech on the March on Rome.[47] In 1927 "was received by Il Duce who kept him a long time in conference asking him news about the situation of Fascism in North America."[48] He represented in New York the Stefani Agency which is for Italy what Havas is for France and Reuters is for England.[49] Only a loyal Fascist could have been put in such a key journalistic position. In 1937 he accompanied Generoso Pope, owner of the *Progresso Italo-Americano*, to Rome on his visit to the tomb of the unknown soldier, and he appears to be in the act of giving the Fascist salute in the picture taken at that time and given by *Il Mondo*.[49A]

25. Francesco M. Ferrari.[50] Banker. Attended many Fascist ceremonies.[51] Knighted by the Rome government in 1927.[52] "He was in familiar reports with the embassy and with the Consulate General, to which he rendered useful services...Member of the Board of Education of the City of New York...His funeral was attended by the Italian Consul General and the President of the Fascist League."[53] After his solemn funeral had taken place it was found that he had left no money in his bank.

26. Count Roberto Fiocca-Novi.[54] In 1926 he spoke at the inauguration of a fascio in the Bronx with other Fascists such as Trombetta and Fioroni.[55] In 1931 he professed to "strong and indissoluble ties of faith and devotion to the Fatherland, to our Duce and to our marvelous regime."[56] In 1932, president of a committee which presented the Duce with a parchment in "homage and gratitude."[57] From 1933 to 1936 president of the Benito

43. Ibid., December 23, 1928.
44. Ibid., December 23, 1928.
45. Ibid., December 23, 1928.
46. Ibid., December 23, 1928.
47. XVIII, p. 407.
48. XXVI, p. 187.
49. On Agenzia Stefani see Cannistraro, *La fabbrica del consenso*, pp. 198-200. [Ed. Note]
49A. April 1941, p. 9.
50. PIA, December 23, 1928.
51. XIX, p. 474; XX, p. 287; XXIV, p. 84; PIA, February 15, 1927.
52. XXV, pp. 355-357.
53. XXIX, p. 138.
54. XVII, p. 610; XIX, p. 248; XX, p. 287; XXVI, p. 460; PIA, August 9, 1924; January 15, 1927; December 21, 1927.
55. PIA, November 2, 1926.
56. GS, January 2, 1931.
57. XXXV, p. 337; GS, January 14, 1933.

Mussolini Dramatic-Musical Society.[58]

27. Remo Fioroni.[59] Fascist agent.

28. Siro Fusi.[60] President of the New York branch of the Banca Commerciale Trust Co., In 1927, attended the celebration of the Birthday of Rome organized by the Fascio Benito Mussolini of New York;[61] attended the Fascist dinner in honor of Colonel Howard. Decorated by the Rome government.[62]

29. Guglielmo Emanuel Gatti.[63] In 1925, spoke at the inauguration of the Fascio Armando Casalini of Brooklyn[64] and at the celebration of the Birthday of Rome which was organized by the *Grido della Stirpe* and attended by the consul general and "the whole Fascist world and numerous supporters of the movement."[65] In 1926 spoke twice in Fascist ceremonies[66] and took part in a dinner in honor of the super-Fascist priest, F. Grassi.[67] Called comrade by the Fascists.[68] "He was among the first to organize the Fasci in North America and was, in them, director of squads. He was Commissioner Extraordinary for the Fascio Mussolini of New York. He has been for many years manager of the combatant *Grido della Stirpe*. President of the Democratic Club F. P. Spinola and Vice-Chairman of the Columbia League in Brooklyn."[69] Decorated by Mussolini.[70]

30. Vincenzo Giordano.[71] In 1928 editor of the Fascist daily *Bollettino della Sera*.[72] Then in charge of the Fascist *Progresso's* office in Rome. Frequent commuter between Italy and New York. Member of the Fascist association of journalists in Italy.[73]

31. Michele Guarini.[74] Unknown to us.

32. Cesare Legiadri-Laura.[75] Admirer of the Fascist magazine *Carroccio*.[76]

58. GS, February 12, 1933; November 3, 1934; June 22, 1935; March 7, 1936.
59. PIA, January 15, 1927; December 21, 1927.
60. Ibid., December 23, 1928.
61. Ibid., March 22, 1927.
62. AF.
63. XIX, p. 248; PIA, August 7, 1924; April 9, 1925; January 16, 1926; January 15, 1927.
64. PIA, January 29, 1925.
65. XXI, p. 456.
66. PIA, April 2, 25, 1926; XXIII, p. 461.
67. XXIII, p. 462.
68. PIA, May 18, 1928.
69. AF.
70. XXIII, p. 269.
71. PIA, December 23, 1928.
72. Ibid., December 21, 1928.
73. *Annuario della stampa italiana, 1937-1938*, p. 345.
74. XIX, p. 248; PIA, August 7, 1924.
75. PIA, December 21, 1927.
76. XVIII, pp. 96, 304.

In 1934, chairman of a committee for a festival where funds were collected to support the Italian school belonging to the Fascist club Arnaldo Mussolini of Hoboken, New Jersey.[77] Accused of having made of the monthly popular medicine magazine *Il Consiglio del Medico* a carrier of Fascist propaganda, he answered: "I am Fascist because I am Italian. Long Live il Duce."[78]

33. Cesare Maccari.[79] Member of the Fascist party.[80]

34. Manganaro.[81] Since his Christian name is not given by the source it is impossible to say anthing about him.

35. Italo Palermi.[82] From 1926 to 1930 vice-president and then president of the Banco di Sicilia Trust Co., a post he would never have received had he not been a loyal Fascist. He left that post — no explanation given — and became one of the editors of the Fascist *Corriere d'America*. One of the directors of Cine-Roma, 51 Street and Broadway, New York City, which was a vehicle of Fascist propaganda.[83]

36. Attilio Piccirilli.[84] The well-known sculptor. In 1926 affirmed that it would be the glory of the Fascist government if he had caused the Leonardo da Vinci Art School in New York to prosper by "ordering all loyal Italians to make of that school a forge of the Fatherland."[85]

37. Giuseppe Previtali.[86] Fascist key man.

38. Miss Rosa Pucci.[87] Unknown to us.

39. Armando Romano. Fascist.

40. Tommaso Russo.[88] Instructor of Italian at Hunter College since 1927 and at Brooklyn College of the City of New York since 1931. On the staffs of the Fascist dailies *Bollettine della Sera*, 1929-32, and *Progresso Italo-Americano*, 1933.[89]

41. Luigi Scala.[90] From 1925 to 1934 vice-president of the Bank of Sicily Trust Co. Delegate of the Italian Red Cross during the Italo-Ethiopian War.

77. GS, September 29, 1934.
78. Ibid., December 29, 1934.
79. PIA, December 21, 1927.
80. Ibid., March 21, 1928; May 18, 1928.
81. Ibid., January 15, 1927.
82. Ibid., December 23, 1928.
83. IAW.
84. XIX, p. 248; PIA, August 7, 1924.
85. XXIII, pp. 550-553.
86. PIA, January 16, 1926; January 15, 1927; December 23, 1928.
87. Ibid., January 16, 1926; January 15, 1927.
88. XIX, p. 248; PIA, August 7, 1924.
89. IAW.
90. PIA, December 21, 1927.

Knighted by Mussolini. More later about his Fascist anti-Semitic zeal.[91]

42. Tullio Serafini.[92] The well-known orchestra conductor. Most likely acted as a patriotic front.

43. Giuseppe Sessa.[93] Banker. Member of the Fascist Italian Historical Society.[94] In 1927 attended a celebration of the Birthday of Rome at the Fascio Benito Mussolini of New York.[95] In 1930 was received by Mussolini,[96] and in 1932 by the director of Italians Abroad.[97] In 1935 took part in the celebration of the Birthday of Fascism,[98] and was guest of honor at a fiesta of the Fascist club Arnaldo di Crollalanza.[99]

44. Rev. Giuseppe Silipigni.[100] Pastor of the church of the Madonna of Loreto. "Worthy patriotic priest,"[101] "most Italian priest,"[102] in 1923 "spoke under the auspices of the Fascio of New York."[103] In 1924, a festa was held on board the steamship *Giuseppe Verdi* to collect funds on behalf of his schools.[104] In 1926, together with Thaon di Revel, Garofalo, G. E. Gatti, and other Fascists spoke at a dinner in honor of the super-Fascist priest, F. Grassi;[105] the Fascio Armando Cassalini of Brooklyn was inaugurated in his church among "enthusiastic acclamations for Mussolini";[106] he took part in the celebration of the March on Rome together with all the Fascist big shots;[107] and he had a place at the head table at a dinner of the Tiro a Segno Nazionale, a Fascist transmission belt, together with the other Fascist big shots.[108] In February 1929, for the Lateran agreements, he sent a message to Mussolini, "wise guide, indefatigable leader, most beloved Duce, political genius of New Italy, sent by divine Providence," in which he "reaffirmed his immovable faith in the Fascist Party."[109] In the same year he took part in a committee in honor of Italo Balbo.[110] Admired by and a shareholder of

91. IAW.
92. PIA, December 23, 1928.
93. Ibid., December 23, 1928.
94. IAW.
95. PIA, April 22, 1927.
96. XXXII, p. 172.
97. XXXVI, p. 232.
98. GS, March 30, 1935.
99. Ibid., May 18, 1935.
100. PIA, December 23, 1928.
101. XVII, p. 147.
102. XXV, p. 378.
103. XVII, pp. 147, 501, 725.
104. XX, p. 90.
105. XXIII, p. 465.
106. XXIV, p. 658.
107. PIA, October 30, 1926.
108. Ibid., November 13, 1926.
109. Ibid., February 12, 1929.
110. Ibid., January 1, 1929.

Carroccio.[111]

   45. Ignazio Thaon di Revel.[112]

   46. Domenico Trombetta.[113]

   47. Alfredo Viscardo.[114] Unknown to us.

The result of the preceding analysis is that if we eliminate the names of the nine ladies among whom only two or three were Fascist (nos. 2, 17, and 22) and the others most probably acted as fronts, thanks to their patriotic leanings; of the other thirty-eight men at least thirty were Fascists or fellow-travelers and, among them we find the most prominent leaders of the movement: Thaon di Revel, Previtali, Trombetta, Comito, etc.

It is not to be marveled at, therefore, when we find that the directors of the Dante Alighieri Society of New York took part in Fascist meetings as representatives of the organization, as, for example, when Fioroni, in 1925, attended the inauguration of a fascio in the Bronx,[115] and when Gatti took part in the festa aboard the Italian ship *Diulio*, in April 1928, "to benefit the New York Fascio."[116]

A survey of the directors of the other local branches of the society would give analagous results.

It is, however, necessary to point out that this organization in the early years of the Fascist regime had very little strength. In 1924, Falbo complained that its work was "hindered by many obstacles" and that its local committees were "far from doing the work corresponding to the importance of the colonies and the scope of Italian interests."[117] In November 1925, when there was a conference of the representatives of the various local chapters, Falbo had to admit that "in the past, disconnected efforts had not turned out to be completely fruitful."[118] In 1927, there existed only twelve chapters all over the United States.[119] Toward the end of 1928 it had been reduced to the point of not having "any seat, any members, any directorate," because its leaders were too much absorbed in their occupations.[120] It acquired importance several years later.

111. XXVII, p. 185; XXX, p. 371.
112. PIA, December 23, 1928.
113. XIX, p. 248; PIA, August 7, 1924; December 2, 1925; January 16, 1926; December 21, 1927.
114. XIX, p. 248; PIA, August 7, 1924; January 16, 1926.
115. PIA, November 2, 1926.
116. Ibid., April 24, 1928.
117. Ibid., January 7, 1924.
118. Ibid., December 2, 1925; Gio., November 30, 1925.
119. XXVI, p. 353.
120. PIA, October 15, 1928.

Italian Chamber of Commerce of New York

No man who had business connections with Italy could afford to ignore the Italian Chamber of Commerce unless he was prepared to face hopeless hardships. Therefore its control was of paramount importance to the Fascists.[120A]

As soon as Mussolini came to power, the Chamber fell in line and sent him a message of good wishes. "It was one of the first pledges sent to the New Regime from Italian associations in America," so boasts its secretary, Bonaschi, in the fiftieth anniversary publication of the Chamber.[121] In his report of January 1923 on the activities of the Chamber, President Vitelli incited the members to "be worthy of what is expected of Italians abroad by the man who, having formed Italian youth into one indissoluble Fascio, has united into one Fascio, equally indissoluble, the spirits of all Italians."[122]

In 1922-23, president of the Chamber was Giuseppe Vitelli; vice-president, M. Mario Prochet; treasurer, Pasquale I. Simonelli; and secretary, Alberto Bonaschi.

A. Bonaschi needs no introduction.

M. M. Prochet. In 1923 he took part in organizing a picnic of the Fascist transmission belt, Tiro a Segno Nazionale, where the excursioners burst forth with "Giovinezza, Giovinezza."[123]

P. I. Simonelli. Decorated twice by Mussolini, in 1924[124] and in 1931.[125]

G. Vitelli. On the board of Naples Trust Co.[126] In 1933 he invoked "fresh acts of heroism" from the Italian race, "Awakened by the voice of the Duce."[127]

Presidents, vice-presidents and treasurers of the chamber from 1924 to 1930 (Bonaschi remaining permanent secretary all the while) were as follows:

Dante Antolini. Vice-president 1924-1925. Unknown to us.

Attilio H. Giannini. President from 1924 to 1930. In 1926 he made a wild Fascist speech at the Chamber of Commerce of Paterson, New Jersey.[128] In

---

120A. On the Italian Chamber of Commerce of New York see Federal Writers Project, *The Italians of New York* (New York, 1938), pp. 110-111. [Ed. Note]

121. *Nel cinquantenario della Camera di commercio italiana di New York* (New York, 1937), p. 148.

122. PIA, January 26, 1923.

123. XVIII, p. 299.

124. XIX, p. 237.

125. XXXIII, p. 179.

126. IAW.

127. GS, July 22, 1933.

128. PIA, October 31, 1926.

1927, "he aroused a hurricane of applause and a weighty alalà" when he exalted Mussolini at a meeting at the Biltmore Hotel.[129] In 1928, at a luncheon on board the *Conte Verde,* he aroused "enthusiastic applause" when he mentioned "the new Fascist State created by Benito Mussolini."[130] In 1929 he assured his listeners that "today Italy is animated by an heroic spirit."[131]

Ercole H. Locatelli. Treasurer in 1924-25 and vice-president from 1926-1930. "One of the wealthiest industrialists of Italy and America."[132] President of the Tiro a Segno Nazionale, 1923-1924. Member of the Italian Historical Society, and of the Italian War Veterans Federation.[133]

No wonder, therefore, that in 1928 the Fascist League of North America could affirm that it had succeeded, "according to instructions received from Rome," in including the Chamber of Commerce in the Fascist united front.[134]

[The New York Italian Chamber of Commerce has registered with the secretary of state as an agent of the Italian government.

In June 1939 it unanimously decided that the commercial counselor of the Italian embassy in Washington should be de jure its honorary vice-president for the duration of his office.[135]

Many of its members had to accept the membership and meekly bow to Fascist control for the sake of their business. But it would really have been very difficult for anti-Fascists or mere a-Fascists to become directors or officials in an institution which received subsidies from the Fascist government.

We have not had time to go profoundly into this point of our research, although *La Rivista Commerciale Italo-Americana,* official organ of the Camera, offered a documentation rich and easy to collect. But as little as we have been able to put together is sufficient to give us an idea of this organization.

According to IAW the following persons had been directors of the Chamber in 1940:

    1. Antonino Corigliano, Fascist by his own admission.
    2. Domenico D'Angiola, past director of the Italian World Veterans Federation; director fo the association of ex-servicemen decorated for acts of valor (Nastro Azzurro); director of the foundation to help needy war

129. Ibid., March 21, 1927.
130. Ibid., April 17, 1928.
131. Ibid., January 31, 1929.
132. AF.
133. IAW.
134. PIA, January 30,, 1928.
135. *La rivista commerciale italo-americana* (July 1, 1939), p. 24.

veterans (Vittorio Emanuele III). It would be a strange thing if this man were not a full-fledged Fascist.

3. Angelo Lizzola, unknown to us.

4. Lionello Perera, unknown to us.

5. Riccardo San Venero, New York manager of the Trieste and Venice Insurance Company; no one would have been able to hold an office of this kind unless he were full-fledged Fascist.

6. Giuseppe Vitelli, member of the executive board of the Bank of Naples Trust Co.; this also is an office to which none but a trusted Fascist would ever have been called.

The president of the Chamber, Italo Verrando, general manager of the Italian Line, on June 19, 1941, "gave the Fascist salute in the United States District Court after a Jury had found ten Italian seamen guilty of sabotage aboard the ship Aosta." Judge William S. Smith said: "He [Verrando] may disagree with the American system of government, but when in my courtroom I hope at least he will respect it."[136]

Everybody knows that in such organizations the executive secretary controls strategic points much more efficiently than any presidents, chairmen or directors. Well, secretary of the Chamber until the end of 1939 was Dr. Alberto Bonaschi, duly enrolled member of the Fascist party.[137] "After the resignation of Dr. Bonaschi, the office of secretary was taken on by Mr. Andrea Brancato, a Fascist by his own admission, who, during the Italo-Ethiopian War returned to Italy and joined the Italian army as *Capomanipolo* [Captain], 321 Legion of the Black Shirts."[138]

The addresses on the radio organized by the Chamber óf Commerce are of course permeated with Fascist propaganda.[139]]

Connected with the action of the Chamber of Commerce was that of the Italian banks: The Bank of Naples, the Banca Commerciale, the Bank of Rome, the Bank of America and Italy, etc. The directors, executives and other employees of these banks had to be full-fledged members of the party. We have already met several of them along our path: Bonanno, Vitelli, Di Marco, Palermi, Boglione, Scala, Fusi, Catinella, Ferrari. Other names must be added to these:

Rosario Catanzaro. Employee at the Banca Commerciale Trust Co. In 1926, one of the directors of the Fascio Benito Mussolini of New York.[140]

Pardo De Renzis. Enrolled as a member of the Fascio of New York in 1923.[141] Director of the War Veterans Association in 1924. In 1925 started,

136. *New York Herald Tribune*, June 20, 1941.
137. XXX, p. 351.
138. IAW.
139. Gio., 1936, pp. 12-13, 45.
140. PIA, May 5, 1926.
141. Gio., December 29, 1923.

together with Garofalo and Simone the Fascist weekly *Il Piave*.[142] In 1926, gave a lecture at the Fascist People's University.[143] In 1927, gave a lecture at the Popular Institute of Fascist Culture on "Fascist Literature and Ethics."[144] On the staffs of many Italian banks in New York and Boston from 1923 to 1938.[145]

Pietro Dinella. Director of the Brooklyn branch of the Bank of Sicily; in 1926 was chairman in a meeting of the Armando Casalini Fascio.[146]

Giuseppe Fazio. An employee of the Commercial Bank. In 1919, "had enrolled in the Fascio of Venice."[147]

Chevalier Fumagalli. An employee of the Bank of Rome. In 1924 was one of the commissioners for the Fascio of New York.[148]

Ernesto Luzzatto. "Fascist ever since 1919," "one of the first members of the New York Fascio Benito Mussolini."[149] In 1924 director of the War Veterans Association.

Frank Zunino. Director of the East River National Bank. "Enthusiastic over the miracles performed by Fascism."[150]

In 1929, the president of the Bank of Sicily, Palermo, and the director of the Commercial Bank, Fusi, contributed $1,700 to help the Ladies' Auxiliary Queen Margherita to obtain "worthy quarters."[151]

War Veterans

In Italy the war veterans began to organize into a national association in 1919. The Fascists tried to capture it, and they succeeded in 1925, after stubborn resistance on the part of the anti-Fascists, and after unbelievable pressure, legal and illegal, exerted by the government.[152]

In the United States, also, several local associations among Italian ex-servicemen were formed spontaneously before the Fascists seized power in

142. XXII, p. 106.
143. XXII, p. 106.
144. XXV, p. 488.
145. IAW.
146. XXIV, p. 658; XXXIII, p. 199.
147. AF.
148. PIA, February 3, 1924.
149. AF.
150. XVIII, p. 297.
151. PIA, January 27, 1929.
152. On the role of the Italian war veterans in the rise of Fascism, see Renzo De Felice, *Mussolini il rivoluzionario* (Turin, 1963), and *Mussolini il fascista*, I (Turin, 1966); Giovanni Sabbatucci, *I combattenti nel primo dopoguerra* (Rome-Bari, 1975); and Ferdinando Cordova, *Arditi e legionari D'Annunziani* (Padova, 1969). [Ed. Note]

Italy (October 1922). The struggles which were rending the organizations in Italy had their counterpart here and there in America. For instance, in Boston, the war veterans had some rows with the fascio.[153] But almost everywhere Fascists and War Veterans, or rather those who had captured their leadership, worked hand in hand.

In Philadelphia,[154] Cleveland, Ohio,[155] Wilmington,[156] and Lawrence, Massachusetts,[157] Hartford, Connecticut,[158] and Omaha, Nebraska,[159] branches of War Veterans were established by the initiative of the fasci or vice-versa. In Philadelphia, the secretary of the fascio was also president of the War Veterans.[160] In Lawrence the vice-secretary of the fascio was the president, and one of the directors of the fascio was the secretary of the War Veterans.[161] In Chicago[162] and in Toronto, Canada,[163] veterans and fascio together took the initiative for patriotic ceremonies. In Boston, the quarrels between War Veterans and Fascists had been patched up by the end of 1925.[164]

In many cases the links of these associations formed in America with that of the War Veterans or the directorate of the Fascist party in Italy or the local consulates in America, were explicitly admitted. In March 1924, the president and the secretary of the Boston branch went to Rome "to settle differences existing between Fascists and Veterans in Boston," and they were received by "the authorities of the Government and of the Fascist Party" including Mussolini.[165] In Cleveland, Ohio, the association of War Veterans arose through the work of a commissioner (*fiduciario*) whom the directorate of the Fascist party at Rome had entrusted with the task of spreading the fascio in Ohio.[166] In Philadelphia, the fascio announced that it was operating "according to directions issued by the central headquarters at Rome."[167] The veterans of Hartford, Connecticut,[168] and Chicago[169] chose the consuls as

153. XVIII, p. 582; Gio., November 10, 1923; May 1, 1924.
154. PIA, February 11, 1923.
155. Ibid., April 14, 1923.
156. Ibid., November 13, 1924.
157. Ibid., December 6, 1924.
158. Ibid., November 4, 1926.
159. Ibid., August 23, 1928.
160. Ibid., August 4, 1923.
161. Ibid., December 6, 1924.
162. Gio., November 10, 1923; PIA, May 29, 1924.
163. PIA, October 22, 1928.
164. Ibid., November 11, 1925.
165. Ibid., March 12, 1924.
166. Ibid., April 14, 1923.
167. Ibid., January 22, 1924.
168. Ibid., May 26, 1924.
169. Ibid., May 16, 1925.

their honorary presidents; those of Trenton, New Jersey,[170] and those of Hartford,[171] announced that they were part and parcel of the association which had been established by "Royal Decree of June 24, 1923." In Worcester, Massachusetts, the branch was created "on invitation from the General Headquarters of the organization in Italy,"[172] and at the inaugural ceremony held in the presence of the consular agent, they sent a telegram to the king of Italy "asserting their unalterable loyalty."[173] Also in Pittsburgh, Pennsylvania,[174] and in Newark, New Jersey,[175] the branches inaugurated their activities in the presence of consular agents.

In New York, as early as 1923, the veterans were presided over by Previtali, and "began work to form branches in the various centers of America, Mexico, and Canada as the result of special orders received from the National Headquarters in Rome."[176] In November 1923, Italian Victory Day was celebrated by the association in a meeting held at Washington Irving High School "attended by the squadrons of the Fascio which performed the service of honor" and under the patronage of the consul.[177]

The directorate of New York association in 1924 was made up of Previtali as president and by the following directors:

1. Caterino Campisano. Unknown to us.

2. Giuseppe Casublol. In 1927 he took part in the commemoration of the March on Rome under the auspices of the Fascist League.[178] In 1933 he was an official at the Italian Consulate of New York; termed comrade by *Grido della Stirpe*.[179]

3. Gennaro Cipriani. In 1923 he was present at a Fascist ceremony at which squads of the fascio of New York performed the service of honor.[180] He held the position of vice-consul, and spoke at a Fascist ceremony.[181]

4. Pardo de Renzis.

5. Armando De Rossi. Unknown to us.

6. Ernesto Luzzatto.

170. Ibid., April 19, 1924.
171. Ibid., March 23, 1925.
172. Ibid., September 10, 1924.
173. Ibid., November 9, 1924.
174. Ibid., September 15, 1924.
175. Ibid., March 6, 1929.
176. XVIII, p. 297.
177. XVIII, p. 498.
178. PIA, October 30, 1927.
179. May 6, 1933.
180. XVII, p. 612.
181. XVIII, p. 499.

7. Raffaele Milella.

8. Carlo Mirabile. In April 1940, he received a certificate of merit from Consul General Vecchiotti for his activities on behalf of the Fascist Educational Club Nicola Bonservizi.[182]

9. Giuseppe Rossini. A clerk at the consulate who in July 1941, returned to Italy along with the Consul General Vecchiotti.

10. Alfonso Sagramoso. During the Italo-Austrian War of 1915-1918, colonel in the shock-troops (arditi).[183] After the war, the arditi formed the framework of the Fascist shock-troops. Most likely Sagramoso was as much a Fascist as the rest.

11. Sebastiano Scire. Fascist.[184]

12. Vincenzo Vedovi. In 1923 spoke at a Fascist ceremony at which the squads of the fascio of New York were performing the service of honor.[185] In October 1927, participated in the commemoration of the March on Rome in the headquarters of the Fascist League of North America.[186] Trustee of the Fascist Italian Historical Society.[187] In 1932, 1934, 1935, and 1936 he participated in the celebrations of the Birthday of Fascism and the March on Rome.[188]

13. Giuseppe Zito. Unknown to us.

In April 1924, the directorate of the association announced that the membership cards had arrived "from Rome."[189] In June 1924, after the Matteotti murder, the association of War Veterans in New York and the Fascist Central Council of North America decided to form a "united front for the accomplishment of the final goal which is identical for the two associations," invited "all Italians to await with calm the future events in Italy and to hinder in no way" the work of Mussolini, and asserted that it was "necessary to meditate on the fact that enemies, internal and external, were finally glad to have a corpse on which to speculate in order to prevent the march of Italy towards her high destiny."[190] These were the same arguments which were used in Italy in those days when protests against the murder were rising up on all sides.

It is not necessary to follow year by year the changes which took place in

182. GS, April 27, 1940.
183. XIX, p. 585.
184. XIX, p. 359.
185. XVIII, p. 499.
186. PIA, October 30, 1927.
187. IAW.
188. GS, December 3, 1932; March 31, 1934; March 30, 1935; March 28, 1936.
189. PIA, April 27, 1924.
190. XIX, p. 695.

the directorate of the association to show that it was always controlled by members of the Fascist party with perhaps occasional fronts now and then. It will suffice to note that in 1925, the president was Castruccio,[191] and from 1926 to 1929, Garofalo,[192] figures well known to us by now.

At the beginning of 1925, the representatives of the local branches of War Veterans assembled in New York and set up a federation "to represent in America the National Association at Rome."[193] Previtali was chosen as president. In April of the same year his place was taken by Castruccio.[194] In July of the same year, ten chapters in the United States were "recognized by the headquarters at Rome" as lawfully constituted members of the federation.[195] In 1926 and 1927 and 1928, Vincenzo Vedovi acted as president.[196] In June 1929, the federation was incorporated according to the law of the state of New York. The board of trustees who signed the act were Vincenzo Vedovi, Raffaele G. Berlinghieri, Giacomo Ganci, Giuseppe Ganci, and Arnaldo Vedovi.

R. Berlinghieri. Decorated by Mussolini in 1934.[197]

Giacomo Ganci. Contributor to the *Grido della Stirpe*.[198]

A. Vedovi. Unknown to us.

According to the act of incorporation, the five trustees are elected at the annual meeting of the federation (section 4); but the annual meeting is attended only by the presidents of the local branches (section 14) who are appointed together with the directors of the local branches each year in December by the board of trustees (section 10), and the annual meeting of the federation is held during the following January (section 12). Thus there is no danger that the local directorates will make trouble for the board of trustees. On the other hand the board of trustees is the arbitrator of all the disputes which arise in the branches and whenever they deem it necessary they may dissolve the councils of directors or the branches themselves (section 9). Thus any troublemaker can be gotten rid of without much difficulty.

Side by side with the organization of War Veterans, [five] other minor associations of ex-servicemen arose.

Blue Ribbon

In 1923, the Rome government created an association among those War

191. XXI, p. 363.
192. PIA, February 6, 1926; February 1;4, 1927; February 25, 1928; May 7, 1929.
193. XXI, p. 459.
194. PIA, April 30, 1925.
195. Ibid., July 29, 1925.
196. Ibid., July 15, 1926; August 20, 1927; September 24, 1928.
197. XXXVI, p. 325.
198. GS, August 29, 1936.

Veterans who had been decorated for acts of bravery (Nastro Azzurro). In 1926 this organization was set up in the United States.[199] In 1927, the branch of Boston, in inaugurating its work, sent a message to headquarters at Rome, hailing the king and the "magnificent Duce."[200] President of the institution "in this land of voluntary exile" in 1927 was Martinez.[201]

War Maimed Men

The Italian National Association of the War Maimed Men, in 1926, also had its offspring in the United States. Martinez, "delegate for the Central Committee in Rome," created the branch in the United States[202] and was its president.[203]

Victor Emanuel III Foundation

Again in 1926 there arose in New York the Victor Emanuel III Foundation, which proposed to aid needy war veterans.[204] President of this organization was Luigi Berizzi, vice-president Thaon di Revel, and among the other directors we find Facchetti-Guiglia, Locatelli, Bigongiari, Castruccio, Garofalo, V. Vedovi, Villa, and Freschi. The association obtained a small subsidy from the Italian government.[205] When the subsidies came to an end, the foundation also came to an end.

Villa could be no other than Silvio Villa, who was a shareholder of *Carroccio*.[206] He would not have been either counselor of the Italian Discount and Trust Co.[207] nor director of the Victor Emanuel Foundation[207] if he had not been a loyal Fascist.

Il Vittoriale

These minor military associations had as their organ in 1924 a monthly review, *Il Vittoriale*, which claimed to be published in both New York and Rome, under the editorship of Favoino di Giura. Secretary of the review was F. Petinella and treasurer Andrea Brancato.

F. Petinella. Unknown to us.

A. Brancato. Fascist by his own admission.[209]

199. Gio., February 15, 1926.
200. PIA, February 18, 1927.
201. Ibid., February 25, 1927.
202. Ibid., May 19, 1926.
203. Ibid., July 15, 1926.
204. Ibid., June 11, 1926.
205. *New York Times*, July 18, 1932.
206. XXX, p. 361.
207. XX, p. 396.
208. Gio., June 30, 1926
209. IAW.

Arts and Trades

In 1927 we find mention of an organization of veterans called Arts and Trades (Arti e Mestieri). Its headquarters for the state of New York were at 302 East 37 Street, New York City. It was to be a branch of an Italian national organization, the center of which was in Leghorn (Italy), and was represented in the United States by Filippo C. Marchella. The latter summoned a meeting in Newark, New Jersey, in March 1927.[210]

F. Marchella. "In 1926 the Italian Minister for Public Education congratulated him personally for his accomplishments and for the work of Italianism he had carried on within the Leonardo da Vinci Art School."[211] In 1936 he was one of the organizers of a great Fascist manifestation.[212]

Tiro a Segno Nazionale

The Tiro a Segno Nazionale soon went over bag and baggage into the Fascist camp. In 1923 and 1924, president of this club was Ercole H. Locatelli.

The club celebrated Labor Day in 1923 with a trip to the farm of Mr. Giuseppe Personeni, "a militant Fascist." "The excursioners sang "Giovinezza, Giovinezza." In that same year, the king's birthday (November 11) was celebrated at a dinner under the chairmanship of Cav. [aliere] Uff. [iciale] Giuseppe Gerli. Addresses "of a distinct Fascist character" were given by Vincenzo Massimiliano, Judge Frschi, and Luigi Reali. Giuseppe Personeni offered to the ladies a candy box "decorated with the emblem of the Roman Fascio."[213] In 1926 and in the following years, Facchetti-Guiglia was president or one of the directors.[214]

Given the small importance of this association, we do not think it necessary to waste more time, paper and ink on it.

The Fascist Longshoremen Federation of North Americca

In 1924 a Fascist dinner was attended by a "commendatore Giani of the Fascist Syndicates."[215] At that time, Fascist syndicates were associations of employers and unions of employees under the leadership of Edmondo Rossoni. Simone was also in America as a delegate of the syndicates "led by Rossoni."[216] In October 1926, the Fascist League of North America announced

210. PIA, March 17, 1927.
211. AF.
212. GS, April 22, 1936.
213. XVIII, pp. 299, 499; Gio., November 24, 1923.
214. IAW.
215. PIA, April 27, 1924.
216. XXIV, p. 88.

that a Fascist Longshormen Federation of North America had been created with its seat at 61 Whitehall Street, Room 406, New York City, and "it had many enrollments." Thaon di Revel broke these good tidings to the headquarters of the federation at Genoa.[217] In December, a certain Terranova organized a chapter of the organization in Baltimore.[218] In Boston, a chapter was created in May 1927.[219] At the beginning of 1928 there was also a chapter in Philadelphia. The organization was incorporated under the laws of the State of New York under the name of Autonomous Fascist Federation of Maritime and Aerial Transportation Employees.[220] The word autonomous was but a lie. When there was no need to fool the gullible Americans, the organization termed itself outright Lega Marinare Fascista (Fascist Union of the Longshoremen).[221] The organization was so little autonomous that in January 1928, the central council of the League delegated Bonaschi to run the federation. Meanwhile Major Filiberto Toselli had been sent from Rome to New York "to run the delegation of the Federazione Marinare Italiana."[222] Therefore Bonaschi asked to be exonerated and the council delegated Toselli[223] who had already been delegated from Rome. Toselli bore the title of president.[224] In October 1928, Toselli resigned and was succeeded by Felice Corradini,[225] also called Velino Carradini.[226]

Giani. We do not know if this is that same Mario Giani that we find later in the capacity of Cultural Agent of the Consulate.

Terranova obviously is the same Fascist whom we have already met and who was secretary of the New York Fascio Benito Mussolini.[227]

F. Toselli. Duly enrolled member of the Fascist Party. Organized in 1928 the Fascio Aurelio Padovani in Brooklyn, Bleeker Street.[228]

In 1928 a collection of funds was started in order to open in New York a Home for Italian Longshoremen.[229] In September 1928, the representative of the Italian Navigazione Generale in New York, in order to raise funds necessary for the maintenance of the institution, allowed the ship *Augustus*

217. PIA, October 24, 1926; Gio., November 30, 1926; XXIV, p. 464.
218. PIA, December 14, 1926.
219. Ibid., May 10, 1927.
220. Gio., March 15, 1928.
221. PIA, January 1, 1929.
222. AF.
223. PIA, January 30, 1928.
224. Ibid., April 18, 1928.
225. Ibid., October 22, 1928.
226. Ibid., January 1, 1929.
227. Ibid., December 10, 1926.
228. Ibid., April 13, 1928.
229. Ibid., April 18, 1928.

to be opened to fifteen hundred paying visitors.[230] The company and the Fascists worked hand in hand.

In July 1928, the federation summoned a group of seamen to appear at 61 Whitehall Street in order to receive their personal documents (*libretti di matricola*); those documents which were not claimed within a month would be sent back to Italy.[231] The longshoremen, having to travel constantly between Italy and America, could be denounced in Italy as disloyal if they lost themselves on illegal paths in America. But an Italian longshoreman, as soon as he had disembarked in an American port, could desert and, in this way, escape the Fascist discipline both in Italy and America. The Italian communities in this country swarm with anti-Fascist longshoremen who deserted from Italian ships.

In August 1930, the longshoremen's home was still a thing of the future and the branch of the federation was still "in the process of formation."[232] In September 1930, a commissioner extraordinary was delegated, most likely from Rome, to reorganize it.[233] In October 1931, this person was expelled from the Fascist ranks, no explanation given, and was readmitted, no explanation given.[234]

These facts tend to make us think that the federation never existed except on paper, and that all the money collected for the longshoremen's home ended up in the pocket of the organizers.

Fascist Association of Italian Journalists of North America

It arose in 1927 "under the auspices of the Central Council of the Fascist League." Its presidency, until the task of organization was finished, was offered to the Fascist agent Commander Antonio C. Quattrini, editor of the super-Fascist Rome daily *Impero*. The first directorate consisted of Agostino De Biasi, Francesco Moschetti, M. Soave de Cellis, Domenico Trombetta and Flavio Pasella. Its first move was to send Mussolini a message of "homage and absolute devotion."[235]

A. De Biasi, M. Soave de Cellis, D. Trombetta are already known to us.

F. Moschetti. One of the wildest Fascists, and co-editor of *Il Grido*. He died in 1933.

F. Pasella. Born in 1884 and emigrated to America in 1912, he found it

230. Ibid., September 12, 1928.
231. Ibid., July 12, 1928.
232. GS, August 16, 1930; PIA, August 9, 16, 1930.
233. GS, September 13, 1930.
234. Ibid., October 24, 1931.
235. XXV, p. 171.

healthy to remain here during the Italo-Austrian War. "Very well known among the Italian societies and among the politicians of New York because he was an assiduous frequenter of celebrations and banquets in the Colony."[236] "Teacher of Italian in New York's public schools." Editor of *Il Corriere del Bronx*.[237]

Italian Medical Association

Founded in 1919. By January 1928, it had entered the ranks of the Fascist united front, if we are to believe the central council of the Fascist League.[138] Previtali often held the office of president, vice-president, or director of this Italian Medical Association. On April 30, 1927, the association gave a dinner in honor of the Ambassador De Martino.[239]

The impact that physicians can exert upon a population is tremendous and, therefore, it would be interesting to ascertain to what point physicians of Italian origin had a hand in spreading Fascist propaganda. We have not had time to make a systematic research in this field. We gather from reliable sources that no less than 90 percent of the approximately thirteen hundred Italian-born physicians in New York are Fascistically inclined.

The Italian Hospital

It does not need to detain us, since its Fascist administrators squandered or devoured its assets, and, therefore, there is no longer any Italian Hospital in New York.[239A]

Vera Art-Alba Club

In October 1923, Pietro Santoro, one of the promoters of the Fascist celebration held at Carnegie Hall.[240] Founded a Vera Art-Alba Club which was inaugurated by A. De Biasi who "spoke of the duties of Italianism" which all emigrants must profess in every manifestation of life among foreigners."[241] In February 1924, a dinner was given in honor of Santoro at which the ultra-Fascist priest, F. Grassi, acted as toastmaster. Among others spoke fellow-traveler Judge Freschi; A. De Biasi, Fascist, and Flavio Pasella, Fascist.[242] It does not seem that this initiative had great success.

236. AF.
237. IAW.
238. PIA, January 30, 1928.
239. XXV, p. 487.
239A. Federal Writers Project, *The Italians of New York*, pp. 112-113. [Ed. Note]
240. XXIII, p. 171.
241. XVIII, p. 411.
242. XIX, p. 243.

Associatione degli Artisti Italiani

Formed in 1925 as one of the lodges of the Sons of Italy. It was presided over by A. Piccirilli.[243] It does not seem to have even attained great importance.

Mutual Aid Societies

We have not had enough time to make a methodical survey of the mutual aid societies for the period 1923-1929.

The most important was the Mutual Aid Society of Italian Barbers of the State of New York. It had a membership of two thousand and before 1930 it was made up of nine branches which every two years elected a central executive council in the convention of its delegates.[244] In 1923, its general president was Paolo Cremona, admirer of the super-Fascist *Carroccio*.[245] But it seems that its leaders did not begin to become affiliated with the Fascist movement before 1926. In this year, a dinner was given in honor of Carlo De Biasi, business manager of the super-Fascist *Carroccio*,[246] and editor of the official weekly paper of the association, *Il Barbiere Moderno*. Consul Vattani attended the dinner, bringing the greetings of the consul general, and arousing "an unending acclamation" when he praised [Umberto] Nobile, who was flying towards the North Pole. Other orators were: F. M. Ferrari, Fascist; fellow-traveler Judge Fraschi; A. De Biasi, publisher of the *Carroccio;* Pasella, Fascist; Cotruvo, a Fascist agent, recently "arrived in America on a patriotic mission"[247] who finished by pitching his tent in Cleveland, Ohio. Di Silvestro sent a message of greeting.[248] In the fall of the same year, the Consul Bollati and the Fascist banker Raffaele Prisco[249] spoke at another dinner.[250] In 1928, the association was presided over by Joseph Mandese[251] who, in 1937, was a contributer to the book *Act of Faith in Mussolini*, compiled by Scilla di Glauco.

In 1929, there arose in the Bronx, among the people originating from Grumo, a little town in Apulia, the idea of donating to the new born University of Bari "an artistic and monumental bust of the Duce." In a

243. XXI, p. 266.
244. XXIII, p. 583; XXIV, p. 662.
245. XVIII, p. 93.
246. XXX, p. 334.
247. XXIII, p. 367.
248. XXIII, p. 583.
249. XVIII, p. 597; XIX, pp. 687-688.
250. XXIV, p. 571.
251. XXVIII, p. 456.

meeting called for this purpose, Rev. D. Fiorentino expressed the opinion that the gift should be given by all the Italians coming from Apulia and not by the citizens of the town of Grumo alone. In January 1929, therefore, [there] began to exist a Federation of Apulian Associations. Its president was Rocco Cortese.[252] It does not seem that this organization was of any consequence up until 1934.

Here and there, Fascists appear as speakers at meetings of mutual aid societies, or as their directors. For instance, in 1928, Agostino De Biasi was the speaker at a meeting of the Società Muro Lucano.[253]

However, all in all, we have the impression that Fascist penetration in these circles was very limited in those first years.

Italian Child Welfare

This charitable institution arose in 1911 by the initiative of a philanthropist, R. Cassetta.

The Fascists realized what great influence could be exerted in Italian circles through its medium. In 1925 a meeting was held to exhort the Italians to support the institution.[254] Besides an Italian vice-consul, the following persons spoke at that meeting: Bernardino Ciambelli, "Ardent Fascist";[255] Judge Cotillo, who, after declaring himself an admirer of Fascism only for Italy, was preparing to leap the fence; A. De Biasi; F. M. Ferrari; Judge Freschi; Judge Francis X. Mancuso; Pasquale Margarella, president of the organization; J. W. Perilli.

F. X. Mancuso. In 1923 he accepted a first decoration from Mussolini,[256] in 1924 a second,[257] and in 1925 a third.[258] In 1926 he was a speaker at a dinner given by the Fascist League of North America in honor of the Fascist aviator, de Bernardi,[259] and cooperated in the drive for the Fascist transmission belt, Italian Hospital.[260] In 1929 he was hard hit by the failure of the Ferrari Bank of which he was one of the directors.

P. Margarella. Shareholder of *Carroccio*;[261] decorated by Mussolini in

252. PIA, January 1, 1929.
253. XXVIII, p. 85.
254. XXI, p. 456.
255. XVII, pp. 612, 719; XXXVI, p. 602.
256. XVII, p. 500.
257. XVIII, p. 362.
258. XXVII, p. 151.
250. XXIV, p. 566.
260. XXIV, p. 567.
261. XXX, p. 371.

1928;[262] "noble compatriot,"[263] "professed a jealous attachment to Italy and his native town."[264] In 1933, treasurer of a committee which organized a dinner in honor of the super-Fascist priest, Grassi.[265]

We see, therefore, that the institution was entrusted to dependable Fascist hands. If it had been otherwise, the Italian Lines would not have permitted its directors to organize dinners and dances on board its liners for the collection of funds.

The institution maintained two schools: one on Sullivan Street, headmaster, Augusto E. Califano, and the other on Hester Street, headmistress Miss L. J. De Ferrari-Weygandt. All the teachers "carried on prodigious work of shaping the minds and the hearts of the young Italians in an Italian frame."[266]

In December 1925, a dance was held aboard the *Conte Rosso*, having a "solemn character of Italian manifestations," for the benefit of the institution. The committee which organized the *festa* was made up of Mancuso, A. De Biasi, F. M. Ferrari, J. W. Perilli and C. De Biasi.[267] In 1926 Judge Mancuso and A. De Biasi became vice-presidents of the association.[268] In 1928, another benefit dance was given on board the *Conte Biancamano*.[269]

The Italian Teachers' Association

[This organization was created in 1920. In December 1922, under the presidency of Mario Cosenza, it presented a parchment to Mussolini, "regenerator of Italy." Mussolini had come to power on October 30. Thus no more than a few weeks had sufficed him to regenerate Italy. Mussolini answered praising "the precious work performed by Italian teachers in foreign lands."[270]

In 1931 the association gave a luncheon in honor of Cosenza. The ambassador presented Cosenza with a gold medal. Those who praised Cosenza in their speeches, besides some Americans who did not realize that they were being used as fronts, were Leonard Covello, vice-president of the association, J. Freschi, and the ambassador.[271]

262. XXVII, p. 184.
263. XX, p. 286.
264. XXII, p. 280.
265. GS, December 12, 1932.
266. XXI, p. 563.
267. XXII, pp. 416, 618.
268. XXIII, p. 262.
269. XVII, p. 444.
270. XVII, p. 383.
271. XXXV, p. 145.

Italian Young Folks League (Brooklyn)

The earliest information we have of this organization dates from 1925. It gathers studious youth, organizes it for a common work of education and trains it to public life." "It gathers bold young people, born here of Italian parents, and wanting to keep Italian ardor alive in their hearts." Their president was August E. Califano,[272] the headmaster of the Italian Child Welfare School. In April 1926, Baron Sergio gave a lecture on Fascism at this club.[273]

In 1932 the League was described as a spirited fraternity of young Italians who have devoted themselves to spreading the Italian culture and ideals among foreigners. It had as its president M. Pasqualle Yuppa.[274]

Leonardo da Vinci Art School

"It led a poor existance" up to 1932, when it came under the direction of A. Piccirilli and Michele Falanga. In 1932 the government began to support it, to the great satisfaction of the *Carroccio* which hoped that it would become "a forge in the service of the mother country." Patrons of the school were the Consul General and G. Gerli.[275]

M. Falango was knighted by Mussolini in 1925.[276]

Columbus Legion (The Bronx)

Carroccio,[277] stated that its purpose was to foster among the Italians of the Bronx the study of the Italian language. Its president was Pasquale D. Badia, M.D., a prominent Fascist. We do not know whether this was the same as the Legione Dei Figlior Colombo, of which in 1927 Vito Contessa was president, E. Guccione, secretary and P. Caruso, treasurer.[278] The latter in 1931 was a member of the Fascio Theodore Roosevelt.[279]

Società Gioventù Nicosiana

It was in existence in February 1929. Its president was Cannelo Amoruso, one of the editors of the Fascist daily *Progresso Italo-Americano*.[280]

272. XXI, p. 457; XXII, p. 620.
273. PIA, April 19, 1926.
274. XXXV, p. 342.
275. XXXV, pp. 98-99.
276. XXII, p. 411.
277. XVII, p. 331.
278. GS, January 28, 1928.
279. Ibid., July 11, 1936.
280. PIA, February 1, 1929.

Roman Forum

Association of professional men under the presidency of Freschi, which existed in Brooklyn in 1931.[281]

Greenwhich House

Erected in 1931, an Italian language directed by Mrs. Legiadri-Laura, the wife of the Fascist physician whom we already know. Greenwich House also maintained a summer colony at Poughkeepsie, New York, for sons of Italians.[282]

Summer Vacation and Tours in Italy

The idea of organizing tours for boys and girls goes back to 1921.[283] In that year the Italy-America Society took the first initiative of this kind.[284] In 1922, twenty-five young people went to spend their vacations in Italy at the expense of the Order of the Sons of Italy and the Italian Chamber of Commerce, under the direction of Bonaschi and under the protection of Di Silvestro.[285]

These tours soon gave opportunity for propaganda. The summer tour of 1925 was conducted by Countess Irene de Robilant, secretary of Italy-America Society.[286] In 1927 Baldo Aquilano founded an Italian Tourist Institute "which specialized in the organization of trips to Italy by teachers and students." His office was at 225 Lafayette Street, the beehive of Fascist activities.[287]

In 1928 the Fascist government began to organize, at its own expense, summer vacations in Italy for boys and girls of Italian parentage living abroad. In that year during a single month 7,200 young people from European and the Mediterranean lands were gathered in Italy.[288]

In 1929 the League solicited donations for sending Italian-American children to the Fascist summer camps in Italy. In July 120 boys and 48 girls

---

281. XXXIII, p. 147.

282. XXXIII, p. 283.

283. See also Salvemini's pamphlet, "Italian Fascist Activities in the U.S.," pp. 12-13; and Diggins, *Mussolini and Fascism*, p. 100. [Ed. Note]

284. *Italy-America Society News Bulletin*, December 30, 1928; February 15, 1921.

285. Aquilano, pp. 128-129.

286. *Bulletin of the American Association of Teachers of Italian*, February 1925, p. 17; *Italy-America Society News Bulletin*, January and March, 1925.

287: AF.

288. P. Parini, "Les Fasces Italiens a L'etranger," in the year book of the *Centre International d'etudes sur le Fascisme* (Lausanne, 1929), p. 173.

of Italian parentage, ranging in age from thirteen to seventeen, sailed for Italy. They wore shields with the fasces. The girls were under the chaperonage of sisters from the Villa Vittoria Convent of Trenton, New Jersey. The mayor of New York, Mr. Walker, and Ambassador De Martino went aboard the ship to see the party off. There were "three cheers for Mayor Walker" and "three cheers for Jimmy." "Jimmy" exhorted the boys and girls to take advantage of that splendid opportunity and keep in mind the fine character "not only of the people but also of the government of Italy":

> Italy is making wonderful and very rapid strides, and under the present administration has won the admiration of the world. From your trip you will bring back a clearer view of the progress of civilization and a stronger sentiment for Italy and its accomplishments.

Upon their arrival in Italy the boys and girls were presented to Mussolini and the pope and then taken to Fascist summer camps, near Naples and Palermo.[289]

The children who were to enjoy these trips to Italy — a coveted gift indeed — were chosen according to a method well calculated to arouse Fascist zeal not only in the fortunate ones selected but also in their class mates. This is what we read in the daily *Stampa* of Turin (Italy) on September 12, 1929:

> As is well-known, each year on the anniversary of the Birthday of Rome, the children in Italian schools abroad are told to express their thoughts about Italy in the form of an essay. This has been going on for five years. The call to the children comes from the Duce. It is the Duce again who supplies the theme within whose limits the children's thoughts must be developed. There is a single theme for all children in all Italian schools throughout all countries, a theme which serves to test both the degree of advancement attained by our schools abroad and the new spirit of the little Italians scattered all over the world.

The children's papers were sent to Rome and there examined. The authors of the best papers in each country were rewarded with the trips to Italy. On the morning of August 1, Mussolini gave a reception to all the boys who had come from foreign countries. He told them: "Be proud of wearing the black shirts and being Italian." In the evening the secretary general of the party addressed them at a grand demonstration:

> Young comrades, you will leave Italy after having gazed beyond (!) the organs of one ancient glory at the organs of the new Italy. Tell your fathers and your mothers, who perhaps only recall a fixed and tormented Italy, the miracle you have witnessed. Tell them the joy and pride you felt in roaming the roads of Italy and the streets of Rome. Tell them, above all,

289. *New York Herald Tribune*, July 6, 1929.

about the magnificent shrine of this morning when before you our Duce appeared. Go, young and proud ambassadors of Fascist Italy.[290]

In the December 1929 issue of the *Carroccio*, A. De Biasi was so indiscreet as to ask the following questions:[291]

> Is it possible to get a report about the children's trip to Italy organized by the general Secretary of the League, Captain Cancli? It was announced that here in America the sum of twenty-five thousand dollars was collected for this purpose. On the other hand, an official communication of the Secretariat for the Fasci Abroad in Rome stated: "There is in Italy a small group of children from the United States, one hundred and thirty in all, and the expenses for this undertaking *have been entirely by the Bank of Sicily*. May we know then, what use was made of the twenty-five thousand dollars collected here? Let us have light.

The light never came and the mystery was never mentioned again by the editor of *Il Carroccio*.

Eighty American students of Italian origin were registered with the University of Rome in 1931 and were received by Mussolini.[292]]

The outcome of our research has always been the same. At the head of those associations which were captured by Fascist agents were to be found directorates made up, entirely or for the most part, of members of fellow-travelers of the Fascist party. If there were here and there a few non-Fascist members, they were made use of as fronts. Moreover, the organizations in America depended on headquarters which had their locations in Italy. The Sons of Italy, who had no headquarters in Italy with which they could coordinate themselves, kept an office in Rome which acted as a link between the Fascist party and the leaders of the Fascist League of North America.

290. Rome daily *Messaggero*, August 2, 1929.
291. XXX, p. 383.
292. XXXIV, p. 177.

3

The Italy-America Society,
The Institute of Italian Culture,
and the
Italian Historical Society

While the two Orders of the Sons of Italy and the other transmission belts of which we have spoken in the preceding pages were working among the citizens and residents of Italian descent, other transmission belts indoctrinated the English-speaking population.

The Italy-America Society

This society was founded at the end of the First World War, and its purpose was "to create and maintain between the United States and Italy an international friendship, based upon mutual understanding of their national ideals and aspirations." At that time Italy was still living, like the United States, under a democratic system and it was not difficult for either country to understand the other. In fact, up until the end of 1922, the society did useful and honest work by spreading correct information about Italian affairs and organizing students' trips to Italy.[1]

---

1. Federal Writers Project, *The Italians of New York*, p. 103. [Ed. Note]

When Mussolini seized power, mutual understanding became difficult indeed, and perhaps the Italy-America Society should have disbanded in 1923 rather than in 1939 as it did. But as early as the spring of 1923 the society fell into line and became the medium through which the high financial and Tory circles of America gave vent to their admiration for the "great man."[2]

> The secretary of the society, Mr. Henry J. Burchell, was knighted by Mussolini in 1923[3] and in September 1923 showed his loyalty to his feudal lord by upholding him even in such an international act of gangsterism as the occupation of Corfu.[4] In 1926 he was received by Mussolini; Mussolini put at his disposal "a precious material" and he announced that he would make a tour of lectures in American cities.[5] The Italian consuls cooperated with the branches of the Italy-America Society in the organization of the tour.[6] Mr. Burchell inaugurated his tour at the Italian embassy at Washington, and then he visited the cities of Baltimore, Nashville, St. Louis, Memphis, New Orleans, Santa Barbara, San Francisco, Sacramento, Seattle, Salt Lake City, Lincoln, Omaha, Chicago, Boston, and New Haven speaking on such subjects as "Rebirth of Imperial Rome" and "Italy and Mussolini." Mussolini rewarded this Fascist enthusiasm by bestowing upon him a second decoration.[7]

The society published a bulletin in which with great glee all kinds of achievements were credited to the Fascist regime. It offered luncheons and dinners to eminent Fascist visitors at the best New York hotels, and occasional lectures, which usually were events in New York society circles. To be a member of the Italy-America Society became a distinction and its gala celebrations were never missed by the social reporters of the important New York dailies. One may form an idea of the work which was carried on by the society from the following instance. In February 1932, the society celebrated a "George Washington evening" at the Mayflower, by dances, music, presentation of an American flag and an Italian flag to the society, etc. A gentleman, Mr. Ernest de Weerth, started the festa by a short address where he described the misery of Italy before Mussolini came to rescue her from Bolshevism. When he subsided, the couples started to dance. Then the dancers subsided and Mr. de Weerth started talking again on the happiness of Italy after Mussolini began to perform miracles. Then he subsided again and the dancers started again their job, and so on until the dancers tired of dancing and Mr. de Weerth tired of speaking and ejaculated his epilogue.[8]

2. The president of the Italy-America Society in 1923 was Paul Cravath, an attorney for the House of Morgan. [Ed. Note]
3. XVII, p. 608.
4. XVIII, p. 267.
5. XXIV, p. 78.
6. XXV, pp. 263, 359; *Bulletin of the Italy-America Society*, March 1927.
7. XXV, p. 636; *Italy-America Society Bulletin*, February 1928, p. 23.
8. *Italy-America Society Bulletin*, February 1932, pp. 26-35.

The yearbook for 1925 of the society gives the names of its directors and members. There are to be found there American bankers like Mr. Thomas W. Lamont, Mr. Clarence Dillon, Mr. Otto H. Kahn or Mr. Charles E. Mitchell who, from 1925 to 1928 were to float Italian loans for three hundred million dollars on the American market, pocketing a 10 percent commission on them;[9] American men and women of Tory complexion who liked in Mussolini "the man who had put the canaille in its proper place," making the trains run on time; American stuffed shirts waiting for some decoration falling from Rome on their breasts; and even some wholly respectable people who sincerely loved Italy and were made use of as fronts. If from American one turns to Italian names, one finds there all the leaders of the Fascist gang — Judge Freschi, Stefano Berizzi, Alberto Bonaschi, Giuseppe Previtali, etc. — aptly intermingled with a few fronts.

Manager of the society from 1923 to 1928 was Countess Irene di Robilant, who had arrived from Italy immediately after the March on Rome and who, besides minding the business of the society, gave Fascist lectures here and there. Miss Robilant was succeeded at the end of 1928 by Lauro De Bosis.[10] This exceptionally well gifted young man came to America as a Fascist, but under the impact of his experiences in this country, changed his mind, started underground anti-Fascist activities in Italy and during the summer of 1930 resigned from the office.[11] De Bosis was succeeded by Mrs. Carla Orlando-Averardi, a full-fledged Fascist, who in 1934 was succeeded by Alberto Carabelli, formerly on the staff of the two Fascist dailies *Progresso Italo-Americano* and *Corriere d'America*, and managing editor of the Fascist magazine *Atlantica*.[12]

9. On these financial dealings with Mussolini see Gian Giacomo Migone, "Aspetti internazionali della stabilizzazione della lira: il piano Leffingwell," in *Problemi di storia*, pp. 43-94; and "La stabilizzazione della lira: la finanza americana e Mussolini," *Revista di Storia Contemporanea*, 2 (1973), 145-185. [Ed. Note]

10. In 1927 a Press Office to bolster Italy's image in American eyes as established within the Italy-America Society as a result of an agreement between the Bank of Morgan and Italian Finance Minister Giuseppe Volpi di Misurata. The headquarters of the society was then transferred to the Casa Italiana of Columbia University, and Burchell also assumed the presidency of the Casa. See Bicocchi, "Propaganda fascista e comunità italiane in USA: la Casa Italiana della Columbia University," pp. 664-668; and the documentation in Archivio Centrale dello Stato, *Ministero della Cultura Popolare*, busta 439, fascicolo "Italy-America Society." [Ed. Note]

11. De Bosis was born in 1901 of an Italian father and an American mother (Lilian Vernon). He studied in Italy and taught briefly at Harvard Unviersity. By 1930 he had associated himself with Mario Vinciguerra in the anti-Fascist Alleanza Nazionale, and on October 3, 1931 he died in a heroic flight from Rome after dropping anti-Fascist leaflets over the Italian capital. In 1933 Salvemini was appointed to the Lauro De Bosis Chair of History at Harvard. See Charles F. Delzell, *Mussolini's Enemies: The Italian Anti-Fascist Resistance* (Princeton, 1961), pp. 67-71; Frances Keene, ed., *Neither Liberty nor Bread* (New York, 1940), pp. 361-62. [Ed. Note]

12. IAW.

To tell the truth, in March 1928, the Italy-America Society gave a reception for Arturo Toscanini,[13] whose scant love for Mussolini was a well-known fact, and a scholar of anti-Fascist opinions, Prof. Lionello Venturi, was one of the speakers in February 1929.[14] But Toscanini had not yet refused to play the Fascist anthem in Bologna and had not yet been insulted and beaten by the Fascists, and Venturi had not yet refused to take the oath of allegiance to the Fascist regime. These facts were to occur in 1931. In 1928 and 1929 the directors of the Italy-America Society were not prophets and could still be hospitable.[15]

The Italy-America Society and its various branches in Boston, Philadelphia, Chicago, San Francisco, Los Angeles, and New Orleans were too aristocratic and exclusive; they catered to a special section of the American public, an influential section to be sure, but still limited in numbers, and people who at the bottom did not need any particular propaganda effort to become pro-Fascist. The Italian government could have used to better advantage the $5,000 a year with which it subsidized the society. It was necessary to reach a larger audience. Such a task was entrusted to other organizations.

The Institute of Italian Culture

In 1923, an Institute of Italian Culture in the United States was created under the direction of an executive council consisting of full-fledged Fascists or fellow-travelers, like Burchell, Bigongiari, Cosenza, Prezzolini (then visiting professor at the summer session), and a few honest people made use of as fronts like Arthur Livingston and Prof. S. P. Duggan. The institute was established in cooperation with the two transmission belts, the Italy-America Society and the Dante Alighieri Society, and fronts like the Institute of International Education and the Instituto de las Españas.[16] As its president,

13. *Italy-America Society Bulletin*, April 1928, p. 73.
14. *Italy-America Society Bulletin*, January 1929, p. 207.
15. Salvemini's references to Toscanini and Venturi were important events in the history of Italian anti-Fascism. In Bologna on the evening of May 14, 1931, Toscanini refused to begin his concert with the Fascist humn "Giovinezza," and as a result was beaten by Fascist *squadristi* led by Costanzo Ciano. He left Italy shortly thereafter and remained in the United States until after the war, during which time he associated himself with Salvemini and the anti-Fascist movement. See Delzell, *Mussolini's Enemies*, p. 200, and the documentation in Archivio Centrale dello Stato, *Segreteria Particolare del Duce, Carteggio Riservata* (1922-43), fascicolo H/R, "Toscanini, Arturo."
Venturi was one of the handful of leading Italian university professors who refused to take an oath of loyalty to the king and to the Fascist regime in August 1931, as a result of which he lost his teaching position. Venturi, an eminent art historian, joined Giuseppe Borgese in exile and took an active part in the Mazzini Society during World War II. See Delzell, *Mussolini's Enemies*, pp. 91-93, and De Felice, *Mussolini il duce* (Turin, 1974), p. 109. [Ed. Note]
16. The Istituto di Cultura Italiana was created with the support of Columbia University

Prof. John L. Gerig of Columbia [Univeristy] was elected. Its secretary was P. M. Riccio,[17] and its executive secretary, Ugo Cocchini, in 1923 one of the directors of the transmission belt Dante Alighieri Society.[18]

The institute claimed to be purely an educational organization. But an institute is not what it claims to be. It is what its directors want it to be, and among its directors those prevail who are possessed with more clear ideas and more determined will. We do not know whether Professor Gerig was ever possessed of any clear or obscure idea about Italy. What we do know is that in February 1924, to explain the "very noble" aims of the institute, he tendered a dinner to Bigongiari, S. Romano, U. Guidi, Luigi Cipolla, Salvatore Parisi, Reverend Serafini, Umberto Billi, L. Lanza, and Trombetta. Also present at the dinner were Ottorino Incoronato, president of the transmission belt Italian War Veterans of Montreal, Canada, and a Chevalier Barricelli from Ohio, who would hardly have been the only white shirt in that company.[19] Professor Gerig was answered by two full-fledged Fascists, Di Silvestro and Licari and one aspiring Fascist, Judge Cotillo, who promised their support to the institute.[20]

In the two summers of 1924 and 1925, the institute organized special courses in the University of Rome for American students. In 1925 Gerig and Bigongiari acted as teachers.[21] There is no danger that the students might have learned from them anything which might conflict with the Fascist doctrine or version of events. The names of the students who went to Rome have not been handed down to posterity with the exception of Mario Pei, graduate of the College of the City of New York.[22]

> M. Pei had no need to go to Italy to study in order to discover the glories of Mussolini and Fascism because he had been a member of the New York Fascio as early as 1923.[23] He knew the achievements of the Fascist government and he had announced them that same year in *Il Carroccio*.[24] But to drink in the primary fountains of truth and light under the guidance of his teacher and comrade, Bigongiari, did him a lot of good. In fact, in 1926,

President Nicholas Murray Butler. Almost immediately the Central Fascist Council's secretary, Ornello Simone, informed Gerig that it would cooperate actively with the institute. See Bicocchi, "Propaganda fascista," p. 676. Gerig was the chairman of the Department of Romance Languages at Columbia. [Ed. Note]

17. *Italy-America Society Bulletin*, September 1923, p. 11. [Peter Riccio was the author of *On the Threshold of Fascism* (New York, 1929), in which he argued that Giuseppe Prezzolini and his collaborators on *La Voce* had been the intellectual vanguard of Fascism. Ed. Note]

18. XVII, p. 610.

19. PIA, February 2, 1924.

20. Ibid., March 2, 1924.

21. *Italy-America Society Bulletin*, November 1924, p. 7; XXI, p. 139.

22. XXI, p. 646.

23. Gio., August 11, December 29, 1923.

24. XVIII, pp. 239-241.

we find him as one of the triumvirs governing the Fascio of New York,[25] and most likely it is due to his pen a bombastic proclamation which the fascio issued in December of that year.[26]

In 1926, Professor Gerig received a decoration from Mussolini.[27]

In 1926, he gave an address at Columbia in which he said:

> Thanks to the efforts of your great leader, Mr. Mussolini, we have seen arise an admiration for Italy and her ideas that has never been paralleled in modern history. While some may shake their heads and criticize, there is no doubt of the hold the Duce has over the spirits of the forward-looking young people the world over...Is it not significant that a French artist and soldier is now preparing a portrait of Mr. Mussolini as a further contribution to what he considers a most worthy cause?[28]

The Italian Historical Society

In 1927 an Italian Digest and News Service was founded as "a center of information and propaganda for Italy and the Fascist regime among Americans." Il Carroccio, in breaking this piece of good news, wrote:

> It proposes to publish books and pamphlets documenting fully the new political and economic order in Italy. These monographs will be such as to enlighten the American spirit and they will be printed in editions of tens of thousands of copies.[29]

A few months later in a luncheon in honor of the Italian ambassador to Washington, De Martino, Previtali announced that the Italian Digest and News Service would be transformed into an Italian Historical Society which, under this new guise, "would continue in its purpose of enlightening public opinion about the political, industrial and social revolution which was going on in Italy." The luncheon was attended, among others, by Judge Freschi.[30]

From the Progresso Italo-Americano, May 22, 1927, and from Giovinezza, June 1, 1927, we learn that the society intended to "make known the problems, ideals and events of the New Italy"; that a bureau in Rome "would furnish original documents, information and explanation, and would help the members who for the purpose of studying went to Italy to get in contact with the suitable persons," so that the society would operate as an "efficient connecting link between the American people and Italian achievements"; and that the society would have the following directors: J. L. Gerig; Previtali;

25. XXIV, p. 357.
26. PIA, December 9, 1926.
27. XXI, p. 355.
28. XXIII, p. 647.
29. XXV, p. 167.
30. XXV, p. 488.

Bigongiari; Harold Lord Varney; A. Portfolio; L. Berizzi; Riccardo Bertelli;
Anthony Campagna; Facchetti-Guiglia; A. Fanoni; J. Freschi; John Laspia;
Howard Marraro; Joseph and Charles Paterno; Mario Pennacchio; Peter
Riccio; Antonio Stella; I. Thaon di Revel.

H. L. Varney. We do not know whether he was giving the society his
time and work free of charge, and if not, who was contributing the money
for his salary. Portfolio, treasurer of the society, might perhaps answer
these questions. What we do know is that in August 1927 he delivered at
the Fascio of Port Chester, New York "an extremely Fascist address."[31]
In January 1929, he discovered that "as time passes, the great similarity
between the ideals and goals of Fascist Italy and constitutional America
become increasingly evident to the thinking American people; the early
tendency of some Americans to condemn is giving place to a wholesome
admiration for the great achievements of Mussolini."[32] In March 1929, he
spoke at Rochester, New York on Fascism "as if he were an Italian and the
Consular Agent had to act as interpreter." According to Mr. Varney, the
"Miracles" performed by Fascism in such a short time were due "solely
to the firm will of a man of great genius who was born for the greater glory
of Italy."[33] In 1931, he presented a film *Fascist Italy* at a meeting of the
Dante Alighieri Society of Jersey City, New Jersey.[34] In 1932, he was
knighted by Mussolini, and in 1933, after Hitler came to power, he left the
Italian American Society and took up the editorship of the Fascist magazine, *Awakening*.[35] But even after that he still took part in Fascist propaganda: for example, in 1933 he introduced a film, "a vivid historical exhibit
of Italy's Nine Fascist Years" at different places, including the Catholic
Don Bosco Community Center of Port Chester.[36]

R. Bertelli. In 1923, appointed as commissioner by the Fascist Central
Council for the Fascio of New York.[37]

M. Pennacchio. In 1923, member of the New York Fascio[38] and in 1926
one of the directors of the War Veterans.[39]

As we have seen or shall see later, all the other directors were Fascists or
fellow-travelers, except perhaps A. Fanoni, a surgeon. In 1926, he was
decorated by Mussolini and *Il Carroccio* flooded him with the most
extravagant praises as if he were one of the world's greatest scientists.[40]
These two bounties could never have been conceded to him had he been
marked as unsympathetic to Fascism.

31. PIA, August 9, 1927.
32. Ibid., January 6, 1929.
33. Ibid., February 21, 1929.
34. GS, March 28, 1931.
35. *Who's Who in America* (Chicago, 1941).
36. GS, February 2, April 1, May 6, 1933.
37. Gio., December 29, 1923.
38. PIA, March 2, 1924.
39. Ibid., February 6, 1926.
40. XXII, p. 547.

In his report to the 1927 convention of the Fascist League of North America, Giurato stated that the Italian Historical Society was "doing a really prodigious work."[41]

The society boasted that it possessed "a complete information service, a library, speakers, etc."[42] In February 1928, *Giovinezza* announced that Previtali, Thaon di Revel, Marraro, Roe, Du Chene de Vere (about whom we know nothing), had given addresses on behalf of the society.[43] In March of the same year, the society, in cooperation with the Institute of Arts and Sciences of Columbia [University], organized a series of lectures on contemporary Italy. The English journalist, S. S. McClure, spoke on the subject "Eighteen Months of Italy: Studying Mussolini and Fascism," and Mr. James J. Walsh, professor at the Catholic Fordham University and worthy contributor to *Il Carroccio*,[44] spoke on "The Cultural Background of Modern Italy." Both were introduced by Previtali, and it is not hard to guess in what direction they addressed their eloquence. The society could not do without having A. F. Guidi as one of its speakers.[45] In December 1928, it offered a dinner in honor of Colonel Howard, "fervent propagandist of the New Italy and its regime."[46]

In February 1929, the society announced that the publications of Mr. James P. Roe would be sent free of charge to whomever asked for them,[47] and it issued a pamphlet written by that same Fascist agent on the Roman Question and against Italian Free Masonry.[47A] In March 1929, the society instituted an information bureau run by Miss Emma Barzini, daughter of the well-known Fascist newspaperman, Luigi Barzini [Sr.].[48]

In that same year, 1929, one of the reporters of the *New York Herald Tribune* paid a visit to the office of the society and had an interview with Mr. Varney. Mr. Varney said that the program of the society was "to encourage and provide historical research," but was willing to admit that Fascist propaganda was also one of the aims of the new organization. He himself was the author of a pamphlet printed and distributed by the society, in which he held the view that Italian Fascism was the most perfect form of democracy and that at some day not far distant the United States would be

41. Gio., December 11, 1927.
42. Ibid., December 15, 1927.
43. Ibid., February 15, 1928.
44. XXXI, p. 196.
45. PIA, November 24, 1928.
46. Ibid., December 15, 1928.
47. Ibid., February 8, 1929.
47A. James P. Roe, "Fascism, Masonry and the Vatican in Italy," Italian Historical Society Pamphlet No. 5. [Ed. Note]
48. PIA, March 24, 1929.

forced to adopt it.[48A] He was kind enough to admit that the society employed paid American propagandists who had the task of explaining to the American people the great accomplishments of Mussolini and of the Fascist regime.[48B] The reporter of the *Herald Tribune* thought that such an institution for historical research must have a library and asked to be permitted to see it. But the society possessed only eight books, four of which were the volumes of the New York telephone directory. In 1931, the society circulated in America that film on the *Achievements of Fascism*,[49] of which we already know that Mr. Varney was a commentator. Varney waxed enthusiastic about "the new Italian constitution under the regime of Mussolini" with all the competence gained from a recent trip to Italy[50] without understanding a single word of Italian. Had he traveled at his own expense or as a guest of the Italian government?

A branch of the society was founded in Baltimore, Maryland, in 1928 by the Italian Consul Orsini-Ratto. Another branch, under the title Massachusetts Italian Historical Society, was established in Boston in 1930. The program stated that the society was to be strictly "cultural and undenominational." But in the list of the founders, side by side with the names of several American gentlemen and some members of the Catholic clergy, there were listed also the names of the ex-president and-vice-presidents and-officers of the dissolved fascio of Boston, as well as the names of other well known Fascists, none of whom, however, had ever made any contribution to or shown any familiarity with historical studies. At the inaugural meeting of the society, the official speaker was no less a person that the Italian Ambassador De Martino who delivered the most fantastic eulogy of Mussolini. The speech was printed and widely distributed by the society as its first contribution to historical learning.

48A. Harold Lord Varney, "The Outlook for Democracy in Italy," Italian Historical Society Pamphlet No. 6. [Ed. Note]

48B. The Italian Historical Society published a number of translations of key works on Fascist policy, including Alfredo Rocco (minister of justice under Mussolini), *The Political Doctrine of Fascism;* Giuseppe Volpi di Misurata (minister of finance), *The Financial Reconstruction of Italy;* Alberto Pennachio, *The Corporate State;* and Howard R. Marraro, *Nationalism in Italian Education.* In addition, its pamphlet series included "The Italo-Ethiopian Controversy" (No. 15), a defense of Mussolini's invasion; Volpi's "Italy's Financial Policy" (No. 1); Willis J. Abbot, "Mussolini Tells Why He Prefers Fascism to Parliamentarism for Italy" (No. 2); Herbert W. Schneider, "Italy Incorporated" (No. 3); and Alice Hunt Bartlett, "Fascism and Poetry" (No. 7). [Ed. Note]

49. GS, March 28, 1931.

50. PIA, October 3, 1928.

4

ROMAN CATHOLIC PRIESTS [1]

When one bears in mind the meanings which the words Italianism, patriotism, Italian culture, [and] Italian language acquired after 1922, one understands what the Italian Fascists in the United States were driving at when they stated that "the recent political and spiritual events of our Fatherland have brought into high relief the important share which the Vatican, strong helpmate, powerful collaborator of Italianism, has assumed

1. See also Salvemini's pamphlet, "Italian Fascist Activities in the U.S.," p. 11; Diggins, *Mussolini and Fascism*, pp. 182-203; and William B. Smith, "The Attitudes of Catholic Americans Toward Italian Fascism Between the Two World Wars," Ph.D. dissertation, Catholic University of America, 1969. In *What To Do With Italy* (New York 1943), pp. 67-68, Salvemini and La Piana made the following observations: "A deeper and more lasting impression was made on Italian minds by the fact that from the beginning of Fascism the joyful chorus that celebrated the merits of the new regime was joined by the robust and pious voices of the Catholic clergy and laymen the world over . . . As soon as Mussolini, shortly after his advent to power, began his courtship of the Vatican, the enthusiasm of the American Catholics for the Duce and his Fascists increased by leaps and bounds. The favorable disposition of the Catholic clergy towards Mussolini showed itself first in America and was more unanimous than in Italy. In Italy the Vatican had to move warily, for large numbers of the lower clergy were still suffering heavily

in the spiritual expansion of Italianism in the world";[2] that "all the priests in
the zone of Pittsburgh, Pennsylvania were cooperating in every work of
faith and patriotism";[3] that "whoever has been in North America has seen
with his own eyes how much our priests are doing here for Italy...The
priests are excellent servants of the Nation, within and outside the borders
of Italy";[4] that the Franciscan friars "leave a deep imprint of profound
Italianism in their footsteps";[5] that "the mission of the ministers of the
Catholic Cult is to educate the sons of the emigrants in Italianism; nothing is
more necessary today than to instill a sense of their national origin into the
spirit of our youth";[6] that the new apostolic delegate, Monsignor Fumasoni-
Biondi, "will break away from the circle of internationalism and keep
himself...within Italianism";[7] that in the activities of Italian Franciscan
friars in the United States there is "national besides religion; in almost all
their schools they teach the national language by means of Italian teachers,
who know how to insert the glorious traditions of our Fatherland into their
lessons";[8] that "the Italian parishes of Brooklyn are an example of ecclesiastic
and civil activity; beside the temple, always an Italian school, the Educational
Afterwork;[9] the organization of the young people and their preparation for
the future."[10]

If anyone should gather together all the utterances of American cardinals
and bishops about Mussolini, all the sermons, all the articles and essays of
Catholic priests and monks, and all the effusions of the Jesuits of America
and of the minor organs of Catholic thought in this country, one would
have the most impressive and astounding anthology of Fascist glorification.[10A]

from Fascist violence, and only at the end of 1926 were the last traces of clerical resistance to
Fascism wiped out. In America there had been no struggle, and enthusiasm flowed unhampered
by memories of bloodshed. It waxed greater when Pius XI, on December 20, 1926, stated that
Mussolini had been sent by Divine Providence. It reached a high pitch at the time of the
Lateran agreement, and finally it reached its climax when Mussolini sent the Fascist legions on
the Spanish 'crusade' and was so highly commended and complimented by the Pope himself."
[Ed. Note]

2. XIX, p. 352.
3. XIX, p. 360.
4. XIX, p. 560.
5. XXI, p. 432.
6. XXII, p. 94.
7. XVII, p. 118.
8. XXIV, p. 389.
9. The Afterwork is a Fascist institution established in Italy in 1925 under the chairmanship
of a prince of the royal house.
10. XXXV, p. 231.
10A. In *What To Do With Italy*, pp. 69-70, Salvemini and La Piana observed that: "We need
not descent to mere archbishops and bishops, many of whom received, at one time or another,
decorations from the Fascist government as a sign of appreciation for their cooperation in
creating a halo of greatness and almost of holiness around the head of the Duce and for their
fostering among American Catholics and non-Catholics the cause of Italian Fascism. Much less

In 1924, Cardinal O'Connell, archbishop of Boston, discovered that "Italy was in the process of undergoing a marvelous transformation since Benito Mussolini had seized the reins of the Government": "I have never in my life witnessed a change so pressing. I see perfect order, cleanliness, work, industrial development."[11] In 1925, the archbishop of Chicago, Cardinal Mundelein, found out that in the city of Rome there was "order" and concluded from this that "Mussolini is a great big man — the man of the times,"[12] and he accepted a high decoration from Mussolini.[13] In 1926, in Frankford, Pennsylvania, at the inauguration of an Italian parochial school attended by representatives of the fascio of Philadelphia, Pennsylvania, and of the Fascist League of North America, speeches "very enthusiastically applauded, exalting religion and Fascist Italy" were given by Cardinal Dougherty, archbishop of Philadelphia, the Italian vice-consul, and Reverend Tonini, "who, in a brillant discourse, referred to the admirable work of the Duce and the Fascist Government, putting special emphasis on the wise work of Fascism in strengthening and revitalizing religious sentiment."[14] Again in 1926 the archbishop of Boston, Cardinal O'Connell, when accepting a high Fascist decoration, defined the Duce as "a genius in the field of government, given to Italy by God to help the nation continue her rapid ascent towards the most glorious destiny."[15] In the fall of 1934, he persisted still in seeing Mussolini [as] "the miracle man." According to him, Mussolini had shown "great forebearance and magnanimity" after King Alexander of Serbia had been assassinated in Marseilles by agents who had enjoyed the protection of Mussolini.[16] The archbishop of New York, Cardinal Hayes, accepted from Mussolini four decorations, [each] one higher than the other.[17] In 1934, when Msgr. Stephen J. Donahue was appointed auxiliary bishop of New York, Il Carroccio[18] hailed this event "with the most respectful friendship and the most heartfelt devotion," owing to the fact that Monsignor

do we need to descend to the level of priests, friars, monks, and nuns, or to the Jesuits of the weekly America, or to the editors of two or three hundred Catholic diocesan bulletins, newspapers, periodicals, and whatnot...A collection of the books, articles, essays, sermons, addresses, an utterances of bishops, priests, sacristans, and Catholic laymen which saw the light during that period, would form a good-size library and stand as a strange but significant monument to the intellectual blindness caused by fanatic devotion and by a reactionary, organized ecclesiasticism...At present we are interested only in the important part that the support given to Fascism by representatives of the Catholic Church of America had in strengthening the hold of the Fascist regime on the Italian people." [Ed. Note]

11. PIA, January 3, 1924. [Also cited in What To Do With Italy, p. 68. Ed. Note]

12. XXI, p. 354. [Also cited in What To Do With Italy, p. 68. Ed. Note]

13. XXII, p. 511.

14. Gio., October 28, 1925. [Also cited in What To Do With Italy, p. 69. Ed. Note]

15. XXIV, p. 553. [Also cited in What To Do With Italy, p. 68. Ed. Note]

16. XXXVI, p. 501.

17. XIX, p. 352; XXIII, pp. 350, 563; XXX, p. 139. [Also cited in What To Do With Italy, p. 69. Ed. Note]

18. XXXVI, p. 95.

Donahue was "a friend of the Italians," (in terms of Fascist ideology [the Italians means] the Fascists), and for many years he had been in "close intellectual contact" with the *Carroccio,* "being a subscriber and an eager reader of it." The archbishop of Philadelphia, Cardinal Dougherty, the bishop of Seattle, Washington, the bishop of Providence,, Rhode Island, the archbishop of San Francisco, and we do not know how many other high American prelates, accepted decorations.[19] In 1929 the bishop of Cleveland took part in the Fascist celebration of the Birthday of Fascism and spoke, "exalting Mussolini, the Man of Destiny."[20] Again in 1929 at a ceremony for the investiture of an Italian-born bishop at Rochester, New York, two Fascist agents, [Ugo] D'Annunzio and De Ritis, appeared in the seats reserved for the authorities.[21]

The reason for this deluge of enthusiasm is easy to detect. In January 1923, Cardinal Gasparri, the secretary of state for Pope Pius XI, and Mussolini had a meeting in the home of Count Santucci, president of the Bank of Rome, and agreed that a final solution of the Roman Question should be reached, and, moreover, the Bank of Rome, with which Italian Catholic institutions and Vatican high prelates had deposited large sums of money, should be saved from impending bankruptcy. It seems that the Bank of Rome-Vatican-Fascist understanding cost the Italian taxpayer 60 million gold dollars. The favor of the Catholic clergy for Mussolini showed itself first and was more unanimous in America than in Italy. In Italy the Vatican had to move more warily owing to the fact that large sections of the lower clergy were still suffering heavily under Fascist violence, and only at the end of 1926 were the last remnants of resistance wiped out. In America there was never any fight and, therefore, the enthusiasm could flow freely. It was enhanced when Pope Pius XI, on December 20, 1926, stated that Mussolini had been sent by Divine Providence. It reached its climax at the time of the Lateran agreements (February 1929) as a result of which a fresh stream of 90 million gold dollars passed from the Italian treasury into the coffers of the Holy See.[22] From coast to coast, bishops, priests, monks, nuns and Knights of Columbus drained the whole dictionary of laudatory adjectives in praising to the skies the wisdom and religious spirit of the great Duce.

Let us add that not even Protestant ministers failed to sacrifice to the new Moloch. Some of them were Italians. Rev. Cosimo Dell'Osso, in 1928 pastor of the Italian Lutheran Church of New York, was a devoted admirer of the

19. XXI, pp. 252, 253; XXV, pp. 91, 455.
20. PIA, March 29, 1929.
21. Ibid., March 23, 1929.
22. On the Lateran Accords and the negotiations leading up to them see De Felice, *Mussolini il fascista,* II, pp. 382-436, and the sources cited in the footnotes of that volume. [Ed. Note]

super-Fascist *Carroccio*.[23] Rev. Pietro Moncada, in 1930, conducted to Italy a group of Evangelical pastors, for the most part Italians, "to clear up the misunderstandings about the state of things in Italy."[24] A Valdensian minister, G. Brun, in 1935, composed a "hymn to Fascism, for restoring the national consciousness of the Italians and guiding Italy towards a future worthy of ancient Rome."[25] Itinerant Valdensian ministers came every year from Italy to lend a helping hand to the propaganda machine.

Even among the English-speaking Protestant clergy, the Duce could count admirers. In 1923, the Most Reverend E. M. Stires, bishop of the Protestant Episcopal Church of Long Island, in an address at a dinner at the Italy-America Society gave vent to his Fascist enthusiasm and in a debate at the Astor Hotel took the Fascist side against Prof. Arthur Livingston of Columbia[26] and again in 1928 gave free rein to his enthusiasm in an address at the Casa Italiana.[27]

In 1924, Reverend Dr. A. Conrad delivered, in the Protestant Church of Park Street in Boston, Massachusetts, a laudatory sermon on Fascism.[28] The Episcopal bishop of Buffalo, Dr. Brent, in 1926 went to President Coolidge to tell him that "Mussolini was giving Italy a new spirit."[29] The one who broke the record was Reverend Dr. Samuel W. Irwin, rector of the Methodist College of Monte Mario in Rome, who, in 1928, had the effrontery to give lectures to show that the Germans of South Tyrol had no ground to complain of any oppression on the part of the Fascist regime.[30] The Protestant ministers who had a share in Fascist propaganda, were few in proportion to the [total] number of them. Moreover, they enjoy a great freedom of movement, whereas the Roman Catholic clergy are strictly controlled by their superiors, and therefore, the whole of the Protestant clergy cannot be regarded as responsible for the utterances of a few, while the moral responsibility of the Roman Catholic priests is that of their bishops. When all this has been said, the fact remains that the lower clergy of Italian origin in this country deserve a certain indulgence if they let themselves be led into the paths of Fascism by the example not only of their legitimate superiors, but also of some Protestant ministers.

We have drawn from *The Official Catholic Directory* of 1927 the Italian churches in the Bronx, Brooklyn, New York, and Queens, with the names of

23. XXVIII, p. 249.
24. XXXI, p. 430.
25. AF.
26. XVIII, p. 498.
27. XXVII, p. 487.
28. XIX, p. 678.
29. XXIV, p. 281.
30. XXVIII, p. 323.

their priests. Then we have tried to find out who among them took part in Fascist demonstrations or other Fascist activities. The date which we have thus been able to collect are rather fragmentary, but they are more than sufficient to show how close and efficient has been the Catholic-Fascist understanding. Those priests who, during the Fascist celebration of the Birthday of Rome, April 21, 1940, received a certificate of merit from the consul general for services rendered in their parochial schools to the "Italian language," i.e. for spreading Fascist thought, are singled out by the letters *Cm.* Their names have been drawn from *Grido della Stirpe.*[31]

A. Rectors of Churches

1. Joseph R. Agrella. Our Lady of Mount Carmel. Brooklyn.

In 1924, spiritual director of the Italian Catholic Union of Brooklyn.[32] In 1928, the Fascio Umberto Nobile, Greenpoint, Brooklyn, opened its schools of Italian language under his auspices.[33] In March 1929, he invited his parishioners to a ceremony of thanksgiving for the Lateran agreements, in which he hailed the "master craftsman, Benito Mussolini, who, with great care and a loving heart, is forging the destinies of the Fatherland."[34]

2. Alfonso Archese. Sacred Hearts of Jesus and Mary. Brooklyn.

Cm. In 1926, together with the consul general, he spoke at a dinner to raise funds for the Fascist transmission belt, the Ospedale Italiano.[35] Very much admired by the *Carroccio* as a "priest of untiring activity, of always brilliant initiatives, recognized leader of the Italian clergy of Brooklyn."[36] In 1932, spoke to a "grand patriotic evening" where the entrance of Italy into the First World War was celebrated.[37] One of the co-editors of the Catholic-Fascist weekly *Il Crociato.*[38] In January 1936, during the Italo-Ethiopian War, spoke at a meeting of the Fascist Academy of Music where money was being raised to help Mussolini's war.[39] In September 1936, took part in the ceremony where a flag, destined for Marshall Graziani, Italian viceroy in Ethiopia, was blessed.[40] In November 1936, blessed the banner of the Fascist club Araldo di Grollalanza, praising the "patriotic" aims of the club.[41] In 1940, not only received the certificate of merit from the consul, but took

31. April 27, 1940.
32. PIA, March 2, 1924.
33. Ibid., October 15, 1928.
34. Ibid., March 2, 1929.
35. XXIII, p. 264.
36. XXXV, p. 231.
37. XXXV, p. 239.
38. XXXVI, p. 95.
39. GS, January 11, 1936.
40. Ibid., February 1, 1936.
41. Ibid., Nobember 4, 1936.

part in the honorary committee for the ceremony for the Birthday of Rome.[42]

3. Gaetano Arcese. Holy Rosary. Manhattan.

The super-Fascist *Carroccio* in 1934 defined him as "beloved leader of the Italian clergy of Brooklyn," and informed us that in Italy he had been received by Piero Parini, director of the Bureau of Italians Abroad at the Foreign Office, and Parini "had renewed the compliments which he had already tendered him in America, for what he was doing in behalf of Italianism [Fascism] among immigrants and strangers."[43] From the *Catholic Directory* of 1937, p. 102, we learn that he succeeded the Fascist Caffuzzi in the office of diocesan consultor. He was also supreme spiritual director of the Italian branches of the Union of the Holy Name Societies. Cardinal Hayes could find but Fascist priests to advise him on Italian affairs in his archdiocese.[43A]

4. Leopold Archese. Saint Lucy. Bronx.

"Always ready to offer his valuable contribution to all manifestations of Italianism."[44] In April 1935, granted the hall of the Church of Nativity in Ozone Park, where he then acted as rector, for a meeting of the Armando Diaz Club, a branch of the Fascist Lictor Association, for a lecture of the chief Fascist agent A. F. Guidi. A group of boys from the parochial school, presented by Arcese, sang "Giovinezza" and a patriotic demonstration was staged in the street, at the head of which marched Arcese.[45] In August 1936, allowed the committee of the Fascist club Pietro Badoglio to hold their meeting in the auditorium of his church.[46]

5. Victor Bassi. Our Lady of Grace. Bronx.

According to the anti-Fascist weekly, *La Parola*,[47] he is "notorious for his Fascist activities"; during the Ethiopian war, collected rings from the Italian women to be sent to Italy to bolster her gold reserves; celebrated the Italian victory in Ethiopia by organizing a demonstration where the Fascist anthem "Giovinezza" was played, in 1941, in a sermon held in his church, he incited his parishioners to protest against the conscription of Catholic youth into the American army.[47A]

6. Joseph A. Caffuzzi. Our Lady of Carmel. Bronx.

In 1923, he was praised by the *Carroccio* for his "religious, educational,

42. Ibid., April 27, 1940.
43. XXXVI, p. 230.
43A. See also Giovanni Schiavo, *Italian-American History*, II (New York, 1949), p. 772. [Ed. Note]
44. GS, August 29, 1936.
45. Iibd., April 20, 1935.
46. Ibid., August 29, 1936.
47. July 12, 1941.
47A. Schiavo, *Italian-American History*, II, pp. 796-797. [Ed. Note]

and patriotic work"[48] and for "fervid patriotic sentiments."[49] He opened an
Italian school in 1925.[50] In 1926, the fasci of New York and vicinity promoted
a *Te Deum* in his church because Mussolini had escaped an attempt upon his
life.[51] He took part in the committee to honor Italo Balbo in 1929.[52] The
archbishop of New York, Cardinal Hayes, "called him to his side in the
College of Advisors."[53] Given his mentality, it is not hard to guess what
criterion he used in choosing and proposing to the archbishop the priests
who were to promote "a more intense educational movement" among the
Italian element of New York. They were: G. Caramanno, A. Buonaccorsi,
G. Bastaglia, S. Cantatore, P. Cantatore, G. Cinfrino, R. Molfitano, C.
Rosselli, and F. Monteleoni.[54] In the *Catholic Directory* of 1927, p. 105, he
appears as one of the diocesan consultors in the archiepiscopal curia of New
York. Died in 1931.[54A]

7. Arsenio Caprio. Our Lady of Loreto. Brooklyn.
Cm. In 1938, the Fascist transmission belt, Columbia Independent League,
held the commencement exercises for its schools of Italian language in the
auditorium of his church.[55]

8. Anthony Catoggio. Saint Joseph. Bronx.
Cm. In 1925 was chairman of the committee which organized the dinner
in honor of Margarella, president of the transmission belt Child Welfare
Committee.

9. Alexander Ciocia. Saint Michael Archangel. Brooklyn.
Co-editor of the Fascist Catholic weekly, *Il Crociato.*[56]

10. A. R. Cioffi. Saint Rosalia. Brooklyn.
Cm. In January 1940, in the auditorium of his parochial school, the
mother's club held a ceremony. Consul General Vecchiotti intervened,
received by a chorus which sang the Fascist anthem "Giovinezza." The
consul praised Cioffi, who "has known how to organize one of the most
beautiful parochial schools which exists in America."[57]

11. Joseph Congedo. Heart of Jesus and Mary. Manhattan.

48. XVII, p. 725.
49. XXXIV, p. 81.
50. *Official Catholic Directory*, 1927.
51. XXIV, p. 456.
52. PIA, January 1, 1929.
53. XXXI, p. 428.
54. XXVIII, p. 243.
54A. Caffuzzi had also been awarded a knighthood by King Victor Emmanuel III. Schiavo, *Italian-American History*, II, pp. 787-788. [Ed. Note]
55. PIA, July 4, 1938.
56. XXXVI, p. 95.
57. GS, January 20, 1940.

Cm. Admired by *Il Carroccio* as a "priest of great heart and foresight."[57A] In 1924 published a pamphlet, *For God and Country: Forward Sons of Italy!* [*Pro Deo et Patria: Avanti Figli d'Italia*] to assert the need of spreading the knowledge of the Italian language as a defense of Italianism.[58] In 1925 he established at Hackensack, New Jersey a summer camp for needy Italian children[59] — a worthy initiative indeed, if besides granting these children a good amount of fresh air, Reverend Congedo did not stuff them with Fascist propaganda. The fact that this was true is proved by the popularity which Reverend Congedo enjoyed among the authorities of Fascist Italy[60] and by the fact that in 1932 Mussolini knighted him[61] and granted $1,500 to the summer camp of Villa St. Joseph.[62] In 1928 he opened the first parochial high school for young Italians of both sexes who wanted to study "in a religious and Italian atmosphere."[63] In 1934 he received a gold medal for spreading Italian culture in America.[64] His work in the summer camp of Villa St. Joseph was much appreciated by the Fascists, and in June 1934 a celebration was held aboard the Italian liner *Rex* under the sponsorship of the ambassador, the consul general and Generoso Pope, to raise funds for the upkeep of the school.[65] In November 1934, he took part in the ceremony where the Federation of Apulaian Associations offered a bust of Mussolini to the University of Bari. More about his Fascist activities will be said later on.

12. Anthony Demo. Our Lady of Pompeii. Manhattan.

In 1925, described by *Carroccio* as "well-deserving rector, a soldier of God and Fatherland."[66] Knighted by Mussolini in 1928.[67] Shareholder of the *Carroccio*.[68] "He served his country in the glorious brigade of Grenadiers, and the national discipline has remained indelibly stamped upon his character."[69]

13. Daniel Di Nonno. Holy Family. Manhattan.

The church of the Holy Family "is an educational center for Italian youth...It is a school of patriotism. The priest keeps intact the pride of the Italian. This year (1934) the Association of Italian War Veterans chose the

57A. XXXVI, p. 199.
58. XX, pp. 469, 476.
59. XXI, p. 264.
60. XXI, p. 674.
61. XXXV, p. 337.
62. *New York Times*, July 18, 1932.
63. XXVIII, p. 759.
64. XXVI, p. 213.
65. XXXVI, p. 110.
66. XXI, p. 459.
67. XXVII, p. 184.
68. XXX, p. 371.
69. XXIII, p. 371.

temple of Rev. Di Nonno to hold the solemn mass in honor of the Unknown Soldier. Grouped around the Consul General, the War Veterans and the guests of honor, the people, led by Di Nonno, joined in the rite consecrated to the far distant Fatherland. This gained the praise of the Italian authorities and of the Veterans' National Association in Rome."[70]

14. Bonaventura Filitti. Saint Theresa of the Infant Jesus. Bronx. Cm. His greatest quality is "his ardor and national enthusiasm."[71]

15. Dominic J. Fiorentino. Saint Dominic. Bronx. Cm. In 1934 he took part in the committee which offered Mussolini's bust to the University of Bari.[72]

16. Francis P. Grassi. Saint Anthony, Wakefield. Bronx.
"He was one of the founders of the Association of War Veterans. He knows how to combine the duties of a priest with those of a disciplined Fascist."[73] "100 percent Italian,"[74] "patriot priest,"[75] "priest of efficient religious, civil and patriotic activity."[76] In 1921, he promoted in New York a first nucleus of Fascist sympathizers.[77] In 1924, "raised a hymn of praise to Fascism."[78] In 1926, he received a decoration for his "outstanding patriotic activities"[78A] and was received by the pope and by Mussolini.[79] In 1928, honorary president of the Fascio Podestà-Priori of the Bronx, he participated in a meeting of the fascio, at which he advised the members to attend the gatherings.[80] In 1929, he took part in the committee to honor Italo Balbo.[80A] In 1929, in a telegram to Mussolini, he claimed to be a "humble pioneer of the Fascist ideal in America."[81] In 1931, he gave vent to his admiration for the Grido della Stirpe,[82] and raised a hymn to the "unconquered and unconquerable Duce."[83] In 1932, became "an authoritative and active member of the Lictor Federation" which took the place of the Fascist League

70. XXXV, p. 55.
71. XXXV, p. 312.
72. GS, November 18, 1934. [At the ceremony dedicating the church in May 1927, Cardinal Hayes and Mayor Walker presided along with Italian Consul General Axerio. Schiavo, Italian-American History, II, p. 794. Ed. Note]
73. XXV, p. 56.
74. PIA, October 21, 1928.
75. XVII, p. 618.
76. XXIII, p. 465.
77. GS, November 25, 1933.
78. XIX, p. 155.
78A. XXIV, p. 89.
79. XXIV, p. 305.
80. PIA, February 3, 1928.
80A. Ibid., January 1, 1929.
81. Ibid., February 12, 1929.
82. GS, May 2, 1931.
83. Ibid., November 14, 1931.

of North America, received a second and higher decoration from Mussolini for his "loyalty as an Italian and a Fascist priest"[84] and praised the *Grido della Stirpe*, "the only Fascist weekly of America that has known how to fight, without human respect, for the triumph of justice and for the affirmation of the Fascist ideal among the Italian masses."[85] In November 1932, after Trombetta's acquittal at the Arena trial, he sent him a "brotherly kiss."[86] In 1932, the golden anniversary of his priesthood was celebrated by a great celebration which was enlightened by a piece of music entitled "Fascist Italy," composed for the occasion and dedicated to the honored priest by Maestro Mauro Bosco. Toastmaster of the banquet was Judge Freschi. "Many speeches hailed the patriotism of the guest of honor, who was one of the first enthusiasts of the Fascist movement in Italy." Telegrams of greeting were sent by President Roosevelt, Governor Lehman and Mayor La Guardia — Father, forgive them, for they knew not what they were doing — and Father Coughlin, who knew perfectly well what he was doing.[87] In May 1936, after the Fascist victory in Ethiopia, he gave a sermon in his church "vibrating with ultra-Fascist faith." At a meeting onMay 10, Mario Lauro, representative of the consul general, certified that Grassi had been "the first and greatest apostle of Fascism among all the priests of America."[88] In 1940, the Dante Alighieri Society in Italy bestowed upon him a gold medal "because of his prominent activities in the United States aimed at spreading the knowledge of the Italian Language and culture."[89] He had never kept any parochial school. He had spread the knowledge of Italian language and culture through his Fascist allocutions and activities.[89A]

17. Vincent Jannuzzi. Saint Joseph. Manhattan.

"Soldier of Italianism,"[90] "exalted spirit of faith and patriotism,"[91] "held in great esteem for his patriotic spirit,"[92] "comrade" who "combines in himself the virtues of a priest and the exemplary activities as a wholehearted Fascist."[93] In 1924, the *Carroccio* published an article in praise of him. In commenting on this article, the magazine said that "the Government of Rome had never shown itself to be so inspired as when it rewarded him with

84. Ibid., February 6, 1936; XXXV, p. 85.
85. GS, March 5, 1932.
86. PIA, November 5, 1932.
87. Ibid., January 18, 20, 1934; GS, January 20, 1934.
88. GS, May 30, 1936.
89. PIA, October 23, 1940.
89A. Grassi, who received the title of commendatore from the Italian government, died in Rome during World War II. Schiavo, *Italian-American History*, II, p. 777. [Ed. Note]
90. XXVI, p. 382.
91. XIX, p. 477.
92. XXII, p. 279.
93. XXXVI, p. 229.

the Cross of Knighthood."[94] On June 14, 1924, a dinner was given on board the Italian steamship *Duillo* to benefit the Church of Saint Joseph and its annexed school, which had been founded by Reverend Jannuzzi. Chairman of the ceremony was fellow-traveler Judge Freschi.[95] In April 1926, the Fascist League, the War Veterans, the Sons of Italy and the consul general picked out the Church of Saint Joseph, "with the ready cooperation of the rector Rev. Chevalier Jannuzzi," to celebrate a Mass thanking God for the salvation of Mussolini from an attempt at his life.[96] In March 1929, Reverend Jannuzzi, together with the Fascists Martinez, Garofalo and Catanzaro, attended an "evening celebration of sublime Italianism" where "the sacred oath of fealty to the Fatherland, the King and the Fascist Regime" was renewed.[97] In 1929, he was a member of the committee to honor Balbo.[98] Shareholder of *Carroccio*.[99] In 1931 he received a higher decoration.[100] In 1934, the director general of the Italians Abroad, Parini visited his school and was "overcome with tenderness by the children, on whose lips flowered the names of Italy and Mussolini with grace and enthusiasm."[101]

18. Gregory Liucci. Most Precious Blood. Manhattan. *Cm.*

19. Alfonso Parziale. Our Lady of Peace. Brooklyn.
Cm. Knighted in 1925. He aimed at making his school on Carroll Street "a temple of Italianism."[102] "Moving spirit of the Italian Catholic Union of Brooklyn."[103] In 1926, he received a second decoration.[104] In 1927, he founded an Afterwork (Dopolavoro, a Fascist club), which was inaugurated in the presence of Reverend Pianigiani, chief of the Italian Franciscan friars in the United States.[105]

20. Valerian Pianigiani. Saint Anthony of Padua. Manhattan.
In 1927, took part in the inauguration of the Fascist Afterwork club founded by A. Parziale.

21. Carmelo Russo. Saint Francis of Paola. Brooklyn. *Cm.*

22. Thomas Sala. Saint Roch. Brooklyn.
Cm. In 1926, the inauguration of Fascio Armando Casalini was held in his

94. XIX, pp. 560-562.
95. XIX, p. 697.
96. XXIII, pp. 169, 461.
97. PIA, March 19, 1929.
98. Ibid., January 1, 1929.
99. XXX, p. 371.
100. XXXIII, p. 368.
101. XXXVI, p. 73.
102. XXI, p. 675; XXII, p. 98.
103. XXXIII, p. 111.
104. XXIV. p. 396.
105. XXV, p. 488. [Schiavo, *Italian-American History*, II, pp. 836-838, 841. Ed. Note]

church, amidst "enthusiastic acclamations to Mussolini,"[106] and he requested to be enrolled in the above mentioned fascio.[107] In 1925, at the inauguration of the parochial school which he founded, the consulate was officially represented;[108] a dinner was given to raise funds for his school, and *Carroccio* favored the school[109] knowing it to be in safe Fascist hands.

23. Joseph Silipigni. Our Lady of Loreto. Manhattan.

24. Ottavio Silvestri. Saint Joseph Patron of the Universal Church. Manhattan.

Cm. On the diocesan Kings County school board. "True priest and fervent Italian, well deserving of Religion and of the Fatherland." In his church, Reverend R. Ferrari invoked divine benediction for the king, Italy and for the "magnificent Duce."[110] In 1934, he spoke at a ceremony of the Fascist Association of Italians Abroad of Brooklyn.[111] In 1936, he took part in a demonstration of that organization, blessed the banner of the Fascist club "Sons of the Wolf, and gave a discourse on the Rome of the Caesars, the Rome of the popes and the present day Rome which witnesses "Mussolini's powerful work."[112] Worthy of the admiration of *Carroccio*.[113] Co-editor of the Catholic Fascist weekly *Il Crociato*.[114] In 1933, on the Birthday of Rome, he took part in the ceremony in which the consul consigned the banner given by Mussolini to the society of the citizens of Sant'Angelo dei Lombardi.

25. Analdo Vanoli. Saint Joachim. Manhattan.

Admirer and shareholder of *Carroccio*.[115] Took part in the ceremony for the Birthday of Rome on April 21, 1933.

26. John Voghera. Transfiguration. Manhattan. *Cm.*

27. Paul Zolin. Mary, Help of Christians. Manhattan.

In May 1935, two branches of the Lictor Association, the Francesco Crispi, and the Maria Josè held a festa in the auditorium of his church.[116] Another festa was held there the proceeds of which went to the *Grido della Stirpe*.[117]

From our survey, the conclusion arises that of the approximately fifty Italian churches of New York City, at least twenty-seven certainly belong to

106. XXIV, p. 658.
107. PIA, December 27, 1926; February 17, 1927.
108. XXII, p. 260.
109. XXII, p. 413.
110. PIA, March 20, 1929.
111. GS, October 13, 1934.
112. Ibid., June 6, 1936.
113. XXXIII, p. 280.
114. XXXVI, p. 95.
115. XXVIII, p. 85; XXX, p. 371.
116. GS, May 18, 1935.
117. Ibid., June 6, 1936.

the Catholic-Fascist denomination of Father Coughlin, and it is likely that more than one among the others would not have escaped our search if it could have been more exhaustive.[118]

Of the fourteen rectors of Brooklyn, no less than nine come out affiliated with the Fascist propaganda machine. The concentration of Fascist forces in Brooklyn is a fact that we will have occasion to observe other times. We do not know if this phenomenon should be connected with the fact that one of the most important shipyards in the United States is located in Brooklyn, or with the fact that the bishop of Brooklyn is a warm protector of the Coughlinite movement, or with both of these circumstances combined.

B. Assistants to Rectors

Besides the rectors of the churches there were in New York other priests who acted as assistants to the rectors. It would be strange if the approximately thirty assistants of Fascist rectors like Caffuzzi, Congedo, Jannuzzi, etc., were politically indifferent or anti-Fascists, or that a politically indifferent or anti-Fascist rector would tolerate a Fascist assistant in his church. We will enumerate here only those assistants about whom we have been able to collect definite information.

28. Francis Cagnina. Assistant at Saint Philip Neri. Manhattan.

Cm. In the *Catholic Directory* of 1937 he appears as rector of the new church of Saint Clare of Assisi. *Il Progresso*[119] gave the news that Professor Maistrelli (one of the cultural agents of the consulate general) had examined the pupils of Reverend Cagnina's parochial school and "showed great enthusiasm to the priest and promised to speak of the brilliant results to His Excellency G. Vecchiotti (the Italian consul general) who so loves our children. Many deserve medals."

29. Anthony Castellano. Assistant of Parziale at Our Lady of Peace, Brooklyn.

Carroccio describes him as a "generous patriot."[120]

30. Ignazio Cirelli. Assistant of Cassuneti at Saint Roch. *Cm.*

Carroccio defines him as "one of the most distinguished Italian priests of the metropolis."[121]

---

118. Fr. Charles E. Coughlin, one of the most consistent and well-known exponents of the rightist philosophy in the United States during the 1930s was a strong admirer of Mussolini and Italian Fascism. See Philip V. Cannistraro and Theodore P. Kovaleff, "Father Coughlin and Mussolini: Impossible Allies," *Journal of Church and State*, 13, 3 (Autumn 1971), 427-443. [Ed. Note]

119. July 2, 1940.

120. XVII, p. 506.

121. XXXII, p. 171.

31. Agostino Doyno. Assistant of Our Lady of Solace. Coney Island. *Cm.*

32. Giacomo Lassandro.
"Egregious cooperator" of Silipigni.[122]

33. Francesco Magliocco. Assistant of Caffuzzi in the Church of the Carmine.
Admirer and shareholder of *Carroccio*.[123]

34. Leonardo Pavone. Assistant of Father Congedo.
"Confirmed patriot, pitiless and sincere Fascist, Italian in his soul," in 1931 he gave a lecture at the Fascio Theodore Roosevelt on "The Foreign Policy of the Fascist State."[124] In 1934 he defended the anti-Semitic policy of Hitler: "Hitler persecutes the Jews not because they adore Javè, but because they had harmed the life of the German nation...They made themselves enemies of Germany, putting themselves at the head of the Communist movement."[125]

35. Salvatore Piccirillo. Assistant at Saint Vincent de Paul. Manhattan.
In 1926 he blessed the banner of the Fascio Benito Mussolini.[126]

C. Priests Not Attached to Parish Churches

36. Antonio De Liberti.
Cm. In the *Catholic Directory* of 1927 he is given as belonging to the diocese of Brooklyn, and it seems that he was the assistant of Leopold Arcese in the Church of Saint Lucy, where he became pastor in 1932.[127] In 1934, he spoke, together with several Fascist big shots at a dinner of the society of the citizens of Sant'Angelo dei Lombardi, a Fascist transmission belt.[128]

37. Germano Formica. Director of the Home for Emigrants.
"Egregious friend and colleague" of *Carroccio*, knighted by Mussolini in 1931.[129] In 1932, on the Birthday of Rome, he assisted at the ceremony at which the society of the citizens of Città Sant'Angelo received a banner donated by Mussolini.[130]

38. Joseph Schiano.

---

122. XXVII, p. 501.
123. XVIII, pp. 408, 510; XXVII, p. 184; XXX, p. 371.
124. GS, November 21, 1931.
125. Ibid., March 17, 1934.
126. PIA, February 4, 1926.
127. IAW.
128. XXXVI, p. 510.
129. XXXIII, p. 196.
130. PIA, April 25, 1933.

The *Catholic Directory* of 1927 places him in Brooklyn. In 1927, he spoke at a meeting of the Fascio Umberto Nobile.[131]

D. Priests Belonging To Neighboring Towns
and
Attending Fascist Ceremonies In New York

39. Ernesto Coppo.

According to the *Catholic Directory* of 1927, he belonged to Port Chester. In March 1933, he was the official speaker at the ceremony in which the "Italian Committee of North America handed over to the Consul General a medal and plaque destined for Mussolini to celebrate the tenth anniversary of the March on Rome."[132] In 1936, he spoke at the patriotic and religious ceremony organized by Zolin announcing that "on his next trip to Italy he would carry to Mussolini the devoted greetings of the Italo-Americans of New York."[133]

40. Antonio D'Annucci. Our Lady of Solace. Coney Island.

War Chaplain. In 1926, he spoke at the inauguration of the Fascio Armando Casalini of Brooklyn.[134]

41. Canello Dattolo.

The *Catholic Directory* of 1927 locates him at Dobbs Ferry. In 1926, on a trip to Italy, he gave a speech in Avellino on "Mussolini as seen from the United States, attended by the authorities of the Fascist Party," giving "much attention to the emigration services."[135] If his opinions on Mussolini and his ideas about the emigration services had been such as not to please the authorities of the Fascist party who heard him, he would not have returned to America in one piece.

42. Raffaele Ferrari.

The *Catholic Directory* of 1927 assigns him to the Church of Saint Antoninus of Newark, New Jersey. In the church of Jannuzzi, in 1929, he gave the panegyric of the Lateran aggrements.[136]

43. Severino Focacci.

In 1927, he was rector of the Church of the Assumption in Tuckahoe.

---

131. Ibid., January 14, 1927.
132. GS, April 1, 1933.
133. Ibid., June 6, 1936. [Coppo, who was made bishop in 1922, served for a brief time as pastor of the Church of Our Lady of the Rosary in Port Chester. Schiavo, *Italian-American History*, II, p. 808. Ed. Note]
134. XXIV, p. 658.
135. XXIII, p. 169.
136. XXIX, p. 234.

After having "cooperated in the ecclesiastical and educational work" of Caffuzzi as his assistant, he succeeded him in 1931.[137]

E. Itinerant Priests Sent From Italy
to
Carry On Propaganda

They are not to be found in the *Catholic Directory* of 1927 or any other year. They are now and then given by dailies and magazines.

44. E. Cilento.

In 1927, he paid a subscription to the super-Fascist *Carroccio* to have it sent to an American writer "to convince him of the good which the Fascist regime had wrought in our Italy."[138] Together with two other priests, Carloncini and Ciminelli, assisted Jannuzzi singing the solemn mass which was celebrated in the Church of Saint Joseph in April 1926 to thank God for Mussolini's escape from an attempted assissination. Ciminelli was a Fascist without any doubt, as will be shown under number 45. It would be strange if among the four priests who sang that mass, Carloncini alone had been indifferent or anti-Fascist.

45. E. Ciminelli.

"Veteran of the war of Mussolini's companion in the trenches." He delivered the official speech at the solemn mass celebrated by Reverend Jannuzzi in the Church of Saint Joseph in April (see the preceding name, Cilento).

46. Carmelo Disano.

In 1925, he began a course of weekly lectures on social, political and religious matters at the Chapel of the Graces, 415 East Thirteenth Street, New York City. Forerunner of Mussolini in preaching the doctrine of anti-Semitism, in 1926 he gave a speech on "our right to protect Italian youth from the Fanaticism of the Jews."[139]

47. Reginald Giuliani.

During the First World War, was chaplain of the shock troops (*Arditi*) and in 1919 joined D'Annunzio at Fiume. In 1929, he made a "speaking tour of the United States."[140] Killed during the Ethiopian War.

48. Monsignor Pellettieri.

In 1926, he participated in the commemoration of the March on Rome,

137. XXXIV, p. 182.
138. XXV, p. 276.
139. XXIII, p. 263.
140. XXX, p. 366.

declaring himself to be a "devoted follower of Mussolini."[141]

49. Filippo Robotti.

War chaplain, decorated for military valor during the First World War.[142] He came to the United States in 1924 as a member of a mission of Dominican preachers, and announced his desire to give addresses of "patriotic propaganda."[143] He spoke at Buffalo and Port Chester.[144] In 1926, "he undertook an interesting tour of sermons and patriotic addresses in California,"[145] speaking at San Francisco on behalf of the Dante Alighieri Society, the Fascist transmission belt, at their commemoration of the Birthday of Rome.[146] In 1926, 1927, and 1928 he was one of the directors of the New York branch of the War Veteran Federation, the Fascist transmission belt of which Garofolo was president,[147] and of course he delivered patriotic addresses here.[148] In 1928, he returned to Italy "to rest."[149] In 1929, he came back to New York. He was chosen as president of the Blue Ribbon Association. The Fascist League of North America chose no other than this "very authoritative missionary of Religion and Fatherland"[150] when it wanted to commemorate Marshall Cadorna, who had been Italian chief of staff during the First World War.[151] Again in 1929, he was a member of the committee to honor Italo Balbo.[152] In 1930, he gave a sermon in the Church of Mount Carmel during the Mass in commemoration of the two Fascists Carisi and D'Ambrosoli who had been killed in New York,[153] and he gave another speech to commemorate these two comrades in 1931 at the consualte general of New York.[154] In 1932 he was knighted by Mussolini, and the War Veterans offered him a dinner to celebrate the decoration.[155] The *Grido della Stirpe* defined him as a "brave and untiring propagandist in this land of America, not only of the religion of God, but also of Fascism."[155A]

A survey of the other cities of the United States and Canada in which there were Italian language priests, would give the same results everywhere:

141. PIA; October 30, 1926.
142. XXVI, p. 381.
143. XIX, p. 242.
144. XIX, p. 362.
145. XXIII, p. 681.
146. XXIII, p. 461.
147. PIA, February 6, 1926; August 20, 1927; February 25, 1928.
148. XXVI, p. 381; XXVIII, p. 105.
149. XXVIII, p. 98.
150. PIA, March 14, 1929.
151. Ibid., January 11, 1929.
152. Ibid., January 1, 1929.
153. XXXI, p. 335.
154. XXXIV, p. 178.
155. XXXV, p. 78.
155A. February 2, 1932.

priests who encourage the founding of fasci, are members and directors of them, offer them their own buildings for their meetings, celebrations and ceremonies; priests who are praised by Fascists as patriots of deep Fascist sentiments, fervent Fascists and so on; priests who celebrate Fascist holidays like the March on Rome, the Birthday of Rome, the Birthday of Fascism, and even the day on which Italy entered the First World War — a barbarous ceremony, 100 percent Fascist; priests who utter the most exaggerated exaltations of Mussolini and defend him even when, on the island of Corfu, he bombs women, children and old people who had fled there from Asia Minor; priests who bless Fascist banners, speaking Fascist words at these ceremonies; priests who are directors of the Fascist transmission belt branches of the Dante Alighieri Society; and everywhere, priests who are knighted by Mussolini for services rendered to the cause of Italianism, that is to say of Fascism. If all these knights garbed in black would go to the conquest of the Holy Sepulchre, they would constitute an army, certainly invincible for its number, if not for its military skill and bravery. In 1925, at least seven priests belonged to the Fascist transmission belt, War Veteran's Association, in Chicago, Illinois.[156]

In the Vatican there exists a high official whose job is to direct the work of religious assistance among the Italian emigrants, the so-called Prelate of Italian Emigration. Under his supervision, a Pontifical College for Italian Emigration prepares the priests who have to come to indoctrinate the Italian emigrants in this country. This prelate was very well informed about what was going on in the United States, and he never deemed it necessary to caution his subordinates to be more prudent. That Father Robotti, who came to the United States in 1924 to spread Fascist propaganda, was chosen by the higher-ups of his order. Another Dominican, Fr. Angelico Bregola, who was in America for two years on a mission, and who, in 1925 when he returned to Italy, was appointed by the Fascist Government chaplain of the military academy of Modena,[157] and therefore, certainly had not come to America to spread anti-Fascist propaganda, was also chosen by the higher-ups of his order. In June 1926, when Msgr. Caccia Dominioni came to the United States as papal delegate, Thaon di Revel sent him a telegram of welcome in the name of the league, and two Fascist leaders of Chicago made their appearance at his reception in Fascist uniform.[158] In the same year, Cardinal Bonzano, papal legate to the Eucharistic Congress of Chicago, granted a special audience to the secretary of the fascio of Chicago, and he saw no harm in the fact that the fascio of Chicago, "in Black-Shirts," should

156. PIA, Apriil 30, 1925.
157. XXVIII, p. 88.
158. Gio., June 30, 1926.

take part in a reception in his honor,[159] and that Rev. Giovanni Longo, who had come to the United States for the Eucharistic Congress, should profit by it to visit various states, spreading "effective Fascist propaganda."[160] In 1928, Monsignor Della Ciappa, sent to New York by the Vatican to collect data for the sanctification of a nun, who had dedicated a disinterested life of sacrifice to the education of the emigrants, Mother Cabrini, took advantage of his religious mission to tell the Italians that "Providence had sent Benito Mussolini, the Duce, reviver of moral consciences, works and of faith, the man who knows how to assert himself, leading Italy back to paths of glory, power and prosperity, respected and feared in the world."[161] Saintly Mother Cabrini could never have suspected in her life that Providence wanted to make Italy a nation feared in the world.

The Jesuit fathers who came from Italy to the United States in 1929 to "labor for the Italian colonies," obtaining, according to the *Carroccio*,[162] "plenty of frutis" had certainly not been instructed by their superiors to create disturbances with Mussolini's consuls before returning to Italy.[163]

159. XXIII, p. 676.
160. XXIV, p. 310.
161. PIA, November 24, 1928.
162. XXIX, p. 133.
163. As Salvemini himself admitted in his pamphlet "Italian Fascist Activities in the U.S.," p. 11, there were a few admirable exceptions to the long list of Catholic priests who, in one way or another, supported Fascism, notably Msgr. Joseph Ciarrocchi of the Church of Santa Maria in Detroit. Ciarrocchi led a successful fight against the Italian consul's (Giacomo Ungarelli) efforts to take over the Italian community in his city. See Philip V. Cannistraro, "Fascism and Italian-Americans in Detroit, 1933-1935," *International Migration Review*, 9, 1 (Spring, 1975), 29-40. [Ed. Note]

PART III

THE FASCIST MOVEMENT

1

Fascist Demonstrations
in New York City[*]

1. [By the end of 1929 the Fascist organizations and their transmission belts had been firmly established in the United States, and in the years that followed their activities and propaganda began to bear fruit as never before. The depression not only plunged America into a deep economic, social, and political crisis, but tended to reinforce and aid Fascist efforts. The economic disaster raised serious questions about the validity of American institutions and disillusionment grew rapidly throughout the nation. From the extreme right were heard the loud and influential voices of demagogues like Huey Long, Francis Townsend, Theodore Bilbo, and Charles Coughlin, each advocating his own particular brand of right-wing ideology to solve the ills of American society. From the left, the Communists moved into high gear as they preached the end of capitalism and worked feverishly for the coming of the proletarian revolution. Many admiring and hopeful eyes in the United

---

[*] Sections 1 and 3 of this chapter were written by the editor of the present volume. Section 2 has been taken from Salvemini's pahmphlet, "Italian Fascist Activities in the U.S.," pp. 14-15. [Ed. Note]

States turned toward Mussolini and his Fascist experiment in the early 1930s as the dictator proclaimed his corporate state and his social institutions as the answer to Italy's own economic problems.[1]

Although the election of Franklin D. Roosevelt in 1933 gave many Americans a renewed faith, the policies and activities of his new administration also helped to boost the image and prestige of the Duce. Some observers believed that the New Deal was merely an imitation of Fascist social and economic policies in Italy, and indeed many administration leaders had actually studied and praised the would-be successes of Mussolini's domestic program.[2] Thus Mussolini appeared to Americans not only as the man who had saved Italy from Bolshevism and had restored his country to a position of order and strength, but who had now offered the entire world a solution to its most serious crisis. Mussolini's prestige in the United States grew rapidly and steadily in these years.[3]

For a variety of reasons New York City remained the chief center of Fascist activities in the United States during the 1930s. Not only did many of the existing organizations including the Lictor Federation, the Italy-America Society, the Institute for Italian Culture, and the Italian Historical Society have their headquarters there, but it was also the focal point for the Italian-American pro-Fascist press. *Il Progresso Italo-Americano*, *Il Carroccio*, and *Il Grido della Stirpe* all were located in New York, where they had a vast readership among the city's millions of Italian-Americans. Moreover, with the election of Mayor Fiorello La Guardia in 1933 and the powerful attraction of the Democratic party for most ethnic-Americans, Tammany Hall Italian-American leaders such as Generoso Pope, Edward Corsi, Charles Poletti,

1. On the rising threat of Fascism in the United States see Arthur M. Schlesinger, Jr., *The Politics of Upheaval* (Boston, 1960), pp. 69-95; and morris Schonbach, "Native Fascism During the 1930's and 1940's," Ph.D. dissertation, University of California, Los Angeles, 1958. [Ed. Note]

2. Maurizio Vaudagna, "Il corporativismo nel giudizio dei diplomatici americani a Roma (1930-1935)," *Studi Storici*, 16, 3 (1975), 764-796; and Diggins, *Mussolini and Fascism*, pp. 164-166. Reports from Italian diplomatic officials in Washington to Rome stressed the similarities between New Deal policies and the Fascist program. See for example Augusto Rosso to the Ministry of Foreign Affairs, January 17, 1935, Archivio Centrale dello Stato, *Ministero della Cultura Popolare*, busta 170, fascicolo 22, and a report by Rosso entitled "Endenze totalitarie del New Deal," August 31, 1940, ibid., busta 163, fascicolo 19, 78/3. [Ed. Note]

3. After Hitler's seizure of power in Germany in 1933 the blatant activities of the German-American Bund and the aggressive Nazi propaganda quickly aroused criticism from many Americans. The Italian government sought to prevent the growing antipathy toward Nazism from compromising the popularity of the Fascist regime. "One thing is certain," warned Fulvio Suvich, Italian under-secretary for Foreign Affairs, "it is necessary that any Fascist programs that we may undertake in this country must remain independent of Nazi action, lest they may be interpreted in the United States as an alliance between Fascist nations which might be dangerous to American democracy." Telespresso, March 5, 1937, Archivio Centrale dello Stato, *Ministero della Cultura Popolare*, busta 163, fascicolo 19/3. [Ed. Note]

and Ferdinand Pecora controlled the vitally important Italian vote in the city. Because Mussolini had such a powerful attraction for so many Italian-Americans, these and other political *prominenti* were often found publicly supporting Fascist activities and were crucial in Fascist plans to seize the Italian-American community. The fact that much of the anti-Fascist effort was also concentrated in New York for many of the same reasons, only increased its importance to the Fascists and their agents.[4]

The cause of Fascist propaganda received a major stimulus in 1930 when the famous Italian writer Giuseppe Prezzolini became director of the Casa Italiana of Columbia University. The Casa Italiana had already become an important vehicle of Fascist propaganda among intellectuals and students since its earlier identification with the Italy-America Society, the Italian Historical Society, and other transmission belts. As we have already seen, a number of professors in Columbia University's Department of Romance Languages had lent their prestige as intellectuals and educators to Fascist propaganda and the various transmission belts. Now, with Prezzolini as its director, the Casa Italiana became one of the most powerful sources of Fascist propaganda in the United States.[5]]

2. It is probably not due to pure chance that all the professors in the Department of Italian at Columbia Unviersity (Bigongiari, Prezzolini, Marraro, Ricio) are endowed with Fascist souls and that Arthur Livingston, a man of wide learning in the field of Italian literature, but of independent mind, was transferred from the Italian to the French department.

The following significant notice appeared in the *New York Times* of February 20, 1938:

> A group of Columbia University students will live for five weeks next summer with Italian families in Perugia, while others visit Rome to study teaching methods...according to an announcement yesterday by Professor Howard R. Marraro, director of the Italian Interuniversity Bureau on Morningside Heights. The work in Rome will comprise ten lectures on the educational and social activities of the Fascist government, with a compar-

4. Many of the reasons that made New York the major center of Fascist activity were described in a report of January 17, 1935, by Augusto Rosso to Rome. See Archivio Centrale dello Stato, *Ministero della Cultura Popolare*, busta 453, fascicolo "Movimento ascista negli Stati Uniti." [Ed. Note]

5. On the Casa Italiana and its propaganda activities see Bicocchi, "Propaganda fascista," pp. 676-697; Diggins, *Mussolini and Fascism*, pp. 255-257; and the documentation in Archivio Centrale dello Stato, *Ministero della Cultura Popolare*, busta 439, fascicolo "Casa Italiana." Since the end of World War II Prezzolini has continued a running and somewhat hollow-sounding campaign to defend himself against his own past by denying his complicity with Fascism. These unconvincing efforts have been recently brought together in a pamphlet by Prezzolini entitled *The Case of the Casa Italiana* (New York, 1976), a work fraught with desperation and many errors of the kind he accused others of committing. [Ed. Note]

ative study of methods in the United States.

One can be sure that the American students who go to Italy under the wing of such a guardian angel run no risk whatever of learning anything in their lectures at Rome which might lead them to the conclusion that educational and social activities of democratic America might have some superior points when compared with those of Fascist Italy. Nor has there ever been any danger that the Italian Interuniversity Bureau could become a channel for information or activities which might displease the cultural agents of the Italian embassy at Washington.[5A]

Being an Italian subject and a loyal Fascist Signor Prezzolini cannot afford to ignore the regulation issued by the Italian minister of education in August 1934, enjoining professors who intend to go abroad to inform the minister "so that measures may be taken for the guidance of our authorized diplomatic representatives concerning proper propaganda to be carried on in the interests of our culture." The meaning of the word culture in Fascist language may be deduced from the fact that the erstwhile Ministry of Press and Propaganda was rechristened Ministry of Popular Culture. Besides teaching Italian literature in the Department of Italian at Columbia University Signor Prezzolini is director of the Casa Italiana at that institution. On October 20, 1935, a rally at the Casa Italiana marked the reception of the newly appointed Italian consul, Signor Vecchiotti; appropriately enough, he was received to the strains of the Fascist anthem "Giovinezza." On July 17, 1939, Mussolini's personal paper, *Il Popolo d'Italia* published the following statement: "The Duce has received Giuseppe Prezzolini, who reported to him on the activities of the Casa Italiana of Columbia University." Manifestly the Casa Italiana is under two different sovereigns: the head of the Italian government and the president of Columbia Unviersity.[6]

3. [The Fascists in New York suffered a minor blow to their prestige in 1931 as a result of the visit of Italian Foreign Minister Dino Grandi to the United States. News of Grandi's impending journey sparked a major protest effort by anti-Fascists, who petitioned President Hoover and attacked Grandi in their newspapers with particular ardor. The anti-Fascists planned such an impressive demonstration against the Fascist leader that city officials feared for his safety; upon his arrival in New York, therefore, Grandi was taken directly to New Jersey by the Coast Guard. He was, however, subsequently

5A. See also "The Italian Interuniversity Bureau at Columbia University," in *School and Society*, 47 (February 26, 1938), 267-268. [Ed. Note]

6. In 1935 Salvemini was invited to speak at the Casa Italiana, but he refused to do so unless he received an official invitation from either President Butler or Prezzolini directly. He undoubtedly felt that the opportunity to expose Fascism in the lion's den would have a real impact only if it was an official invitation, and of course Prezzolini refused to issue such an invitation. [Ed. Note]

feted at the Casa Italiana, at the White House, and by publisher Adolph Ochs.[7]

It was in this atmosphere that a new figure came on the scene. In late November 1932 Antonio Grossardi arrived in New York as the new Italian consul general. Grossardi's appointment was part of a systematic effort on the part of the Italian Ministry of Foreign Affairs to expand its network of consular agents throughout America and the world by the appointment of younger, highly aggressive consuls trained in the methods and ideology of the Fascist Blackshirts.[8] Grossardi made little attempt to hide his aggressiveness and indicated that he would set about immediately to spread Italianism to New York's Italian-American masses.[9]

Hardly had Grossardi settled into his new position when the local agents and representatives of the Fascist movement demonstrated their solidarity with his work. In December the Italian Historical Society honored the consul with a dinner,[10] and the following day an elaborate reception was held for him at the Casa Italiana, presided over by Prezzolini.[11] In turn Grossardi began immediately to mobilize the numerous Fascist organizations and their transmission belts throughout the city in a vigorous and increasingly blatant campaign of public demonstrations, speeches, and celebrations which culminated in a ceremony in which Grossardi placed a wreath on the bier of Italian aviator Francesco De Piendo.[12] But demonstrations themselves were not enough, and Grossardi set his mind to creating for his subjects a whole new network of local Fascist clubs, social organizations, schools, children's camps, civic committees, and educational centers to spread the regime's propaganda. Perhaps more insidious than this, however, was the skillful way in which Grossardi used the resources of the American and New York City governments to further his own work.]

4. The years of 1933 and 1934, which witnessed Grossardi's activities, were the worst years of the American economic depression. The great majority of the Italians belonging to the laboring classes lived on relief.

7. Diggins, *Mussolini and Fascism*, pp. 123-125. [Ed. Note]

8. In addition to Grossardi, other recently appointed consuls in the United States included Giuseppe Brancucci in Yonkers *(New York Times*, February 24, 1933), the consul in Newark *(New York Times*, October 4, 1935), Consul General Segrè in Boston, Consul Yannelli in Johnstown, Pennsylvania, and Consul General Pervan in Philadelphia. See the testimony of Girolamo Valenti before the Dies Committee in House of Representatives, 75th Congress, 3rd Session, *Special Committee on Un-American Activities*, Report 282, II (Washington, D.C., 1940), October 4, 1938, pp. 1182-1186; Diggins, *Mussolini and Fascism*, pp. 102-104; and Santarelli, *Storia*, I, p. 481. [Ed. Note]

9. *New York Times*, November 23, 1932. [Ed. Note]

10. Ibid., December 18, 1932. [Ed. Note]

11. Ibid., December 19, 1932. [Ed. Note]

12. Ibid., September 7, 1933. [Ed. Note]

They were not in a position to support by their own means the institutions which Grossardi was creating and which needed headquarters, teachers, teaching supplies, and so forth. No one will ever know how much Grossardi's successes cost the Italian taxpayer. An accountant who knew Italian and was not a Fascist agent might clear up this matter by going through the financial records of each institution.

We do not need such an investigation to state that the depression favored the work of Grossardi. At a meeting of the Apulian Federation held on the evening of September 21, 1936, its head, Vincenzo Rossini, described the work done by his organization on behalf of its members. He gave the following information:

> It was possible to obtain work for them from the WPA, the Emergency Relief Bureau and other civic institutions. He mentions the success achieved in getting from the City Hall a license for the retail dealers in ice and coal, who make up the largest group of the members of the Federation, after a campaign to fight and destroy the racket which had existed in that industry for years. He mentions the contract obtained by the ice-distributors from Commissioner Morgan of the Department of Public Sales, thanks to the personal interest of Mr. Di Serio. A good 6,200 permits were obtained in this way.

We do not know to whom was given the direction of the WPA in New York. From the anti-Fascist weekly *La Parola*,[13] we learn that in 1924, a Fascist, Francesco Mancini, killed an anti-Fascist, was acquitted by a Brooklyn jury and during the depression was made foreman in the WPA. It is not difficult to guess how much pressure in the interests of the consulate could be exercised by WPA officials belonging to the Fascist movement upon unemployed of Italian extraction. We lack the means of examining the names of the WPA officials in charge of the Italian population in New York.

Another circumstance which certainly favored Grossardi's work was the election of La Guardia as mayor of New York in the year 1933. La Guardia never held any brief for Mussolini or Fascism. But he had to try to get votes from an Italian electorate among whom the Fascists were becoming well organized, vociferous and aggressive. Therefore he was forced to make concessions to the Fascist bosses now and then. It was clear, however, that he was not overenthusiastic about such bedfellows nor, to keep their favor, was he willing to lose the allegiance of the non-Italian population of New York and of those Italians who had remained indifferent or hostile to Fascist propaganda. On Columbus Day of 1936, after the Ethiopian War, he did not take part in the ceremony at Columbus Circle, thus causing the *Progresso Italo-Americano* to wonder and arousing protests on the part of the *Grido*

13. July 31, 1943.

della Stirpe.[14] This paper suggested that La Guardia should change his name to Mr. Ward. Not only had La Guardia abstained from taking part in the meeting, but he had not prevented an anti-Fascist demonstration from taking place, to antagonize the Fascist ceremony. The Fascist Guarrata proclaimed in *Grido della Stirpe*[15] that "it was high time to stop it":

> La Guardia not only fails to be present at the solemn exaltation of the great Navigator from Genoa, but he allows a few Bolshevist sympathizing Jews, renegades and refugees to give vent to their rage, insulting and outraging Italy and its magnificent Duce, at the same time and on the same Square. La Guardia ignores the fact that Fascism and Italy are one and the same thing.

In 1937, when La Guardia was up again for reelection as mayor of the city, Trombetta, the enfant terrible of Fascism, charged La Guardia with "always humiliating" the Italian element and maintained that it would be better to give the vote "to a mayor of Chinese origin who respected the Italians, rather than to a mayor with an Italian name but a Jewish-Bolshevist soul, who avoids the Italians owing to the fact that in Italy there is a government which gets on the nerves of the subversive elements in New York, who are La Guardia's friends and who are protected by him."[16]

Trombetta found himself alone. Comrade Vinci protested against comrade Trombetta.[17] Facchetti-Guiglia, Previtali, Bonavita and Macaluso came out for La Guardia. An Italian committee, pro-La Guardia, headed by Lionello Perera, was joined by many prominent Fascists, headed by Stefano Miele and Frank Catinella. Corsi headed the Republican committee for La Guardia. An Italian committee for the Tammanist candidate, O'Mahoney, headed by Paul Rao, was joined mostly by people of no account.

Macaluso stated that La Guardia, in the course of no more than four years, had chosen from among New Yorkers of Italian descent eight magistrates, four assistant attorneys, many district office administrators, two members of the board of education, etc.[18] *Il Progresso*[19] gave the names of seventy Italo-Americans who had been appointed to municipal posts. If one scrutinizes them one by one, eleven persons might have been listed as Fascist or fellow-travelers:

---

14. La Guardia learned a political lesson as a result of the Columbus Day ceremony, and the following year he did attend the rally and gave a major address, to the disappointment of the anti-Fascist leaders. See the *New York Times*, October 13, 1937. On La Guardia's period in office see Arthur Mann, *La Guardia Comes to Power, 1933* (New York, 1965). [Ed. Note]
15. GS, October 17, 1936.
16. *L'Impero*, September 7, 1937, p. 2.
17. Ibid., October 15, 1937, p. 21.
18. Ibid., October 15, 1937, p. 20.
19. October 15, 1937.

1. Juvenal Marchisio; 2. Emond L. Palmieri; 3. Antonio Calitti; 4. Stefano Miele; 5. Alberto Bonaschi; 6. Michele Fiaschetti; 7. Edward Corsi; 8. Lionello Perera; 9. Peter Sammartino; 10. Frank Barbieri; 11. F. X. Giacione. We are already acquainted with nos. 4, 5, 7, 8, 9, 11.

J. Marchisio. Teacher at Saint John's College, Brooklyn. Described by *Il Grido*[19A] as "strong champion of Italo-American youth, powerful upholder of the great Italian name." Spoke at a meeting of the Diciotto Novembre fascio.[20]

E. Palmieri. Took part in the celebration of the Birthday of Fascism in 1934.[21]

A. Calitri. Spoke at the demonstration of "fervent patriotism and clamorous homage to Mussolini" of the Federation of Apulian Associations in 1934.[22]

M. Fiaschetti. In 1930 attended the celebration of the Birthday of Fascism promoted by *Il Grido*.[22A] Member of the committee which in 1933 organized the celebration of the tenth anniversary of the birth of the *Grido della Stirpe*.[23]

Frank Barbieri. Described in Scilla di Glauco's *Act of Faith* in 1937 as "vigilant sentinel of Italianism abroad."

Andrew Luotto. Gave a lecture on Fascism in New Haven, Connecticut, in the presence of the local ultra-Fascist consular agent P. De Cicco in 1923.[24] His name "Luotto, Hon. Andrew" is to be found among the words of prominent Fascists who sponsored the Barber's Association grand Mussolinian affair of November 1936.[25]

Others, Magistrate Frank Giorgio, Magistrate George B. De Luca, Dominic Trotta, were not loathe to participate together with well-known Fascists in the ceremonies in honor of the ultra-Fascist priest Grassi in January 1934. Others, Alex Pisciotta, Nicola Soldanieri, took part, together with many well-known Fascists, in the huge demonstration of the Fascist transmission belt at Jackson Villa Park on August 30, 1936.[26]

However, to be fair to the latter individuals one has to bear in mind that Mayor La Guardia and President Roosevelt also sent their good wishes to the ultra-Fascist priest, and that some of them may have been made use of as fronts in demonstrations which in their own opinion were patriotic and not Fascist. Every politician had to fish votes in the Fascist pond.

Among the men who had been appointed by La Guardia was a militant anti-Fascist (Dr. Fama), and none of the others as far as we know ever

19A. October 20, 1934.
21. GS, February 2, 1936.
21. Ibid., March 31, 1934.
22. XXXVI, p. 506.
22A. April 5, 1930.
23. GS, May 27, 1933.
24. XXVII, p. 265.
25. PIA, November 30, 1936.
26. Ibid., August 30, 1936.

showed Fascist proclivities. Thus one has to admit that, all in all, he might have made even greater concessions to electoral expediency. In 1941 he explained the appointment he had made of an unworthy judge by a wisecrack: "When I make a blunder, it is a beaut!" A certain margin for beauts has to be allowed to any man in La Guardia's position.

But when all this has been said, the fact remains that Grossardi and his agents were in a position to derive great advantage from the fact that, for instance, Edward Corsi had become the head of the Home Relief Board, to the great satisfaction of Trombetta. Other well-known Fascists or fellow-travelers like Alberto Bonaschi, Stefano Miele, Peter Sammartino, Lionello Perera, had been chosen for other positions. An Italian shoeshiner or taxidriver who read in his Italian daily those names and of their good luck, was led to think that friendship with powerful men might be useful and would join some fascio or at least some society which was under the protection of a well-known Fascist. Who could blame him? So the fasci and the transmission belts swelled and multiplied.

Under Grossardi's auspices Fascist celebrations and demonstrations increased rapidly in number, size and significance.

In January 1934, the golden anniversary of the priesthood of the Fascist Rev. Francis P. Grassi, pastor of Saint Anthony, Wakefield, Bronx, was celebrated. A spectacular dinner was given in his honor. A "March of Fascist Italy," composed and dedicated to the honored priest by Maestro Mario Bosco, enlivened the evening. When the guest of honor arrived, the orchestra played the American anthem, the Italian royal march, and "Giovinezza." Bishop Walsh of Newark, New Jersey, gave the blessing. Then many speeches "hailed the patriotism of the guest of honor who had been one of the first enthusiasts of the Fascist movement in Italy." Telegrams of greeting were sent by President Roosevelt, Governor Lehman, and Mayor La Guardia[27] who were seeking votes, by Cardinal Hayes, Father Coughlin, three ministers in Mussolini's cabinet, and two cardinals from Italy. President Roosevelt and Governor Lehman, even more than Mayor La Guardia, will be forgiven since they did not know what they were doing.

> Among the speakers the following were recorded: 1) the Mussolinian Count Anthony Campagna; 2) Judge Freschi; 3) Rev. Giovanni Daraio, who spoke "eloquently about the mission of the Catholic minister" meaning, no doubt, that the support of Mussolini was a part of that mission; 4) Judge G. Hartman; 5) A. F. Guidi who "hailed comrade Grassi"; 6) Count L. Criscuolo; 7) Generoso Pope; 8) Edward Corsi; 9) Judge Cotillo; 10) Bishop Walsh; and 11) Grossardi. Other guests of honor were 12) Cas-

27. Ibid., January 18, 20, 1934; GS, January 20, 1934.

tellani, vice-consul at Newark; 13) Judge Caponigri; 14) Assistant District Attorney Di Giovanna; 15) G. di Silvestro; 16) Judge Frank Giorgio; 17) Reverend Monteleone; 18) A. Palanca; 19) A. Portfolio; 20) Paul P. Rao; 21) Rev. Ercole Rossi; 22) Ruis (misprint for Reiss-Romoli?); 23) Judge D. Frank; 24) the Honorable Suglia; 25) Domenico Trotta; 26) Judge Valente; 27) Vicario; 28) Judge Alberto Vitale.

The committee which organized the ceremony was under Mayor La Guardia's high patronage, and included besides some of the above-mentioned names, 29) P. Margarella; 30) L. Covello; 31) Peter Hickey; 32) Edwin Agostini; 33) Pasquale Badia; 34) Adamo Ciccarone; 35) Gaetano Clemente; 36) Antonio d'Angelo; 37) Domenico J. Dall'Aquila; 38) Anthony De Pace; 39) A. Di Marco; 40) Luigi Gerbino; 41) Jerome Cristina; 42) Antonio Guarino; 43) Vincenzo Laviosa; 44) Francesco Maglietta; 45) John N. Malnati; 46) Luigi Massa; 47) Charles Pagnozzi; 48) Michael Paterno; 49) Charles A. Perilli; 50) G. Spatafora; 51) John Suglia; 52) Domenico Trombetta; 53) Antonio Vena; 54) Diodato Villamena; 55) Francesco Vitale.[28]

If we do not count Judge Hartman (no. 4), Bishop Walsh (no. 10), or Peter Hickey (no. 31), who do not belong to the Italian group, we find that of the other fifty-two, the great majority, that is at least forty, were connected with the Fascist movement. Of the twelve others who participated in a ceremony markedly Fascist in character, possibly some took part in this business solely in order to fish votes, or to revolve, like moths, around the light and get a decoration.

In March 1934, a "worthy commemoration" of the Birthday of Fascism was held at the Hotel Ambassador. It was promoted by the *Grido della Stirpe* and by "very dear and faithful friends" of the paper, among whom were Carlo Agrò, Thaon di Revel, Giuseppe Carlino and Luigi Criscuolo.

Consul Grossardi's entrance was greeted with the singing of the anthem "Giovinezza." He was accompanied by Thaon di Revel; Vinzo Comito, as representative of Generoso Pope, who was unable to take part; four officials of the consulate (Spinelli, Caradossi, Spatafora and Melani); A. F. Guidi, commissioner of the Italian Press Abroad; V. Vedovi, president of the War Veterans Federation; S. Bonanno, president of the New York War Veterans Association; G. Previtali, president of the Italian Historical Society; and other celebrities of the Italian community.

The following institutions were represented at the celebration: The Order of the Sons of Italy; the Independent Order of the Sons of Italy; the Arnaldo Mussolini Fascio and the Aurelio Padovani Fascio of Hoboken; the Association of Italians Abroad; the Abraham Lincoln Club; and the clubs affiliated with the Lictor Association, i.e. Giovinezza of Hoboken, represented by Mario De Nicolò, Antonino Gigante, and Francesco Poveromo; the Francesco

28. PIA, January 18, 19, 1934; GS, January 20, 1934.

Crispi Club, represented by Carmelo Casablanca, and Antonio Armeli; the Margherita di Savoia Club. The central council of the Lictor Association was represented by Joseph Santy and Calogero Diana. Three of the directors of the Barbers' Benevolent Association and the entire directorate of the Association of Italian Industrialists and Workers attended the ceremony officially. From Reading, Pennsylvania, a telegram arrived to greet "in a Fascist fashion" the consular authorities and the old leaders, especially Thaon di Revel, and concluded: "We swear loyalty to Il Duce."

The official speeches were given by Trombetta, Thaon di Revel, A. F. Guidi, Grossardi and Mrs. Giulia Morelli. Also Mary Pickford, "admirer of Italy and of Fascism," spoke "with heartfelt enthusiasm of Italy, noting the good fortune of our native land in knowing how to create a leader every time that there is need of one; she concluded her speech, singing the praises of the Duce, Benito Mussolini, and Fascist Italy." A. F. Guidi and Trombetta, in the name of those present, sent a telegram to Parini "begging him to express to the Duce their feeling of gratitude and their unalterable devotion."[29]

In April 1934, the Association of Italians Abroad sent out a circular reminding "all good Italians" that Mussolini had linked that day with the "continuous creative activities of New Italy which, by virtue of the Fascist regime, advances with Roman constancy and spreads over the furrow plotted by Romulus and Remus 2,687 years ago, the fecund seeds of a rejuvenated civilization which brings welfare and peace to the world."[30] According to *Il Progresso*[31] the speakers at the ceremony were G. A. Bonavita, "enthusiastic animator of the Association," and Consul Grossardi. The time had ended when the consuls had to pretend that there were no fasci in the United States. He expressed his approval of that "group of brave men" who "while living among a foreign race, know how to preserve intact their love for their mother land." He also reminded his listeners that "from the furrow traced by Mussolini had sprung the street upon which the whole of the Italian people march today." A street which springs from a furrow is difficult to visualize, but a Fascist consul did not have to worry about mixed metaphors.

The committee which organized the celebration consisted of the following persons, who must be regarded as full-fledged Fascists: R. Avati, U. Barboni, G. Bonavita, U. Canessa, F. De Grassi, G. De Santi, A. Di Giovanni, A. Gianuzzi, T. Grancelli, La Fiadra, P. Pellegrino, P. Pizzo, P. Pugliese, A. Scimone.[32]

29. GS, May 31, 1934.
30. PIA, April 19, 1934.
31. May 6, 1934.
32. PIA, May 6, 1935.

We do not know whether this ceremony was the same as that which was reported by *Grido della Stirpe*[33] as having been held at Hoboken by the Lictor Association, and in which the secretary general of the association, Giuseppe Santy, acted as chairman. The speakers included Ugo Vittozzi, G. Cataldo, Facchetti-Guiglia, who had recently returned from Italy, the consul general of New York; Macaluso, an official of the consulate of Newark, New Jersey; and an official of the consulate general of New York.

In October 1934, the Lictor Association, "advanced sentinel of the Fascist idea on American soil,"[34] in cooperation with the Abraham Lincoln Club of the Bronx, promoted a celebration of the March on Rome at the New Terrace Garden of the Bronx. The fighting Fascist element of greater New York as "fully represented" and the ceremony turned out to be "grandiose." Orators were Gerolamo Cristina, chairman of the celebration committee, Grossardi, and A. F. Guidi.[35] Among those who were recorded by *Il Progresso*[36] and *Grido della Stirpe*,[37] A. F. Guidi was listed immediately after the consul, and Facchetti-Guiglia immediately after A. F. Guidi. These were evidently the most authoritative party chiefs. Three persons sent telegrams of greetings and approval; Edward Corsi; magistrate, F. X. Giacone, and Generoso Pope. Pope was one of the chief key men in the New York Fascist movement. Magistrate Giacone may be classified among the moths attracted by the light. As far as Corsi is concerned, one cannot imagine that he sent his greetings to such a ceremony without knowing anything about the Abraham Lincoln Club or the Association of Italians Abroad, or without realizing that he was joining a demonstration of definite and unequivocal Fascist nature.

These are the names of the persons who took part in the ceremonies of March, April, and October, 1934 according to *Grido della Stirpe* and *Il Progresso*:[38]

1. Edmund Agostini; 2. Edward Agostini; 3. Edwin L. Agostini; 4. Elena Agostini; 5. Carlo Agrò; 6. Arturo Alleva; 7. "Comrade" Fred Alterio of the Alterio Detective Bureau; 8, Carmelo Amoruso; 9. Vincenzo Anastasio; 10. G. Andronaco, M.D.; 11. Lucio Angeli; 12. Adolfo Arena; 13. Raimondo Ariola; 14. V. Ascrizzi; 15. Teresa Badagliano; 16. Vito Bagnato; 17. Arturo Balsimelli; 18. U. Barbani; 19. Attilio Barbera; 20. Gino Barone; 21. Giuseppe Barone; 22. Attilio Barrano; 23. Ippolito Bartolini; 24. R. Bertelli, "once member of the Central Council of North America"; 25. Roseline Boeuf; 26. S. Bonanno; 27. G. Bonavita; 28. Louis A. Bonvicino, M.D.; 29. W. Borea; 30. Mauro Bosco; 31. Angelo Caggiano; 32. Mario Calamai;

33. May 12, 1934.
34. GS, October 27, 1934.
35. XXXVI, p. 506.
36. October 29, 1934.
37. November 3, 1934.
38. GS, March 31, 1934; PIA, May 6, October 29, 1934.

33. M. Campitiello; 34. Renzo Campolini; 35. Ignazio Cancelliere; 36. Vito
C. Cannella; 37. Francesco Canzano; 38. Francesco Capria; 39. Lorenzo
Caputo; 40. G. Carlino; 41. Prime Carnera; 42. F. Cassola, M.D.; 43. G.
Pasquale Catalano; 44. Frank Catinella; 45. James Ciancaglini; 46. Rina
Ciancaglini-Gera; 47. Camillo Cianfarra; 48. Claire Ciani; 49. William
Ciervo; 50. Eugenio Cilento; 51. Vincenzo Ciuti; 52. V. Comito; 53. Emilio
Coppotelli; 54. Giuseppe Cosulich; 55. L. Criscuolo; 56. Giuseppe Cupparo;
57. Gussie Currieri; 58. A. D'Angelo; 59. Vincenzo d'Antona; 60. A. De
Biasi; 61. C. De Biasi; 62. Frank De Caro; 63. M. S. De Cellis; 64. Vincenzo
de Crescenzo; 65. Vincenzo Del Cupolo; 66. Florindo Del Gaizo; 67. Lucia
Della Malva; 68. Lelio De Ranieri; 69. Ettore De Stefano; 70. Calogero
Diana; 71. Vittorio Di Bari; 72. Antonio Di Givo; 73. A. Di Marco; 74. G.
Di Prima; 75. E. Dragoni; 76. J. Fargione; 77. Carmelo Favazza; 78. Filippo
Fazio; 79. Armando Ferraro; 80. Antonio Ferrayorni; 81. G. Ferruggia; 82.
Luigi Fiammenghi; 83. Bortolo Filippone; 84. Remo Fioroni; 85. Dominic
Florio; 86. Leandro Forno; 87. Leonardo Fragomeni; 88. Giuseppe Frasca;
89. Miss Gagliardo; 90. J. Gambatesa; 91. Giacomo Ganci; 92. Giuseppe
Ganci; 93. Giuseppe Genovese; 94. G. Gerli; 95. O. Ghelli; 96. Gaetano
Giallorenzi; 97. A. Giannuzzi; 98. Gennaro Giorgi; 99. Carlo Giovannardo;
100. Guido Giovannozzi; 101. G. Godono; 102. G. Grasso; 103. John
Grieco; 104. Enrico Guarrata; 105. Jerome A. Jacobi, U.S. Ambassador to
Ethiopia (!); 106. Vincenzo La Rossa; 107. Antonietta Latella; 108. Nicola
Lattoraca; 109. Angelo Lauria; 110. Giovanni Lettieri; 111. Salvatore
Limoggio; 112. Anacleto Locatelli; 113. E. Locatelli; 114. Lorenzo Lucarelli;
115. C. Luisi; 116. Miss Giovanna Luisi; 117. Bruno Lupia; 118. E. Luzzatto;
119. F. P. Macaluso; 120. Enzo Maddaloni; 121. Salvatore Mangiaracina;
122. Domenico Marafioti; 123. Salvatore Marchetti; 124. Liborio Marino;
125. Giovanni Marsico; 126. F. M. Martucci, M.D.; 127. Mario Masi; 128.
Ugo Maugeri; 129. Frank G. Melchionna; 134. Miss Eimila Meloni; 135.
Carlo Meola of Chicago; 136. F. Mercurio; 137. Stefano Miele; 138.
Edoardo Migliaccio; 139. Ernest Migliaccio; 140. Gregorio Morabito; 141.
Enrico Morelli; 142. G. M. Mortati; 143. W. G. MacAdoo; 144. MacDowell;
145. Giuseppe Nardella; 146. G. Nardone; 147. P. Occhipinti; 148. Guido
Orlando; 149. Francesco Palleria; 150. Edmond Palmieri; 151. Salvatore
Paone; 152. Salvatore Parisi; 153. Nino Parrello; 154. Carlo Pascarella;
155. Rev. L. Pavone; 156. Frank Pecora; 157. P. Pellegrino; 158. Laurence
Penza; 159. Toto Pescetti; 160. Mrs. Maria Piazza; 161. A. Piccirilli; 162.
Pirrone; 163. Andrea Pisciotta; 164. P. Pizzo; 165. Luigi Podesta; 166. A.
Portfolio; 167. P. Portfolio; 168. Rosa Pucci; 169. Earl Purpura; 170. A.
Raccasi; 171. Giuseppe Radaelli; 172. Salvatore Reina; 173. Anthony S.
Renzi; 174. Anthonio Rispettabile; 175. Roberto Roberti; 176. V. Rossini;
177. Bruno Rovere; 178. A. Ruspini; 179. C. Sabella; 180. G. Salvi, M.D.;
181. Raimondo Sanfilippo; 182. Joseph Santy; 183. G. Sardo Gardalano;
184. Francesco Saroli; 185. Rev. Silvestri; 186. Fred Smith, "organizer of a
new Fascist movement among American intellectuals"; 187. Sabino
Solofrizzo; 188. Spinelli; 189. Ernesto Staiti; 190. Rinaldo Stroppaquaglia;
191. G. Susca; 192. Vittorio Tamagnini; 193. A. Terranova; 194. Vincenzo
Titolo; 195. F. Tomaselli; 196. Miss Torini; 197. Paolo Tornabene; 198.
Antonio Torrente; 199. Carlo A. Tosi; 200. Domenico Tripepi; 201.
Giuseppina Troisi; 202. D. Trombetta; 203. M. Tumolo, M.D.; 204. Valerio
Valeri; 205. V. Vedovi; 206. Gerlando Verruso; 207. Paolino Versace; 208.
W. S. E. Whitestone; 209. E. Zoppa.

R. Airola. Admirer of Trombetta[39] and co-editor of the *Grido della Stirpe*.[40] Special assistant of District Attorney Dewey.[41]

V. Anastasio. In October 1940, together with V. Ascrizzi, L. Angeli and other Fascists, he attended a dinner during which toasts were drunk "to the destiny of the distant Fatherland."[42]

G. Andromaco, M.D. Admirer of the *Grido della Stirpe*.[43] Attended the celebration of the Birthday of Fascism in 1935.[44]

V. Bagnato. Participated in the celebration of the Birthday of Fascism also in 1935.[45]

A. Balsimelli. Secretary of the San Marino consulate in New York. Repatriated in 1942 with the personnel of the Italian embassy.

Giuseppe Barone. "Ready for any sacrifice for the triumph of every Fascist cause in America."[46] Chief of the press bureau of the Abraham Lincoln Club.[47] Volunteered as a member of a Fascist unit during the Ethiopian War.

I. Bartolini. In 1935 celebrated the March on Rome with a message full of Fascist enthusiasm.[48]

M. Bosco. In 1934, he composed a "March of Fascist Italy" dedicating it to Reverend F. Grassi.[49]

M. Campitiello. Admirer of the *Grido della Stirpe*.[50] Participated in the commemoration of the Birthday of Fascism also in 1935.[51]

R. Campolini. "Black shirt of the first hour."[52]

P. Carnera. The well-known Fascist prize fighter.

G. Catalano. Executive of the Bank of Sicily Trust Company. In 1937, contributed to Scilla di Glauco's *Atto di Fede* [Act of faith] with an *evviva, evviva, evviva* for Italy and the Duce.

W. Ciervo. Participated in the celebration of the Birthday of Fascism also in 1935.[53]

E. A. Cilento. Admirer of the *Carroccio* which "makes us feel proud to call ourselves Italians in our adopted country."[54] Participated in the celebration of the Birthday of Fascism also in 1935[55] and in October 1935, wished "long life to our Duce."[56]

V. Ciuti. "Modest but enthusiastic and preserving propagandist of Italianism" *(italianita)*;[57] "well deserving of the Italian Red Cross and the

39. GS, July 12, 1930.
40. Ibid., July 8, 29, 1933.
41. Ibid., August 3, 1935.
42. Ibid., October 5, 1940.
43. Ibid., April 16, 1932.
44. Ibid., March 30, 1935.
45. Ibid., March 30, 1935.
46. Ibid., October 11, 1930.
47. Ibid., March 24, 1934.
48. Ibid., October 26, 1935.
49. PIA, January 18, 1934.
50. GS, April 18, 1931.
51. Ibid., March 30, 1935.
52. Ibid., February 20, 1936.
53. Ibid., March 30, 1935.
54. XXXV, p. 275.
55. GS, October 30, 1935.
56. Ibid., October 26, 1935.
57. XX, p. 400.

War Veterans Association; first in patriotic demonstrations of our colony."[58] Rewarded with a gold medal by the Rome headquarters of the Dante Alighieri Society.[59]

E. Coppotelli. Admirer of the *Grido della Stirpe* and Mrs. Giulia Morelli.[60] One of the directors of the Fascio Sandro Mussolini in 1935.[61]

G. Cosulich. Director of the New York office of the Cosulich Shipping Co. Decorated in 1932.[62]

G. Currieri. Participated in the commemoration of the Birthday of Fascism also in 1935.[63]

A. D'Angelo. Participated in the commemoration of the Birthday of Fascism also in 1935.[64]

V. D'Antona. On the staff of the Fascist daily, *Progresso Italo Americano*. In 1940, awarded a certificate of merit for his service to the Italian language by Consul General Vecchiotti.[65]

V. De Crescenzo. Enrolled as a member of the fascio of New York in 1923.[66] Participated also in the commemoration of the Birthday of Fascism in 1935.[67] Often took charge of directing muscial programs in Fascist ceremonies.

F. Del Gaizo. One of the directors of the Fascism transmission belt Italian Chamber of Commerce of New York.[68] Decorated in 1926.[69]

E. De Stefano. Decorated in 1932.[70]

V. Di Bari. In 1931, President of the Fascio Theodore Roosevelt.[71] Participated in the commemoration of the Birthday of Fascism also in 1935.[72]

E. Dragoni. Executive of the Bank of Rome Trust Co.

G. Fargione. Admirer of the *Grido della Stirpe*.[73] In 1935, protested against "the defamation of the Duce by the press."[74]

A. Ferraro. Admirer of the *Grido della Stirpe*.[75] Participated in the celebration of the Birthday of Fascism also in 1935.[76] Called "our dearest friend" by the *Grido della Stirpe*.[77]

B. Filippone. Wrote in the *Grido della Stirpe*: "For the glory of Italy; hail Fascism."[78]

58. XXI, p. 670.
59. XXXII, p. 244.
60. GS, April 15, 1935.
61. Ibid., August 24, 1935.
62. XXXV, p. 236.
63. GS, March 30, 1935.
64. Ibid., March 30, 1935.
65. PLO, p. 151.
66. Gio., December 29, 1923.
67. GS, March 30, 1935.
68. XIX, p. 208.
69. XXIV, p. 299.
70. XXXV, p. 337.
71. GS, February 28, 1931.
72. Ibid., March 30, 1935.
73. Ibid., June 30, 1933.
74. Ibid., August 31, 1935.
75. Ibid., April 16, 1932.
76. Ibid., March 30, 1935.
77. Ibid., July 13, 1935.
78. Ibid., April 21, 1934.

L. Forno. Participated in the commemoration of the Birthday of Fascism also in 1935.[79] Well-known Fascist radio commentator.

L. Fragomeni. Contributor of the *Grido della Stirpe*.[80]

G. Frasca. Spoke at a meeting of the Fascio Roma Imperiale in 1936.[81]

O. Ghelli. "Old comrade, wounded and maimed in the service of the Fascist cause."[82]

A. Giannuzzi. In 1932 vice-president of the Fascio Theodore Roosevelt.[83] Participated also in 1935 in the celebration of Fascism.[84]

G. Giorgi. Very active in the Lictor Federation.[85]

G. Giovannozzi. Fascist by his own admission.[86]

J. Grieco. Commissioner of the Mario Sonzini Club in 1936.[87]

E. Guarrata. One of the wildest Fascists of Brooklyn.[88] Repatriated with his wife in 1942.

N. Latorraca. "Fascist of the very first hour."[89] Participated in the celebration of the Birthday of Fascism also in 1935.[90]

A. Lauria. Executive of the Italian Line[91] and therefore a Fascist.

L. Lucarelli. A Fascist poet who published in the *Grido della Stirpe* the results of his inspiration.[92]

Miss Giovanna Luisi. Member of the Fascio Iolanda di Savoia.[93]

E. Maddaloni. In 1935, took part in a "Fasicst action" against persons who demonstrated against Italy in her quarrel with Ethiopia.[94]

D. Marafioti. In 1934 and 1935, one of the directors of the Abraham Lincoln Club.[95]

L. Marino. "One of those Fascists who never compromise," in 1930 one of the directors of the Independent Order of the Sons of Italy.[96]

G. Marsico. Employee of the Western Union.[97] Excellent vantage point for anyone wishing to indulge in espionage.

F. Martucci. Contributor to *Grido della Stirpe*.[98]

M. Masi. "Gave himself entirely to the Fascist cause."[99]

U. Maugeri. In 1926, one of the directors of the Fascio of New York.[100]

79. Ibid., March 30, 1935.
80. Ibid., August 5, October 28, 1933; September 21, October 26, November 9, 1935.
81. Ibid., September 5, 1936.
82. Ibid., June 10, 1936.
83. Ibid., February 28, 1931.
84. Ibid., March 30, 1935.
85. Ibid., February 7, 28, October 24, 1931; April 30, May 14, 1932.
86. IAW.
87. PIA, January 8, 1936; GS, January 29, 1936.
88. GS, June 16, August 25, September 15, 1934; March 23, 1935; passim.
89. XXXI, p. 65.
90. GS, March 30, 1935.
91. Ibid., March 31, 1934.
92. Ibid., July 4, August 8, October 24, 1936.
93. Ibid., March 5, 1932.
94. Ibid., August 10, 1935.
95. Ibid., February 24, 1934; February 16, 1935.
96. Ibid., January 4, 1930.
97. Ibid., March 31, 1934.
98. Ibid., December 19, 1931; March 11, July 22, 1933.
99. XXV, p. 492.
100. PIA, May 19, 1926.

In 1927, member of the court of the Fascist League of North America.[101]

M. Melani. Employee of the consulate.

F. G. Melchionna. Attended the celebration of the Birthday of Fascism in 1935.[102]

Edoardo Migliaccio. Participated in the celebration of the Birthday of Fascism also in 1935.[103]

Ernesto Migliaccio. Attended the celebration of the Birthday of Fascism in 1935.[104]

G. Morabito. Attended the celebration of the Birthday of Fascism in 1936.[105]

E. Morelli. "Our faith makes us sure that Fascism will soon benefit the whole of mankind."[106]

G. Nardone. Attended the celebration of the Birthday of Fascism in 1935.[107]

G. Orlando. "Six and half (!) million Americans of Italian descent rightly regard Mussolini as their idol."[108]

S. Paone. Admirer of the *Grido della Stirpe*.[109] Attended the celebration of the Birthday of Fascism in 1935.[110]

N. Parrello. In 1924, one of the directors of the Fascio of New York.[111] Died in 1935.

Francesco Pecora. Participated in the celebration of the Birthday of Fascism in 1935.[112] In August 1936, participated in the Fascist mass meeting of Morristown.[113]

P. Pellegrino. "The March on Rome that we Fascists celebrate."[114]

T. Pescotti. In 1935 member of the Fascist Italian American Union.[115]

M. Piazza. In 1936, one of the directors of the Fascio Edda Ciano-Mussolini.[116]

A. Raccasi. Participated in the commemoration of the Birthday of Fascism also in 1935.[117]

S. Reina. Attended the celebration of the Birthday of Fascism in 1935.[118]

A. Rispettabile. In 1934, one of the officials of the Abraham Lincoln fascio.[119]

R. Roberti. "Fascist from the very first hour, took part in the March on

101. Ibid., November 8, 1927.
102. GS, March 30, 1935.
103. Ibid., March 30, 1935.
104. Ibid., March 30, 1935.
105. Ibid., March 28, 1936.
106. Ibid., February 23, 1935.
107. Ibid., March 3, 1935.
108. Ibid., January 6, 1934.
109. Ibid., May 27, 1933.
110. Ibid., March 30, 1935.
111. XIX, p. 473.
112. GS, March 30, 1935.
113. Ibid., August 22, 1936.
114. Ibid., October 27, 1934.
115. Ibid., November 2, 1935.
116. Ibid., November 14, 1936.
117. Ibid., March 30, 1935.
118. Ibid., March 30, 1935.
119. Ibid., February 24, 1934.

Rome."[120]

B. Rovere. Director of the Bank of Sicily Trust Co. Admirer of Trombetta and of the *Grido della Stirpe*.[121] In 1935 published an article glorifying the the "lira and the policy of national reconstruction of Mussolini"[122] just at the time when the economic and monetary situation in Italy was going from bad to worse. Took part in the celebration of the Birthday of Fascism.[123] "Fervid defender of the Fascist regime in America."[124]

C. Sabella. Manifested his Fasicst faith in 1937, in Scilla di Glauco's book *Atto di Fede [Act of faith]*.

Spinelli. An Employee of the consulate.

R. Stroppaquaglia. An employee of the consulate.

F. Tomaselli. Active contributor of the *Grido della Stirpe*. Much admired by the *Carroccio* as one of those *franc-tireurs* who are always ready to defend Mussolini and Fascism.[125] In 1930, he wrote: "I am not a Fascist but I admire Fascism and take pride in subscribing to it."[126] He did not explain what he would have done differently had he been a Fascist.

P. Tornabene. In 1933, he "greeted the King and the Duce of Fascism with the Roman salute."[127] In 1934, he was gratified to know that the "spiritual rapprochement of all Italians with the country of their origin is due to Fascism: long life to Benito Mussolini."[128]

C. Tosi. One of the directors of the Bank of Naples Trust Company.[129] Participated in the celebration of the Birthday of Fascism also in 1935.[130]

M. Tumolo. Took part also in 1935 in the celebration of the Birthday of Fascism.[131]

P. Versace. In 1934, president of the Sant'Eufemia d'Aspromonte Society. The fact that he not only is found in the company of full-fledged Fascists in the directorate of that transmission belt, but that he also participated in demonstrations of a specifically Fascist nature, permits us to state that he certainly belonged to the movement.

Out of the 109 persons listed above there are only 52 for whom we have not found other evidence of their affiliation with the Fascist movement.

When in February 1935, Grossardi left New York, a dinner was given in his honor aboard the liner *Rex*.[132] The dinner was attended by almost all the

120. Ibid., October 28, 1933.
121. Ibid., November 3, 1934.
122. Ibid., March 2, 1935.
123. Ibid., March 30, 1935.
124. Ibid., July 21, 1935.
125. XXIV, p. 308.
126. GS, September 9, 1930.
127. Ibid., October 28, 1933.
128. Ibid., October 27, 1934.
129. XXXI, p. 322.
130. GS, March 30, 1935.
131. Ibid., March 30, 1935.
132. Grossardi was replaced as consul general in February 1935 by Gaetano Vecchiotti, an equally aggressive diplomat whom *Fortune* identified in 1940 as one of the leading Fascist agents in the United States. See "The War of Nerves: Hitler's Helper," *Fortune*, 22 (November 1940), 86. [Ed. Note]

well-known members of fellow-travelers of the Fascist movement in the city. At the table of honor with him were: G. Pope, J. Freschi, E. Corsi, V. Vedovi, and R. Angelone, an official of the Italian embassy. *Il Progresso*[132A] gave the names not only of the prominents who had the honor of sitting at the same table as Grossardi, but also of those who formed the chorus around those protagonists.

    1. Edwin Agostini; 2. C.Agrò; 3. A. Angelone; 4. A. Arbib-Costa; 5. J. M. Anfiero; 6. P. Badia; 7. Maestro Vincenzo Bellezza of the Metropolitan; 8. L. Berizzi; 9. Riccardo Bertolli; 10. D. Bigongiari; 11. S. Bonanno; 12. A. Bonaschi; 13. Peter Brancato; 14. Giuseppe Brancucci; 15. A. Campagna; 16. Mario Calamai; 17. Umberto Cardossi; employee of the consulate; 18. G. Carlino; 19. F. Cassola; 20. Augusto Castellani, employee of the consulate; 21. Rev. J. Congedo; 22. A. Corigliano; 23. E. Corsi; 24. M. Cosenza; 25. Domenico D'Angiola; employee of the consulate; 26. Attilio D'Antona; 27. A. De Biasi; 28. Pasquale De Cicco, vice-consul at New Haven; 29. Arturo Ferrari; 30. Nadia Del Papa; 31. George De Luca; 32. F. Di Giura; 33. L. Dionisi; 34. A. Facchetti-Guiglia; 35. I. C. Falbo; 36. I. J. Freschi; 37. Siro Fusi; 38. Giuseppe Gambatesa; 39. Alberto Garabelli; 40. L. Gerbino; 41. F. X. Giaccone; 42. G. Giallorenzi; 43. Guido Giovannozzi; 44. Marcello Girosi; 45. Romolo Giudici; 46. A. F. Guidi; 47. Luigi Gullini, M.D.; 48. A. Lauria; 49. E. H. Locatelli; 50. Longhi Rossi, councilor of the embassy; 51. John Lo Re; 52. F. P. Macaluso; 53. D. Malnati; 54. H. Marraro; the consulate; 57. G. Mortati; 58. Paolo Occhipinti; 59. Alberto Ottino; 60. A. Palanca; 61. Michael Palermo; 62. I. Palermi; 63. Ettore Panizza, the well-known conductor; 64. Goffredo Pantaleoni; 65. P. Parisi; 66. M. Paterno; 67. Judge Ferdinando Pecora; 68. Luigi Pesenti; 69. A. Piccirilli; 70. Ezio Pinza, the well-known singer; 71. L. Podesta; 72. G. Pope; 73. A. Portfolio; 74. G. Previtali; 75. G. Prezzolini; 76. Reiss Romoli, executive of the Banca Commerciale; 77. G. Revedin; employee at the embassy; 78. P. M. Riccio; 79. Luigi Risso; 80. Bruno Rovere; 81. Guglielmo Roselli; 82. A. Ruepini; 83. A. Sala; 84. Guido Sansoni; 85. F. Sardi; 86. F. Saroli, executive of the Banca Commerciale Trust Co.; 87. Carlo Savini; 88. F. Scalvini; 89. L. Scaramelli; 90. E. Secondari, M.D.; 91. Meriggio Serrati; 92. Joseph Sessa; 93. Giulio Setti; 94. Rev. O. Silvestri; 95. P. Simonelli; 96. S. Solofrizzo; 97. G. Spatafora, employee at the embassy; 99. G. Sterni; 100. Renato Tasselli; 101. I. Thaon di Revel; 102. Guido Tieri; 103. D. Trombetta; 104. V. Vedovi; 105. G. Vitelli; 106. B. Zirato.

    J. M. Anfiero. Industrialist who in the autumn of 1935, when the Italo-Ethiopian War broke out, in his capacity as their "director and fellow worker," requested all his workers to give two days wages to the Italian Red Cross. The workers contributed as much as about five thousand dollars.[133]

    G. Brancucci. In 1924, consular agent at Bridgeport, Connecticut.[134] In 1927, attended the celebration of the March on Rome.[134A] Knighted in

132A. February 27, 1935.
133. *Pro Opere Assistenziale Italiane*, p. 73.
134. XX, p. 400.
134A. October 30, 1937, PIA.

1934.[135] In 1934 on the Birthday of Rome, sent "Fascist greetings" to Trombetta.[136] In 1936, vice-consul in Yonkers. In 1937, transferred from Yonkers to Vancouver, British Columbia.[137]

N. Del Papa. Employee of the Italian Line.[138]

A. Garabelli. Manager of the Fascist review *Atlantica* and secretary of the transmission belt, Italy-America Society.[139]

L. Gerbino. In 1928 contributed to endowing the transmission belt Casa Italiana.[140] Decorated in 1932.[141]

G. Giovannozzi. Fascist by his own admission.[142]

R. Giudici. "Comrade."[143] Stated in 1935 that "Fascism is bringing to life again the pride of race in all the Italians in the world."[144]

G. Pantaleoni. Fascist by his own admission,[145] up till June 1940.

A. Scalvini. In 1935, attended the celebration of the Birthday of Fascism.[146]

E. Secondari. One of the wildest Fascists among the New York physicians.[147]

M. Serrati. In 1927, attended the celebration of the Birthday of Rome.[148]

G. Sessa. Knighted in 1926.[149] In 1927, attended the celebration of the Birthday of Rome.[150] Received by Mussolini in 1930.[151]

S. Setti. "Militant Fascist."[152]

G. Sterni. Actor. In 1933 sent a message of greeting to the *Grido della Stirpe*.[153] In 1935 announced to the world that "Italy owes a debt of gratitude to Fascism."[154] More about him later.

R. Tasselli. "Former Secretary of the London Fascio."[155] In 1935, one of promoters of the Fascist Italian American Union.[156]

B. Zirato. Shareholder of the *Carroccio*.[157]

To sum up, out of 106 persons who attended the dinner, proof that they were militant Fascists is lacking for only 21 of them. Probably some of these persons, for example the tenor (no. 55), the basso (no. 70) and the two

135. XXXVI, p. 325.
136. GS, April 21, 1934.
137. *Impero*, April 30, 1937, p. 6.
138. IAW.
139. Ibid.
140. XXVII, p. 153.
141. XXXV, p. 230.
142. IAW.
143. GS, November 9, 1935.
144. Ibid., October 26, 1935.
145. IAW.
146. GS, March 30, 1935.
147. PIA, April 21, 1927.
148. XXIV, p. 300.
149. PIA, April 21, 1927.
150. XXXII, p. 172.
151. XXXVI, p. 232.
152. XXV, p. 268.
153. GS, May 27, 1933.
154. Ibid., October 26, 1935.
155. IAW.
156. GS, August 31, 1935.
157. XXX, p. 371.

conductors (no. 7 and no. 63) were there in the capacity of moths revolving around the light.

2

The McCormack-Dickstein Committee

In his book *Gli Italiani nel Mondo*, published at the beginning of 1935, Parini stated that there were 775 fasci abroad and they were "the most loyal co-operators of our diplomatic and consular authorities:"[1]

> In the lands across the Ocean [North and South America] not all those who are Italian by origin are still Italian citizens. For obvious reasons, interests formed over a period of fifty years bind the Italian generations born under those skies to the destiny of their new countries...In those countries what we ask is that all Italians, whether still our citizens or naturalized, *and the latter more than the former* [italics ours],...feel the pride of belonging to this glorious race of ours, do honor to its name, know its language and *serve and protect its traditions* [italics ours]...We can assert with pride...that in the vast and hostile (!) world the Italian emigrant no longer feels alone. A vast spiritual bond has been formed above political boundaries, across continents and seas, wherever our people have migrated.[2]

1. Piero Parini, *Gli italiani nel mondo* (Rome, 1935), p. 36.
2. Ibid., pp. 37-39.

Parini described the work of the Bureau for Italians Abroad, which he directed, in the following terms:

> The Bureau of Italians Abroad, faithful to the directions by which the Duce wanted to reattach the Italian Communities abroad to the life of our nation, has devised new instruments and sharpened and perfected those already on hand. Each Fascio abroad...is a center of that faith which has...put Italy back on the map among the peoples of the world...The Fascist Regime has increased the number and scope of the Italian schools abroad...Lectures in the Italian language in foreign universities and regular courses in Italian language for foreigners not only help to spread our language and our culture, but fan the spark of Fascist thought in the modern world...Added to this is the work of the "Dante Alighieri" Society made to correspond in action and in spirit to the necessities of the new times...
> There has arisen a foreign section of the "National Union of Discharged Officers" ("Unione Nazionale degli Ufficiali in Congedo") whose purpose is to create and maintain a bond of national and military solidarity among the ex-officers...who want to feel...perpetually and intimately united to their Fascist fatherland...In its work of propaganda, the Bureau for Italians Abroad brings together and coordinates all the tools and means for the purpose either of keeping alive in the communities of emigrants the love for the Fatherland and the faith in the Regime, or of bringing to the attention of the foreigners the achievements...of Fascist Italy. It keeps strict watch over the Italian newspapers abroad; they represent centers of loyalty beyond the frontiers...From time to time orators sent from Rome, and chosen from among those who through life and study are the best acquainted with the problems abroad, go out and inspire their fellow Italians with the most glorious moments of Italian life, bring to them the greetings and thoughts of the Regime, and maintain the moral ties between the Mother country and the emigrants. Special agreements with the best suited Institutions allow us to project the most significant movie films, distributed all over the world, according to schedules preordained with the Royal Consuls and the local Fasci. The most significant and glorious anniversaries in our national life, like the Birthday of Fascism, the March on Rome, Victory Day, are celebrated every year in the Italian communities abroad and always with the intervention of orators selected by, or sent over from Rome. One of the initiatives which has given the best results is the organization of group excursions of Italians to Italy. Thus a real bath of "Italianism" is given them...We mustn't forget, in speaking of publications, the school text-books, purposely edited, illustrated and printed for the Itlaian schools abroad...The Italians abroad are today an immense and united legion which follows the Duce with a well-disciplined and steady step towards the future, silently obedient to his orders, ready for all the battles.[3]

Hitler did nothing more than follow Mussolini's path, when he created the Foreign Division of the National Socialist Party (Gau Ausland) under Ernst Wilhelm Rohle.

---

3. Ibid., pp. 53-56, 64-67.

Officially, the purpose of this organization [the Gau Ausland] is to bring all those of German citizenship living outside Germany into the ranks of the National Socialist Party. The Government has also taken over such organizations as the League of German Societies Abroad, established in 1892, the purpose of which had been to promote cultural relations between Germany and other countries, and has fashioned them into an agency of propaganda. This organization and a number of others have been coordinated into the League for Germanism Abroad, which does not confine its activities to German citizens, but reaches out to all so-called "Volksgenossen," or racial comrades.

The city of Stuttgart has been officially designated as the city of foreign Germans. Annual conventions held there have attracted from 70,000 to 80,000 persons from all over Europe and the Americas. Various other agencies of the German government, the Student Exchange Service, the Academic Exchange Service, lecture Bureaus and travel organizations, are stimulated by the government to work for the establishment, in every country, of German racial groups devoted to the interests of the German Reich.

In the past the Pan-Germanic activities of the Nazi regime have been particularly strong in those countries which border on Germany. Recently, however, there has been a marked intensification of this campaign of propaganda on the American continent. German newspapers in the United States are supplied with free news services, German schools with free educational materials, German radio listeners with special short-wave broadcasts. This propaganda is all directed toward one goal; to instill in the American citizen of German descent a consciousness of the German "race" and a feeling of allegiance toward the German Reich...If this agitation is permitted to continue unchecked, it cannot fail to create a cyst in the body politic of the American people. It will result in setting apart a large group of inhabitants of the United States whose duty it would be to render primary allegiance to the ruler of a foreign power. Friction between this group and the rest of the American people might result in unrest and possible bloodshed.[4]

Ernst Wilhelm Rohle was simply the Nazi-German Parini. In February 1935, a committee appointed in 1934 by our House of Representatives to investigate un-American propaganda reported that agents of the Nazi government were very active.[5] Nazis were conducting youth summer camps where children were taught to regard Chancellor Hitler as their leader and to believe that the principles of government taught by him were superior to the principles of democratic American government. It was quite a common occurrence for steamship lines to invite residents of this country to parties on board ships while in port, where those who attended were addressed by representatives of Nazi organizations on the subject of Nazism and its philosophy. Gigantic mass meetings were being held and every kind of effort and influence, short of violence and duress, was being brought to bear

4. *The German Reich and the Americans of German Origins* (New York, 1938), pp. v-vi.
5. On the McCormack-Dickstein Committee, see the introduction to this volume. [Ed. Note]

in order to weld all persons of German birth or descent into one group subject to dictation from abroad. But it was quite a different matter with the Fascists. The committee devoted no more than eleven lines to stating that they had had evidence tending to show Fascist activitiy by an Italian vice-consul at Detroit, Michigan and had submitted it to the State Department. (As a result of the ensuing investigation the Italian vice-consul of Detroit, Signor Ungarelli, had to pack his bags for Italy.)[6] But the committee was as considerate towards that Italian vice-consul of Detroit as not to publish anything about his activities, while they had brought into the open the activities of the German consuls. As for the remaining Fascist activities the committee dispatched them in no more than three lines stating that "organization which seemed to be guided by Fascist principles had made no progress" in this country.[7]

The committee would not have needed any Secret Service to discover that, when inviting people to attend social gatherings and Nazi addresses on board their ships, the German authorities were but aping what had been practice of the Italian Fascists for many years. Here is the information we came across about such gatherings, though we had no intention whatsoever of making an exhaustive survey:

> 1923, July 22. Luncheon aboard the *Colombo*. Over two hundred guests.[8]
> 1923, October 28. "Commemoration of the March on Rome aboard the *Conte Rosso*." Speakers: A. Olivetti, Attorney Littleton, Congressman Tinkham of Boston and I. C. Falbo.[9]
> 1926. "The Italian newspapermen of New York gathered to a dinner aboard the *Conte Rosso*, to welcome Commander Freddi,"[10] a Fascist big shot who had come to the United States in a propaganda and inspection tour.
> 1927, November 6. Celebration of the March on Rome aboard the *Roma*.[11]
> 1928, April. Celebration of the Birthday of Rome aboard the *Duilio*, the proceeds to go to the Fascio of New York. Groups of Fascists wearing black shirts took part. The consul was welcomed by Thaon di Revel, G. Previtali, F. P. Macaluso, Countess Facchetti-Guiglia, V. Martinez, V. Vedovi.[12]
> 1928, September. Dinner held aboard the *Augustus* by the transmission [Italian] Chamber of Commerce of New York. Ambassador De Martino

6. On the Ungarelli affair see Cannistraro, "Fascism and Italian-Americans in Detroit." [Ed. Note]
7. 74th Congress, 1st session, Report 153, February 15, 1935.
8. XVIII, p. 86.
9. XVIII, p. 407.
10. XXVI, p. 460.
11. PIA, November 6, 1927.
12. Ibid., April 24, 1928.

"invited the attendants to turn their thoughts to the Man who, in his in-comparable genius, was untiringly working for the greatness of Italy, under the august sign of the Lictorial Fasces Benito Mussolini."[13]

1928, November 3. The Fascist League of North America made an official celebration of the March on Rome aboard the *Saturnia*, "by this means testifying [to] its highest admiration for the Duce and the prodigious work he is doing for the Fatherland."[14] "The Ambassador walked through two rows of Fascists, keeping his arm raised in the Roman salute." I. Falbo, L. Podestà, G. Previtali, P. Garofalo, V. Martinez, G. De Silvestro, A. Facchetti-Guiglia, P. Catinella, Judge Freschi, A. Bonaschi, S. Miele, D. Trombetta, S. Pino, A. Schisano, V. Rossini, P. Parisi, M. S. De Cellis, C. Maccari were among those attending the ceremony.[15]

In 1934, while the committee was carrying on its investigation, three receptions were held on the transatlantic liner *Rex*. The first, on April 27, was aimed at collecting funds for the educational bureau of the Casa Italiana,[16] and was attended by the Italian ambassador. The second was organized to collect money for the Fascist club Dopolavoro formed by the personnel of the liner.[17] The third, on November 7, was held for the benefit of the Fascist transmission belt, the Association of War Veterans, and was attended by the consul general.[18]

The committee did not notice that a Fascist priest, Reverend J. Congedo, had managed since 1928 an Italian summer camp which had nothing to envy in the Nazi summer camps, and that that summer camp was subsidized by the Italian government; that "every year, on board some transatlantic liner a party was given for the benefit of this Camp, and a substantial sum collected";[19] and that in 1934, besides the three already mentioned receptions, another reception had been given on the *Rex*, to the benefit of Reverend Congedo's camp.[20]

The committee ignored the fact that an official of the Bureau of Italians Abroad, Torquato Giannini, in 1930, 1932, and 1934 had made propaganda tours in the United States.[21] They ignored everything about Parini's January-February 1934 tour in Mussolini's American empire. They took care not to know that American boys and girls were sent to summer camps in Italy. They did not take any notice of what *The Nation* had published on the Casa Italiana.[21A] They did not know anything about the Fascist celebrations and

13. Ibid., September 12, 1928.
14. Ibid., October 11, 1928.
15. Ibid., November 5, 1928.
16. XXXVI, p. 71.
17. XXXVI, p. 107.
18. XXXVI, p. 504.
19. XXXVI, p. 202.
20. XXXVI, p. 110.
21. XXXII, p. 313; XXXV, p. 150; XXXVI, p. 104.
21A. *Nation*, 139 (November 7-12, 1934), 523-524, 550-552, 565, 590; 140 (January 30-April

ceremonies which in 1934 had become so numerous and obstreperous.

Had they really wanted to know what, in actual fact, was happening, they would have, by then, come to the conclusion reached by the review *Fortune* in November 1940:

> There is an almost exact parallel in the operations of the Fascist and the Nazi International. The difference, such as it is, is quantitative: where Hitler has been discreet, Mussolini has been bold.

On March 25, 1941, Representative Dickstein, who had acted as vice-chairman of the committee which had dismissed the Fascist matter, made in the House the following statement:[22]

> About 1932, or 1933, or 1934 the McCormack Committee got some information on the Black Shirts in this country. I have the original documents that I found in my file about the Black Shirts in this country. I went to Gene Pope, the gentleman who is now charged with being a Fascist, and he, himself, gave me and the Committee all the assistance possible to go after these groups that called themselves the Black Shirts. In my presence he condemned their action and absolved the Italian people in this country of any participation in this movement. He did everything he could as an American to destroy the so-called Black Shirts.

From these words one would reach the conclusion that Mr. Dickstein, with the help of Mr. Pope, unearthed a good deal of damaging evidence about Fascist activities. The fact is that Vice-Chairman Dickstein never unearthed anything either with or without Mr. Pope's assistance, since Mr. Pope was one of the key-men of the movement which should have been investigated. The lamb asked the wolf whether there were wolves in the vicinity.

Mr. Girolamo Valenti, editor of the anti-Fascist weekly *La Parola*, May 24, 1941, stated that in September 1934, he had been subpoenaed by the McCoramck Committee; that he had complied with the summons and was expecting to be questioned by Representative Dickstein, but he was dismissed, and never was summoned again.

The report of the McCormack-Dickstein Committee was like a go signal

3, 1935), 129-130, 377-378, 388; 141 (November 27, 1935), 610. [Ed. Note]

22. *Congressional Record*, vol. 87, Part 3 (Washington, D.C., 1941), p. 2570. Dickstein's statement about Pope refers to the charges made by Goffredo Pantaleoni before the executive session of the Dies Committee in December 1940, and which were published in the *New York Post* and the *Daily News* on March 20, 1941. Similar accusations had been made by Girolamo Valenti to the Dies Committee in October 1938, and Valenti repeated them in the May 24, 1941 issue of his newspaper, *La Parola*, adding that there was a Dickstein-Pope collusion. In June, Dickstein made an extended statement to the House defending Pope and attacking Valenti and other anti-Fascists as communists or Fascists in disguise. See *Congressional Record*, vol. 87, Part 5, Appendix (Washington, D.C., 1941), pp. 5278-5280, June 17, 1941, and the *New York Enquirer*, June 23, 1941. [Ed. Note]

given to the Fascist movement. Soon after the committee had stated that there was no vestige of Fascism in America, in the following March, a solemn celebration of the Birthday of Fascism took place in New York under Mr. Dickstein's insensitive nose. The celebration was promoted by the *Grido della Stirpe* and was attended by "an immense crowd comprising elements of every social class, all imbued with blind faith in Fascism and in its great creator." The speakers were Domenico Trombetta, Agostino De Biasi, Angelo Flavio Guidi, Consul Spinelli, and the secretary general of the Dante Alighieri Society who had come from Italy for a tour in the United States. "The presence of the Fascists in their black shirts with their glorious pennants, struck a vibrant note. The crowd was carried away by the strains of Giovinezza and other war songs." "The dawn of March 23 found the best and most fervent exponents of Italianism and Fascism assembled and fraternizing in irresistible enthusiasm. About five thousand miles away from the dazzling light of Rome an overwhelming ovation for our Duce was concluded with shouts of Eja, Eja, Eja, Alalà, for the King, for Fascist Italy, for the Duce." The *Grido della Stirpe*, March 30, 1935, which regales us with this dithyrambic description, gives us also the names of all those who attended. It is clear that all of them belonged to the movement.

1. Carlo Agrò; 2. G. Arcieri, M.D.; 3. J. M. Anfiero; 4. Ed Agostini; 5. Raymond Ariola; 6. G. Andronaco, M.D.; 7. A. Albini, drugist; 8. Lucio Angeli; 9. V. Ascrizzi; 10. Miss Santina Alongi; 11. Romolo Avati; 12. S. Bonanno; 13. Atillio Barbera, M.D.; 14. L. Bloisi; 15. Vito Bagnato; 16. A. Bonvicino, M.D.; 17. John Bonfatto; 18. Solla Bentivoglio; 19. Giuseppe Barone; 20. Frank Bagnato; 21. William Borea; 22. Nicholas Barbieri; 23. B. Bartoli; 24. Luigi Crisouolo; 25. Vito Cannella; 26. Vinzo Comito; 27. Miss Grazia Cucinotta; 28. Joseph Cona; 29. C. Cupparo; 30. E. A. Cilento; 31. James Ciancaglini; 32. Capuano; 33. Alfredo Corvi; 34. Miss Josephine Ciaccio; 35. D. Cotroneo; 36. V. J. Curcio; 37. William Ciervo; 38. Miss Frances Ciervo; 39. N. Catalano; 40. Frank Capria; 41. Miss Capozzi; 42. M. Conti; 43. Renzo Campolini; 44. Miss Giulia Gallo; 45. Frank Catinella; 46. C. Campanelli; 47. M. Campitiello; 48. Gussie Curreri; 49. Salvatore G. Ciancio; 50. Emilio Coppetelli; 51. S. D'Agostini; 52. Mrs. Grazietta Durante; 53. Frank De Rosa; 54. Frank De Caro; 55. G. De Sanctis; 56. Annibale Di Befo; 57. Calogero Diana; 58. Rose De Pasquale; 59. G. D'Arista; 60. G. D'Angelo; 61. A. D'Angelo; 62. A. De Marco; 63. A. Dussich; 64. Mrs. Lucia Della Malva; 65. F. Di Cicco, M.D.; 66. Vittorio di Bari; 67. Michele Dellino; 68. V. De Crescenzo; 69. A. Erriquez; 70. H. G. Filippi; 71. F. Fazio; 72. A. Ferraro; 73. L. Fragomeni, M.D.; 74. John Finizio; 75. Louis Fredda; 76. L. Fiammenghi; 77. R. Fioroni; 78. Leandro Forno; 79. A. Giaquinto; 80. Ernesto Guccione; 81. Giuseppe Ganci; 82. P. Giovannozzi; 83. G. Gerli; 84. Giorgio Gennaro; 85. Ettore Frisina; 86. G. Giallorenzi; 87. Mario Giani; 88. J. Cristina; 89. Vito Guariglia; 90. Antonio Giannuzzi; 91. Angelo Gloria; 92. Vincenzo Jannone; 93. Lentini; 94. Joe La Sala; 95. Bruno Lupia; 96. E. Luzzatto; 97. Giovanni Luisi; 98. Nicola Latorraca; 99. James Lanzetta; 100. L. Mossa; 101. Edward Migliaccio; 102. Ernesto

Migliaccio; 103. F. Martucci; 104. Miss Marinaro; 105. Torquato Manousi;
106. Liborio Marino; 107. Mario Melamo; 108. Mrs.Nollisi; 109. E. Man-
fredi; 110. Pasquale Medici; 111. F. G. Melchionna; 112. Charles Muscatel-
lo; 113. Ugo Maugeri; 114. P. Mannerini; 115. Enrico Morelli; 116. Guilia
Morelli; 117. D. Maloscia; 118. Peppino Milano; 119. D. Marafioti; 120.
Adolfo Mariotti; 121. S. Nicotra; 122. G. Nardone; 123. Thomas Novia;
124. Raffaele Oggiano; 125. Nino Parrello; 126. Antonio Piccinni; 127.
Francesco Palleria; 128. F. A. Panucci; 129. Francesco Pecora; 130. R. L.
Pavone; 131. Elizabeth Purpure; 132. Paolo Pizzo; 133. S. Paone; 134.
Leopoldo Polizzi; 135. Decio Pugliese; 136. Pecoraro; 137. Aroldo Palonoa;
138. Luigi Pallone; 139. Enzo Pascarella; 140. Salvatore Pini; 141. Salvatore
Reina; 142. Bruno Rovere; 143. O. Ruotolo; 144. Alfonso Raccasi; 145.
Ottavio Rossi; 146. V. Rossini; 147. R. Renna; 148. N. Rossi; 149. Julio
Roig; 150. A. Scalvinci; 151. G. Sessa; 152. J. Susoa; 153. C. Sinagra;
154. Joseph Santy; 155. Carlo Toai; 156. M. Tumolo; 157. G. Traina;
158. Ruggero Tortoreto; 159. V. Vedovi; 160. E. Valle; 161. Frank Velardi.

In April 1935, when the Birthday of Rome was celebrated by the
Association of Italians Abroad at 225 Lafayette Street, "several Italian
Fascists attended the ceremony wearing black shirts."[23]

It seems likely that, if the Congressional committee had not announced
that there was no Fascist danger in the United States, Mayor La Guardia
would not have appointed A. Bonaschi to the board of education in May
1935. This appointment was made upon request of the New York [Italian]
Chamber of Commerce, one of the Fascist transmission belts.[24] *Il Grido
della Stirpe* termed, on that occasion, Bonaschi as "our dear friend and
comrade."[25]

The go signal was given just at a moment when it was most wanted. Since
1933, Mussolini was preparing war against Ethiopia.[26] The incident of Wal-
Wal in Eastern Africa (December 1934) marked officially the opening of the
dispute which was to lead to actual war in October 1936. In Italy the
campaign against Ethiopia became lively only during the summer of 1935.
Large sections of the population were hostile towards Mussolini's warlike
contortions, and only when actual war broke out, and the British government
did everything it could to make its action both hateful and inefficient,[27] the
Italians rallied around Mussolini to pull through. On the contrary in the

23. PIA, April 30, 1935.

24. *La rivista commerciale italo-americana*, December 1939, pp. 15-17.

25. CS, May 18, 1935.

26. Salvemini traced the origins of the Italian-Ethiopian War in his volume *Prelude to World
War II* (London, 1953). [Ed. Note]

27. In 1935 Salvemini debated with Alberto Tarchiani on the nature and impact of British
policy toward Mussolini's invasion of Ethiopia, asserting that the sanctions were a farce and
that the British Tories had given Mussolini a free hand. See for example his article "Mussolini,
l'Inghilterra e l'Etiopia," *Giustizia e Libertà*, June 21, 1935, and "Il prossimo atto della commedia,"
ibid., August 30, 1935. [Ed. Note]

United States the campaign against Ethiopia was started as soon as the incident of Wal-Wal had been engineered. Most Italian language papers and all radio commentators, an army of lecturers in the English and Italian languages, all priests of the Catholic-Fascist denomination, servile correspondents from Rome, Paris and London, methodically indoctrinated day in and day out, in the course of 1935, the population of Italian origin in this country to the effect that "Mussolini was always right."

The Italo-Ethiopian War marks a turning point in the history of the Italians in the United States. In 1935 and 1936 Fascist control asserted itself over the majority of them without contest. Mussolini's American empire actually arose. While the masses of Italian origin were grouping themselves solidly behind Mussolini, the great majority of the American population condemned the policy of the Fascist government. Mussolini lost in America in a few weeks all the prestige that he had succeeded in building up in many years of methodic misinformation. Of the cleavage thus created between the Italian communities and the rest of the population the Fascist agents took advantage to cultivate from then on among the Italians a feeling of protest and anger against that which they described as preconceived, unjust and malicious hostility against an Italy that was seeking a place in the sun. A never-ending campaign of slander and hate was then launched against England. The dangerous situation which surprised so many people in 1930-1940, became ripe in 1936.[28]

---

28. On the American and Italian-American reaction to the war, see Diggins, *Mussolini and Fascism*, pp. 302-312, and Brice Harris, Jr., *The United States and the Italo-Ethiopian Crisis* (Stanford, 1964). [Ed. Note]

3

The Ethiopian War

A new personage, Piero P. Carbonelli, appeared in New York in June 1935. Officially he was a correspondent of the Milan daily *Corriere della Sera*. In actual fact, he had come to take the place of Angelo Flavio Guidi who, since the previous year, had become a commuter between Italy and America, always keeping, though, his title of commissioner of Italians Abroad.[1] Carbonelli too had the title of commissioner (*fiduciario*) of the Italian Fasci Abroad,[2] or commissioner of the National Fascist party.[3] He also was called "Representative of the Fatherland's Government,"[4] and "our Party Chief" (*nostro gerarca*).[5] Any time there was no commissioner for a Fascist club, Carbonelli appointed its directors.

In the same summer of 1936, Thaon di Revel decamped from New York

---

1. GS, June 15, 1935.
2. Ibid., June 6, 1936.
3. PIA, October 28, 1936.
4. GS, June 27, 1936.
5. Ibid., August 8, 1936.

and from then on he worked in Rome, as the national executive of the Fascist party, in charge of the fasci of the United States, Canada and Mexico.

In July 1936, shortly after Carbonelli had taken the floor, a new organization arose to take up the leadership of the Fascist movement in the United States, in view of the imminent war, the Unione Italiana d'America.[6] This name should have been translated into Italian Union of America — that is to say: an organization of Italians in America. But for the benefit of the gullible American, it was translated into American Italian Union, which might convey the idea either of a union among Italo-Americans, or of friendship between America and Italy.

The promoters of the new organization were Ugo Veniero D'Annunzio,[7] Eugenio Casagrande di Villaviera, G. Previtali, R. Bertelli, S. Bonanno, H. Marraro, R. Tasselli, G. Bigongiari, E. Locatelli, and V. Vedovi.

> U. D'Annunzio. In following years, he was to run the Italian Library of Information, a propaganda institution maintained by the Italian government.[8]

The union was linked with the Italian Historical Society and had its headquarters at the Italian consulate general (Palazzo d'Italia). It was directed by a triumvirate composed of D'Annunzio, president; Casagrande, secretary; and Facchetti-Guiglia[9] who, most likely, acted as commissioner. Its aims were "to strengthen more and more the excellent links of friendship existing" between Italy and America, "to fight the campaign of press which, blinded by racial prejudice, was attempting to corrupt public opinion of this country," and "to try to gather together all those, individuals and associations, who could not fail to recognize the necessity of an ever increasing cohesion and more precise unity of purpose."[10]

6. The Unione Italiana d'America was apparently created at the suggestion of Bernardo Bergameschi, an envoy of the Ministry for Press and Propaganda sent to the United States at the time of the Ethiopian War. The Unione sought to unite all Fascist propaganda in America and to coordinate efforts among Italian-Americans with those aimed at the rest of American society. See Bicocchi, "Propaganda fascista," pp. 670-671, and Diggins, *Mussolini and Fascism*, pp. 289-290, 303. [Ed. Note]
7. Ugo V. D'Annunzio was the son of the famed literary-political figure, Gabriele D'Annunzio. He came to the United States in 1918 and became a United States citizen in 1925, working as an aviation engineer. He died in 1945. *New York Times*, January 18, 1945. [Ed. Note]
8. The Italian Library of Information, established in 1938, was a prolific source of Fascist propaganda. With its headquarters in New York and substantial funds from the Ministry of Popular Culture, it published a popular "Outline Series" of pamphlets on all aspects of Fascism. See Diggins, *Mussolini and Fascism*, pp. 97-98, 258; Bicocchi, "Propaganda fascista," p. 696; and Salvemini's pamphlet "Italian Fascist Activities in the U.S.," p. 14. There is also a substantial amount of material on the library in the Archivio Centrale dello Stato, *Ministero della Cultura Popolare*, busta 443, fascicolo "Italian Information Service." It closed in July 1941 by order of the State Department. [Ed. Note]
9. PIA, August 1, 1935.
10. GS, July 27, 1935.

Even before D'Annunzio's union got started, the War Veterans Association of New York came to the fore at the beginning of August and passed "amidst unspeakable enthusiasm a resolution of unconditional support to the Duce's action." The text of the resolution deserves to be given in full because it perfectly represents the attitude that propaganda was creating among the Italian masses in America:

> Whereas the Italian Government in connection with the Ethiopian prob-
> lem is inspired by reasons of moral, political and economic nature, the
> Italian War Veterans of New York affirm 1) their unalterable attachment
> and devotion to the Italian Fatherland; 2) their full and unconquerable
> faith in the action of the Italian Government; 3) their absolute confidence
> that under the guidance of Benito Mussolini, Prime Minister of His Majesty
> Victor Emmanuel III, Italy will attain the goals set up for her by her glorious
> traditions and the just desires of her people; 4) their firm will to support the
> action of the Italian Government by every means and if necessary even
> with the sacrifice of their own lives.
>
> Whereas, furthermore, certain exponents of the press and of public
> opinion in the United States have assumed a hostile attitude, they vigor-
> ously protest against their inopportune interference with a question of
> exclusively Italo-Abyssinian concern and absolutely foreign to American
> interests. They reject all insinuations offending the dignity of Italy and the
> courage of the Italian army victorious in the greatest conflict of modern
> history. They express the wish and the confidence that the same part of
> American public opinion, of the press and of the associations may in the
> future attain a higher sense of justice and prudence.

Then at the consulate general, on August 28, 1936, the delegates of "about fifty" associations gathered, numbering as a whole more than two hundred fifty thousand members, if we are to believe what was said by *Il Progresso*[11] and *Il Grido*.[12] But the figure of two hundred fifty thousand members, which would indicate an average of five thousand members for each association, was certainly imaginary, according to Fascist dynamic statistical habits. Those who took part in the discussion were: E. Casagrande, G. Luigi, G. Previtali, Count L. Criscuolo, S. Miele, Santo Modica, A. Caputo, V. Comito, R. Ganci, F. P. Macaluso, J. Cristina, G. Susca, and Carbonelli.

> S. Modica — at the time of the quarrel between Cotillo and Di Silvestro,
> he took Cotillo's side. Then together with Cotillo, went bag and baggage
> into the Fascist camp.

A motion by Carbonelli was adopted in which the presidents of the would-be two hundred fifty thousand members of the would-be fifty clubs were very much concerned with "making safe the friendship between Italy

11. August 30, 1935.
12. August 31, 1935.

and America," declared "their loyalty to the United States of America of which many were citizens, and at the same time, their unceasing devotion to the Italian Fatherland," urged that the United States remain neutral in the conflict, decided to "consider themselves spiritually mobilized" and summoned the directors of all Italo-American associations to form a united front any time circumstances required it. A telegram was sent to President Roosevelt advocating the neutrality of the United States, and another was sent to Mussolini. This second telegram was signed by D'Annunzio, president of the union, Casagrande, secretary of the union, and Carbonelli who had no office in the union but obviously was the highest authority among the Fascists,   after the consul.

In September 1935, a circular letter sent out by D'Annunzio to the comrades who ran the Italian associations, made the following announcement:

> The entire world must realize that all Italians, under any sky and in whatever latitude, are a solid and formidable mass, obedient to the orders of His Majesty the King, and of our admirable Duce, and dedicated to the service and to the greatness of our beloved Fatherland.

The circular ended with the Fascist formula *"A noi!"* ("To Us!").

In another circular of the same day, D'Annunzio asked the president of each association dependent on the union to make known to the consulate the figure of those among its members who, as Italian citizens, "were to declare their absolute and enthusiastic support of the decisions taken by the supreme national authorities." As for the members of Italian origin who were American citizens, "it would be lawful and even opportune, nay dutiful, owing to their Italian origin, to indicate their number too to the Consulate, and assert their devotion to the land of their birth, and their desire for the triumph of the just cause."[13]

At the beginning of autumn, a new consul general, Gaetano Vecchiotti, took office in New York. From that time on, three men, Vecchiotti, Carbonelli, and Pope, were constantly on the forefront as leaders of the Italians in New York.

When the war was started, in October 1935, monster demonstrations were put up everywhere in the United States, to show that all Italians were siding with Mussolini. The Federation of War Veterans donated a field hospital, with doctors and nurses.[14] The local branches of the War Veterans Federation publicly recruited volunteers for the fighting front, not only

13. GS, September 21, 1935.
14. *Impero*, October 1, 1936, p. 18.

among the Italians resident in the United States, but also among American citizens of Italian origin, without the federal government taking any step to discourage such a movement or to denationalize those who enrolled.[15]

After the League of Nations enacted economic sanctions against Italy, the Italian Chamber of Commerce organized a series of weekly radio broadcasts "to defend and spread the consumption of Italian products." Together with other well known Fascists like P. Sterbini, F. Quattrone, V. Vedovi, L. Podestà, three Italo-American intellectuals participated in this campaign: L. Covello, M. Cosenza, and P. M. Riccio.[16] They intermingled their praises for Italian spaghettis and cheeses with exhortations to learn the Italian language. Covello, who had been decorated by Mussolini recently, explained that "there are two main things that help differentiate the one people from the other: in the first place, the language *with all it implies* [italics ours] and with the vast culture of which it is the expression; and secondly, the habits, among which the most typical ones are those related to foods and beverages."[17] The national cells were putting even the kitchen to Mussolini's service.

On December 27, 1935, there appeared a new weekly *La Settimana*, "founded by Edward Corsi." It unconditionally upheld the policy of Mussolini in the Ethiopian War. It was printed with a certain lavishness of paper and pictures, and it must have cost a pretty penny. Its offices were at 626 Fifth Avenue, Palazzo d'Italia, the quarters of the Italian consulate general. On its board of directors and editorial staff, besides E. Corsi, there were the following persons: Alfonso Arbib-Costa; Adriano Cacace; Costantino Catanzaro; Basilio Cavallaro; Carlo De Vio; Felix Forte; G. Prezzolini; James V. Ricci; Pietro Rosa; Amerigo Ruggiero; Nino Sparacino.

> E. Corsi, G. Prezzolini and A. Arbib-Costa are already known to us.
> P. Rosa of Stamford, Connecticut. In July 1933 sent "Fascist greetings" to the *Grido della Stirpe*, stating that "Fascist achievements make us proud of feeling more and more Italian."[18] In October 1935 he sent through the Italian Union of America to the Duce the applause of the Italian Institute of Stamford, comprising fifty societies with fifteen thousand members, believe it or not.[19]
> A. Ruggiero. "He often returned to Italy, and has been received many times by Mussolini and other ministers. When the illustrated weekly re-

---

15. Mussolini asked for volunteers in the fall of 1935, but when the American press expressed alarm at the possibility of Americans being recruited by Fascist agents, the Italian ambassador announced that no American citizens would be accepted. Nevertheless, between October and December almost two hundred Italian-Americans volunteered. *New York Times*, September 16, October 20, December 8, 1935. [Ed. Note]

16. Gio., January, February, March, April 1936.

17. Ibid., January 1938, p. 13.

18. GS, July 22, 1933.

19. Ibid., October 12, 1935.

20. AF.

view, *La Settimana*, was established, founded by Hon. Edward Corsi, he was asked to take the editorship of it."[20]

N. Sparacino. "In 1921, he took an active part in the Fasci. . .In October 1934, he returned to New York, taking a position on the *Corriere d'America* as art director. At this time he is on the staff of the review, *La Settimana*, as art director."[21]

G. Vassallo. "He is enrolled in the Fascist University organization of Italy. Since 1935 he has been in New York editing the literary weekly *La Settimana*."[22]

We have no information on the others.

In December 1936, the offices of the weekly were moved to 225 Lafayette Street, the well-known beehive of Fascist organizations. In May 1937 the review died.

In January 1936, the grand venerable of the Sons of Italy in New York State, F. P. Catinella, exhorted the members "to show that the influence and opinion of American citizens of Italian extraction must no longer be ignored, and must, instead, be esteemed and respected."[23]

Innumerable meetings, ceremonies, and demonstrations took place in New York from the autumn of 1935 to the summer of 1936. We shall mention only the most typical ones.

On the evening of September 13, 1935, the Club of the Italians Abroad, Ridgewood, in Brooklyn, held a big meeting. Rosario Ganci, president of the club, and A. Cornella, G. Susca, F. P. Catinella, Facchetti-Guiglia, U. D'Annunzio, V. Comito, F. P. Macaluso and G. Bonavita spoke. Among the participants E. Casagrande, C. Amoroso, Carlo Mariani, F. P. Pizzo, A. Brancato, G. d'Angelo, G. Marsico, Rosario Romeo, Mannecchia, Nunzio Sozi, A. Vitale, Salvatore, Bertuglia, Domenico Abramo, G. Napoli, Vincenzo Pizzone, Louis Topazio, Luke Materi, Salvatore Li Vecchi, Carmelo Franco and A. Balsimelli were recorded. The meeting adopted a message to Mussolini which ran as follows:

> Members and friends of "Club of Italians Abroad" in Brooklyn acclaim our Italy's rights asserted under your guidance, and manifest their unfailing faith in their Fascist fatherland. Alberto Cornella, Rosario Ganci.

In October 1935 the March on Rome was clamorously celebrated in the Bronx by the Abraham Lincoln Club and the Italian House. The consul arrived accompanied by Francesco Cottafavi, general of the Fascist militia in Italy, Facchetti-Guiglia, Carbonelli, two officials of the consulate and A. Palanca. He was received by a committee, composed of P. Badia, G. Luisi, J.

21. Ibid.
22. Ibid.
23. Gio., January 1936, p. 9.

Cristina, A. Di Marco, by the venerables of the Order of the Sons of Italy and of the Independent Order of the Sons of Italy. The bells of the Carmine church, of which Rev. Severino Focacci was the pastor, joined their music to that of the band of the Italian House led by Maestro Mauro Bosco. Addresses by Badia, Luisi, Carbonelli, demonstration for the king and the Duce.[24]

On the evening of November 4, the Unione Italiana d'America together with the War Veterans Association, the Victor Emmanuel III Foundation, and the Association of Italians Abroad sponsored a celebration of Italian Armistice Day in Carnegie Hall. The official speaker was Judge Freschi.[25] The Italian ambassador to Washington, a former American ambassador to Germany, Gerard, who most likely did not know what he was doing there, Consul Vecchiotti and Generoso Pope were received by the organizing committee consisting of U. D'Annunzio, E. Casagrande, V. Vedovi, S. Bonanno, M. Calamai, R. De Felice, R. Tasselli, C. De Regibus, Facchetti-Guiglia, while the orchestra was playing the royal march and "Giovinezza." Then the crowd sang another Fascist song, "Black Shirts." Speakers were Bonanno, president of the War Veterans Association, the Italian ambassador, ex-ambassador Gerard, Judge Freschi, General Giuseppe Garibaldi, one of the unworthy grandchildren of the hero of the Italian Risorgimento, and Casagrande.

On December 14, 1935, another mass meeting was held at Madison Square Garden, with the official aim of launching a drive on behalf of the Italian Red Cross. Mayor La Guardia attended, stating that he "exclusively" meant to help the campaign for the benefit of the Italian Red Cross, "that noble institution functioning independently from every political or religious creed." But Pope, Judge Ferdinand Pecora, Judge Cotillo, and Consul Vecchiotti assailed Great Britain and the League of Nations and upheld Italy's right to civilize Ethiopia.[26] The event was handed over to posterity in a volume entitled: *14 Dicembre, XIV E. F. — Pro Opere Assistenziali Italiane*, i.e.: *Fourteenth of December of the Fourteenth Year of the Fascist Era — For the Benefit of the Italian Welfare Institutions.* On the first page of the volume a slogan by Mussolini was printed; a message by Generoso Pope followed the Duce's saying. After Pope's memorable sayings came the ambassador's; after these came Judge Freschi; and finally, the Unione Italiana d'America, the War Veteran Association and the procession of associations and business men who had contributed to the printing expenses. On pages 60 and 81 of the volume, the names of the 365 members of the organizing committee of the mass meeting were given.

24. PIA, October 28, 1935.
25. GS, November 11, 1935.
26. PIA, November 15, 1935.

On January 22, 1936, a great rally was held at the Brooklyn Academy of Music. *Il Progresso* commented upon this event in the following terms:[27]

The Italian community of this great metropolis multiplies its demonstrations of infinite love for the distant Fatherland, giving by its spontaneous and passionate initiatives evidence of indubious spiritual unity with the brothers of Italy.

Rev. Alfonso Arcese "amidst ovations" invoked the heavenly blessing on the king and on the "Duce who has led the people of Italy back to the best traditions of Rome, educating its spirit to a high morality and bringing it together in a powerful and feared spiritual solidarity." Pasquale Medici "sang the praises of Italy and the Duce and emphasized the magnificent proof of solidarity given by the Italians of America." Generoso Pope, "the most accredited symbol of Italianism" *(italianità)*, stated that the Italians of America wanted Italy and America to be forever bound by chains of sincere friendhsip and therefore advocated American neutrality in the Italo-Ethiopian War. He said:

Imposing and moving is the evidence of unity among all the Italians around the Man who has had the courage to tell the fifty-two powers combined against Italy: "We will answer you with the sacrifices and heroism of the sons of Italy." We are proud to be sons of that Italy which today has Benito Mussolini for her Duce.

Consul Vecchiotti said he was happy to "ascertain more every day the cult of the Italian masses for Italy." The evening netted three thousand dollars and concluded with acclamations to Italy, the king, the Duce, the army.

In February 1936, in the auditorium of the Church of Mary the Helper, the Salesian Bishop Coppo explained how and why the Italian clergy abroad "were side by side with the Fatherland's Government, supporting the Welfare Institutions of the Fascist regime, morally and financially."[28]

In March 1936, the Birthday of Fascism was celebrated at the Grand Northern Hotel. The room was decorated with Italian flags and coats of arms supplied by the De Caro and D'Angelo firm, owned by fervent patriots. Guests of honor were: Vecchiotti, G. Pope, Carbonelli, B. Rovere, A. Palanca, G. Susca, Brancucci, and the officials of the consulate general, M. Giani, Spatafora, Carlo Cimino, and Umberto Caradossi. A. F. Guidi, A. Facchetti-Guiglia and J. Ingegnieros sent telegrams of greetings. D. Trombetta introduced the master of ceremonies, Mrs. G. Morelli, who, after a short speech, "every word of which was a warm praise to *Il Progresso Italo-Americano,*" introduced, in her turn, Generoso Pope, "greeted with an

27. Ibid., January 24, 1936.
28. *La Settimana,* February 7, 1936.

enthusiastic ovation."

> Pope congratulated Trombetta upon the magnificent struggle for "Ital-
> ianism" [Fascism] he had valiantly led for years. He recorded that *Il Grido
> della Stirpe* had been the first paper ever to print his [Pope's] picture,
> many years before. He observed that the 1936 celebration of the Birthday
> of Fascism coincided with exceptionally important events which were
> revealing to the world the material and moral strength of Mussolini's Italy
> and the gallantry of *our* [italics ours] Army gloriously fighting on the
> battlefields of East Africa. He extolled the magnificent unity of the Italo-
> Americans who had given the most eloquent answer to those trying to
> detract *our* [italics ours] Fatherland. "In a short while — he concluded —
> we shall celebrate the final victory of *our* [italics ours] troops in Africa.
> This will be an impressive celebration and will more and more persuade
> the American people of the strength of our unity and our love for both
> Italy and America."

Speeches were also given by Carbonelli and Vecchiotti.[29] *Il Grido della
Stirpe* commented on the ceremony with this sentence: "Our community is
being more and more Fascistised."

Another great artistic evening party, for the benefit of the Italian Red
Cross, was held at Williamsburg, Brooklyn, in April 1936. Vecchiotti,
Carbonelli, Mrs. Giulia Morelli, Congressman J. L. Pfeifer, and all the local
authorities attended. Filippo Ticone was the master of ceremonies. Carbonelli
and the consul were the official speakers. "The Fascist anthem played by the
Orchestra was then sung by the whole audience." Jerome Licari reminded
the audience what Pope was doing on behalf of the Italian Red Cross and
Pope was made the object of a great demonstration. Other speakers were an
Abyssinian who "sang, once more, the Fascist anthem amidst the enthusiasm
of the audience" and Congressman Pfeifer. Count Criscuolo acted as vice-
chairman.[30]

During the same month a great rally for the benefit of the Italian Red
Cross took place at the coliseum in the Bronx, under the high patronage of
the consul general, chairman of the ceremony being Nicola Tangredi.[31]

In all the speeches the fact was emphasized that the Italians in America
and in Italy formed a united mass, and that the only way of securing the
loyalty of the Italians to America and keeping America and Italy on friendly
terms, was not to antagonize Mussolini's initiatives.

At all the gatherings, money was raised for the Italian Red Cross and the
Fascist Welfare Institutions in Italy. The international regulations interdict
to the Red Cross of a country to raise money in other countries. But the

29. PIA, March 23, 1936; GS, March 28, 1936.
30. PIA, April 10, 1936.
31. *Impero*, March 1936, p. 78.

federal government kept its eyes closed.

The victory of the Italian army and the proclamation of the empire were celebrated on the evening of June 13, 1936, in a mass meeting at Madison Square Garden. This gathering was officially summoned by Consul Vecchiotti in person.[32] He acted by now as if all people of Italian origin, whether American or Italian citizens, were under his jurisdiction. The American authorities never dreamt of calling him to order, as they had once done with Rolandi-Ricci and Thaon di Revel. If they had such an idea, they didn't take any action in view of the coming presidential elections of November 1936.

In this rally G. Pope handed over to the consul a check for one hundred thousand dollars, this being the seventh check for the same amount. The money had been collected through his two dailies.[33] Joseph Gerli offered 100,000 lire. The sums collected in New York by the consulate and Pope's papers amounted to $741,862, without taking into account the money sent to the Italian government directly, without intermediaries.[34]

Mussolini sent to Pope a telegram of thanks which was published in *Il Progresso*[35] and read as follows:

> Sincerest thanks for the conspicuous contributions you sent to the *Royal Treasury* [italics ours]. The very efficient initiative taken by *Il Progresso Italo-Americano* and *Il Corriere d'America* has offered to the Italians in America a way of showing their glowing and patriotic devotion. Signed: Mussolini.

A man who, on the occasion of the Ethiopian War, got extremely busy, was Count Criscuolo. *Il Grido*[36] gave the following account of his fervent activities:

> At the time of the Ethiopian war Criscuolo was accorded hospitality of the editorial pages of the greatest American newspapers such as the *New York Times*, and the *New York Herald Tribune*. His work rated the praise of the Duce, the high Fascist Chiefs and the authorities of the Royal Army Royal Navy, among whom Marshall Badoglio, Marshall Balbo, Count Galeazzo Ciano, Dino Alfieri, Piero Parini, etc., not to mention various Italian ambassadors abroad such as His Excellency Rosso, His Excellency Suvich, His Excellency Cerruti, His Excellency Grandi, etc.

Yet he never succeeded in becoming as prominent as Carbonelli, Facchetti-Guiglia or Pope, not to speak of Consul Vecchiotti or Ambassador Rosso.

---

32. GS, July 4, 1936.
33. *Impero*, July 15, 1936, p. 40.
34. Ibid., December 1, 1936, p. 11.
35. PIA, May 5, 1936.
36. March 27, 1937.

4

The Morristown Demonstration: August 1936

The June mass meeting did not wholly exhaust Fascist enthusiasm. A monster open air demonstration was held at Morristown, New Jersey on August 16, 1936.

Carbonelli and Facchetti-Guiglia, our "untiring and well-deserving Party Chiefs" (*gerarchi*)[1] were the promoters. On this occasion, Facchetti-Guiglia appeared to the Fascist crowd as having the same rank as Carbonelli in the Fascist hierarchy. *Il Grido*[2] gave him the title, seemingly comparable to that once held by Thaon di Revel, of permanent commissioner and party chief (*fiduciario permanente e gerarca*).

Il Grido devoted to the Morristown demonstration a report covering three pages, in its issue of August 22, 1936. This is an exceptionally important document, as far as the history of the Fascist movement is concerned. Through it we learn that, after the disbandment of the Fascist League of

1. *Impero*, September 1, 1936, p. 12.
2. August 22, 1936.

North America, "according to the desire of the Italian authorities," there did not exist any longer "an *officially* recognized Fascist organization" in the United States.

> Those faithful to the Duce, *rigorously abiding by the orders* received from their Heads, always abstained from any initiative which might create *organic* groups. As a consequence, even at the present time, the Italian Fascists in the United States are the only ones in the world who do not possess an *officially recognized* organization of their own.

The words in italics are ours. They permit us to understand the difference that existed between the conditions of the United States and those in other countries. No Fascist organization was officially recognized by the Italian government in the United States, and no organic center existed that could serve as a target for hostility. But Fascists did exist, who obeyed the Italian authorities and had heads. In the ceremony of March 1934, Trombetta said: "Although diplomatic exigencies forced us to disband the Fascist organizations in America, the old Fascists have never ceased to consider Count Revel as their high leader," and the audience greeted these words with a "great ovation."[3]

In 1936, Facchetti-Guiglia and Carbonelli had taken Thaon Di Revel's and A. F. Guidi's place. Their pictures were enthroned in the center of the second page of *Il Grido:*[4]

> American Fascists never had hauled down the pennant of their faith. . . . When the Fascist organization in the U.S.A. was disbanded, owing to diplomatic exigencies, at the end of 1929, we wrote in this paper that it was easy to disband an organization, but it was impossible to destroy, to annihilate, to choke our idea. Thanks to the work of our comrades, Commander Piero P. Carbonelli and Count Facchetti-Guiglia, our mass meeting at Morristown, the first held to celebrate the birth of the Fascist Empire, was the most eloquent demonstration of what we have been constantly asserting for years. For the first time after many years of enforced [?] silence [!], were the old Black Shirts of America finally allowed to see the shining dawn of a new era. On order of our Chiefs [and the orders of the chiefs are not to be questioned], the old squads had been disbanded, the the glorious pennants had been put back in their sheaths, the remembrance of our unforgettable martyrs had been entrusted to the hearts of the comrades. . . But the loyalty to the Duce and the Regime still was the ideal discipline of the old phalanxes. Then the Ethiopian war came and victory once again kissed the three colors of the Fatherland's flag. A passionate upsurge of national sentiment revealed itself among the Italians in the United States. The ancient faith has become gigantic. Spontaneously, [!] without anybody's command [!], the old and glorious formations were spiritually reborn. The old comrades met again on the same route of duty,

3. GS, March 31, 1934.
4. August 22, 1936.

recognized each other, embraced each other. New recruits flocked from everywhere and welled up the ranks. A new and greater certitude unfolded itself for the Italians of the U.S.A. The announcement of this certitude was heralded to us in Morristown. We were at Morristown not for a meeting of heterogeneous masses though prompted by the same patriotic fervor. We were there to accomplish a religious rite inspired by the Duce and Fascist ideals. The old Black Shirts belonging to the squads of the Fascist League of North America were there, together with the young recruits mostly coming from the ranks of our good and honest workers. These have understood, at last, the social meaning of Mussolini's Fascism. Women and girls were there. There were "Piccole Italiane" [Fascist Girls] and "Balillas" [Fascist Boys]. There was the mass of our comrades organized in our National Clubs who for the first-time, had gathered behind their flags to cry unanimously one single name; "Duce, Duce, Duce." The hearts of the old Black Shirts were overflowing with pride, as one of their dreams in their lives of exiles and patriots had finally become a reality; to see at last Fascist units, at the service of the King-Emperor and the Duce, marching before the representative of the Fascist Government.

F. P. Macaluso, too, was pleased that "the seed sown in 1922 and 1923, and which had already become a flourishing shrub when it was out in 1929, is blossoming again, is anew giving fruits which grant good hopes":[5]

> The thousands of Fascists of the first hour are joined now by thousands and thousands of new Fascists. Many of these were absent at the beginning of the Fascist movement because, in good faith, they did not understand it. Their conversion — we have no reason to doubt it — is sincere and profound. They are welcome among the old Black Shirts. Then there are the young and the very young — and these are crowds too. They were not with us in the first years, because they were not yet grown up. They were the "Balillas" who became "Avanguardisti" and then Fascists. They have now grown up in the historic climate of New Italy. They have withstood adverse currents in public schools. They have withstood the overbearing communist influence of their classmates and teachers. As they became men, 21 and over, they spontaneously joined our ranks, proud of their Italian and Roman heritage, proud of their privilege of originating with the land that Fascism, under Benito Mussolini's leadership, restored to the glories and splendors of ancient imperial Rome...This is the essential point. The youths of our extraction born and raised in America, know how to keep one hundred per cent American, but spiritually stick to our Fascist ideals because they deeply feel the pride of their race. This pride they intend to be their highest contribution to their land, America. They shouted with us and will shout again in the future "Duce, Duce, Duce."

The rally was held in a vast ground owned by the Maestre Pie Filippine nuns.[6] These nuns manage many Italian schools in the United States. Their school in Trenton, New Jersey, was attended in 1936 by nearly one thousand

5. *Impero*, September 1, 1936, p. 12.
6. Ibid., August 15, 1936, p. 20.

girls.[7]

> The Reverend "Maestre Pie Filippine" knew how to live up to their great spiritual mission among the Italian masses in America. At Morristown they had had an altar erected in front of their Holy House...The Reverend Nuns had also provided for an excellent system of loudspeakers being installed, and had put on a terrace the musical instruments of their renowned Schola Cantorum.

Not only the Fascists of New York, but also those of many neighboring localities — [such] as Newburgh, Tarrytown, Peekskill, Yonkers, Staten Island, Inwood and other Long Island and New Jersey towns — participated in the rally. "Most of the comrades were wearing black shirts." The Fascist women, the Italian girls and the Balillas also were mostly in uniform. A photo showing many participants wearing black shirts was given in *Impero*.[8]

The clubs marched in front of the consul general who, "wearing the black shirt," exchanged with them the Fascist salute. In Vecchiotti's retinue were Commissioners Carbonelli and Facchetti-Guiglia, who "wore black shirts, too," the consulate's officials — among them, Prof. Mario Giani — and a group of representatives of the Fascist-Catholic clergy, i.e.: Monsignor F. Di Persia, of Jersey City, on behalf of Bishop T. J. Walsh; Reverend Umberto Donati, pastor of Saint Roch in Newark, New Jersey; and Reverend Ferrecchia, pastor of Saint Joseph in Lodi, New Jersey.

> Reverend U. Donati sent his "unqualified approval" to the Lictor Federation in 1930[9] and took part in the celebration of the March on Rome in 1936, proclaiming that "blind selfishness and ingratitude would not succeed in stopping Italy's genius in the Italo-Ethiopian war."[10]
> Reverend F. Di Persia, on the anniversary of the March on Rome, in October 1933, expressed the wish that "the Good Lord might preserve the great Duce for many years to come."[11] On the anniversary of the Birthday of Rome, in 1934, he sent "wishes of ever growing success" to *Il Grido della Stirpe*.[12] In October 1935 he prayed that "the Almighty God might help the right cause of our Fatherland" in the Ethiopian war.[13] Bishop Walsh could not have been represented by a more suitable person than Monsignor Di Persia at the Morristown Fascist demonstration.

In order to show that an ideal and unbroken bond existed between the Fascist League of North America and the Fascist organizations of 1936, the flags of three clubs of the former League proceeded in the first ranks of the

7. GS, August 29, 1936.
8. September 1, 1936, pp. 12-13.
9. GS, January 25, 1930.
10. Ibid., October 25, 1935.
11. Ibid., October 28, 1933.
12. Ibid., April 21, 1934.
13. Ibid., October 26, 1935.

procession. The clubs were: the Benito Mussolini, the primogeneous club of New York; the Michele Bianchi, and the Aurelio Padovani. The flag of the Benito Mussolini club was carried by Miss Amelia Maghina.

This person had contributed a great deal to making the Fascist movement efficient. The *Grido della Stirpe* described her as "a Fascist from the very first day and of sincere faith whom, from the beginning of the movement, we have always seen in the front line in the hours of struggle and who, for many years has dedicated herself entirely to a work of silent organization"; she "cooperated with Thaon di Revel and continues to cooperate in the patriotic work of our permanent Party Chief" (*gerarca*), Count Alfonso Facchetti-Guiglia. Miss Maghina was an employee of the consulate and was repatriated to Italy in July 1941, together with the other consular employees — or at least with those who did not remain in New York to direct secretly the fifth column. It was said among the Fascists that she and Facchetti-Guiglia were the keepers of the list of the Fascists all over the United States.

Immediately after those three flags marched the members of the clubs Mario Sonzini and Benito Mussolini of the Bronx, and Arnaldo Mussolini of Hoboken. This privilege was granted to them in consideration of the fact that the former ones had counted among their members Carisi and D'Ambrosoli — the two Fascists murdered in 1927 — and the latter, Salvatore Arena — the Fascist gangster killed in 1932.

When the defile was completed, Monsignor Ferrecchia celebrated the Mass, which was served by "two comrades wearing black shirts." During the rite, a concert with accompaniment of songs was given by the Schola Cantorum of the Filippini nuns.

The Mass was followed by a series of speeches, "all inspired to a perfect Fascist style." First spoke Reverend Donati, explaining that Villa Lucia (the house of the nuns) is one of the centers in America best endowed with Christian faith and Italianism:

> The Fatherland is protected with weapons, and it asserts itself by spreading its own culture. Carrying out the Duce's will, our soldiers gave Italy an Empire. Upon us, Italians in America, falls the duty of spreading the Italian language and culture, particularly among the Italo-American youths. The "Maestre Pie Filippino" are on the forefront in this field.

Vecchiotti followed Monsignor Donati. He called the names of Carisi, D'Ambrosoli, and of the gangster Arena. He estimated that the participants numbered ten thousand and announced that in coming years not ten thousand but "twenty thousand, thirty thousand, one hundred thousand men and women would be drawn up to extol Imperial Italy."

The Italians of America, though loyal and devoted to this nobly hospitable nation, will never efface from their mind and heart the sacred remembrance of their Fatherland. They will never forget having Italian blood in their veins. They will never renounce to feel tied to their Mother-Country in a spiritual unity which causes all the Italians, in every part of the world, to feel members of a single and great family.

When all the speeches were over, the consul general, the two Commissioners Carbonelli and Facchetti-Guiglia, and a selected group of comrades and American journalists were the guests of the nuns for supper. After the supper, the Schola Cantorum sang, among other Italian patriotic songs, the royal anthem and "Giovinezza."

As the consul and Facchetti-Guiglia took leave from the nuns, the mother superior, Sister Ninette, illustrated what her institution was doing "to spread the Italian language in America and to bring up Italian girls in the spirit of the Christian religion and the sentiment of the Fatherland." In all these speeches, the word fatherland meant, of course, Italy and not America, the country in which those thousands of people and their children were destined to live and die.

When the motorcars made their trip back to New York, "in villages inhabited by Germans, the people crowded the sidewalks, came to the windows, and answered the Fascist salute to our comrades by giving the Hitlerian salute of the German comrades."

To understand how so grandiose a demonstration of aggressive Fascist nature became possible, one should bear in mind the fact that not only Fascist agents but also daily papers, weeklies, schools, churches, the radio, the movies, the theatres in the Italian language were cooperating with the consulate to keep the citizens and residents of Italian origin in a state of stupefied exaltation.

The fact is worthy of note that all the New York papers agreed to ignore the event, though their men had attended it and had been dined and wined by the nuns. The technique of the McCormack-Dickstein Committee was always working. The American public was not to realize that a serious Fascist movement existed in this country.

5

Fascist Clubs

In the demonstrations of 1935-1936 all the members of the Fascist movement parade before us. But together with them we find also persons for whom we lack definite evidence that they were full-fledged Fascists, or even fellow-travelers. Citizens and residents of Italian origin were, day in and day out, told that Ethiopia had for many years been wronging Italy in all possible ways, that in Ethiopia there were gold and coal mines and oil wells and immense agricultural opportunities the use of which was withheld from Italian labor through sheer bad will by the Ethiopians and the British, that a Catholic crusade would open a savage country to Christian civilization, that the whole world was afraid of Italy's power and envious of her glory and wanted to strangle her. Never had Italian patriotism and Fascism been intermingled with greater skill in America. On the other hand, the United States was keeping aloof from the Ethiopian dispute. As a consequence, no Italo-American ever felt a clash of loyalties between the native and the adopted country. He felt free to shout at one and the same time, and with equal enthusiasm, "Long live Mussolini!" and "Long live Roosevelt!" Therefore. in connection with this war, more than with any other event, it would be unfair to bring in names of persons whose capacity as Fascists or fellow-travelers is not shown by other more definite evidence than their mere appearance at such demonstrations.

A definite Fascist character was shown in the demonstration of Morristown. Carbonelli and Facchetti-Guiglia, in their capacity as leaders, summoned only Fascist clubs and left out all other organizations, though "those too had served well the national cause."[1]

The list of the participating clubs was given by *Il Grido*.[2] Not only the Fascist organizations of New York, but also organizations of neighboring towns — Hoboken, New Jersey, Inwood, Long Island, Union City, New Jersey, etc. — took part in the demonstration. We shall limit our survey to those which had their quarters in New York City, and for each club we shall give whatever information we could gather up to August 1936. As we did not have the means for a systematic research, our information will be fragmentary, to be sure; but it will give a fair idea of the Fascist movement in New York City from the beginning of 1935 to the middle of 1936.

Italian-American Union

In December 1935, [Ugo] D'Annunzio, on behalf of the union, sent a "vibrant" telegram to Father Coughlin to thank him for his campaign against the League of Nations.[2A]

In January 1936, Judge Alessandroni; Judge Cotillo; S. Miele; Judge Leveroni, a well-known Fascist of Boston; Judge Sabbatino; P. F. Catinelle; F. Palleria; and others went to Washington on behalf of the union, to present the union's (i.e. Mussolini's) point of view. At a meeting held under the auspices of the union, the officers representing organizations in New York State, Pennsylvania, New Jersey, Connecticut, Rhode Island, and Massachusetts branded as "vicious and unfair" the neutrality bills introduced by Senators Nye and Clark and Representative Maverick and urged an "absolute" neutrality "based upon sound, tested and accepted international law, existing since the days of Grotius."[3]

In February 1936, the union began to issue individual membership cards (*tesseramento*) for American citizens of Italian birth who did not participate

1. *Impero*, September 1, 1936, p. 12.
2. August 22, 1936.
2A. GS, December 7, 1935.
3. Gio., January 1936, p. 3. [Because of the growing threat of war between Italy and Ethiopia, in the spring of 1935 Sens. Gerald P.Nye and Bennett Champ Clark and Cong. Maury Maverick introduced bills to impose absolute neutrality on the United States by taking from the president his ability to make a distinction between aggressors and victims. The bill finally passed by Congress and signed by Roosevelt on August 31 provided for an automatic embargo on goods to all belligerents. See Rovert Divine, *The Illusion of Neutrality* (Chicago, 1962), and Harris, *The United States and the Italo-Ethiopian Crisis*. Ed. Note]

in any association,[4] and it announced that it had four hundred branches all over the United States.[5] D'Annunzio alone knew just how much truth there was in this figure.

Again in February 1936, the union sponsored the celebration of a solemn memorial mass for Fr. Reginaldo Giuliani in the Dominion Church of Saint Vincent Ferrer, Lexington Avenue at Sixty-sixth Street. Father Giuliani had once made a tour of Fascist propaganda in the United States, and was killed in Africa during the Ethiopian war. Four members of the New York Chapter of the Italian War Veterans Association: V. Rossini, Antonio Signore, F. Fazio, and E. Rodilosso, kept guard of honor around the tumulus. Rev. Egidio Rutolo delivered the oration in Italian. Rev. R. E. Cavanaugh spoke in English. The War Veterans were represented by S. Bonanno and G. Cristina; the Blue Ribbon Association by A. D. Felice, and the Disabled Veterans by A. D'Angiola.[6]

In March 1936, the union delivered a proclamation to the Italians in America, summoning them to unite so that "their clear, vibrant, and above all sincere voice might be heard in the councils which control the destinies of the most powerful and most just country in the world."[7]

In August 1936, the union promised that it would "withstand with all possible energy the disastrous effects of the unfair and aggressive English propaganda which in a very short time had upturned public and official opinion of America against Italy,"[8] and announced that a conference among the dependent organizations of New York state would soon be summoned.[9] It was represented at the Morristown demonstration by its president, Ugo D'Annunzio, who flew in a plane over the field.

Abraham Lincoln, Mario Sonzini, and Casa D'Italia (The Bronx)

In June 1935, the Abraham Lincoln Club still had its school of Italian language under the auspices of the Dante Alighieri Society and its teacher was still Mrs. Rina Ciancaglini-Gera.[10]

In September 1935, Dr. Pasquale Badia succeeded G. Luisi as president of the Abraham Lincoln Club. He defined the club as "A patriotic and Fascist association in a foreign land."[11] The "fine Black Shirts" of the Abraham Lincoln Club elicited the admiration of the *Carroccio*.[12]

4. GS, February 8, 1936.
5. Gio., February 1936, p. 49.
6. Ibid., February 1936, p. 49.
7. GS, March 28, 1936.
8. Ibid., August 15, 1936.
9. *Impero*, August 15, 1936, p. 20.
10. GS, January 29, 1935.
11. GS, September 10, 1935.
12. XXXVIII, p. 88.

In October 1935, the Club made a solemn celebration of the anniversary of the March on Rome. Consul General Vecchiotti, General Francesco Cottafavi, apparently an itinerant Fascist higher-up, Facchetti-Guiglia, Carbonelli, A. Palanca, and three officials of the consulate intervened. The guests were welcomed by Dr. P. Badia, the president of the Club, G. Luisi, J. Cristina, A. Di Marco, the presidents of the Italo-American clubs and association, and the dignitaries of the Sons of Italy and the Independent Sons of Italy. "The bells of the Carmine church (pastor, Rev. Severino Focacci) joined their sound to the concert of the Italian Bronx Band." Addresses were given by Badia, Luisi, Vecchiotti, Carbonelli. The salute to the Duce was ordered and given and the participants hailed the king and the Duce.[13]

The club was represented at the celebration of the Italian Armistice Day (November 4, 1935) by P. Badia, upon whom the decoration of Commander of the Crown of Italy had been bestowed in those very days.

On December 27, 1935, "in an atmosphere of pure and sincere Fascist comradeship and discipline," the Club decided to dismiss the name of Abraham Lincoln and to take up the title of Circolo Italiani Uniti Mario Sonzini. The following directors were chosen: G. Acciani, P. Badia, Giovanni Corradini, Giacinto Mancusi, C. Scicchitano, A. Zulli.[14]

At the time of the Fascist League of North America, there existed a Mario Sonzini Fascio in the Bronx. Most likely, this Fascio took the name of Abraham Lincoln when the League was forced to disband, but, in 1936, Abraham Lincoln was no longer needed as a front, and Mario Sonzini came back again into light. A curious evidence might well corroborate our hypothesis. PLO, which was published in 1940, put the establishment of the Sonzini Club as far back as 1925, and the Club celebrated in 1940 its "fifteenth" birthday.[15] (In Boston, Massachusetts, a Fascist club is called even today, 1943, by the name of Abraham Lincoln. The picture of Mussolini which adorned its hall disappeared prudently in the spring of 1941.)

The Mario Sonzini Club inherited the Abraham Lincoln's school of Italian language,supported by the Dante Alighieri Society. In addition, it had an Afterwork (Dopolavoro) club, entrusted to Alfredo D'Amato, Renato Mancusi, and Antonio Pontillo, all "old Blackshirts."[16] The club also had a ladies' auxiliary.[17]

Meanwhile, in July 1935 a Casa d'Italia ("House of Italy") had arisen in

13. PIA, October 28, 1935.
14. Ibid., January 1, 1936.
15. GS, May 25, 1940.
16. PIA, January 8, 1936.
17. GS, January 29, 1936.

the Bronx, a "very pure sentinel of Fascism in America."[18] Trombetta greeted
the new institution "with frank Fascist enthusiasm and with the feelings of a
comrade." The Dante Alighieri Society was expected to establish a school
under that same Mrs. Rina Ciancaglini-Gera,[19] who had been running the
school of the Abraham Lincoln Club.

In *Il Progresso*[20] we read:

> The Italians abroad know that the fatherland has given them common
> hearths on which burns the unquenchable fire of Italianism. These hearths
> are represented by the "Houses of Italy" ("Casa d'Italia"), symbols of the
> nation abroad, centers of life that assemble in themselves all the activities
> aimed at protecting, helping and melting our communities into a single
> block of will and sentiments. Since they represent Italy, Fascism even in
> their exterior, in their architectural lines and in their structure, has wanted
> them to keep aloft the prestige of our country...In America (North and
> South) there are 80 Houses of Italy. Marked with that spirit of benevolence
> and comradeship that distinguishes Fascism, the Houses of Italy carry out,
> with incomparable nobility, their hospitable task for all persons — even
> strangers — who ask to become a part of them, provided that they are of
> good will.

Obviously, the Casa d'Italia of the Bronx (not to be confused with the
Casa Italiana of Columbia University) arose through the initiative and at
the expense of the consulate. In October 1935, the institution was managed
by a triumvirate consisting of Giovanni Luisi, Jerome Cristina and Antonio
Di Marco.[21] The ceremony by which its school was inaugurated was the
occasion for an "ardent display of Italianism." The speakers were Giani on
behalf of the consulate, Lucia Della Malva and Jerome Cristina. Facchetti-
Guiglia, Prezzolini, M. A. Delagi, Edward Corsi, James Ciacaglini and Susca
sent messages of greeting.[22]

The institution was represented at the demonstration of November 4,
1935, by F. Latella. But it did not have a very long life, and at the beginning
of 1936 it merged with the Mario Sonzini Club. The new institution took the
name of Benito Mussolini Club and depended on the Lictor Association.

In January 1936, the Benito Mussolini Club held a meeting in which A.
Grisco and G. Luisi spoke exhorting all the "old and good Italian elements of
the Bronx to gather under a single and pure banner of Italianism." "The
audience, standing, could not refrain from shouting with all its might a
name which is the symbol of a new faith, a new flame: Duce, Duce, Duce!"

18. Ibid., August 3, 1935.
19. Ibid., August 24, 1935.
20. July 2, 1938.
21. PIA, October 28, 1935.
22. GS, October 12, 1935.

Directors were to be: G. Grieco, M.D., commissioner, and Enzo Maddaloni, G. Luisi, Cosmo Masillo, Giorgio Bragalini, A. Settineri, Jerome Cristina, D. Pepe, Attilio Parrino, Nicola Piccinni, Antonio Bellitti.[23]

It appears that the harmony between the members did not last very long since toward the end of January 1936, we find that again there exists a Mario Sonzini Club which announces that "owing to its activities, more and more worthy of the Fatherland and of our most beloved Duce," the number of members had been more than tripled, and that the ladies auxiliary would sponsor an artistic soirée which would be attended by G. Sterni, "the artist who works so tirelessly for the moral betterment of our people in this foreign land."[24]

Benito Mussolini (The Bronx)

It seems that this club severed relations with the Mario Sonzini Club in January 1936. Certainly in June 1936, it had a life of its own.

Jerome Cristina was its commissioner, and it celebrated the Italian victory in the Ethiopian war. American schoolboys of Italian origin, Fascist women and Balillas were in attendance. J. Cristina exhorted the Italians of New York to keep united for the victories of tomorrow. G. Luisi stated that "the members of the Club would go on being the sentinels guarding the Fatherland's and Fascism's outposts in the Bronx." P. Carbonelli, too, exhorted the members to keep united, "so that the Italo-Americans might benefit from the Italian victory," and praised Generoso Pope. The meeting ended with the audience shouting "Duce, Duce, Duce" and singing "Giovinezza."[25]

In July 1936, we find among the directors Ernesto De Simone.[26]

In August 1936, comrades Giacinto Mancusi, Ernesto De Simone, Renato Mancini, Antonio Bellitti, Francesco Capria, R. Altieri, and S. Siclari were recorded among the members of this Club, and J. Cristina was its president.[27]

In the Morristown demonstration, the pennant of this club proceeded side by side with that of the Mario Sonzini Club.

"Something new had happened," was the comment of *Il Grido della Stirpe* "and a spirit of real Fascist cooperation and of final brotherhood had, at long last, developed, in the Duce's name, between the two old Clubs of the Bronx. Also, by the will of the Commissioners [Carbonelli and Facchetti-Guiglia], the squads of the two Clubs had mingled together, and it almost

23. PIA, January 8, 1936.
24. Ibid., January 29, 1936.
25. Ibid., June 14, 1936; GS, June 20, 1936.
26. PIA, July 2, 1936.
27. *Impero*, August 1, 1936, p. 39.

seemed as if they were a single Club, which, by the way, would be everybody's wish."

It is obvious that there still existed grudges between the two clubs.

In consequence of the fact that in the Morristown demonstration the members of this club marched mingled with those of the Mario Sonzini Club, it is impossible to decide which man belonged to which club. For our purpose, however, it suffices to take note of the "old comrades" listed by *Il Grido della Stirpe*: Alfredo Di Donato, Salvatore Stuto, Renato Mancini, Giovanni Luisi, Gerardo De Sanctis, G. Mancusi, Frank Capria, N. Piccini, Giovanni Costa, and the De Lillo brothers.

Lictor Association

The association held a meeting in September 1935, to which the secretary general, J. Santy, brought the "fervent greetings" of A. Facchetti-Guiglia and P. Carbonelli. Those present at the meeting "made unanimous votes for the victory, the glory and the ever-increasing greatness of the Fatherland which is marching steadily towards the future under the shield of Fascism and of the Duce."[28] At another meeting, in October, they declared themselves "ready for any event."[29]

In December 1935, the association held a meeting at its headquarters (434 East Fourteenth Street) in the honor of P. Carbonelli, General Francesco Cottafavi and A. Facchetti-Guiglia. Besides Cottafavi and Carbonelli, J. Santy also gave a speech.[30]

Seven clubs depended on the Lictor Association. It marched immediately after the Mario Sonzini, Benito Mussolini, and Arnaldo Mussolini Clubs in the Morristown demonstration. They were: Francesco Crispi, Colonel Ivo Oliveti, Maria Josè, Michele Bianchi, Giovinezza, Margherita di Savoia, and Rosa Maltoni Mussolini. Of these, only the first three had their headquarters in New York City; Giovinezza and Margherita di Savoia had them in Hoboken, New Jersey, Michele Bianchi and Rosa Maltoni Mussolini in Inwood, Long Island. The Benito Mussolini Club of the Bronx, which in January, 1936 was dependent on the Lictor Association, had now become autonomous.

Francesco Crispi (Manhattan)

Dependent on the Lictor Association.

In June 1935, it had an amateur actors' branch in which F. Polizzi took

28. GS, September 14, 1935.
29. Ibid., October 19, 1935.
30. Ibid., December 7, 1935.

part.[31] In the same month, in cooperation with the Maria Josè Club, it held in the auditorium of the Church of Saint Mary the Helper, a festival during which ninety dollars was collected and offered to *Il Grido della Stirpe*, "the flame of our most holy ideals."[32]

In November 1935, one of the directors, F. Polizzi, left for Italy to volunteer for service in the war against Ethiopia.[33] On his return he was given the first membership card *ad honorem* in the club.[34]

In a meeting on January 12, 1936, Leopoldo Polizzi read the financial report for 1935. As a consequence, the meeting ousted the present directors and chose a temporary triumvirate composed of Antonino Alessandro, Leopoldo Polizzi, and Antonio Massari, "giving them the duty of taking immediate possession of all that which belonged to the Club." Moreover a committee was appointed for collecting money and golden objects to be offered to the Italian Red Cross and the Fascist Welfare Foundation (Opere Assistenziali) in Italy.[35]

Maria Josè (Manhattan)

Dependent on the Lictor Association.

In March 1935, Mrs. Agnanno was organizing a group of Balillas connected with this club.[36] On January 18, 1936, the club held its annual dance in the auditorium of the Parochial Church at 437 East Eleventh Street. Representatives of Giovinezza, Margherita di Savoia, Mario Morgantini, Francesco Crispi Clubs, and other associations attended. Also present at the dance was P. Carbonelli who was "greeted warmly." The speakers were the chairman of the festa, Antonino Mazzari, and Joseph Santy. "Money and gold were collected for the Fatherland." The directorate of the club consisted of Mrs. Mamie Casabianca, A. Mancari, A. Ficalora, G. Pancaldo, G. Alonzi, G. Ferrara, E. Mirabelli, F. Santoro, V. Velardi, G. Troncone, G. Finizio, L. Mancusi, G. Zingone, A. Casabianca, A. Cardella.[37]

In the Morristown demonstration, the club was associated with a Balilla club, probably the same group of Fascist children which was being organized in March 1935.

Association of Italians Abroad (Manhattan)

This organization held a meeting in July 1935, at which A. F. Guidi was

31. Ibid., June 16. 1935.
32. Ibid., June 29, 1935.
33. Ibid., November 16, 1935.
34. Ibid., July 18, 1936.
35. PIA, January 18, 1936.
36. GS, March 23, 1935.
37. PIA, January 26, 1936.

welcomed and greeted with the anthem "Giovinezza." Much applauded speakers, in praise of Italy and the Duce, were Victor Anfuso; P. Badia, president of the Abraham Lincoln Club of the Bronx; Attorney Saitta; C. Amoruso; V. D'Antoni; and Giovanni D'Angelo for the Fascist Club Armando Diaz of Ozone Park. Guests of honor were: U. D'Annunzio, E. Casagrande, A. Facchetti-Guiglia, F. P. Macaluso, V. Comito, F. Catinella, G. Susca, A. Brancato, Mannecchia. Chairman of the ceremony was Alberto Cornella.[38]

The Association was represented by A. Facchetti-Guiglia and A. Cornella at the celebration of Italian Armistice Day, November 4, 1935.

Thirty-seven members of the Association enlisted as volunteers and served under the Italian flag in the Italo-Ethiopian War.[39]

At the manifestation of Morristown, the Association was represented by the following members: Attilio Barbera, M.D.; Sara Bonavita, Faustino Carbo; Leonardo Curreri, Vincenzo De Angelis; Aniello De Vivo; Filippo Di Benedetto; Giuseppe Ganci; Gennaro Giorgi; Giovanni Idone; Gioacchino Ingegnieros; Aldo Lombardi; Tommaso Lucente; Isidoro Maidi; Attilio Majone; Liborio Marino; Ugo Maugeri; Francesco Pecora; Pasquale Pellegrino; Paolo Pizzo, commissioner of the Association; Decio Pugliese; Rocco Rettura; Luigi Rossi; Francesco Scaduto; Pietro Scancarelli; Vincenzo Triviso.

The review *Impero*[40] gave a picture of members of this club, wearing black shirts.

Edmondo Rossoni (Brooklyn)

Named after an agitator of the IWW in the United States who had become a minister [of corporations] in Mussolini's cabinet.

In the Morristown demonstration, its members, "mostly workers," were led by G. Ganci and Sara Bonavita.

Associated Italian Education Clubs (Brooklyn)

In October 1935, this Association was led by a directorate of superior triumvirs. Those superior triumvirs were comrades G. Ceseri, G. Marullo, and S. Otera,[41] the same who had signed its act of incorporation in August 1934. Their title most likely was intended to distinguish them from the directors of the dependent branches.

During the fourteenth year of the Fascist era (i.e. from November 1935 through October 1935) the organization was directed by G. Ceseri, Generoso

38. Ibid., August 1, 1935.
39. *Impero*, July 15, 1936, p. 41.
40. September 1, 1936, p. 26.
41. GS, October 26, November 14, 1935.

Lombardo, L. Rossi, "member of a Fascist squad in Italy," and "comrade" S. Lo Presti, "once member of the 'Fighting Fasci.' "[42]

The AIEC [Associated Italian Education Clubs] was also termed Lictor Federation. The Fascists, like the Communists, have always made skillful use of the device of giving different names to the same organization and similar names to different organizations. Thus they created confusion, made it difficult to assign to each one its own responsibilities, and, in addition, made it appear that there were many more organizations than really existed. We shall make use of the official title Association of Italian Education Clubs, to avoid confusion with the Lictor Association.

In March 1936, the organization was represented at the celebration of the Birthday of Fascism by comrade Ettore Rodilosso.[43]

In April 1936, it celebrated the Birthday of Rome by a proclamation announcing that "it was closing its ranks" and ending with the words: "Salute to the Duce! For Benito Mussolini and the Empire. A. Noi!"[44] *A Noi!* ("To us!") is one of the Fascist war cries.

In June 1936, the association inaugurated its Fascist pennant, with seven hundred comrades attending.[45] Its headquarters in Brooklyn were inaugurated in August 1936, by Carbonelli who brought a message from the Duce.[46]

According to *Impero*,[47] "animators" of the association were Carbonelli and Facchetti-Guiglia, that is to say the two party chiefs (*gerarchi*) who had taken over the positions of A. F. Guidi and I. Thaon di Revel as leaders of the Fascist movement.

Speaking of the branches of the AIEC whose members took part in the Morristown demonstration, *Il Grido della Stirpe* informs us that the development of the organization during the recent months had been "miraculous," and that it had made an "important" show at Morristown. "This Association had only about fifty members last year. Today it has two thousand." The credit for this progress had to be given to comrades Giacomo Ceseri, Stefano Lo Presti, Attilio Rossi and their cooperators. The organization was preparing to carry out a plan of action "entirely inspired by the Duce's sacred commandment."

The following clubs depended on the AIEC in August 1936: Costanzo Ciano, Luigi Rizzo, Enrico Toti, Angelo Rizza, Eleonora Roosevelt, Arnaldo

42. Ibid., November 14, 1935.
43. Ibid., March 28, 1936.
44. Ibid., April 18, 1936.
45. Ibid., June 6, 1936.
46. Ibid., August 8, 1936.
47. August 1, 1936, p. 45.

di Crollalanza, Eolian Islands, and Circolo Pozzallese, Francesco Paolo Giunta.

Costanzo Ciano (Brooklyn)

Named after the father of Foreign Minister [Galeazzo] Ciano.

This club is mentioned for the first time in *Impero*.[48] Most likely it did not yet exist on June 6, 1936, as *Il Grido della Stirpe* does not mention it among the clubs depending on the AIEC at that date.

Luigi Rizzo (Brooklyn)

Named after a navy officer who sank two Austrian battleships during the war of 1915-1918.

According to PLO,[49] this club was founded in 1933. It certainly was in existence in 1935 and had specialized in organizing "patriotic performances."[50] Comrade Generoso Lombardi, M.D. and G. Marullo were among its Directors in November 1935.[51]

Seventeen of its members volunteered for the Ethiopian War.[52] G. Ceseri, one of the directors of the AIEC, was its president in June 1936.[53]

Enrico Toti (Brooklyn)

Named after an Italian hero of the First World War, who was killed in Italy during the Civil War.

This club seems not to have existed yet in June 1936, as *Il Grido della Stirpe*[54] does not mention it among those dependent on the AIEC.

Angelo Rizza (Brooklyn)

Also termed Circolo Siracusano Angelo Rizza.[55] An Angelo Rizza Fascio existed in Brooklyn at the time of the Fascist League of North America. One wonders whether the club we deal with now, was the old Fascio which had gone underground from 1929 to 1935, or a root and branch new club.

The Educational Club Angelo Rizza, "based on principles of perfect Italianism," was being formed in September 1935. Its directors were Angelo Giardinella, Angelo Giudice, and Salvatore Urso.[56] It was regularly working

---

48. Ibid.
49. PLO, pp. 42, 101.
50. GS, January 23, 1937.
51. Ibid., November 16, 1935.
52. Ibid., February 13, 1937.
53. Ibid., June 6, 1936.
54. June 6, 1936.
55. *Impero*, November 1, 1936, p. 5.
56. GS, September 9, 1935.

in November 1935, as a branch of the AIEC,[57] and it was represented at the mass meeting of November 4, 1935, by Ettore Rodilosso, its commissioner.[58]

In February 1936, Ettore Rodilosso promoted a dance in the quarters of this club to raise money for the Italian Red Cross and the Italian Welfare Foundation,[59] and in April 1936, he issued a message on behalf of the club to celebrate the Birthday of Rome.[59A] A. Giardinella was still president of the club in June 1936.[60]

Eleonora Roosevelt (Brooklyn)

The name given for this Club by *Il Grido della Stirpe* is Eleonora Duse, after the famous Italian actress. But no other source ever gave the same name during those years. What did exist was a feminine Fascist club which used the name of Mrs. Roosevelt as front, just as other clubs used the names of Theodore Roosevelt and Abraham Lincoln.

Mrs. Giovanna Cillè was the president of this club in 1935 and 1936.[61] Its pennant was dedicated in June 1936 with a patriotic address by Mrs. Cillè.[62]

Araldo Di Crollalanza (Manhattan)

In March 1935, the directorate of this club consisted of Francesco Abbruzzi, Felice Bello, Giovanni Campanile, Nicola Campanile, Giuseppe Capo, Albertino Cavicchia, Giuseppe Crisanzio, Giacomo De Fonte, Nicola De Fonte, Gaetano De Leonibus, Vito Deliso, Francesco Del Re, Antonio Di Benedetto, Vincenzo Furio, Rocco Laudadio, Giavanni Lemo, Giuseppe Lepore, Domenico Liotine, Vincenzo Luciano, Leonardo Marsico, Michele Marsico, Leonardo Mossa, Nicola Panzini, Angelo Pignataro, Giuseppe Rizzi, Pietro Roca di Francesco, Pietro Roca Di Nicola, Francesco Valletta, and Vitantonio Verga.[63]

In May 1935, "this flourishing club, composed of active and disciplined Fascists," commemorated "with Fascist solemnity" its second year of life with addresses by Trombetta and A. F. Guidi, who in his capacity of the club's director "praised the idealism of the club which carries on its activities in the light of the sun," and "praised Roosevelt, the King and the Duce." Guests of honor at the ceremony were Giuseppe Sessa and A. Facchetti-Guiglia. The club described itself as an "Educational Club."[64]

57. Ibid., November 2, 1935.
58. PIA, November 5, 1935.
59. GS, February 1, 1936.
59A. Ibid., April 18, 1936.
60. Ibid., June 6, 1936.
61. Ibid., November 16, 1935; June 6, 1936.
62. Ibid., June 6, 1936.
63. Ibid., March 16, 1935.
64. Ibid., May 18, 1935.

In September 1935 the club summoned a meeting of the Italian associations to discuss the Italo-Ethiopian dispute. Trombetta and Facchetti-Guiglia addressed the meeting, which was attended by L. Mossa, president of the club, V. Rossini and delegates of four clubs.[65]

In April 1936, L. Mossa sent a message to *Il Grido della Stirpe* on behalf of the club, stating that "though far away from Italy, we are ready to take up our place for her, if our Duce commands us to do so; for Imperial Italy alalà!"[66]

In June 1936, the club had become a branch of the AIEC, its president still being Leonardo Mossa.[67]

The Arnaldo di Crollalanza Club sent to the Morristown demonstration a group of Boy Scouts. The members were led by comrade Leonardo Mossa. Comrades Leonardo Marsico, Vincenzo Luciano, Giovanni Mossa, Giuseppe Mossa, Michele Marsico, Nicola De Fonte, the Del Re brothers, Rocco Laudadio and Giuseppe Falco wree among those present.

Isole Eolie ("Eolian Islands") (Brooklyn)

Names after a group of islands in the Tyrrehenian Sea, among which there is the island of Lipari on which the opponents of the Fascist regime were interned. It existed in September 1935 as an "Educational Club"[68] and in June 1936, it depended on the AIEC. Its president was Vincenzo Taranto,[69] "an old Black Shirt," who together with Gaetano Ferlazzo, led the club at the Morristown demonstration. Among its members were the brothers Stefano and Gaetano Rando, "old Black Shirts."

Francesco Paolo Giunta — Pozzallese (Brooklyn)

This was the Rinascente Pozzallese rechristened after a local Brooklyn politician. It was also termed Circolo Pozzallese F. P. Giunta.[70]

In 1934 this club kept a school of Italian language, the teacher of which was F. Priolo.[71] In February 1935, it had as its president, P. Francesco Giardinella, and its headquarters were at 117 Carroll Street.[72] The club sent its delegates in March 1935 to the celebration of the Birthday of Fascism;[73]

65. Ibid., September 25, 1935.
66. Ibid., April 18, 1936.
67. Ibid., June 6, 1936.
68. Ibid., September 28, 1935.
69. Ibid., June 6, 1936.
70. *Impero*, November 1, 1936, p. 5.
71. XXXVI, p. 216.
72. PIA, February 24, 1935.
73. GS, March 30, 1935.

in April 1935, to the celebration of the Birthday of Rome;[74] and in May 1935 to a ceremony of the Arnaldo di Crollalanza Club[75] and to the commemoration of Carisi and D'Ambrosoli.[76] It is obvious that the club was an integral part of the Fascist network, although it is not possible to say definitely at what moment it passed from the group of transmission belts to that of out-and-out Fascist organizations.

In August 1935, the club had its flag and the pennant of its school blessed.[77] Mario Giani, cultural agent of the consulate, was present at the ceremony and praised the club for its school.[78] Directors of the club were Cesare Colombo, Ferdinando Emilio, Giovanni Modica. Francesco Carnemolla was teacher in the club's school.[79] In September 1935, the club sent its delegates to a meeting of the Arnaldo di Crollalanza Club[80] and to the meeting of the Association of Italians Abroad of Brooklyn.[81] In November 1935, the club had as one of its directors, A. F. Guidi, who represented it at the rally of Madison Square Garden.

In February 1936, we find among its directors comrades Emidio Fernando, C. Colombo, and Guglielmo Modica.[82]

The club, termed Educational Club, was a branch of the AIEC, Giovanni Modica being its president in June 1936.[83] Besides G. Modica, its members, comrades Giovanni Carnemolla, Francesco Gullaro, Salvatore Gullaro, and Giovanni Rendo participated in the Morristown demonstration.

Nuova Italia ("New Italy") (Ridgewood, Brooklyn)

This club was up till the end of 1935 a branch of the Association of Italians Abroad. It was presided over by Rosario Ganci and had its headquarters at 396 Knickerbocker Avenue. In 1935 its school was still conducted by Maria Todaro and Alfonso Rizzuto.[84]

On the evening of January 6, 1936, the club held a meeting at which P. Carbonelli and Rev. Ottavio Silvestri were guests of honor. The president after sending his greetings to comrade G. Bonavita who had volunteered in the war against Ethiopia, announced that a vast Italo-American organization, under the name of Lictor Federation, had been established. Its aim was to

74. PIA, April 30, 1935.
75. GS, May 18, 1935.
76. PIA, May 31, 1935.
77. GS, August 17, 1935.
78. Ibid., August 24, 1935.
79. Ibid., August 31, 1935.
80. Ibid., September 28, 1935.
81. PIA, September 15, 1935.
82. GS, February 22, 1936.
83. Ibid., June 6, 1936.
84. Ibid., February 2, 1935; June 29, 1936.

"gather around itself all the educational clubs in order to discipline them under a single directorate"; and he proposed that the Brooklyn branch of the Association of Italians Abroad join the Lictor Federation. The motion of the president was seconded by Anthony Di Palma, G. D'Angelo, Giovanni La Cagnina, Carlo Diana, Antonio Di Miceli, and Giuseppe Di Stefano, and it was passed unanimously.[85] The Lictor Federation was nothing else but the Associated Italian Educational Clubs. Thus as of January 1936, the Brooklyn branch of the Association of Italians Abroad passed under this new jurisdiction, taking up the title of Nuova Italia. It is also sometimes called Association of Italians Abroad of Brooklyn.[86]

Il Progresso[87] speaks of it as if it were a new club, whose commissioner (fiduciario) is comrade Pasquale Biancavilla. Promoters of the foundation of the club, together with the commissioner, were: Salvatore Sucasera, J. Perez, Salvatore Di Franco, Giuseppe Ragusa.

At the first meeting, John J. Visani, M.D., sent his greetings. Rev. Ottavio Silvestri, pastor of the Saint Joseph Church, was present as spiritual advisor, and was pleased to attend such a meeting "inspired by high sentiments of religion and patriotism." Attorney Saitta was the speaker. Albert Cornella was made honorary president and Alderman Baldassarre Lamberto honorary member. The directorate consisted of the following persons: P. Biancavilla, commissioner, and Salvatore Bertuglia, Luigi Rossi, Charles Greco, Gaetano Aleo, Giovanni D'Angelo, Benedetto Rallo, Antonino Castagnaro, Vincenzo Macaluso, Pietro Butera, Emilio Premori, and Antonino Brigagliano.[88]

The club met on January 17, 1936, in the auditorium of the Church of St. Joseph, Suydan Street. The meeting "was made important by the presence" of P. Carbonelli.[89] Reverend O. Silvestri blessed the members. F. Biancavilla, S. Bertuglia, A. P. Cornella, Giuseppe Ganci, and Mrs. Cacico were the speakers. Reverend Silvestri said that "he was happy to see, after so many years he had spent in America, his dreams consisting of a limitless devotion to the Church and to Italy come true." P. Carbonelli proposed a vote of thanks to G. Pope and his daily papers, and the assembly unanimously agreed. Commissioner P. Biancavilla adjourned the meeting with the salute to the Duce.[90]

In June 1936, the club, which had been reorganized, held a ceremony for the closing of its school. Consul General Vecchiotti, Carbonelli, commissioner

85. PIA, June 10, 1936.
86. GS, June 26, 1936; Impero, July 15, 1936, p. 40.
87. January 11, 1936.
88. PIA, January 11, 1936.
89. Ibid., January 17, 25, 1936.
90. Ibid., January 27, 1936.

for the Fasci Abroad, Mario Giani cultural attachè of the consulate, Jerome Ambro, Pietro Giambalvo, Mutolo, and Monsignor Silvestri were present. A squad of Black Shirts, aligned in the center of the hall, crowded with attendants, welcomed the representative of the government with an enthusiastic ovation, and gave the Roman salute. The children of the school sang "Giovinezza" and other patriotic anthems, [with] comrade Rosario Ganci, and the teachers, Mrs. De Pasquale and Mrs. Todaro conducting. Commissioner Giuseppe Ganci, while declaring that he himself would observe an attitude of rigid discipline towards the "authorities," demanded that all the members of the club should observe the same attitude towards him and the Fascist officials. Besides Giuseppe Ganci, Reverend Silvestri, Jerome Ambro, Carbonelli, Giuseppe Maltese, M.D. in charge of the cultural activities of the club, and V. D'Antoni on behalf of Il Progresso spoke. Consul Vecchiotti "praised the loyalty of Italo-Americans towards the land of their origin"; he made the prediction that from then on, Italian emigrants would seek work in Ethiopia and not in America, and therefore, "the duty of keeping the flame of Italianism and the racial conscience alive, rests with the Italo-Americans who already are in this country." The meeting closed with the public shouting "Duce, Duce, Duce."[91]

In July 1936, the club celebrated the foundation of the empire with a ceremony in which Vecchiotti, Mario Giani, Carbonelli, and Monsignor Silvestri took part. The children of the school of which comrade Rosario Ganci was director and Mrs. Maria Todaro teacher, gave with great success evidence of their abilities. The school was sponsored by the Dante Alighieri Society.[92]

During that same month, the club gave a party in honor of its two members, Reverend Silvestri and A. P. Cornella. Comrade P. Biancavilla, commissioner of the club, Carbonelli and F. P. Macaluso made speeches.[93]

The squad which the club sent to the Morristown demonstration, was headed by P. Biancavilla, and comrades Filippo Marchella, Nicola Scala, Giovanni D'Angelo, Lorenzo Caputo, Giuseppe Frisone, Vincenzo Macaluso, and Giuseppe Macaluso were in his retinue, along with the ladies auxiliary, the youth group, and the sport branch of the club.

We do not know whether the ladies auxiliary is the same organization as that which in March 1936 was called Women's Educational Club of Bensonhurst, Brooklyn.[94]

91. Ibid., June 19, 1936; GS, June 27, 1936..
92. Impero, July 15, 1936, p. 40.
93. Ibid., August 1, 1936, p. 37.
94. PIA, March 23, 1936.

Nove Maggio ("Ninth of May") (Brooklyn)

Names after the day in which Mussolini proclaimed the revival of the Roman Empire, in 1936, as a result of the victory in the Ethiopian War.

Here is the story of the club, as it is given by *Il Progresso:*[95]

> In May 1936, a group of Italians of Avenue U in Brooklyn, who had collected and sent to Italy large quantities of iron, copper and gold, felt the urge of celebrating the Italo-Ethiopian victory, not with sporadic and isolated manifestations, but by uniting in a marvelous "fascio" the pure forces of this section of Greater New York. In this way the "Ninth of May" Club of Brooklyn was born. From its incorporation until today, the life of the "Ninth of May" Club has been a continual and gradual ascent. This part of the city, which was cold and hostile to Italian manifestations, almost prey to subversive doctrines, today has pledged itself completely to Italy and to the Duce, and of such faith has given ample and indisputable proof in its two celebrations of the first and the second anniversary of the Italian Empire, in May of 1937 and 1938. The first ones to initiate the idea and the summons were: Attorney Gennaro Cipriani, Giuseppe Oddo, Nando Riggio, Francesco Mosca, Vincenzo Lucchesi, Amedeo Forzano, Gaetano Liotta, Antonio Buongiorno, Giuseppe Trapani, Pietro Mazzoli, Carlo Carulli, D. De Francesco, Francesco Maiorca, Aristide Sigismondi, Salvatore Valenti, Michele Zotta, Antonino Grillo, Ottavio Graziano. His Excellency Fulvio Suvich, ex-Ambassador of Italy, Consul General Gaetano Vecchiotti, Commander P. Carbonelli, Count Facchetti-Guiglia, and others have repeated again and again their satisfaction and given their encouragement for the Club's marvellous activities. In 1938, by unanimous vote, the Club established a school for the teaching of the Italian language under the patronage of the "Dante Alighieri" Society, in the section of Gravesand, Brooklyn. This school was able permanently to show an effective force of at least 200 pupils and gained a large percentage of awards in the final competitions.

In July 1936, the club celebrated the victory of the Fascist forces in the Ethiopian War, with a ceremony in which its president comrade De Francesco, Reverend Della Pietra, and F. P. Macaluso made speeches, and "also Comrade Leo De Stefano pronounced vibrant words inspired with the purest Fascist faith."[96]

Nove Maggio Del Bronx (Ninth of May of the Bronx)

This club had its headquarters at 690 East 226 Street. It was affiliated to the NUIA [National United Italian Associations], its charter bearing the number 113. In August 1936, youth groups and schools of Italian language, music and choral singing were being organized.[97] The club had also a band which took part in the Morristown demonstration together with the

95. October 5, 1938.
96. *Impero*, July 15, 1936, p. 40.
97. Ibid., August 1, 1936, p. 38.

members.

Diciotto Novembre 1935, XIV
("Eighteenth of November 1935, Fourteenth Year of the Fascist Era)
(Brooklyn)

On November 18, 1935, the League of Nations decided sanctions against Italy on account of Mussolini's aggression against Ethiopia. The club was named after the date of the event. It was first mentioned, according to our records, in December 1935, and was incorporated under the laws of New York State. Its official title in the incorporation act was "November 18, 1935, XIV, Association, Inc.," the item XIV meaning fourteenth year of the Fascist regime, and it was adopted in an official document of the State of New York. The club's headquarters were at 8787 Bay Parkway, Brooklyn. It was a member not only of the Association of Italian Educational Clubs, but also of the National United Italian Associations, its charter bearing the number 102.[98]

Among the founders of this club were Antonio Dussich[99] and F. Amorello.[100]

In January 1936, its directorate consisted of Salvatore Aragona, Michele Florio, Umberto Penza, John Petraglia, and Tommaso Secli.[101]

The club held a "great Italian Red Cross Rally" on the evening of January 18, 1936, in the auditorium of the New Utrecht High School, under the chairmanship of Gennaro Cipriani. The rally had been organized by Antonio Dussich, Arturo Egitto, Michele Florio, Bernardino Genchi, and Tommaso Secli. Consul General Vecchiotti affirmed that the sanctions applied by the League of Nations against Italy had "brought all the Italians to the maximum of devotion toward their head, Benito Mussolini." He brought forth "tumultuous applause and shouts of Duce, Duce, Duce." E. Casagrande tendered the greetings of the Italian American Union. Mrs. Carla Adgate De Viti urged the women to show their loyalty to Mussolini by offering their wedding rings. Gennaro Cipriani offered a hymn to Fascist Italy and Il Duce. Other speakers were Jouvenal Marchisio and Vito Guariglia. The ceremony was attended by V. Comito, V. Rossini, Vice-Consul Mario Giani, P. Carbonelli, F. P. Macaluso, D. Trombetta, L. Matrogiovanni, Domenico Dellino. Directors of the club were: Giovanni Petraglia, Tommaso Secli, Umberto Penza, A. Vinciguerra, Michele Florio, Salvatore Aragona.[102]

In June 1938, ten children of the Italian school of this club got medals

98. PIA, January 11, 1936.
99. GS, December 28, 1935.
100. Ibid., February 8, 1936.
101. Ibid., February 8, 1936.
102. PIA, January 27, 1936; Gio., January 1936, p. 9; GS, February 8, 1936.

from the consul general, as a premium for the result they had achieved.[103]

Comrade Dussich was described as the "sole of the Club,"[104] whose premises were at 7713 New Utrecht Avenue, Brooklyn.[105] According to comrade Dussich "Fascism is Italy, and Italy is il Duce."[106]

Flatbush Italo-American Association (Brooklyn)

A Flatbush Club with headquarters in Nostrand Avenue, Brooklyn, existed in 1927. In 1938, a Flatbush Italo-American Association, too, had its headquarters at 1565 Nostrand Avenue, Brooklyn. This circumstance makes plausible the assumption that the old club went underground in 1930 (after the Fascist League had been disbanded) and reappeared in the clear light in 1936.

On January 1936, the Flatbush Italo-American Association was a branch of the Federation of Apulian Association and decided to become a member of the National United Italian Associations, changing its name to Italian Educational Club of Flatbush, Brooklyn. Its Charter as member of the NUIA bore number 101. Directors were Michele Dellino, Antonio Gagliardi, Mike Tufariello, Pietro Cappiello, Giacomo Di Vincenzo, John Sebatini, Antonio Sangiovanni, Michele Maio, Giuseppe Petrucelli, Salvatore Di Vincenzo, Francesco Taormina, Gaetano Catanea, Antonio Mancino, Vincenzo Messina. The club had a school committee made up of Mike Tufariello, John Sabatini, Pasquale Ramunni, Antonio Sangiovanni. It also had a sport committee made up of Giuseppe Petrucelli, Pietro Mazzei, and Mario Abbene. The club announced that "owing to the unexpected number of new pupils," the school would be open two days per week, Tuesdays and Fridays, from 7 to 9 p.m. It finally decided to take part en masse in the meeting "Pro America's Neutrality" sponsored by the NUIA and to be held on January 18, 1936, at the New Utrecht High School.[107]

In March 1936, its delegates attended the celebration of the Birthday of Fascism.[108]

In June 1936, the club held a festival at which P. Carbonelli was the official speaker, with A. Facchetti-Guiglia attending.[109]

Armando Diaz (Ozone Park, Long Island)

This club, once depending on the Lictor Association, was one of the first,

103. PIA, June 6, 1938.
104. GS, August 22, 1936.
105. Impero, September 15, 1936, p. 20.
106. GS, October 26, 1935.
107. PIA, January 13, 1936.
108. Ibid., March 23, 1936.
109. GS, January 26, 1936.

if not the very first, to assume the name of Educational Club, back in April 1935, when A. F. Guidi honored it with one of his lectures on the "Progress and Development of the New Italy, Under the Guidance of the Duce." After Guidi's address, the club made a "patriotic parade" in the streets of Ozone Park.[110]

In January 1936, the directors were: Gastone Napoli, Emilio Di Prima, Domenico Vicari, Charles Penna, Bernardo Rotondi, Francesco Sala, Giovanni Papariello, Filippo Monachino, James Petrosino.[111]

In February 1936, the club inaugurated its new headquarters at 8920 101 Avenue, Ozone Park,[112] and this event was celebrated with a ceremony in which the speakers were Emilio Di Prima and William F.Mayer, alderman of Ozone Park.[113]

In March 1936, its president was comrade Gastone Napoli.[114] In June 1936, Carbonelli gave an address.[115]

Roma Imperiale ("Imperial Rome") (Manhattan)

This club was inaugurated in July 1936, with P. Carbonelli and P. Garofalo giving speeches, and A. Facchetti-Guiglia attending.[116] Its aims were: "cult of New Italy," and "observance of laws in America." Giovanni Finizio was one of the directors.[117]

The Roma Imperiale Club was led, at the Morristown demonstration, by the club's commissioner, Carmelo Casablanca, and Angelo Messina, Giovanni Finizio, Francesco Azzarelli and Pietro Spadaro, directors.

Its headquarters seem to have migrated from 216 to 337 East Fourteenth Street. According to *Almanacco*[118] the Roma Imperiale was a women's organization established by Mrs. Mamie Casabianca, to educate the Italian children of East Fifteenth, Fourteenth, Thirteenth, and Twelfth Streets. It was a branch of the NUIA.

Antonio Locatelli (The Bronx)

Named after an Italian aviator who, in 1924, cabled from America to Mussolini approving of the murder of the anti-Fascist Representative Matteotti, and was killed in the Ethiopian War.

110. Ibid., April 20, 1935.
111. PIA, January 12, 1936.
112. Ibid., January 30, 1936.
113. GS, February 29, 1936.
114. Ibid., March 28, 1936.
115. Ibid., June 20, 1936.
116. Ibid., July 11, 18, 1936.
117. Ibid., July 4, 1936.
118. *Almanacco*, pp. 56-57.

Ferruccio Pietravalle, Girolamo Magnoli, Pasquale Russo led this club at the Morristown demonstration. Among its members were comrades Silverio Sandolo, Alessandro Chiaro, Alfonso Bove, Ernesto Magliacane, Aniello Gaiano, Saverio Scotto, the Raimondo Brothers, Giuseppe Bentivegna, and comrade Staniscià, a seventy-seven year-old man, who had been a member of the fascio of Chieti (Italy) and had volunteered in the Italo-Ethiopian War.

Domenico Mastronuzzi (Manhattan)

A Domenico Mastronuzzi Club existed at the time of the Fascist League of North America. When the Fascist League disbanded, the club in February 1930, decided to send half of its money to Mussolini and to give the other half to the Italian Hospital of New York. At that time its directorate consisted of Leonardo De Vito, Giacomo Scarangella and Giovanni D. Cataldo.[119]

In July 1936, a committee was intent on the setting up of a club bearing the same name. Members of the committee were comrades Carlo Di Stefano, Salvatore Brillanti, Giuseppe Di Grazia, Salvatore Cusimano, Giuseppe Pizzo, Antonio Palombella, Lorenzo Cannizzaro, Franco Lo Guidice, Prospero Lo Giudice, and Sebastiano Lo Giudice. Giuseppe Bosco, "an old Fascist storm trooper," was made commissioner.[120] The name Domenico Mastronuzzi was chosen to comply with the wish of Commissioner Carbonelli. The club gathered about five hundred members, mostly workers.[121] Its premises were at 62 Delancey Street.

The club was inaugurated in August 1936, comrades Bosco, Luisi, and Carbonelli being the speakers.[122] It adopted a resolution to the effect that a laurel wreath should be put in its name, in the town of Taranto (Italy), on the memorial of the martyr Mastronuzzi, "to attest the spiritual unity existing between the Italians in America and the Fascist living in the Fatherland."[123]

Tito Minniti (Manhattan)

Named after an Italian officer who was killed by the Abyssinians during the war.

According to *Il Progresso*,[124] in January 1936 a social club named after Donna Lydia, an editor of the Fascist daily *Progresso Italo-Americano*, decided to change its name, assuming that of Tito Minniti. Its directorate consisted of R. Infantino, P. De Luca, E. Curti, G. Bernucci, Di Dantemaria,

119. GS, February 22, 1930.
120. Ibid., July 4, 1936.
121. Ibid., August 22, 1936.
122. *Impero*, July 15, 1936, p. 40.
123. GS, August 22, 1936.
124. January 9, 27, 1936.

Mrs. Giorgenti, Mrs. G. Cesullo, Mrs. L. Brongi, G. Palumbo, P. Massaro, G. Daidone, S. Abrosiano, Miss M. Sicuro. On the other hand, according to *Almanacco*[125] this Educational Club was established on June 26, 1936 by Pietro de Luca, who obtained for it a charter of membership in the NUIA. Cooperating with him were the other founders: Nicola Pernice, M.D., Salvatore Amico, Vincenzo Valentino, Achille Venditti, Vincenzo Lo Piccolo, Mary Morasco, Giuseppe Palumbo, Benny Santamaria, Ersilia Cappetta, Pietro Massaro, Cesare Storti, Mary and Chiarina Inciardi, Carlo D'Alia, Nicolina Ventriglia, and Anne Storti. The directors of its ladies auxiliary were: Ersilia Capetta, Mary Cascone, Mary Marucco, Jennie Falzone, Giuseppina Todaro, and Margherita Todaro. Future historians will decide which of the two versions is the true one.

In July 1936 a patriotic evening was held. Dancing was interrupted so that R. Infantino, P. De Luca, Attorney Marsico, honorary member, Enzo Maddaloni and Scali, M.D. could "raise lofty hymns to the distant fatherland."[126]

At the Morristown demonstration the club's members were led by comrade Raffaele Infantino. Among them were Cesare Storti, Anne Storti, Achille Bernini and Giuseppe Mannarino.

Risorgimento Italo-Americano; Roma Eterna
("Italo-American Rival"; "Eternal Rome") (Brooklyn)

An association termed Risorgimento Italo-Americano was established in Williamsburgh, Brooklyn, in February 1936, Carbonelli making the inaugural speech. Gaspare Mutolo was made Commissioner; L. Galatioto, Giuseppe Cantales, Arturo Greco, Vincenzo Costa, Alfredo Alfano, Giuseppe Smurra, and Augusto Contessa were the directors.[127]

In April 1936, the club had an Italian school sponsored by the Dante Alighieri Society,[128] of which comrade Domenico Abramo was the director and Mrs. Rosa Leone the teacher.[129]

Risorgimento Italo-Americano changed its named to Roma Eterna in July 1936, at which time the directorate consisted of Domenico Abramo, D. Fasano, Arturo Greco, Gaspare Mutolo, Vincenzo Marsilla, A. Contessa, G. D'Avanzo, G. Cantales, Angelo Guerriero, and Vincenzo Costa.[130]

The club appeared with its new mane at the Morristown demonstration, in which its members were led by the faithful comrade G. Mutolo surrounded

125. *Almanacco*, p. 28.
126. PIA, August 2, 1936.
127. GS, March 7, 1936.
128. PIA, July 5, 1938.
129. GS, April 18, 1936.
130. Ibid., August 1, 1936.

by comrades Filipo Fazio, Gaetano Uzzo, Giuseppe Smurra and Domenico Baldari.

Due Ottobre 1935 ("Second of October," 1935)

Named after the day in which Mussolini started war on Ethiopia.

At Morristown, its members were led by Enrico Guarrata and comrade Romolo Giudice.

Quadrumviro De Bono (Brooklyn)

Named after the Italian general who, during the Fascist uprising of October 1922, had been one of the four chieftains of the Black Shirts, and in 1935 had led the Italian troops against Ethiopia, before Badoglio went to his rescue. Termed also General De Bono.

Comrades Carmelo Muscatello and Michele De Mutis were its representatives at the Morristown demonstration.

Ventotto Ottobre (Twenty-Eighth of October) (Brooklyn)

Named after the day in which the Fascist uprising of 1922 overwhelmed Italy.

Its premises were at 610 Myrtle Avenue, Brooklyn.

At the Morristown demonstration, this club was led by comrades Giuseppe De Luna and Giuseppe Brancato, M.D.

Mario Morgantini (Manhattan)

Named after the first officer of the Italian Army killed in the Ethiopian War.

It was founded on December 2, 1935 through the initiative of A. De Pasquale, G. Iengo, P. Tenore, E. Anzalone, F. Buongiovanni and Enzo Battiparano. At its inauguration, in December 1935, the speakers were comrades Enzo Battiparano, Arturo Faccini, V. Lamattina and Giuseppe Santy, secretary general of the Lictor Association, who outlined the overwhelming vitality of Fascist Italy. E. Battiparano, Pasquale Buongiovanni, L. Caputo, Paolo Del Bagno, Eugenio Formichella, Domenico Letterese, Ciro Salzano, and Gabriele Starace were made directors.[131]

The club's first meeting was held on January 3, 1936, at 354 116 Street, P. Carbonelli delivered one of his innumerable addresses, which brought forth in the hall shouts of Duce, Duce, Duce. Other speakers were A. Tassini and G. Iengo. Pasquale Parino was made honorary member, and a telegram signed Del Bagno was sent to the mayor (Podestà) of Naples in which "the

131. Ibid., December 14, 1935.

Italians of Harlem swore allegiance to the Duce."[132]

At another meeting, during the same month of January 1936, the club decided to establish groups of Balilla and Vanguards for the sons of the members. The meeting was adjourned with the ritual shouting Duce, Duce, Duce.[133]

Quoting from *La Settimana*,[134]

> One of the largest demonstrations [to celebrate the Italian victory in the war with Ethiopia] took place in Harlem. Organized by the "Mario Morgantini" Club, and under the direction of its President, Paolo Del Bagno, an imposing procession moved from the headquarters of the Club, at the corner of 1st Avenue and 115th Street, through the Italian Streets of that section, amid thundering applause, shouts of 'evviva' and the warm enthusiasm of the crowd applauding from windows and sidewalks. Three bands playing patriotic songs and accompanied by the singing of thousands of voices preceded the parade. The demonstrators carried posters with pictures of the Duce and of his brave Army Chiefs.

In July 1936, R. Abbondandolo was chosen as one of its triumvir,[135] and from now onwards he acted as the undisputed boss.

In August 1936, the club held a grandiose meeting at Pleasant Park Bay, the Bronx. Consul General Vecchiotti, Carbonelli, Facchetti-Guiglia, Rev. Enrico Mezzatesta — who blessed the pennants of the Club — [and] an imposing crowd attended. This was "a very interesting Italian demonstration."[136]

The magazine *Impero* gave the picture of the members of this club,[137] and the picture is to be found also in *Il Mondo*.[138] Two vice-consuls and Carbonelli appear in it. Many members wear black shirts and give the Fascist salute. The girls wear the same uniform as the Piccole Italiane ("Fascist Girls") in Italy.

Five hundred members of this club took part in the Morristown demonstration, led by comrade Renzo Abbondandolo, and comrade Paolo Del Bagno. Among them *Il Grido della Stirpe* listed comrades Pasquale Bongiovanni, Enzo Battiparano, Domenico Letterese, Pasquale Tenore, Gabriele Starace, Marzio Rotoli, Aniello D'Abrienzo, M.D., Rocco Lamattina, and Salvatore Vassallo, "member of the G.U.F.," i.e. member of the University Student

132. PIA, january 10, 29, 1936.
133. Ibid., January 26, 1936.
134. May 15, 1936.
135. GS, July 25, 1936.
136. *Settimana*, August 14, 1936.
137. August 15, 1936, p. 41.
138. December 1940, p. 5.

Fascist Organization in Italy.

Sandro Mussolini (Brooklyn)

Named after a nephew of Mussolini who died young.

Its establishment was announced in August 1935. "Its basic aim is to represent, uphold and preserve Italian prestige abroad, supporting in this cosmopolitan environment those political principles that have been outlined and dictated by the great pioneer, Mussolini." Mrs. Giulia Morelli took the initiative and was seconded by Count Guido Magnoni, M.D., Louis Bonvicino, M.D., D. Trombetta, G. Sessa. The provisional directorate consisted of Francesco Romano, Emilio Coppetelli, Pietro Starti and Salvatore Tocci.[139]

In September 1935 the club pledged itself "to offer to all good patriots a distinct atmosphere of Italian fervor. Foremost among its activities will be schools of Italian language and lectures. Films giving the immortal works of the Fascist regime will be part and parcel of the educational plan."[140]

In October 1935, the club numbered seventy-five members. It was represented at the Madison Square Garden rally on November 4, 1935 by Salvatore Tocci. The official inauguration of the club occurred in December 1935. Vecchiotti, Giani, Trombetta were received to the strains of the royal march and "Giovinezza." Francesco Romano, one of the directors, delivered an address "filled with burning patriotism." Mrs. Morelli surveyed the club's activities: four classes of Italian and two classes of hygiene and elementary medicine conducted by Dr. Bonvicino. She offered the consul her wedding ring. Several ladies did the same. Consul Vecchiotti added his own rhetoric and was greeted with "Giovinezza" and "Duce, Duce, Duce."[141]

Giovanni Piccione, M.D. was one of the directors in February 1936, when P. Carbonelli delivered an address at 1819 Eighty-second Street, "pointing out the difference between the theoretical democracy of the United States and the practical one of Italy."[142]

> He showed, with history at his hand, that the present regime in Italy is the only true Democracy. The boast of the other nations pretending to govern under a pure Democracy is disproved by the facts. The great number of unemployed, the method with which help is given to the needy, the influence and impunity of criminal gangs show that those nations are living under the most hateful plutocracy. . . The Ethiopian war is but an episode in the struggle of the Italian people to free itself from a very wicked interference. . . Under the knowing leadership of the Duce, Italy cannot fail

139. GS, August 24, 1935.
140. Ibid., September 7, 1935.
141. Ibid.., September 7, 1935.
142. Ibid., February 8, 1936.

to attain the brilliant future which is its due.

Prof. Mario Giani represented the consulate and received from Mrs. Antonietta Borelli, Mrs. Italia Amatucci, and Giacomo Giglio their wedding rings to be sent to Rome.[143]

In April 1836, the club had a dramatic branch headed by Rosario Romeo.[144] Teachers of Italian language in the school depending on the club, were, in the summer of 1936, Ninfa Alfano and Anna Romano.[145]

The awarding of prizes to the pupils of the school took place in the auditorium of Public School 186. Mrs. Morelli announced that the teaching would be continued in the coming year. The club's headquarters were at 1819 Eighty-second Street in Brooklyn.[146] Giuseppe Amatucci, Leone Gaddi, Faustino Palmieri and Emanuele Romano were recorded among its members in August 1936.[147]

Edda Ciano Mussolini (Ozone Park, Long Island)

Women's club named after Mussolini's daughter, who married Foreign Minister Ciano. It was founded in January 1936 by Calogero and Lilly Diana, "who worked tirelessly and in every possible way to keep lighted the flame of Italianism; a hundred or so members and friends joined with them to keep high the flame of faith and love for the land of their birth." Headquarters at 1493 Myrtle Avenue.

The other directors were: G. Di Meglio, Kitty Mazzara, and Mrs. M. Pezzino. Rev. Leopold Archese, Miss A. Picone, A. F. Guidi were honorary members, Miss A. Stabile was the teacher.[148]

The club depended on the Lictor Association.

Pietro Badoglio (Ozone Park, Long Island)

Named after the chief of the Italian army who defeated the Ethiopians in 1936.

The club was founded in June 1936 through the amalgamation of the Unity Democratic Club and the Italian Community House, Alfonso Mercorella, Fiorentino Catalano, Arturo Di Liva and Louis Lo Grosso made speeches at the inaugural ceremony.[149] Active workers for the formation of the club had been Calogero Diana, president of the Lictor Association in

143. PIA, February 5, 1936.
144. Gio., April 1936, p. 98.
145. GS, July 18, 1936.
146. Settimana, August 7, 1936, p. 14.
147. GS, August 15, 1936.
148. Almanacco, p. 55.
149. Impero, June 15, 1936, p. 40.

1934, and Giuseppe Piazza who, in 1934, had been treasurer of the committee for the establishment of the Armando Diaz Club.[150] G. Piazza, Quirino D'Urgolo, Flavio Squizzero, Vincenzo Cella and Alfonso Crociano were directors.[151]

Camillo Benso Di Cavour (Brooklyn)

The first news that we have about this club, is dated November 1935. Comrades Giuseppe Bonanno, Attilio Braschi, Giovanni Giordano, Giovanni Potenzani, Nazzareno Raffa and Attilio Rossi were its directors at that time.[152]

In February 1936 it gave an artistic soirée.[153]

In June 1936 it depended on the AIEC and its president was Attilio Rossi.[154]

G. Pacca (Brooklyn)

The first news about this club is found in November 1935, when Vittorio Manca was its commissioner, and Randazzo its president.[155] V. Manca went to fight as a volunteer under the Italian flag during the Ethiopian war. In 1939, he sent a telegram overflowing with Fascist enthusiasm to *Il Grido della Stirpe*.[156]

Comrades (Morristown)

The *Grido della Stirpe*, in its report of the Morristown demonstration, recorded also:

"Comrades" of New York who had taken part in the parade, but were not mentioned under their own clubs: 1. Mario Cobianchi; 2. Alessandro Pugliese; 3. Pietro Bonelli Bassano; 4. Silvio Teobaldo Bianchi; 5. Victor Beano; 6. A. Franceschina; 7. Lelio De Ranieri; 8. Oscar Cenci; 9. Ernesto Luzzatto; 10. Mario Ragosta; 11. Alfredo Fanelli; 12. Egidio Di Genova; 13. Bartolo Chimienti; 14. Antonio Signore; 15. Ottavio Rossi; 16. Luciano Mobilio; 17. Alfredo Spina; 18. Italo Marsico; 19. Mario Quarello; 20. Aldo De Vecchi; 21. Efio De Vecchi; 22. Attilio Mascheroni; 23. Carlo Rossi; 24. Emilio Biglia; 25. Salvatore Galeffu; 26. Carmine Bua; 27. Giuseppe Bocache; 28. Giuseppe Livoti; 29. Pietro D'Arpa; 30. Serafino Severini; 31. Antonino Canto; 32. Giovanni Graniero; 33. Salvatore Graniero; 34. Pasquale Badia; 35. Vincenzo Grossi, M.D.; 36. Salvatore Sanzeri; 37. Giuseppe Trapani; 38. Alfredo Consiglio; 39. Umberto Penza; 40. Michele Dellino; 41. Guido

150. GS, September 29, 1934.
151. Ibid., August 29, 1936.
152. Ibid., November 16, 1935.
153. Ibid., February 15, 1936.
154. Ibid., June 6, 1936.
155. Ibid., November 16, 1935.
156. Ibid., April 29, 1939.

Bignami; 42. Gaspare Napoli; 43. Giuseppe Cappuccio.

"Comrades" who had sent greetings from New York and other towns of the United States: leaving aside those living out of New York, we find mentioned: 1. V. Vedovi; 2. Guglielmo Romoli Reiss; 3. Aroldo Palanca; 4. Gaetano Spatafora; 5. Francesco L. Saroli; 6. Domenico D'Angiola; 7. G. Favoino Di Giura; 8. V. Comito; 9. V. Rossini; 10. Ettore Nicoletti; 11. Rev. V. Jannuzzi; 12. Rev. Giovanni Volpe; 13. Angelo Mililli; 14. Filippo Agrò, M.D.

Conclusion

Many people have been injected with the opinion that if a totalitarian regime has accomplished miracles in Italy, the same medicine should deserve at least a fair trial in America. In 1934, nine out of ten of the leading citizens of a town in Vermont, Brattleboro, expressed the belief that Italian Fascism "might be a fine thing for America" (*Harper's Magazine*, November, 1934). If such a state of mind has been created among people having no sentimental bond with Italy, one can readily imagine the results that Fascist misinformation cannot fail to have had among people of Italian extraction.

Fascist propaganda in the United States can strongly affect the younger generations in the long run only if they are left to themselves without any other guidance. I know of a young man who was brought to this country by his parents when he was two. Later he attended a New York parochial school. When he was in high school, his class was visited by an Italian consul who asked the children to write a description of Fascist Italy and Mussolini, pointing out that the writer of the best paper would receive as a prize a free trip to Italy. "Of course, I exaggerated," the young man admits, "and I got it." The Italian consul general came to the school when the prizes were assigned and made a speech about Italy and Mussolini. The winner of the prize and three hundred other Italian-American boys led, for two months, the lives of wealthy people as guests of the Italian government. Before returning to America, the boy in question and his fellows were received by Mussolini, who pinned a medal on the breast of each of them and told them that they must remember Italy once they had returned home. Today, the same youth earns a meager livelihood as a delivery-boy in a vegetable store. Italy is the land of his dreams. He is homesick. He cares nothing for America. When told to go to the World's Fair or the Metropolitan Museum, he refuses."What does all this mean compared to Italy?" On the day when Mussolini needs men in New York to gather around his banner, that boy will not hesitate one moment in answering the call. Should someone then hand him a gun, you may be sure that he would use it without thought or scruple against anyone who would be pointed out to him as Mussolini's enemy.

Among the older generation, success has not been so overwhelming, at least until the present, as the Fascists assert. They have never succeeded, for instance, in capturing the two organizations composed of sixty thousand prevalently Italian dressmakers. They have made some headway in certain local groups, but the central headquarters and most of the local directorates remain beyond their control.

If I might venture to give definite figures on phenomena which by their very nature are fluctuating and nebulous, I should say that 50 percent of the Italo-Americans share the views of my friend, the Boston banana vendor, and therefore tend to be concerned only with their own affairs.

Ten percent are anti-Fascist. The majority, belonging to all shades of conservative or liberal opinion, are not organized and remain inactive. The politically active minority is split up into many groups — anarchists of at least two denominations, revolutionary syndicalists, left-wing socialists, right-wing socialists, Mazzinians, not counting the communists who, for the present and while awaiting fresh orders, walk hand and hand with the Nazis. All these groups are at loggerheads with one another, make as much noise as possible, and do not accomplish very much. Italians cannot do anything without noise and they often make noise without doing anything.

The out-and-out Italian-American Fascists constitute no more than 5 percent of the Italian population. Most of the successful businessmen and professionals are pro-Fascist. For one who was himself or whose father before him was a day laborer only twenty years ago, it is the consummation of felicity to be knighted by Mussolini. The more rich and ambitious are ever so bold as to hope that they may become Senators of the Realm when they stop making money and go back to Italy. Two emigrants to South America have obtained that reward for their patriotic zeal. Why should not others hope to do likewise? To pave the way for such triumphs, they contribute generously to all kinds of Fascist activities.

The Fascist agents are strongly organized, active and as noisy as Italians can be. Around this small nucleus clusters the remainder of the population, about 35 percent, a halo of people with a mentality which has not yet clearly become Fascist and antidemocratic but which might crystallize at the first emergency.

When war broke out in September 1939, the Italian Fascists made common cause with the German Nazi, the Coughlinite anti-Semitic Catholics, the Communists and their fellow-travelers, the Irish persistent in their hatred of England, and the brainless pacifists. Tolstoi and Ghandi, even more than Colonel Lindbergh and Representative Fish became holy water for Mussolini's minions. Peace, peace, peace — this became the slogan of the men who had applauded Mussolini's attack on Ethiopia, his intervention in Spain and the rape of Albania. They suddenly grew most punctilious in their love of American democratic institutions. They showed deep concern lest civil liberties be curtailed in the land of the free if there were war; that would be an unbearable disgrace — freedom must be jealously guarded in America while it is being wiped out in Europe. When Hitler and Mussolini have triumphed in Europe, then there will be a good chance that civil liberties in America will not be temporarily curtailed in time of war but permanently discarded in time of peace. "America for the Americans."

As long as Mussolini remained nonbelligerent and no clash with the policies of the United States seemed possible, the Fascist-pacifist attitude could be maintained without undue difficulty. The end of Mussolini's nonbelligerency, the harsh condemnation uttered by President Roosevelt against him, and the consent given by the overwhelming majority in this country to the president's judgment, have brought about a serious dislocation in Fascist activities.

Most Italians, even those who believe that Mussolini has made Italy rich, prosperous, respected, and feared have been shocked in their moral sense and the Fascists have lost much ground among them. Few Fascists have been as stupid as that consular agent who, on June 12, announced that all "6,000,000 people" of Italian origin in the United States "are secretly backing the aspirations of Mussolini" (New York Times, June 13, 1940). The others either have sought refuge in prudent silence or have proclaimed to the four winds their unshakeable loyalty to American institutions. To be sure they hope for Italy's victory. Are they not of Italian origin? Are they not in duty bound to love the land of their birth? Are not the English praying for their country's victory? My country right or wrong. But nobody has the right to doubt their loyalty. They are second to none in their devotion to the United

States. It is not among them that traitors to America can be found. Whoever is looking for fifth columnists should look for them not among Fascists-pacifists loyal to America but among those who are opposed to Fascism and to Italy. A committee of vigilantes is needed to purge the United States of fifth columnists. If such a committee had the close cooperation of the Italian consulates, there is no doubt that every fifth columnist of Italian descent would at once vanish into thin air.

There is something to be gained in listening to these strange arguments. Rowdies who broke the shop windows of Italians in London and in Toronto, or urged the dismissal of Italian waiters from Chicago restaurants, show that they are unworthy citizens of a free country. Worse is the case of the English Home Office. When Mussolini declared war, wholesale arrests were made all over England of anti-Fascists, Fascists and indeterminate Italians. Many were herded together with Nazi and anti-Nazi Germans onto a ship which was subsequently torpedoed by a German submarine. Perhaps a Home Office which was directed until a few months ago by one of Hitler's and Mussolini's intimate friends, Sir Samuel Hoare, could not have done otherwise. But this entire business has been playing into the hands of the Fascist propaganda agents.

A blind wave of hysterical and indiscriminate anti-Italian persecution would strike not at the handful of men who are really dangerous and who already are prepared to show all the necessary papers and affidavits to prove their eternal American loyalty, but at the great mass of innocent men and women whose only guilt lies in bearing an Italian name. This tragic mistake should be avoided.

To be sure, Fascist activities must be disorganized.

The staffs of the Italian embassy and the consular offices and agencies should be reduced to the numbers of their personnel in 1922. They should limit their activities to the seven hundred thousand Italian immigrants who still retain their Italian citizenship and refrain from cultural activities among those who have obtained American citizenship. The education of these new citizens should be directed by the country of adoption and not by the country of origin.

An inquiry should be made into the sources of the funds which support Fascist propaganda on the radio and in the Italian language press. Another inquiry should be conducted on the ways and means by which Fascist propaganda is being carried on in American schools. It is not difficult to list the teachers of Italian in the after-school clubs, high schools and colleges and to examine the textbooks they use.

Radio speakers, journalists, parish priests and lecturers of Italian origin who have carried on Fascist propaganda among Italians or English-speaking people during the last few years should be deprived of their citizenship if they have become American citizens and deported to Italy. American rights and privileges belong to those who were born in America and to immigrants who have taken their oath of allegiance to American institutions in all sincerity. A Fascist of Italian origin who lives in America is a foreigner who hates American institutions. If he has sworn allegiance to them, he has perjured himself. He has no right to invoke the protection afforded by the very institutions he seeks to destroy. No American citizen would be allowed to live in Italy if he tried to organize democratic and anti-Fascist activities in that country. Democratic America should apply to Italian Fascists the same treatment Mussolini would apply in Italy to anti-Fascists protected by American citizenship even if American born. An Italian Fascist deported to Italy would be deprived of no liberty except that of living an unhappy life under the rotten and hated democratic Constitution of the United States. He could then live happily in the country of his dreams under the rule of the man he worships as "sent by Divine Providence," as Pope Pius XI put it. He would have no grounds for complaint. For the rich, deportation would only serve as a sort of badge of honor which would help them to their wished-for goal: to become Senators of the Realm. Moreover, their names would be added to the Book of Martyrs.

It would not be difficult to compile from the Italian press a list of many of these persons and find therein ample proof of their activities.

Repressive measures, however, would not be sufficient to remedy the evil that has already been done or to prevent the recurrence of the old evil as soon as the Fascist agents have weathered the present crisis. When Fascist activities have been disorganized, democratic education must fill the vacuum thus created. Millions of human beings must be reclaimed. They should not be abandoned to intellectual and moral starvation at the very moment democratic institutions have broken down in Europe and are on the defensive in the United States. Democracy must be constructive and aggressive if it is not to end in defeat.

New radio programs will have to be substituted for those containing Fascist propaganda. Radio commentators in Italian will have to adapt themselves to the interests of their special public, using some of the methods successfully used by the Fascist agents. They should insert news and comments in the course of musical or dramatic programs. They should strive to inform their public about American legislation aimed at protecting their rights as workers and promoting their welfare as human beings. This work is most urgently needed and would yield effective results.

Institutions should be established to care for boys and girls after school. They cannot produce rapid results. But this work is as vital as that which ought to be carried out on the radio. The slower its results, the sooner it should be set up on the broadest possible scale.

New textbooks should be prepared for the various schools and teachers should be warned against texts tainted with Fascist misinformation.

The diffusion of the few Italian weeklies worthy of an audience should be encouraged. Another half dozen such weeklies should be founded in the most important centers of the United States.

An information bureau should be established. Its duties would consist in checking information circulated through American press agencies and papers, and to contradict, on the basis of documented evidence, deceitful news.

No one should ever consider suppressing the teaching of the Italian language in schools or making Americans of Italian extraction forget the fatherland of their ancestors and its tongue. After Mussolini entered the present war, some radio announcers in New York were dispensed with and a ban was put on the Italian language by radio stations in New York City and Boston. At the time of writing, I do not know what is happening in other sections of the United States. I maintain that the ban on the Italian language is a gross blunder. People who are accustomed to their daily dose of propaganda in Italian now get it in broken English and are angered against this democracy which does not respect the rights of national minorities. Forbidding is easier than creating, but it leads nowhere. Let the Italian language flow over the radio, but see to it that it carries the voice of eternal Italy, which existed before Mussolini was born and will go on long after Mussolini is dead. There is no clash whatever between the spirit of American institutions and that of the Italian Risorgimento. Nor is there any basic difference between the education which the American receives when he studies the history of his country and that which the Italian would receive if he were taught that Italy was a civilized and progressive country before Mussolini came to power and that the Fascist dictatorship has destroyed human dignity and lowered the standard of living of the Italian people. This is not to suggest the suppression of any truth in any school, newspaper, book, lecture hall or radio address. This is merely a plea for the protection of democratic principles against totalitarian deceit.

Private initiative is unable to cope with all these needs. The flood of Fascist activities is financed by the Italian government. On May 6, 1938, the United States reported that the Italian Ministry of Foreign Affairs was spending $6,500,000 on propaganda in foreign countries, of which the schools alone absorbed $3,000,000. These schools have been chiefly in the United States, South America and France. Between $250,000 and $300,000 was assigned to support other Fascist organizations abroad. The Ministry of Popular Culture was given $100,000 to keep Italian press attachès in the most important embassies. To these sums should be added the money expended by the Fascist party, the Dante Alighieri Society, the tourist agencies and the funds placed at the personal disposal of Mussolini as head of the Italian government for propaganda abroad. During the past two years, appropriations have steadily and substantially increased. How can private initiative alone stem such a flood? Unconditional laissez-faire policies in the intellectual as well as in the economic field lead not to competition but to butchery when individuals or groups of unequal strength confront one another. If the city, state and federal governments of the United States expect private enterprise to oppose Fascist activities by its own unaided effort, the outcome of the contest can be but defeat.

Can a democratic country abandon large sections of its population to the antidemocratic activities of a foreign government?

Index

NOTE — Dotted entries indicate organizations and clubs.